BLACK FEMALE
PLAYWRIGHTS

BLACKS IN THE DIASPORA

Darlene Clark Hine, John McCluskey, Jr., and David Barry Gaspar
General Editors

KATHY A. PERKINS

BLACK FEMALE PLAYWRIGHTS

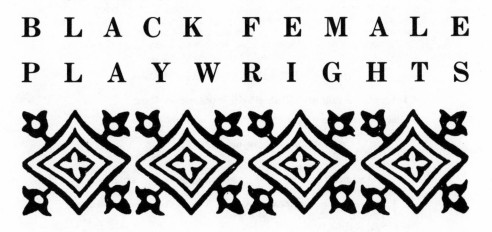

An Anthology of Plays before 1950

Indiana University Press

BLOOMINGTON & INDIANAPOLIS

Manufactured in the United States of America

Library of Congress Cataloging-in-Publication Data

Black female playwrights: an anthology of plays before 1950 / Kathy
A. Perkins, editor.
     p.   cm.—(Blacks in the diaspora)
  Bibliography: p.
  ISBN 0-253-34358-5
    1. American drama—Afro-American authors. 2. Women and
literature—United States. 3. American drama—Women authors.
4. Afro-American women—Drama. 5. Afro-Americans—Drama.
I. Perkins, Kathy A.   II. Series.
PS628.N4B54 1989
812'.008'09287—dc 19   88-46040
                                              CIP

1 2 3 4 5 93 92 91 90 89

Contents

ACKNOWLEDGMENTS

In 1981, with the assistance of a Ford Foundation Fellowship, I began extensive research on the contributions of blacks in the non-performing areas of the American theatre—designers, directors, producers, choreographers, musical directors, technicians and other craftspeople behind the scenes. While researching the life of Shirley Graham (DuBois) during the summer of 1984, for her work as a producer, director, and composer, I became acquainted with her collection of plays. Although it was never my intention to focus on playwrights, Graham's work sparked my interest in other black female playwrights prior to the Civil Rights Movement of the 1950s. I was fascinated by their interpretation of life through drama. Within a short period, I found myself collecting plays and investigating the lives of these writers.

Tremendous gratitude must be expressed to the numerous individuals whose support and assistance have made *Black Female Playwrights* a reality. Much of the ground work and inspiration for this project is credited to the published works and personal assistance from James V. Hatch of the Hatch-Billops Collection in New York City. I owe appreciation to the scholarly works of Jeanne-Marie A. Miller, John Monroe Gilbert, and Doris Abramson, as well as Nellie McKay and Ted Shine. I am indebted to the assistance of the staff members at the following research centers: Esme E. Bahn, Moorland-Spingarn Research Center of Howard University; Beth Howse, Fisk University Special Collections Library; Rosemary Hogg, Federal Theatre Project Collections, George Mason University; Schomburg Center for Research in Black Culture; The Center for the Study of Women and Center for Afro-American Studies at the University of California, Los Angeles (UCLA); Nancy McKinney of the California Afro-American Museum, Los Angeles and Lonnie Bunch, III, of the Smithsonian Institution. I am grateful to Delores Hudson and Pamela Watkins for their editorial assistance, and to the following friends on the East Coast who assisted in gathering information while I was on the West Coast: Michon Boston, Ruby Sales, Nancy Davis, and Patricia Bainer.

Thank you to the family members and friends of the writers for sharing material and information: Patricia Hart, Lorenz Graham, David Graham DuBois, Dolores Sheen, and Rowena Jelliffe.

To May Miller, the lone survivor of the playwrights presented in this anthology, for allowing me to vicariously relive the Washington, D.C., and

Harlem Renaissance through our infinite hours of conversations in her Washington home.

Black Female Playwrights would not have been possible without grants and fellowships from the National Endowment for the Humanities, Money For Women/The Barbara Deming Memorial Fund, Smith College, and the Institute of American Cultures/Center for Afro-American Studies (UCLA). Thanks to my parents, Marion and Minerva Perkins, for their support in all of my endeavors.

My greatest gratitude is to my sister, Linda, for encouraging and convincing me that I could take on such a research project. Linda's own scholarly research on early black women has served as a major inspiration for *Black Female Playwrights*.

This book is dedicated to Linda Perkins and May Miller.

BLACK FEMALE PLAYWRIGHTS

INTRODUCTION

The colored woman of today occupies, one may say, a
unique position in this country. In a period of itself tran-
sitional and unsettled, her status seems one of the least
ascertainable and definitive of all the forces which make
for our civilization. She is confronted by both a woman
question and a race probblem, and is as yet an unknown
or an unacknowledged factor in both.

—Anna J. Cooper (1892)[1]

DURING THE CIVIL RIGHTS MOVEMENT, Lorraine Hansberry emerged as
the first black woman to present a drama on Broadway with her 1959 production of *A Raisin in the Sun*. Never before had a black female playwright
commanded such attention in the American theatre. In *Raisin*, Hansberry
was able to realistically address an array of issues such as the strength and
survival of the black family, their dreams, racism, abortion, manhood, and
womanhood. She defied the stereotypical portrayal of blacks commonly seen
on the American stage by substituting realistic images. One of the factors
that precipitated Hansberry's writing *A Raisin in the Sun* is expressed in
a 1959 *New York Times* interview: "One night, after seeing a play I won't
mention, I suddenly became disgusted with a whole body of material about
Negroes. Cardboard characters. Cute dialect bits. Or hip-swinging musicals
from exotic sources."[2]

While Hansberry and the black women writers of her period must be
praised for their courageous and outstanding works, it was the black women
during the first half of the twentieth century who set the stage for this new
group of writers. Prior to the 1950s, black women published over sixty discovered plays and pageants, as well as numerous unpublished scripts. However, many of these works are rare and hard to find.

Overall, blacks in drama did not achieve any significant status in the
American theatre, and playwriting, at that time, was considered a profession for men. During the first half of the twentieth century, black women,
who had to bear the double burden of racism and sexism, burst upon the
scene. However, in this climate, their contributions remained unheralded.
Recently, articles and books have been published establishing the tremendous impact that black women have made not only in black theatre, but in
American theatre in general. Even with these publications, there is still a
paucity of information on the achievements that black women have made as
playwrights. Except for the section on plays of early black women writers
presented in James Hatch and Ted Shine's *Black Theatre U.S.A.* (1974),

there has not been an anthology totally devoted to the works of these pioneer writers.

The impetus behind this anthology grew out of a need to acknowledge the works of these black women in a single volume. These plays—most of which were written when blacks were just learning the art of playwriting—represent a historical perspective that reflects the lives of the early black women. It would be unfair to view these plays based on technical and creative writing skills alone. The main objective in presenting these works is to illustrate how these plays conveyed the attitudes of black women—issues which were rarely voiced on the stage at the time. Many of the topics that these women focused on were issues that could only be expressed by a black woman. Neither the white nor the black male playwright could express the intense pain and fear a black woman experienced concerning her children—wondering, for instance, if the child that she carried for nine months would be sold into slavery, or be a son who might one day be lynched. Along with this excruciating pain, black women were also preoccupied with the safety of their husbands.

Although the black male and female wrote plays on similar topics, their works also differed in many respects. While many of the male playwrights wrote about life in Harlem and other major cities, black women were more diverse in their geographic location, providing a greater sense of the black community on a national level by setting the action in rural communities throughout the country as well as in large cities. The main characters in plays by black women were usually female. These women were often placed in major decision-making roles. In many instances the husband was dead, or absent from the household—perhaps working in another town. The central focus in these women's plays was usually on the children, with the mother being overly protective because of the times in which they lived. The action for the most part occurred in a domestic setting—the kitchen, dining room, or living room, and the play usually opened with a woman sewing, cooking, cleaning, or praying—rarely outside or far from the home. Because of this domestic setting, white characters were often absent in these works. However, the effects of racism reverberated in the home. Plays and pageants based on the lives of famous black heroes and heroines were also prevalent among black women, particularly those who worked as educators.

One of the earliest black female playwrights to have her work produced was Pauline Elizabeth Hopkins, who was raised and educated in Boston during the late 1800s. One of Hopkins's earliest aspirations was to become a playwright. In 1879, Hopkins wrote a musical drama entitled *Slaves' Escape: or the Underground Railroad*. This play was performed by the Hopkins' Colored Troubadours at the Oakland Garden, Boston, July 5, 1880. The cast consisted of members of Hopkins's family and friends. *Slaves' Escape*, a drama with Jubilee songs sung throughout, focuses on how the underground railroad was instrumental in assisting slaves in their flight to freedom. The production was acknowledged in the *Boston Herald*, where it received favorable reviews. Pauline Hopkins also wrote a second play entitled *Drama of Early Days*, which dramatized the biblical story of Daniel in the Lion's Den. There are no known records of this play being produced. Unfortunately, financial circumstances during the latter part of the nineteenth century forced Hopkins to forego her writing activities for a more stable occupation. Hopkins could not give up writing entirely, so early in the twentieth century she took up her pen again as a writer of fiction and one of the editors of the *Colored American Magazine*. In 1899 her novel, *Contending Forces*, was published. This novel, which Hopkins referred to as a romance story, explores mob violence, lynching, and the Negro problem in this country.

Pauline Hopkins is just one example of many black women who attempted to make a career as a playwright prior to the 1950s in the United States. The promotion of plays by black women was often difficult, forcing these women to pursue other areas of writing such as poetry and fiction, which were considered more acceptable.

A major catalyst behind the promotion and recognition of plays by early black women writers came through the efforts of three Harvard graduates: Dr. W. E. B. DuBois, one of the founders of the National Association for the Advancement of Colored People (NAACP), and Professors Montgomery T. Gregory and Alain Locke of Howard University. These three men provided the opportunity for plays by a large number of blacks, especially women, to be recognized, published, and performed. DuBois, Gregory, and Locke encouraged blacks to write plays about the black experience. These plays were called "native dramas."

"Native drama" emerged in Harlem during the early 1920s as part of the Little Negro Theatre Movement. These plays, which included both drama and comedy, depicted a more realistic and richer spectrum of the black experience than the plays written by whites about blacks. This type of drama could be divided into two distinct categories: "race or propaganda plays" and "folk plays." The former included those plays that dealt with the issue of racial oppression as experienced by black people. "Propaganda plays" were written primarily to effect social change. The latter, "folk plays," sought to depict the black experience without focusing on the oppressive issues blacks faced daily and racial tensions. Therefore, the main goal of the "folk play" was to educate and entertain without offending its audience. Although black playwrights may have taken different paths, their goal at this time was to depict the race in a realistic light. W. E. B. DuBois, one of the leaders in the Movement, noted:

Today, as the renaissance of art comes among American Negroes, the theatre calls for new birth. . . . The Negro is already in the theatre and has been there for a long time; but his presence there is not yet thoroughly normal. His audience is mainly a white audience and the Negro actor has, for a long time, been asked to entertain this more or less alien group. The demands and ideals of the white group, and their conception of Negroes, have set the norm for the black actor. He has been a minstrel, comedian, singer and lay figure of all sorts. Only recently has he begun to emerge as an ordinary human being with everyday actions. And he is still handicapped and put forth with much hesitation, as in the case of "The Nigger," "Lulu Belle" and "Emperor Jones."[3]

"Native drama" was a response to the works of white dramatists who in the 1920s attempted to capture the black experience through dramatic works. These writers included white playwrights such as Eugene O'Neil (*The Emperor Jones* and *All God's Chillun Got Wings*), Dorothy and DuBois Heywood (*Porgy*), Marc Connelly (*Green Pastures*), and Paul Green (*In Abraham's Bosom*). But these writers, all of whom achieved fame for their plays on black life, when compared with "native drama," merely brought to the stage superficial aspects of black life. While many blacks sympathized with the efforts of white writers to portray blacks dramatically, they also felt that these plays lacked the "true spirit and soul" of the Negro. Also, despite the claims of authenticity, white-authored plays did not change substantially the prevailing view on blacks.

The views white authors had about blacks stemmed from the white minstrel shows, dating back to the early 1800s, which provided the basis for the stereotypes imposed upon black people in America. The dominant image of the black character was that of a singing, dancing, shiftless, oversexed, and carefree individual. Even with the demise of the minstrel shows at the turn of the twentieth century, these images prevailed in the Tom Shows (dramatizations of Harriet Beecher Stowe's *Uncle Tom's Cabin*), Coon Shows (early name given to black musicals), and Vaudeville/Variety shows.

During the 1920s, black people felt that the time had come for them to be responsible for the presentation of their own images. Blacks were encouraged by individuals such as DuBois to create their own spaces to stage their own works, and present their own images. They were aware that these efforts would probably not be accepted by the larger society, but they were not deterred by that fact. These plays became an alternative to the numerous musical revues and white-authored plays which were popular at the time.

DuBois displayed a major interest in Negro drama. In 1910, he founded the NAACP's *Crisis* magazine, which he edited for twenty-four years and used as his platform to speak out against racial injustices in America. In 1913 he wrote, staged, and directed his pageant, *The Star of Ethiopia*, in New York City. This production traced fifty years of emancipation from slavery. By 1915, the NAACP initiated a Drama Committee to provide a method of utilizing the stage to effect social change. The goal was to encourage the writing of plays by blacks, since most dramatic works written about the black experience flowed from the pens of white authors.

In 1925 DuBois, along with his rival editor, Charles S. Johnson of the National Urban League's *Opportunity* magazine, launched a literary contest;

the best one-act plays submitted would be published in *Crisis* and *Opportunity*. The plays selected would receive cash awards and a ceremony would be given for the winners, thereby providing exposure for the writers. The contest also included other areas in the literary field—short stories, essays, poetry—and illustrations. The *Crisis* and *Opportunity* magazines contest took place during the years 1925, 1926, and 1927.

According to Regina Andrews, who had worked with DuBois and was for years the chief librarian with the 135th Street Library in New York City, the 1925 *Crisis* contest had over 628 manuscripts submitted for all areas.[4] *Opportunity* attracted 732 competitors for the same year.[5] Ironically, although the contests in drama were open to both black men and women, women outnumbered men in submitting plays, and most of the winners were women. Two of the three *Crisis* honors for 1925 went to women: *The Church Fight* by Ruth Gaines-Shelton, and Myrtle Smith Livingston's *For Unborn Children*. For 1926 one of the two went to Eulalie Spence for *Foreign Mail*, and the 1927 prize was awarded to Marita Bonner for *The Purple Flower*. The judges for the *Crisis* contests included such notables as playwright Eugene O'Neil; Montgomery T. Gregory, former head of Howard University's Dramatic Arts Department and Supervisor of Schools, Atlantic City, New Jersey; Lester Walton of the *New York World*; and Charles Burroughs, director of the Krigwa Players' Little Negro Theatre.

Of the seven winners of the 1925 *Opportunity* playwriting awards, four were women: Zora Neale Hurston for *Colorstruck* and *Spears*, May Miller's *The Bog Guide*, and Eloise Bibb Thompson's *Cooped Up*. In 1926, of the four winners, the lone female recipient was Georgia Douglas Johnson for her play *Blue Blood*. Three of the four awards in 1927 were received by women: Eulalie Spence for her two plays *The Starter* and *The Hunch*, and Georgia Johnson's *Plumes*. *Opportunity*'s judges included playwrights Paul Green and Lula Vollmer; Edith Isaacs, of *Theatre Arts Monthly*; actor/singer Paul Robeson; Montgomery Gregory; Robert Benchley, critic and editor of *Life*; and drama critic Alexander Woollcott.

To further encourage the development of drama written by blacks, DuBois organized the Krigwa Players in 1926. Krigwa was the acronym for the Crisis Guild of Writers and Artists. (The "C" was later changed to "K".) During this period, DuBois had a definite philosophy of what Negro theatre should represent. The 1926 inaugural playbill for the Krigwa Players outlines DuBois's philosophy:

The movement which has begun this year in Harlem, New York City, lays down four fundamental principles. The plays of a real Negro theatre must be: *One: About us.* That is, they must have plots which reveal Negro life as it is. *Two: By us.* That is, they must be written by Negro authors who understand from birth and continual association just what it means to be a Negro today. *Three: For us.* That is, the theatre must cater primarily to Negro audiences and be supported and sustained by their entertainment and approval. *Fourth: Near Us.*

The theatre must be in a Negro neighborhood near the mass of ordinary Negro people.

However, DuBois did emphasize that "artists of all races" would be welcomed. While the Krigwa Players existed for only a short time, DuBois was successful in encouraging the formation of other small theatre groups throughout the country. Krigwa Players groups were organized in such cities as Washington, D.C., Denver, and Baltimore.

While DuBois was promoting "race" or "propaganda" plays, Montgomery T. Gregory and Alain Locke were promoting "folk plays" at Howard University. Gregory brought national attention to the Howard Players of Howard University in 1921 when he organized the Department of Dramatic Arts for the purpose of establishing the first National Negro Theatre in the United States. The department offered three areas of professional training—acting, playwriting, and production. Prior to this period, there was virtually no institution that provided professional theatre training for blacks in this country, especially in the areas of playwriting.

On March 3, 1921, the *New York Globe and Commercial Advertiser* presented an article entitled "Negro University Has Dramatic Department on Lines of Harvard's." In this article, the renowned theatre editor Kenneth McGowan stated:

Howard has gone farther than Harvard in one respect. It gives full credit towards a degree for work in the courses in acting and production. Harvard has not yet recognized in this fashion the value of training which Professor Baker gives volunteer students through his production group, the "47 Workshop." . . . Now, why should a small university and a Negro university give all of this time and energy to the study of theatrical production? Not alone because of mind and emotion, which is the primary business of a university. The vision of Professor Gregory, who is director of the Howard Players as well as chief of the department of dramatics, goes beyond that.[6]

Gregory envisioned the Department of Dramatic Arts as the number one professional training ground for blacks in the theatre. In order to achieve this level of professionalism, Gregory believed that support would be needed from both blacks and whites. The Howard Department of Dramatic Arts formed an advisory board which solicited some of the top white names in American theatre and the academic arena. The Advisory Board for the Howard Players boasted such individuals as Professor George Baker of the famous Harvard 47 Workshop, novelist Winston Churchill, playwrights Ridgeley Torrence and Eugene O'Neill, Joel Spingarn of the NAACP, editor Kenneth McGowan, drama critic Robert Benchley, Harvard University's President Charles W. Eliot, President Samuel Eliot, Jr., of Smith College, Frederick Koch, director of the University of North Carolina Players, and

Broadway designer Robert L. Jones. James W. Johnson was one of the few blacks to serve on the committee.

Gregory's philosophy of the Negro theatre differed greatly from that of DuBois. Gregory felt that in order for Negro drama to survive and be accepted in this country, it would have to be exposed to the larger society. In McGowan's article, Gregory was quoted as saying that

> "the Negro has a wonderful opportunity through drama to win a better standing in the community. Not through the production of plays of propaganda; that would be a mistaken effort. I believe that we can win a broader recognition of our rights and responsibilities as citizens by demonstrating our abilities as artists. . . . My hope is that we can train actors and producers who will be able to organize Negro players in a few of the bigger cities. They should not establish theatres in the Negro districts, for that would tend to prevent the white community from seeing their art."[7]

It was through the Howard Players that many black women received their initial training in playwriting. This opportunity allowed black women to see their works produced throughout the northeastern portion of the country. The majority of plays by students of Gregory and Locke (now housed in the Gregory and Locke Collection at Howard University) were written by women. Also, many letters from non-students in reference to plays were sent to Locke and Gregory by females. According to speculation, the large number of plays written by women could be attributed to the fact that since black women were not in any leadership position as compared to black men, these plays provided a unique opportunity for their voices to be heard. Also, black women had never been allowed much of an opportunity to express themselves in the dramatic form and therefore seized the chance to do so.

Although the works of black dramatists rarely reached Broadway, the black male produced "native drama" on the Great White Way prior to the 1950s. These creative works included Willis Richardson's *The Chip Woman's Fortune* (1923), Garland Anderson's *Appearances* (1925), Frank Wilson's *Meek Mose* (1928), Wallace Thurman's *Harlem* (1929), Langston Hughes's *Mulatto* (1935), Richard Wright's *Native Son* (1941), and Theodore Ward's presentation of *Our Lan'* Off Broadway in 1946. Frank Wilson's *The Wall Between* was scheduled to open on Broadway in 1929 but was cancelled. (The crash of 1929 seems to have been a contributing factor.) Then, in 1955, Alice Childress's play *Trouble in Mind* was presented Off Broadway. Lorraine Hansberry's *A Raisin in the Sun* hit in 1959. Broadway had finally heard from the black woman.

Of the many black women who would later become well known in the literary field, particularly for their plays, a large percentage either studied under Gregory and Locke or were influenced by the Howard community. A representative group includes such writers as Zora Neale Hurston, Shirley

Graham, Mary P. Burrill, Angelina Grimké, Thelma Duncan, May Miller, Helen Webb Harris, Georgia Douglas Johnson, Myrtle Smith Livingston, Eulalie Spence, and Lucy White.

While the Harlem Renaissance was in its infancy, Gregory, Locke, and the Howard community were laying the groundwork for this rapidly burgeoning Renaissance in Washington, D.C. Locke, considered one of the trailblazers of the Harlem Renaissance, was already promoting large numbers of works by blacks. Washington, D.C., had the first twentieth century full-length play written, performed, and produced by blacks—*Rachel*.

Billed as "a race play in three acts," Angelina Weld Grimké's *Rachel* was presented by the Drama Committee of the District of Columbia Branch of the NAACP at Myrtilla Miner Normal School on March 3 and 4, 1916. The Drama Committee consisted of such notables as Anna J. Cooper, Ernest E. Just, and Clara Burrill Bruce, as well as Locke and Gregory. Locke has been credited with enabling Grimké to get *Rachel* produced, although it is not quite clear what role he played in this effort. The play is also significant because—as stated in the playbill for *Rachel*—"it is the first attempt to use the stage for race propaganda in order to enlighten the American people relative to the lamentable condition of ten million of colored citizens in this free Republic."

Rachel addresses the psychological impact of racism on the lives of blacks in this country. Set in New York City during the early 1900s, the play deals with a family called the Lovings, who have migrated from the South to escape racial oppression. The main character, Rachel, is a bright young woman whose greatest desire is to become a mother. During the first act, Mrs. Loving reveals to Rachel and her brother, Tom, that their father and half-brother were murdered by a lynch mob ten years earlier in the South. The play covers a period of about four years, and it is during these years that Rachel realizes that she and her family are still victims of racial oppression, even in the North. Rachel and Tom, both well educated, cannot find work for which they are qualified. Rachel also witnesses the brutal treatment of young black children by their white classmates and by the end of the play she questions God's justice in this society. Affected by a society that seems to offer no hope for blacks, Rachel vows never to marry nor conceive. In spite of the very romantic style and the extremely long speeches by Rachel, both of which were typical of the period, Grimké and her pioneer play hold a special place in American theatre history.

The presentation of *Rachel* caused a great deal of controversy in Washington, D.C., especially among some of the NAACP members who had sponsored it. Many members felt the play was too political and criticized it as pure propaganda. There were very few known reviews written at the time of the production in the local papers. In his anthology *Plays of Negro Life*, Gregory's comment on *Rachel* is that it merits attention because it was "apparently the first successful drama written by a Negro and interpreted by Negro actors."[8] He also speaks of the artistic limitations of the play. Although he mentions no names, Gregory states: "A minority section of this committee dissented from this propagandist platform and were instrumental later in founding the Howard Players organization, promoting the purely artistic approach and the folk-drama idea."[9] *Rachel* had subsequent performances at the Neighborhood Playhouse in New York City (1917) and Brattle Hall in Cambridge, Massachusetts (1917). The play was later published in 1920 by Cornhill in Boston. The publication of *Rachel* drew a large number of reviews that were primarily favorable. However, there were those critics who charged *Rachel* with advocating genocide.

A response to the criticism surrounding her play can be found in Angelina Weld Grimké's papers, located in the Moorland-Spingarn Research Center at Howard University. It is not clear whether this response was written for a large audience, the NAACP Drama Committee, or an individual. In her statement, Grimké justifies her reason for writing *Rachel*:

> Since I have been given to understand that "Rachel" preaches race suicide, I should like to state at the start, that that was not my intention. To the contrary, the appeal is not primarily to the colored people, but to the whites. . . . Because of environment and certain inherent qualities, each of us reacts correspondingly and logically to the various forces about us. For example, if these forces be of love, we react with love, and if of hate, with hate. Very naturally all of us will not react as strongly or in the same manner—that is impossible. . . . Now my purpose was to show how a refined, sensitive, highly-strung girl, a dreamer and an idealist, the strongest instinct in whose nature is to be a mother herself—how, I say, this girl would react to this force.

> The majority of women, everywhere, although they are beginning to awaken, form one of the most conservative elements of society. They are, therefore, opposed to changes. For this reason and for sex reasons, the white women of this country are about the worst enemies with which the colored race has to contend. My belief was then that if I could find a vulnerable point in their armour, if I could reach their hearts, even if only a little, then perhaps instead of being active or passive enemies they might become, at least, less inimical and possibly friendly.

> Did they have a vulnerable point and if so what was it? I believed it to be motherhood. . . . If anything can make all women sisters underneath their skins, it is motherhood. If, then, I could make the white women of this country see, feel, understand just what their prejudice and the prejudice of their fathers, brothers, husbands, sons were having on the souls of the colored mothers everywhere, and upon the mothers that are to be, a great power to affect public opinion would be set free and the battle would be half won.[10]

Shortly after the production of *Rachel*, there followed a series of protest or "propaganda" plays authored by black women. The issue of lynching remained a dominant topic until the 1930s. This is understandable given the climate of America during this period. An estimated 3,589 blacks, including 76 women, were lynched between 1882 and 1927.[11] According to historian

John Hope Franklin, "In the very first year of the new century more than 100 Negroes were lynched, and before the outbreak of World War I the number for the century had soared to more than 1,100."[12]

Georgia Douglas Johnson, one of the most prolific and versatile playwrights of the era, wrote several plays focusing on the theme of lynching. Johnson, a member of the Anti-Lynch Crusade Organization which was organized by black women, authored *A Sunday Morning in the South* (1925) in which a young black man's life could have been saved from a lynch mob if only the white judge had interrupted his Sunday morning church service to come to his rescue. Johnson's play *Safe* (193?) looks at a mother who decides to murder her baby son to keep him "safe" from the hands of the lynchers. In her *Blue-Eyed Black Boy* (193?), a mother prevents the lynching of her young black son who accidentally brushes into a white girl. The end of the play reveals that the boy's father is the white governor, who halts the lynching to prevent a scandal. Regina Andrews's *Climbing Jacob's Ladder* (1931) centers around a lynching that occurs while blacks are praying during Sunday church service.

Marita Bonner was possibly the first black woman to use surrealism in her revolutionary play *The Purple Flower* (1926). The play is set in "The-Middle-Of-Things-as-They-Are" and the scene takes place in "the middle of an open plain." The characters are the "Sundry White Devils" and the "Us's." The Us's, who represent black people, are attempting to get to the hill where the purple flower of life thrives. The Sundry White Devils, who live atop the hill, have prevented the Us's for ages from reaching the purple flower in spite of the Us's hard labor and education. Once the Us's reach the hill, they will enjoy life at its fullest. The Us's eventually realize that much blood has to be shed in order to get to the flower. Bonner's message is that no matter how hard blacks work and become educated in this country, the only solution to the race problem is a blood revolution.

Black women also addressed issues dealing with blacks and the military. Alice Dunbar-Nelson and Mary Burrill, both of whom were contemporaries as well as friends of Angelina Grimké and Georgia Johnson, wrote plays during World War I that questioned the black man's loyalty in wartime to a country that offered him none. Nelson's *Mine Eyes Have Seen* (1918) presents Chris, a young black draftee debating whether he should serve his country. He reflects on how his father was murdered by whites, and how as a result of his father's death, his mother died. Chris is also faced with leaving his crippled brother and sister. He eventually concludes that America is his country also, and in spite of all the injustices, he must go off to war and defend his land. In Burrill's *Aftermath* (1919), John, a young black hero, returns from the war to visit his parents only to find that his father has been lynched. John's solution to the problem for the injustices perpetrated against blacks is to take the law into his own hands in order for justice to prevail. In anger he exclaims: "This ain't no time fu' preachers or prayers! You mean to tell me I mus' let them w'ite devils send me miles erway to suffer an' be shot up fu' the freedom of people I ain't nevah seen, while they're burnin' an' killin' my folks here at home! To Hell with 'em!"

May Miller's chilling *Stragglers in the Dust* (1930) takes us to the Tomb of the Unknown Soldier in Washington, D.C. This play is worth noting because Miller, unlike many of her contemporaries, used white characters to illustrate racism in this society. Miller was also one of the few female writers to venture from the home environment in terms of location of her plays. While many of her plays had a domestic setting, she also created several works where the action occurred in such places as a pool hall, an African jungle, a Haitian palace, and the open countryside, as well as the home of a white family. In *Stragglers in the Dust*, Nan, a Negro charwoman, is convinced that the body in the tomb is that of her son killed in action during World War I. A politician and the old white watchman are discussing Nan's belief that her son rests in the tomb:

> BRADFORD: But how could she think that?
> MAC: She kinda misunderstood some of the speeches she's heard out here—took everything to herself.
> BRADFORD: Such a thing has never even crossed my mind. Why that isn't even possible.
> MAC: Of course not, Nan's just a poor old colored woman with nothing left but her dreams.
> BRADFORD: But if it were—what a terrible joke on America!

Another topic that was prevalent among black women, as well as male and white playwrights, was that of miscegenation. These plays usually depicted the negative impact that "mixing of the races" had on blacks, particularly women. Myrtle Smith Livingston examined the ultimate crime in America —the relationship of a black man and a white woman in the South—in *For Unborn Children* (1926). This play is rather unusual: most plays of this period examine the pairing of the white Southern man and the black woman. Smith's pairing of the black man and white woman may be attributed to the fact that as a woman she is expressing the sentiment that was shared by many black women regarding interracial coupling. Marion, the sister of the black man, clearly displays her anger toward him when she exclaims:

> You poor fool! If it's color you want, why couldn't you stay in your own race? We have women who are as white as any white person could be! My God! What is to become of us when our men throw us down? . . . Well, if you marry her, may God help me never to breathe your name again.

Ottie Graham concentrated on the tragic mulatto in her play *Holiday* (1923), showing how a mulatto mother, passing for a white stage actress, leaves her brown-skinned daughter to be raised by friends. Years later, the mother decides to reveal herself to the daughter during the summer holidays. Overwhelmed that her mother had abandoned her, the daughter commits suicide by drowning. Unable to bear the guilt, the mother takes her life by following the daughter into the sea.

Dark-skinned Emmaline in Zora Neale Hurston's *Color Struck* (1925) is threatened by every mulatto that comes near her lover. Emmaline is so self-conscious and insecure about her dark complexion that her behavior causes her to lose the man who really loves her. Georgia Johnson's tragicomedy *Blue Blood* (1926) explores the absurdity and sorrows of the "mixing of races." Two black mothers are bragging about their mulatto son and daughter, who are about to marry each other, when it is later discovered that the children both have the same father. Both mothers had been raped by the same white man.

Poverty and education were also topics handled by various writers. In Georgia Johnson's drama *Plumes* (1928), the poor mother, Charity, is faced with deciding whether to use her last fifty dollars to pay for her dying daughter's operation or to use the money for a "fancy funeral" in the event of her death. Superstition also plays a role in this play. Charity's friend, Tildy, has "read the coffee beans" and insists that the operation would be useless because the coffee beans indicate death.

Mary Burrill's *They That Sit in Darkness* (1919) reveals a poverty-stricken mother and father with eight children, who labor hard to make ends meet. Mrs. Jasper, the mother, is very ill from her day-to-day chores as a domestic, as well as the need to care for her own family, exacerbated by her numerous births. In spite of these hardships, the parents insist that their oldest daughter, Lindy, who is also the greatest help to the household, go to Tuskegee Institute to become a teacher. A visiting nurse, Eilizabeth Shaw, comes by to check on Mrs. Jasper and is disturbed because state laws do not allow her to inform blacks regarding the availability of birth control. Mrs. Jasper dies, preventing the oldest daughter from continuing her education because she must remain to raise the younger ones. Burrill's play is about education. Her message is that every woman should have access to birth control information, and she warns us of the dangerous results that may occur when this knowledge is withheld. She also stresses the importance of blacks' gaining an education to help each other.

While many black women created "race" or "propaganda plays," a large number wrote "folk plays." Because of the numerous unfound plays, it is difficult to assess whether "propaganda" or "folk plays" dominated. Many of the "folk plays" focused on the lighter side of the black experience. Topics involving the church, class conflict, morality, and love relationships were prevalent. There were some "folk" dramatists, such as West Indian–born Eulalie Spence, who avoided racial themes altogether. Spence, whose characters were undeniably black, stressed universal themes. Spence felt that blacks shouldn't be burdened with the problems they faced on a daily basis when they went to the theatre. In her June 1928 article in *Opportunity* magazine, Ms. Spence states:

May I advise these earnest few—those seekers after light—white lights—to avoid the drama of propaganda if they would not meet with certain disaster? Many a serious aspirant for dramatic honors has fallen by the wayside, because he would insist on his lynchings or his rape. The white man is cold and unresponsive to this subject, and the Negro himself, is hurt and humiliated by it. We go to the theatre for entertainment, not to have old fires and hates rekindled. . . . A little more laughter if you please, and fewer spirituals.[13]

Spence's plays usually centered around lovers involved in a love triangle. Except for *Her* (1927), *Undertow* (1929), and *La Divina Pastora* (1929), Spence plays are all comedies. *Undertow*, a melodrama set in Harlem, as were most of her plays, deals with a woman who has returned from the South after many years to reclaim the man she loves—from his wife. Spence's *Fool's Errand* (1927) explores the humorous side of the black church and some of the "busybodies" of the congregation who constantly foster confusion within the community. Spence's comedy *The Hunch* (1927) looks at another love triangle set in Harlem. A couple is about to wed when the fiancée's ex-boyfriend, Bert, discovers that the intended groom has a wife living in Baltimore. Bert travels to Baltimore and returns with the wife to halt the wedding. The play ends happily with Bert marrying his old sweetheart. In an early mystery play, *Her* (1927), Spence juxtaposes religion and superstition. A very religious couple, living in a tenement building, are convinced that their neighbor is a young female ghost. With proper staging, *Her* can be a very suspenseful play. May Miller's comedy *Riding the Goat* (1925) deals with class struggle and the conflict that arises when the people in a small black community are convinced that a young couple have become "too educated" to understand the importance of certain cultural traditions.

Other women, such as Ruth Gaines-Shelton, were to try their hand at comedy. Her play, *The Church Fight* (1925), hilariously reveals some of the familiar characters prevalent in the black church. Another church council has gathered to discuss dismissing the minister who is living beyond his means—off of church funds. When the minister happens to drop by in the midst of the meeting, the members quickly deny any such rumor of expelling him. Gaines goes a step further than Spence with this comedy by giving her characters such names as Brother Judas, Brother Investigator, Sister Two-Face, Sister Meddler, Sister Experience, Sister Instigator, and Sister Take-It-Back.

Also exploring the religious theme was Marita Bonner's melodrama *The Pot Maker* (1927), which finds a recently "called" rural black minister attempting to teach a lesson to his unfaithful wife and her lover through a morality story. The minister also sets a trap for his wife's lover to be killed, but his plan backfires when the wife is also killed.

Some "folk" writers wrote about black heroes and heroines. These plays were often performed in schools and were considered a method of educating young blacks about their heritage. May Miller, who was encouraged by Carter G. Woodson, coauthored with Willis Richardson the anthology *Negro History in Thirteen Plays* (1935). Miller wrote several historical pieces such as *Sojourner Truth* and *Harriet Tubman*. Miller's *Christophe's Daughters* (1935) takes us to the island of Haiti during King Henry Christophe's defeat. The play explores the strength of his two daughters, Athénaire and Améthiste, who have decided to fight to the end to protect their father's honor. Helen Webb Harris wrote *Genifrede* (1922), about a princess who is the daughter of General Toussaint L'Ouverture, the head of the island of San Domingo. The play takes place during L'Ouverture's battle with Napoleon. Harris's play shows Genifrede's strong influence over her father. Harris also wrote the historical play *Frederick Douglass* (1923). Georgia Johnson, who wrote both "propaganda" and "folk" plays, focused on historical characters in *William and Ellen Craft* (1935) and *Frederick Douglass* (1935).

Some of America's greatest black female educators and civil rights activists wrote plays and pageants as a means of educating the race. Mary Church Terrell and Anna J. Cooper, both graduates of Oberlin and educators in Washington, D.C., wrote major pageants. Anna J. Cooper wrote *From Servitude to Service* in 1940 for the July Fourth American Negro Exposition in Chicago, dedicating the production to Eleanor Roosevelt. The piece traced the contribution of blacks in America, starting with the landing at Jamestown. The pageant consisted of three episodes and fourteen scenes. Mary Church Terrell's *Phillis Wheatley: A Bicentennial Pageant* (1932) was presented in Washington, D.C., under the auspices of the District of Columbia George Washington Bicentennial Commission. Harriet Gibbs Marshall, another great educator and Oberlin graduate, wrote the musical drama *The Last Concerto* (1936), which was based on the life of the black classical musician Samuel Coleridge-Taylor. The Washington Conservatory of Music, where Marshall was the director, staged *The Last Concerto*. The cast consisted of close to two hundred members, which was typical of major pageants.

Other history plays, such as Shirley Graham's *It's Morning* (1940) explored the ills of slavery. This drama, which takes place on the eve of emancipation, finds a slave mother contemplating the murder of her young daughter to prevent the child from being sold to a distant slave master. The style of this play is very much like a Greek tragedy: slaves act as the chorus, providing information and setting the action. The murder occurs off stage, also typical of a Greek tragedy.

Of the numerous black women playwrights who were writing prior to the 1950s, seven diverse authors—Georgia Douglas Johnson, May Miller, Zora Neale Hurston, Mary P. Burrill, Eulalie Spence, Shirley Graham, and Marita Bonner—will be the focus of this anthology.

Although diverse in their writing, the seven women presented here had many things in common. They had all been a part of the Washington, D.C., community at some point. They had either studied at Howard University, taught at the famous M Street High School, which later became Dunbar High, or worked with the Krigwa Players in New York, Washington, D.C., or Baltimore. They all knew DuBois and Locke, and often sought their advice regarding their plays. Not only were these women influenced by DuBois, Locke, and Gregory, but they also influenced and inspired each other during this period when it was difficult for women to have their works acknowledged.

Georgia Douglas Johnson, the most prolific writer of the group as well as one of the most experienced, influenced and inspired many women writers of the day. In the home of Johnson the famous "S Street Salon" was held, bringing together many renowned black writers, poets, and dramatists, particularly from the Harlem Renaissance period, to read their works. Johnson encouraged young Marita Bonner to try her hand at playwriting; and Johnson's home was the place Zora Neale Hurston would frequent during her trips to Washington. Hurston also sought refuge in Johnson's home on her final trip from New York back South. May Miller remembers Johnson as a close friend of her parents while a little girl growing up in Washington, D.C. Later, Miller would become a member of the "S Street" group and a close friend. It was May Miller who sat at Johnson's bedside during her last hours. Contemporary Mary Burrill was also a participant in the "S Street" group, as well as a teacher with the M Street School where Johnson would often substitute.

May Miller encouraged close friend Zora Neale Hurston to transfer from Morgan College, in Baltimore, to Howard University to study with Locke and Gregory and to gain experience in the theatre and literature. Hurston started her career as a playwright and folklorist at Howard. In her autobiography, *Dust Tracks on a Road*, Hurston tells of her first meeting with Ms. Miller:

> When it came time to consider college, I planned to stay on at Morgan. But that was changed by chance. Mae [sic] Miller, daughter of the well-known Dr. Kelly Miller of Howard University, came over to Morgan to spend a week-end with her first cousins, Bernice and Gwendolyn Hughes. So we were thrown together. After a few hours of fun and capers, she said, "Zora, you are Howard material. Why don't you come to Howard?"[14]

Hurston and Miller remained friends until Hurston retreated to Florida during the late 1940s and subsequently discontinued communications with many close friends. While working as a secretary/researcher in the home of Dr. Kelly Miller, Shirley Graham met May Miller. It was as a student of Mary Burrill's at the M Street School that Miller would be inspired to write drama. In fact, it was under the supervision of Burrill that Miller had her first play, *Pandora's Box* (1914), printed in the *School's Progress* magazine.

The writers of these plays were usually well educated, and came from a protective environment. Although many of the women were graduates of Howard and Oberlin, they also represented such schools as Columbia, New York University, Radcliffe, Barnard, Emerson, the Sorbonne in Paris, and Yale—primarily New England colleges. Some were very idealistic. They thought that their exceptional education would give their works credibility and acceptance into the larger society on equal grounds. Once out of their protected shell, many of them, such as Marita Bonner and Mary Burrill, assertively spoke out in their plays against the ills of society.

The voice of the black woman playwright was slow to emerge because of racial and sexual barriers. Many of these women, such as the propagandist playwrights, wrote plays not expecting ever to see them staged. Bonner would write on her plays "a play to be read," as opposed to being performed. Georgia Johnson, who submitted several plays on lynching to the Federal Theatre Project, never saw them staged. The few plays that were performed were usually put on by libraries, churches, schools, or clubs within the black community.

Unfortunately, "native drama" written by females never gained the proper recognition it deserved. Many factors were involved with the short-lived "Negro drama" companies that sprang up throughout such cities as New York, Washington, D. C., and Baltimore before the 1950s and particularly during the 1920s and 1930s. A major problem facing black dramatists was the quality of their productions. During the early years in this country, the majority of black professionals in the theatre had been trained in music and comedy. These artists were provided support by the commercial producers. Blacks of the Little Negro Theatre Movement had to compete with professional shows such as *Shuffle Along*, *Black Birds*, *Green Pastures*, and *The Emperor Jones*. Although the Little Theatre Movement was composed of committed individuals, these members for the most part lacked experience in acting and directing. The few that were highly experienced would eventually leave the community for the professional stage. Productions by black dramatists of the Little Negro Theatre Movement also lacked the technical knowledge and the finances to purchase sophisticated staging equipment. The plays themselves often presented a problem. It must be emphasized that blacks during this period were still developing as playwrights and directors. One could only expect so much from these novices. W. E. B. DuBois should undoubtedly be commended for his writing and staging of his *Star of Ethiopia*, but, one must admit, DuBois was neither a playwright nor a director. Hurston's awkwardly written play *Color Struck* was her first attempt at playwriting. Historically it offers an incredible insight into the problem of the color issue within the black race. However, in its present form, the play presents a monumental challenge for even the most experienced director.

Another issue facing many of the little theatre groups was subject matter, particularly from the propaganda plays and, at times, the "folk plays." During a period of escalating lynchings, two world wars, and a major depression, many black people had little desire to go to the theatre, to be educated and subjected to the trials and tribulations of the race problem in America. As writer Sterling Brown simply stated: "But the Negro audience frequently wants flattery instead of representation, plaster saints instead of human beings, drawing rooms instead of the homes of the people. And the typical white audience wants stereotypes."[15]

The black woman playwright persevered. She wrote, produced, directed, and staged her plays no matter how awkward and technically inept they were. The subject, theme, and message were of utmost importance to these dedicated, inspired, and courageous black women. This anthology acknowledges their uniqueness and spirit.

NOTES

1. Anna J. Cooper, *A Voice from the South* (Xenia, Ohio: Aldine Printing House, 1892), p. 134.

2. Interview with Lorraine Hansberry by Nan Robertson in "Dramatist Against Odds," *New York Times*, March 8, 1959 (Schomburg Collection, *A Raisin in the Sun* folder).

3. W. E. B. Dubois, Krigwa Players Inaugural Playbill, season of 1926.

4. Loften Mitchell, *Voices of the Black Theatre* (Clifton, New Jersey: James T. White & Company, 1975), p. 70.

5. Abby Arthur Johnson and Ronald Maberry Johnson, *Propaganda and Aesthetics: The Literary Politics of Afro-American Magazines in the Twentieth Century* (Amherst: The University of Massachusetts Press, 1979).

6. Montgomery T. Gregory Manuscript Collection, Newspaper clipping file on Howard Players. Moorland-Spingarn Research Center, Howard University.

7. Ibid.

8. Montgomery T. Gregory and Alain Locke, *Plays of Negro Life* (New York: Harper & Row, 1927), p. 414.

9. Ibid.

10. Angelina Grimké papers, Moorland-Spingarn Research Center, Howard University.

11. Walter White, *Rope and Faggot: A Biography of Judge Lynch* (New York: Alfred A. Knopf, 1929), p. 229.

12. John Hope Franklin, *From Slavery to Freedom: A History of American Negroes*, 3rd ed. (New York: Alfred A. Knopf, 1967), p. 439.

13. Eulalie Spence, "A Criticism of the Negro Drama," *Opportunity* (June 28, 1928), p. 180.

14. Zora Neale Hurston, *Dust Tracks on a Road*, 2nd ed. (Urbana: University of Illinois Press, 1984), pp. 155–56.

15. Sterling Brown, *Negro Poetry and Drama and the Negro in American Fiction* (New York: Atheneum, 1978), p. 123.

Georgia Douglas Johnson

(1880–1966)

Georgia Douglas Johnson around the early 1920s. *(Courtesy of the Schomburg Center for Research in Black Culture)*

Then came drama. I was persuaded to try it and found it
a living avenue and yet—the thing left most unfinished,
less exploited, first relinquished, is still nearest my heart
and most dear.[1]

ONE OF THE FIRST black modern female poets of the twentieth century,
Georgia Douglas Johnson was an inspiration and role model for the many
black women writers who emerged during the 1920s. A prolific poet and
playwright, Johnson gained recognition as an established writer with the
publication of her collection of poems, *The Heart of a Woman* (1918). Her
Washington, D.C., home was the site of a weekly gathering for many
prominent writers of the Harlem Renaissance known as the "S Street Salon." Such writers as Mary P. Burrill, Countee Cullen, Alain Locke, Marita
Bonner, Jessie Fauset, Willis Richardson, May Miller, Randolph Edmonds,
Jean Toomer, Carter G. Woodson, and Langston Hughes would frequent
Johnson's home to introduce new works.

Georgia Douglas Johnson was born September 10, 1880, to George and
Laura Jackson Camp in Marietta, Georgia. Her father was a well-educated
and wealthy Englishman of whom Johnson knew very little. Because her
mother worked all day away from home, she grew up a very lonely child.
She had no brothers or sisters wholly related, but three brothers and one
sister through a third marriage of her mother.

Johnson began her early education at various private and public schools
in Rome and Atlanta, Georgia. She attended Atlanta University, where she
experienced her first "real homey sympathetic atmosphere." After complet-
ing her education at the university, she taught in Marietta and later worked
as an assistant principal in Atlanta. The late 1890s found Johnson pursuing
musical training at Oberlin Conservatory in Ohio.

Returning to Atlanta, she married Henry Lincoln Johnson in 1900 and
bore two sons, Henry Lincoln, Jr., and Peter Douglas. In 1910 the Johnsons
moved to Washington, D.C., where her husband, "Link" senior, established
a law practice and later was appointed Recorder of Deeds under President
Taft. With the sudden death of Link in 1925, Johnson was forced to provide
for her sons. She assumed various jobs with the government and taught pe-
riodically as a substitute teacher in the Washington, D.C., public school
system. She also furthered her education by taking courses at Howard
University.

A poem written by poet William Stanley Braithwaite, about a lone flower
and a lonely little girl who tended it, inspired Johnson to write poetry. According to Johnson: "Something in this poem together with the associated
idea that he [Braithwaite] had a drop or so of colored blood, gave me a kind
of lift and fed my ambition to emulate him."[2]

While they were living in Washington D.C., May Miller's father, Dean Kelly Miller of Howard University, introduced Johnson to Braithwaite, and they developed a long-time friendship. Braithwaite would also be instrumental in assisting Johnson with her early publications.

Through a friendship with white playwright Zona Gale, Johnson was encouraged to write plays during the early 1920s. Although Johnson was known to have written close to thirty plays, only a few scripts have survived. Of this small group, five were published—*A Sunday Morning in the South* (1925), *Blue Blood* (1926), *Plumes* (1927), *Frederick Douglass* (1935), *William and Ellen Craft* (1935). Only *Plumes*, *Blue Blood*, and *Frederick Douglass* are known to have been produced. *Blue Blood*, which was staged in New York City, featured the talents of Frank Horne and May Miller. In 1933, at Howard University, along with two other one-act plays, *Blue Blood* was produced again.

Because of the unavailability of many of her works, it is difficult to determine which script was her first. In 1926, *Blue Blood*, the only tragicomedy she was known to have authored, won the *Opportunity* contest as one of the four best plays. *Plumes*, which is about poor, rural blacks, captured first prize in the 1927 competition.

Johnson, along with May Miller, was one of the more versatile dramatists. Her works included "folk dramas" as well as "propaganda." Because of Johnson's interracial background, many of her plays such as *Blue Blood* and *Blue-Eyed Black Boy* dealt with miscegenation.

Lynching was another topic Johnson focused on in her works. As an active participant in the anti-lynching campaign during the 1920s, Johnson became aware of the impact drama could have on effecting social change. During the Federal Theatre Project (1935–1939), Johnson submitted four plays that she categorized as her "plays on lynching"—*A Sunday Morning in the South* (versions I & II), *Safe*, and *Blue-Eyed Black Boy*. She also submitted two history plays—*Frederick Douglass* and *Willian and Ellen Craft*. The latter two dramatized the efforts of slaves to escape and gain their freedom. Unfortunately, none of her plays were produced by the Federal Theatre Project.

Johnson continued to write plays into the late 1940s. However, during this period she also wrote poetry and over a dozen musical compositions. During the 1930s, Johnson submitted articles and poems for numerous black papers and journals. She was also a contributing editor for *The Negro Woman's World Magazine* and an associate editor with *The Women's Voice*, both Washington, D.C., based magazines.

Known as an individual with a big heart, Johnson opened her home to anyone seeking refuge. She also ran a correspondence club for "lonely people all over the world." A great lover of movies, Johnson continued to live at her famous S Street home until her death in 1966.

NOTES

1. "The Contest Spotlight," *Opportunity*, July, 1927, p. 204.
2. Autobiography of Georgia Douglas Johnson, Biography File, Fisk University Library, Nashville, Tennessee.

PLUMES

CHARACTERS

CHARITY BROWN,	the mother
EMMERLINE BROWN,	the daughter
TILDY,	the friend
DOCTOR SCOTT,	physician

Scene: A poor cottage in the South.
Time: Contemporary.

SCENE: *The kitchen of a two-room cottage. A window overlooking the street. A door leading to street, one leading to the back yard and one to the inner room. A stove, a table with shelf over it, a washtub. A rocking-chair, a cane-bottom chair. Needle, thread, scissors, etc. on table.*

Scene opens with CHARITY BROWN *heating a poultice over the stove. A groaning is heard from the inner room.*

CHARITY. Yes, honey, mamma is fixing somethin' to do you good. Yes, my baby, jus' you wait—I'm a-coming.

(*Knock is heard at door. It is gently pushed open and* TILDY *comes in cautiously.*)

TILDY. (*Whispering*) How is she?

CHARITY. Poorly, poorly. Didn't rest last night none hardly. Move that dress and set in th' rocker. I been trying to snatch a minute to finish it but don't seem like I can. She won't have nothing to wear if she—she—

TILDY. I understands. How near done is it?

CHARITY. Ain't so much more to do.

TILDY. (*Takes up dress from chair, looks at it*) I'll do some on it.

CHARITY. Thank you, sister Tildy. Whip that torshon on and turn down the hem in the skirt.

TILDY. (*Measuring dress against herself*) How deep?

CHARITY. Let me see, now (*Studies a minute with finger against lip*) I tell you—jus' baste it, 'cause you see—she wears'em short, but—it might be—(*Stops.*)

TILDY. (*Bowing her head comprehendingly*) Huh-uh, I see exzackly. (*Sighs*) You'd want it long—over her feet—then.

CHARITY. That's it, sister Tildy. (*Listening*) She's some easy now! (*Stirring poultice*) Jest can't get this poltis' hot enough somehow this morning.

TILDY. Put some red pepper in it. Got any?

CHARITY. Yes. There ought to be some in one of them boxes on the shelf there. (*Points.*)

TILDY. (*Goes to shelf, looks about and gets the pepper*) Here, put a-plenty of this in.

CHARITY. (*Groans are heard from the next room*) Good Lord, them pains got her again. She suffers so, when she's 'wake.

TILDY. Poor little thing. How old is she now, sister Charity?

CHARITY. Turning fourteen this coming July.

TILDY. (*Shaking her head dubiously*) I sho' hope she'll be mended by then.

CHARITY. It don't look much like it, but I trusts so—(*Looking worried*) That doctor's mighty late this morning.

TILDY. I expects he'll be 'long in no time. Doctors is mighty onconcerned here lately.

CHARITY. (*Going toward inner room with poultice*) They surely is and I don't have too much confidence in none of 'em. (*You can hear her soothing the child.*)

TILDY. (*Listening*) Want me to help you put it on, sister Charity?

CHARITY. (*From inner room*) No, I can fix it. (*Coming back from sick room shaking her head rather dejectedly.*)

TILDY. How is she, sister Charity?

CHARITY. Mighty feeble. Gone back to sleep now. My poor little baby. (*Bracing herself*) I'm going to put on some coffee now.

TILDY. I'm sho' glad. I feel kinder low-spirited.

CHARITY. It's me that low-sperited. The doctor said last time he was here he might have to oparate—said, she mought have a chance then. But I tell you the truth, I've got no faith a-tall in 'em. They takes all your money for nothing.

TILDY. They sho' do and don't leave a cent for putting you away decent.

CHARITY. That's jest it. They takes all you got and then you dies jest the same. It ain't like they was sure.

TILDY. No, they ain't sure. That's it exzactly. But they takes your money jest the same, and leaves you flat.

CHARITY. I been thinking 'bout Zeke these last few days—how he was put away—

TILDY. I wouldn't worry 'bout him now. He's out of his troubles.

CHARITY. I know. But it worries me when I think about how he was put away . . . that ugly pine coffin, jest one shabby old hack and nothing else to show—to show—what we thought about him.

TILDY. Hush, sister! Don't you worry over him. He's happy now, anyhow.

CHARITY. I can't help it! Then little Bessie. We all jest scrooged in one hack and took her little coffin in our lap all the way out to the graveyard. (*Breaks out crying.*)

TILDY. Do hush, sister Charity. You done the best you could. Poor folks got to make the best of it. The Lord understands—

CHARITY. I know that—but I made up my mind the time Bessie went that the next one of us what died would have a shore nuff funeral, everything grand,—with plumes!—I saved and saved and now—this yah doctor—

TILDY. All they think about is cuttin' and killing and taking your money. I got nothin' to put 'em doing.

CHARITY. (*Goes over to washtub and rubs on clothes*) Me neither. These clothes got to get out somehow, I needs every cent.

TILDY. How much that washing bring you?

CHARITY. Dollar and a half. It's worth a whole lot more. But what can you do?

TILDY. You can't do nothing—Look there, sister Charity, ain't that coffee boiling?

CHARITY. (*Wipes hands on apron and goes to stove*) Yes it's boiling good fashioned. Come on, drink some.

TILDY. There ain't nothing I'd rather have than a good strong cup of coffee. (*Charity pours Tildy's cup.*) (*Sweetening and stirring hers*) Pour you some. (*Charity pours her own cup*) I'd been dead, too, long ago if it hadn't a been for my coffee.

CHARITY. I love it, but it don't love me—gives me the shortness of breath.

TILDY. (*Finishing her cup, taking up sugar with spoon*) Don't hurt me. I could drink a barrel.

CHARITY. (*Drinking more slowly—reaching for coffeepot*) Here, drink another cup.

TILDY. I shore will, that cup done me a lot of good.

CHARITY. (*Looking into her empty cup thoughtfully*) I wish Dinah Morris would drop in now. I'd ask her what these grounds mean.

TILDY. I can read em a little myself.

CHARITY. You can? Well, for the Lord's sake, look here and tell me what this cup says! (*Offers cup to Tildy. Tildy wards it off.*)

TILDY. You got to turn it 'round in your saucer three times first.

CHARITY. Yes, that's right, I forgot. (*Turns cup 'round, counting*) One, two, three. (*Starts to pick it up.*)

TILDY. Huhudh. (*Meaning no*) Let it set a minute. It might be watery. (*After a minute, while she finishes her own cup*) Now let me see. (*Takes cup and examines it very scrutinizingly.*)

CHARITY. What you see?

TILDY. (*Hesitatingly*) I ain't seen a cup like this one for many a year. Not since—not since—

CHARITY. When?

TILDY. Not since jest before ma died. I looked in the cup then and saw things and—I stopped looking . . .

CHARITY. Tell me what you see, I want to know.

TILDY. I don't like to tell no bad news—

CHARITY. Go on. I can stan' anything after all I been thru'.

TILDY. Since you're bound to know I'll tell you. (*Charity draws nearer*) I sees a big gethering!

CHARITY. Gethering, you say?

TILDY. Yes, a big gethering. People all crowded together. Then I see 'em going one by one and two by two. Long line stretching out and out and out!

CHARITY. (*In a whisper*) What you think it is?

TILDY. (*Awed like*) Looks like (*Hesitates*) a possession!

CHARITY. (*Shouting*) You sure!

TILDY. I know it is. (*Just then the toll of a church bell is heard and then the steady and slow tramp, tramp, of horses' hoofs. Both women look at each other.*)

TILDY. (*In a hushed voice*) That must be Bell Gibson's funeral coming 'way from Mt. Zion. (*Gets up and goes to window*) Yes, it sho' is.

CHARITY. (*Looking out of the window also*) Poor Bell suffered many a year; she's out of her pain now.

TILDY. Look, here comes the hearse now!

CHARITY. My Lord! ain't it grand! Look at them horses—look at their heads—plumes—how they shake 'em! Land o' mighty! It's a fine sight, sister Tildy.

TILDY. That must be Jer'miah in that first carriage, bending over like; he shorely is putting her away grand.

CHARITY. No mistake about it. That's Pickett's best funeral turnout he's got.

TILDY. I'll bet it cost a lot.

CHARITY. Fifty dollars, so Matilda Jenkins told me. She had it for Bud. The plumes is what cost.

TILDY. Look at the hacks—(*Counts*) I believe to my soul there's eight.

CHARITY. Got somebody in all of 'em too—and flowers—She shore got a lot of 'em. (*Both women's eyes follow the tail end of the procession, horses' hoofs die away as they turn away from window. The two women look at each other significantly.*)

TILDY. (*Significantly*) Well!—(*They look at each other without speaking for a minute. Charity goes to the washtub*) Want these cups washed up?

CHARITY. No don't mind 'em. I'd rather you get that dress done. I got to get these clothes out.

TILDY. (*Picking up dress*) Shore, there ain't so much more to do on it now. (*Knock is heard on the door. Charity answers knock and admits* DR. SCOTT.)

DR. SCOTT. Good morning. How's the patient today?

CHARITY. Not so good, doctor. When she ain't 'sleep she suffers so; but she sleeps mostly.

DR. SCOTT. Well, let's see, let's see. Just hand me a pan of warm water and I'll soon find out just what's what.

CHARITY. All right, doctor. I'll bring it to you right away. (*Bustles about fixing water—looking toward dress Tildy is working on*) Poor little Emmerline's been wanting a white dress trimmed with torshon a long time— now she's got it and it looks like—well—(*Hesitates*) t'warn't made to wear.

TILDY. Don't take on so, sister Charity—The Lord giveth and the Lord taketh.

CHARITY. I know—but it's hard—hard—(*Goes into inner room with water. You can hear her talking with the doctor after a minute and the doctor expostulating with her—in a minute she appears at the door, being led from the room by the doctor.*)

DR. SCOTT. No, my dear Mrs. Brown. It will be much better for you to remain outside.

CHARITY. But, doctor—

DR. SCOTT. NO. You stay outside and get your mind on something else. You can't possibly be of any service. Now be calm, will you?

CHARITY. I'll try, doctor.

TILDY. The doctor's right. You can't do no good in there.

CHARITY. I knows, but I thought I could hold the pan or somethin'. (*Lowering her voice*) Says he got to see if her heart is all right or somethin'. I tell you—nowadays—

TILDY. I know.

CHARITY. (*Softly to Tildy*) Hope he won't come out here saying he got to operate. (*Goes to washtub.*)

TILDY. I hope so, too. Won't it cost a lot?

CHARITY. That's jest it. It would take all I got saved up.

TILDY. Of course, if he's goin' to get her up—but I don't believe in 'em. I don't believe in 'em.

CHARITY. He didn't promise tho'—even if he did, he said maybe it wouldn't do no good.

TILDY. I'd think a long time before I'd let him operate on my chile. Taking all yuh money, promising nothing and ten to one killing her to boot.

CHARITY. This is a hard world.

TILDY. Don't you trus' him. Coffee grounds don't lie!

CHARITY. I don't trust him. I jest want to do what's right by her. I ought to put these clothes on the line while you're settin' in here, but I jes hate to go outdoors while he's in there.

TILDY. (*Getting up*) I'll hang 'em out. You stay here. Where your clothes-pins at?

CHARITY. Hanging right there by the back door in the bag. They ought to dry before dark and then I can iron to-night.

TILDY. (*Picking up tub*) They ought to blow dry in no time. (*Goes toward back door.*)

CHARITY. Then I can shore rub 'em over to-night. Say, sister Tildy, hist 'em up with that long saplin' prop leaning in the fence corner.

TILDY. (*Going out*) All right.

CHARITY. (*Standing by the table beating nervously on it with her fingers—listens—and then starts to bustling about the kitchen*) (*Enter Doctor from inner room.*)

DR. SCOTT. Well, Mrs. Brown, I've decided I'll have to operate.

CHARITY. MY Lord! Doctor—don't say that!

DR. SCOTT. It's the only chance.

CHARITY. You mean she'll get well if you do?

DR. SCOTT. No, I can't say that—It's just a chance—a last chance. And I'll do just what I said, cut the price of the operation down to fifty dollars. I'm willing to do that for you. (*Charity throws up her hands in dismay.*)

CHARITY. Doctor, I was so in hopes you wouldn't operate—I—I—And yo' say you ain't a bit sure she'll get well—even then?

DR. SCOTT. No. I can't be sure. We'll just have to take the chance. But I'm sure you want to do everything—

CHARITY. Sure, doctor, I do want to—do—everything I can do to—to—Doctor, look at this cup. (*Picks up fortune cup and shows the doctor*) My fortune's jes' been told this very morning—look at these grounds—they says— (*Softly*) it ain't no use, no use a-tall.

DR. SCOTT. Why, my good woman, don't you believe in such senseless things! That cup of grounds can't show you anything. Wash them out and forget it.

CHARITY. I can't forget it. I feel like it ain't no use; I'd just be spendin' the money that I needs—for nothing—nothing.

DR. SCOTT. But you won't though—You'll have a clear conscience. You'd know that you did everything you could.

CHARITY. I know that, doctor. But there's things you don't know 'bout—there's other things I got to think about. If she goes—if she must go . . . I had plans—I been getting ready—now— Oh, doctor, I jest can't see how I can have this operation—you say you can't promise—nothing?

DR. SCOTT. I didn't think you'd hesitate about it—I imagined your love for your child—

CHARITY. (*Breaking in*) I do love my child. My God, I do love my child. You don't understand . . . but . . . but—can't I have a little time to think about it, doctor? It means so much—to her—and—me!

DR. SCOTT. I tell you. I'll go on over to the office. I'd have to get my— (*Hesitates*) my things, anyhow. And as soon as you make up your mind, get one of the neighbors to run over and tell me. I'll come right back. But don't waste any time now, Mrs. Brown, every minute counts.

CHARITY. Thank you, doctor, thank you. I'll shore send you word as soon as I can. I'm so upset and worried I'm half crazy.

DR. SCOTT. I know you are . . . but don't take too long to make up your mind. . . . It ought to be done to-day. Remember—it may save her. (*Exits.*)

CHARITY. (*Goes to door of sick room—looks inside for a few minutes, then starts walking up and down the little kitchen, first holding a hand up to her head and then wringing them. Enter Tildy from yard with tub under her arm.*)

TILDY. Well, they're all out, sister Charity— (*Stops*) Why, what's the matter?

CHARITY. The doctor wants to operate.

TILDY. (*Softly*) Where he—gone?

CHARITY. Yes—he's gone, but he's coming back—if I send for him.

TILDY. You going to? (*Puts down tub and picks up white dress and begins sewing.*)

CHARITY. I dunno—I got to think.

TILDY. I can't see what's the use myself. He can't save her with no operation—Coffee grounds don't lie.

CHARITY. It would take all the money I got for the operation and then what about puttin' her away? He can't save her—don't even promise ter. I know he can't—I feel it . . . I feel it . . .

TILDY. It's in the air. . . . (*Both women sit tense in the silence. Tildy has commenced sewing again. Just then a strange, strangling noise comes from the inner room.*)

TILDY. What's that?

CHARITY. (*Running toward and into inner room*) Oh, my God! (*From inside*) Sister Tildy—Come here—No,—Some water, quick.
(*Tildy with dress in hand starts toward inner room. Stops at door, sighs and then goes hurriedly back for the water pitcher. Charity is heard moaning softly in the next room, then she appears at doorway and leans against jamb of door*) Rip the hem out, sister Tildy.

CURTAIN

A SUNDAY MORNING
IN THE SOUTH

C H A R A C T E R S

SUE JONES,　　　the grandmother, aged seventy
TOM GRIGGS,　　her grandson, aged nineteen
BOSSIE GRIGGS,　her grandson, aged seven
LIZA TRIGGS,　　a friend, aged sixty
MATILDA BROWN,　a friend, aged fifty
A WHITE GIRL
FIRST OFFICER
SECOND OFFICER

Place: A town in the South.
Time: 1924.

(*Scene: Kitchen in* SUE JONES'S *two room house. A window on left, a door leading to back yard and another leading to front room. A stove against the back wall, a table near it, four chairs, an old time safe with dishes and two bottles—one clear and one dark—a wooden water bucket with shiny brass bales, and a tin dipper hanging near it on a nail.*

As the curtain rises Sue Jones is seen putting the breakfast on the kitchen table. She wears a red bandanna handkerchief on her grey head, a big blue gingham apron tied around her waist and big wide old lady comfort shoes. She uses a stick as she has a sore leg, and moves about with a stoop and a limp as she goes back and forth from the stove to the table.)

SUE. (*calling*) Tom, Tom, you and Bossie better come on out here and git your breakfast before it gits cold; I got good hot rolls this mornin!

TOM. I reckin I oughter had but I didn't know how heavy they was till I started and then he was gone.

at rolls, then begins humming and singing)

> Eugh . . . eu . . . eugh . . .
> Jes look at the morning star

Eugh . . . eu . . . eugh . . .
We'll all git home bye and bye . . .

(*As she finishes the song* TOM *and* BOSSIE *come hurrying into the kitchen placing their chairs at the table; there is one already at the table for Sue. Sue takes rolls out of stove with her apron and brings them to the table*) It's as hard to git yawll out of the bed on Sunday morning as it is to pull hen's teeth.

TOM. (*eating. The church bell next door is heard ringing*) Eugh—there's the church bell. I sho meant to git out to meeting this morning but my back still hurts me. Remember I told you last night how I sprained it lifting them heavy boxes for Mr. John?

SUE. (*giving Bossie a roll and a piece of sausage*) You hadn't oughter done it; you oughter ast him to let somebody hep you—you aint no hoss!

TOM. I reckin I oughter had but I didn't know how heavy they was till I started and then he was gone.

SUE. You oughter had some of my snake oil linament on it last night, that's whut?

TOM. I wish I hader but I was so dead tired I got outer my clothes and went straight to bed. I muster been sleep by nine er clock I reckin.

SUE. Nine er clock! You is crazy! Twant no moren eight when I called you to go to the store and git me a yeast cake fur my light rolls and you was sleeping like a log of wood; I had to send Bossie fur it.

BOSSIE. Yes, and you snored so loud I thought you would a choked. (*holding out his plate and licking his lips with his tongue*) Grannie kin I have some more?

SUE. Whut? Where is all thot I jest give you?

BOSSIE. (*rubbing his stomach with his other hand and smiling broadly*) It's gone down the red lane struttin'.

SUE. Well this is all you gointer git this mornin. (*helping him to more rolls and sausage*) When you git big and work like Tom you kin stuff all you wants to.

BOSSIE. I aint never gointer break my back like Tom working hard—I'm a gointer be a—a preacher that's whut and . . .

SUE. (*catching sight of someone passing the window as she approached the back door*) I bleve that's Liza Twiggs must be on her way to church and smelled these light rolls and coffee. (*a knock is heard at the back door*) Let her in, Bossie!

(*Bossie jumps up from the table, hurries to the door and opens it*)

LIZA. (*enters sniffling*) Mawning yawll.

SUE. Morning Liza—on your way to church?

LIZA. Yes the first bell just rung and I thought I'd drop in a minute. (*whiffs again*) Coffee sho smells good!

SUE. Tastes better'n it smells—Pull up a cheer and swaller a cupful with one of these light rolls.

LIZA. (*drawing up a chair*) Dont keer if I do. (*she is helped to coffee and rolls while Bossie looks at her disapprovingly. To Sue*) How is your leg gitting on?

SUE. Well as I kin expect. I won't never walk on it good no mo. It eats and eats. Sho is lucky I'm right here next door to church (*to Tom*) Open that winder Tom so I kin hear the singing. (*Tom opens window. To Liza*) Folks don't like to set next to me in church no mo. Tinks its ketching—a cancer or somethin'. (*then brightly*) Whut you know good?

(*From the church next door is heard the hymn, drifting through the window:* "Amazing grace how sweet the sound / That saves a wretch like me . . . ")

LIZA. (*listening*) They done started "Amazing grace." (*music continues as a background for their talk*) (*still eating*) That music she is sweet but I got to finish eatin first, then I'll go . . .

SUE. I ast you whut you know good.

LIZA. Well, I don't know nothin tall good, but I did hear as how the police is all over now trying to run down some po Nigger they say that's tacked a white woman last night right up here near the Pine Street market. They says as how the white folks is shonuff mad too, and if they ketch him they gointer make short work of him.

SUE. (*still drinking coffee*) Eugh, eugh, eugh, you don't say. I don't hold wid no rascality and I bleves in meeting out punishment to the guilty but they fust ought to fine out who done it tho and then let the law hanel 'em. That's what I says.

LIZA. Me too, I thinks the law oughter hanel 'em too, but you know a sight of times they gits the wrong man and goes and strings him up and don't fin out who done it till it's too late!

SUE. That's so. And sometimes the white uns been knowed to blackin they faces and make you bleve some po Nigger done it.

TOM. They lynch you bout anything too, not jest women. They say Zeb Brooks was strung up because he and his boss had er argiment.

LIZA. Sho did. I says the law's the law and it ought er be er ark uv safty to pertect the weak and not some little old flimsy shack that a puff of wind can blow down.

TOM. I been thinking a whole lot about these things and I mean to go to night school and git a little book learning so as I can do something to help—help change the laws . . . make em strong . . . I sometimes get right upset and wonder whut would I do if they ever tried to put something on me . . .

LIZA. Pshaw . . . everybody knows you . . . nobody would bother you . . .

SUE. No sonnie, you won't never hafter worry bout sich like that but you kin hep to save them po devels that they do git after.

(*Singing comes from the church next door:*

        Shine on me, shine on me.
        Let the light from the lighthouse shine on me,

Shine on me, shine on me,
Let the light from the lighthouse shine on me.

TOM. It takes a sight of learning to understand the law and I'm a gointer . . . (*a quick rap is heard at the door and it is almost immediately
pushed open and an* OFFICER *enters as the four at table look up at him
in open mouthed amazement*)

FIRST OFFICER. Tom Griggs live here?

SUE. (*starting up excitedly*) Yes Sir (*stammering*)

FIRST OFFICER. (*looking at Tom*) You Tom Griggs?

TOM. (*puzzled*) Yes sir.

FIRST OFFICER. (*roughly*) Where were you last night at ten o'clock?

SUE. (*answering quickly for Tom*) Right here sir, he was right here at
home. Whut you want to know fer?

FIRST OFFICER. (*to Sue*) You keep quiet, old woman. (*to Tom*) Say, you answer up. Can't you talk? Where were you last night at ten o'clock.

TOM. (*uneasily*) Gramma told you. I was right here at home—in bed at
eight o'clock.

FIRST OFFICER. That sounds fishy to me—in bed at eight o'clock! And who
else knows you were here?

SUE. Say Mr. Officer, whut you trying to do to my granson. Shore as God
Amighty is up in them heabens he was right here in bed. I seed him and
his little brother Bossie there saw him, didn't you Bossie?

BOSSIE. (*in a frightened whisper*) Yessum, I seed him and I heered him!

FIRST OFFICER. (*to Bossie*) Shut up. Your word's nothing. (*looking at Sue*)
Nor yours either. Both of you'd lie for him. (*steps to back door and makes
a sign to someone outside, then comes back into the room taking a piece
of paper from his vest pocket and reads slowly, looking at Tom critically
as he checks each item*) Age around twenty, five feet five or six, brown
skin . . . (*he folds up the paper and puts it back into his vest*) Yep! fits
like a glove. (*Sue, Liza and Tom look from one to the other with growing
amazement and terror as* SECOND OFFICER *pushes open the door and
stands there supporting a young white girl on his arm*)

SECOND OFFICER. (*to girl*) Is this the man?

WHITE GIRL. (*hesitatingly* I—I'm not sure . . . but . . . but he looks something like him . . . (*holding back*)

FIRST OFFICER. (*encouragingly*) Take a good look, Miss. He fits your description perfect. Color, size, age, everything. Pine Street Market ain't
no where from here, and he surely did pass that way last night. He was
there all right, all right! We got it figgered all out. (*to* GIRL, *who looks
down at her feet*) You say he looks like him?

WHITE GIRL. (*looking at him again quickly*) Y-e-s (*slowly and undecid-
edly*) I think so. I . . . I . . . (*then she covers her face with her arm and
turns quickly and moves away from the door, supported by second officer.
First officer makes a step toward Tom and slips handcuffs on him before
any one is aware what is happening*)

SUE. (*holding on to her chair and shaking her cane at the officer, while Bossie comes up close to her and snivels in her apron*) Whut you doing? What you doing? You can't rest my granson—he ain't done nothing—you can't rest him!

FIRST OFFICER. Be quiet, old woman. I'm just going to take him along to the sheriff to question him and if he's telling the truth he'll be right back home here in no time.

SUE. But you can't rest him; he don't know no mo bout that po little white chile than I do—You can't take him!

TOM. (*utterly bewildered*) Granma, don't take on so. I'll go long with him to the sheriff. I'll splain to him how I couldn't a done it when I was here sleep all the time—I never laid eyes on that white lady before in all my life.

SUE. (*to Tom*) Course you ain't. (*to officer*) Mr. Officer, that white chile ain't never seed my granson before—All Niggers looks alike to her; she so upset she don't know whut she's saying.

FIRST OFFICER. (*to Sue as he pulls Tom along*) You just keep cool Grannie, he'll be right back—if he's innocent. (*to Tom*) And the quieter you comes along the better it will be for you.

TOM. (*looking back at his grandma from the doorway with terror in his eyes*) I'll be right back granny—don't cry—don't cry—Jest as soon as I see—(*the officer pulls him out of the doorway*)

LIZA. (*standing with her hands clasped together, her head bowed and swaying from side to side with emotion. She prays*) Sweet Jesus, do come down and hep us this mornin. You knows our hearts and you knows this po boy ain't done nothing wrong. You said you would hep the fatherless and the motherless; do Jesus bring this po orphan back to his ole cripple grannie safe and sound, do Jesus!

BOSSIE. (*crying and pulling at his grandma's apron*) Grannie, grannie, whut they gointer do to my brother? Whut they gointer do to him?

SUE. (*brokenly*) The good Jesus only knows, but I'm a talking to the Lord now asting Him to . . . (*a rap is heard at the door; it is almost immediately pushed open and* MATILDA BROWN *enters hurriedly and excitedly*)

MATILDA. (*breathlessly*) Miss Liza, as I was coming long I seed Tom wid the police and there was some white mens wid guns a trying to take him away from the police—said he'd done been dentified and they want gointer be cheated outen they Nigger this time. I, I flew on down here to tell you, you better do somethin'.

SUE. (*shaking nervously from side to side as she leans on her cane for support*) Oh my God, whut kin I do?

LIZA. (*alertly*) You got to git word to some of your good white folks, that's whut and git em to save him.

SUE. Yes . . . That's whut . . . Lemme see . . . (*she stands tense thinking a moment*) I got it . . . Miss Vilet . . . I got to git to Miss Vilet . . . I nused her when she was a baby and she'll do it . . . Her pa's the Jedge.

LIZA. That's right! I'll go. You can't go quick.

MATILDA. No. Lemme go; I kin move in a hurry, lemme go!

SUE. All right Tildy. Tell Miss Vilet her ole nuse Sue is callin on her and don't fail me; tell her they done took Tom and he is perfect innercent, and they gointer take him away from the police, and ax her to ax her pa the Jedge to go git Tom and save him fur God's sake. Now hurry, Tildy, fly!

BOSSIE. (*to Sue*) Lemme go long; I knows how to git there quick cutting through the ole field.

LIZA. Yes they knows Bossie and he kin hep tell.

SUE. Yes Bossie, gone, yawll hurry, hurry! (*Matilda and Bossie hurry out of the back door and Sue sinks down into a chair exhausted while Liza comes over to her and pats her on the back*)

LIZA. Now, now evrything's gointer be all right . . . Miss Vilet 'll fix it . . . she ain't gointer let her ole mammy call on her for nothing . . . she'll make her pa save him.

SUE. Yes, she's a good chile . . . I knows she'll save him.

(*Sue moves her lips in prayer. From the church next door comes the sound of singing; the two women listen to the words with emotion*

Alas, and did my savior bleed
And did my sovereign die
Would he devote his sacred head
For such a worm as I.

Must Jesus bear the cross alone
And all the world go free,
No, there's a cross for every one
And there's a cross for me.

Sue rocks back and forth in chair, head buried in her apron. Liza walks up and down the floor, throws her hands up imploringly now and then)

LIZA. Oh Lord, hep us to bear our cross! Hep us!

SUE. (*drooping*) Liza I'm feeling sorter fainty lack; git me my bottle of camphor out of the safe yonder.

LIZA. (*going to safe*) Yes chile, I'll git it. You done gone through a whole lot this mornin, God knows. (*takes up a bottle and holds it up for Sue to see*) This it?

SUE. (*shaking her head*) Eugh eugh, that's my sweet oil. It's the yuther one in the black bottle . . . see it?

LIZA. (*taking out bottle and smelling it*) Yes here it is. Strong too. It'll do you good. I has them sinking spells too sometimes (*comes over to Sue with stopper out of bottle and holds it to her nose*) There draw a deep bref of it; feel better?

SUE. I'll feel better tereckly. My old heart is gittin weak.

LIZA. Set back comfortable in your cheer and listen to the singin; they all sho talkin to the Lord fur you in that church this mornin. Listen! (*The church is singing*):

> I must tell Jesus, I cannot bear my burdens alone
> In my distress he surely will help me
> I cannot bear my burdens alone.
>
> I must tell Jesus, I cannot bear my burdens alone
> Jesus my Lord he surely will help me
> Jesus will help me, Jesus alone

LIZA. That's all, that's all we kin do jes tell Jesus! Jesus! Jesus please bow down your ear! (*walks up and down mumbling a soft prayer as the singing continues mournfully*)

SUE. I reckin Tildy's bout on her way back now. I knows Miss Vilet done got her pa by now, don't you reckin, Liza.

LIZA. (*sympathetically*) Course; I spects Tom'll be coming back too any minit now. Everybody knows he ain't done no harm.

SUE. (*listening to running feet at the door and sitting up straight in chair*) Who dat coming? (*Matilda pushes open the door and comes in all excited and panting while Bossie follows her crying*) Whut's the matter? Didn't you find Miss Vilet?

MATILDA. (*reluctantly*) It want no use.

SUE. No use?

LIZA. Whut you mean?

MATILDA. I mean—I mean—

LIZA. For God's sake Tildy, whut's happened?

MATILDA. They—they done lynched him.

SUE. (*screams*) Jesus! (*gasps and falls limp in her chair. Singing from church begins. Bossie runs to her, crying afresh. Liza puts the camphor bottle to her nose again as Matilda feels her heart; they work over her a few minutes, shake their heads and with drooping shoulders, wring their hands. While this action takes place the words of this song pour forth from church:*

> *Lord have mercy.*
> *Lord have mercy,*
> *Lord have mercy over me.*

Sung first time with words and repeated in a low hum as curtain slowly falls)

BLUE BLOOD

CHARACTERS

MAY BUSH
MRS. BUSH
MRS. TEMPLE
RANDOLPH STRONG
These characters are Negroes

Place: Georgia.
Time: Shortly after Civil War.

Scene: Large kitchen and dining-room combined of frame cottage, show-ing one door leading into back yard. One other door (right side of room fac-ing stage) leading into hall. One back window, neatly curtained. Steps on right side of room leading upstairs.

Enter RANDOLPH STRONG *with large bunch of white roses and a package. He places the package, unnoticed, on the table—still holding the roses)*

RANDOLPH STRONG. How is my dear Mother Bush?

MRS. BUSH. Feeling like a sixteen-year-old! That's right, you come right on back here with me. (*Notices roses.*) Oh! what pretty roses! Snow white!

RANDOLPH STRONG. Like um? Thought you would. . . . May likes this kind!

MRS. BUSH. She sho'ly do. Pore chile! She's turning her back on the best fellow in this town, when she turned you down. I knows a good man when I see one.

RANDOLPH STRONG. You are always kind to me, Mother Bush. I feel like the lost sheep to-night, the one hundredth one, out in the cold, separated by iron bars from the ninety and nine! Bah! what am I doing? The milk's spilt! (*Arranging flowers.*) Put these in here?

MRS. BUSH. Sure! My, but they look grand. There ain't many young doctors so handy-like!

RANDOLPH STRONG. (*half to himself*). The first time I saw her she wore a white rose in her hair. . . .

MRS. BUSH. Jest listen! May's plum blind! Oh! if she'd a only listened to me, she'd be marrying you to-night, instead of that stuck up John Temple. I never did believe in two "lights" marrying, nohow, it's onlucky. They're jest exactly the same color . . . hair . . . and eyes alike too. Now you . . . you is jest right for my May. "Dark should marry light." You'd be a perfect match.

RANDOLPH STRONG. (*groans*). Hold, hold for goodness sake! Why didn't you lend that little blind girl of yours your two good eyes?

MRS. BUSH. Humph! She wouldn't hear me. (*Goes up to him, speaking confidentially.*) 'Tween you and me, I shorely do wish she'd a said "yes" when you popped the question las' Christmas. I hates to see her tying up with this highfalutin' nothing. She'll re'lize some day that money ain't everything, and that a poor man's love is a whole sight better than a stiff-necked, good-looking dude.

RANDOLPH STRONG. It can't be helped now, Mother Bush. If she's happy, that's the main thing!

MRS. BUSH. But is she going to be happy . . . that's jest it!

RANDOLPH STRONG. Let us hope so! And yet, sometimes I think—do you know, Mother Bush, (*lowering his voice*) sometimes I think May cares for me.

MRS. BUSH. (*confidently*). Do you know, honey, somehow, sometimes I do too!

RANDOLPH STRONG. (*excitedly*). You do too!! Oh, if I could fully believe that—even now—at the last minute—(*Snaps his finger*). Oh, what's the use? (*Constrainedly.*) Is everything ready?

MRS. BUSH. You bet! I'm all dressed under this apron. (*Swings it back and discloses a brilliant and much decorated gown. Then with a start.*) Lord save us! That Lyddie Smith ain't brought that my'nase dressing yet. Vowed she'd have it here by eight sharp, if she was alive. What time you got?

RANDOLPH STRONG. (*looking at his watch*). Eight thirty.

MRS. BUSH. Eight thirty? Good gracious!

RANDOLPH STRONG. I'll run over and get it for you.

MRS. BUSH. Oh yes, honey! Do hurry. Oh, what a son-in-law you would'a' made!

RANDOLPH STRONG. Good joke . . . but I can't laugh!

(*He goes. Mrs. Bush busies herself with the table arrangements and finally notices a package that had been left by Strong; she opens it and discloses a beautiful vase and reads aloud the card attached.*)

MRS. BUSH. (*reading*). For May and her husband, with best wishes for your happiness, Randolph. (*She sets it aside without saying a word—only wiping her eyes—thinks a while; shakes her head; picks up the vase again and calls toward the stairway:*) May! May! run down here a minute. I've got something to show you. (*Mrs. Bush polishes the vase with her apron and holds her head to one side looking at it admiringly. Enter* MAY *in negligee. Mrs. Bush—with vase held behind her:*) Not dressed yet? . . . Gracious! There . . . look . . . Randolph brought it!

MAY BUSH. Oh! . . . did he? (*Reads card.*) Randolph is a dear! (*Fondles vase and looks sad.*)

MRS. BUSH. He brought these roses, too . . . said you liked this kind.

(*May Bush takes roses and buries her face in them, then thoughtfully changes them into Randolph's vase; looks at it with head one side, then breaks off one rose, fondles it, places it in her hair.*)

MRS. BUSH. May—May—are you happy?

MAY BUSH. Why—why—(*dashing something like a tear from her eye*) of course I am.

MRS. BUSH. Maybe you is . . . May . . . but, somehow, I don't feel satisfied.

MAY BUSH. (*kisses her mother*). Oh, Ma, everything is all right! Just wait until you see me dressed. (*Noise at door.*) Oh, somebody's coming in here! (*May retreats partly up the stairway.*

Enter MRS. TEMPLE, *talking. Voices and commotion heard as if coming from the front of the house, where heated argument is going on at front door, Mrs. Temple's muffled voice being heard. Hall kitchen door opens suddenly. Enter Mrs. Temple, excitedly.*)

MRS. TEMPLE. Heavens! They tried to keep me from coming out here! The very idea of her talking that way to me—the groom's own mother! Who is that little upstart that let me in at the front door? I told her I was coming right out here in the kitchen, for even though we have not called on each other in the past, moving around—as you know—in somewhat different social circles, and, of course, not being thrown very closely together, yet *now*, at this particular time, Mrs. Bush, since our two children are determined to marry, I feel that my place to-night is right back here with you! (*Glancing upward, Mrs. Temple discovers May upon the stairway.*) Why, May, are you not dressed yet! You'll have to do better than that when you are Mrs. John Temple!

MRS. BUSH. Don't you worry 'bout May; she'll be ready. Where's John? Is he here?

MRS. TEMPLE. Sure—he brought me in his car, but the fellows captured him and said they were going to keep him out driving until the last minute. (*Again glancing upward toward May.*) Better hurry, May; you mustn't keep John waiting.

MAY BUSH. (*slowly walking upstairs*). Oh, John will get used to waiting on me. (*Exit May.*)

MRS. TEMPLE. (*to Mrs. Bush*). What's this . . . chicken salad? Is it finished?

MRS. BUSH. No, it ain't. The my'nase ain't come yet. I sent Randolph for it. I jest got tired waiting on Lyddie Smith to fetch it.

MRS. TEMPLE. My gracious . . . give me the things and I'll make the dressing for you in a jiffy.

(Mrs. Temple removes her white gloves and gets ready for her new rôle in the kitchen. Without waiting for Mrs. Bush's consent, she rapidly walks over to wooden peg on wall, takes down extra gingham apron and removes her hat and lightweight coat, hanging both upon the peg.)

MRS. BUSH. *(remonstratingly).* I'm 'fraid you'll git yo'self spoiled doing kitchen work. Sich folks as you'd better go 'long in the parlor.

MRS. TEMPLE. Oh, no indeed. This is my son's wedding and I'm here to do a mother's part. Besides—he is a Temple and everything must be right.

MRS. BUSH. *(Takes materials for making the mayonnaise from kitchen safe and reluctantly places them before Mrs. Temple).* You needn't worry 'bout this wedding bein' right. It's my daughter's wedding—and I'll see to that!

MRS. TEMPLE. *(breaking and stirring eggs for the dressing).* You'll have to admit that the girls will envy May marrying my boy John.

MRS. BUSH. *(stopping her work suddenly, and with arms akimbo).* Envy MAY!!! Envy MAY!!! They'd better envy JOHN!!! You don't know who May is; she's got blue blood in her veins.

MRS. TEMPLE. *(laughing sarcastically).* You amuse me. I'll admit May's sweet and pretty, but she is no match for John.

MRS. BUSH. *(irately).* She's not, eh? If I told you something about my May—who she is—you'd be struck dumb.

MRS. TEMPLE. *(nervously stirring the mayonnaise, replies in a falsetto or raised tone, denoting sarcasm).* Remarkable . . . but I am curious!

MRS. BUSH. *(proudly).* I bet you is—you'd fall flat if I told you who she is.

MRS. TEMPLE. *(suspending the operation of the mayonnaise and curiously assuming a soft, confidential tone).* Pray, Mrs. Bush, tell me then. Who is May?

MRS. BUSH. Who is May? Huh! *(Proudly tossing her head.)* Who is May? *(Lowering her voice, confidentially.)* Why . . . do you know Cap'n WINFIELD McCALLISTER, the biggest banker in this town, and who's got money 'vested in banks all over Georgia? That 'ristocrat uv 'ristocrats . . . that Peachtree Street blue blood—CAP'N McCALLISTER— don't you know him?

MRS. TEMPLE. *(starts at the mention of the name but recovers herself in a moment).* Y—e—s, I've heard of him.

MRS. BUSH. *(like a shot out of a gun).* Well, I'd have you to know—he's May's daddy!

MRS. TEMPLE. *(agitatedly).* W-h-y . . . I . . . I . . . I can't believe it!

MRS. BUSH. *(flauntingly).* Believe it or not, it's the bounden truth so help me God! Ain't you never seed him strut? Well, look at May. Walks jest like him—throws her head like him–an' she's got eyes, nose and mouth jest like him. She's his living image.

MRS. TEMPLE. *(almost collapsing, speaking softly and excitedly).* You . . . you terrify me. Mrs. Bush . . . Captain McCallister can't be May's father!

MRS. BUSH. Can't be May's father! Well, I reckon I ought to know who May's father is! Whut do you know 'bout it anyhow? Whut do you know 'bout Cap'n McCallister?

MRS. TEMPLE. Do you mean to tell—

MRS. BUSH. (*interrupting*). I mean jest whut I said. I'm telling you that my daughter—May Bush—has got the bluest blood in America in her veins. Jest put that in your pipe and smoke it! (*Mrs. Bush here proudly flaunts herself around the kitchen, talking half at Mrs. Temple and half to herself.*) Huh! Talkin' 'bout May not bein' a match fur John. I should say they don't come no finer than May, anywhere.

MRS. TEMPLE. (*again collecting herself and speaking in a soft, strained, pleading voice*). Mrs. Bush, Mrs. Bush, I have something to say to you and it must be said right now! Oh, where can I begin? Let me think—

MRS. BUSH. This ain't no time to think, I'm going to act! (*Takes mayonnaise from Mrs. Temple's apathetic hands.*) My chile's gotter get married and get married right. I . . .

MRS. TEMPLE. (*breaking in*). Please, please, be still a minute for heaven's sake! You'll drive me mad!

MRS. BUSH. Drive you mad! The devil I will. (*Abruptly runs and stands in a belligerent attitude in front of Mrs. Temple.*) Say, look here, Miss High-and-Mighty, what's you up to? Git out of here, you ain't going to start no trouble here.

(*Tries to force Mrs. Temple toward the door.*)

MRS. TEMPLE. (*breaking down in tears and reaching for Mrs. Bush's hands*). Please, please, Mrs. Bush, you don't understand, and how can I tell you—what a day!

MRS. BUSH. (*standing squarely in front of Mrs. Temple*). Look here, is you crazy? or just a fool?

MRS. TEMPLE. Neither, Mrs. Bush, I'm just a broken-hearted mother and you must help me, help me, for May's sake, if not for mine!

MRS. BUSH. For May's sake! 'Splain yourself! This is a pretty come off. For May's sake.

(*Sarcastically.*)

MRS. TEMPLE. It's a long story, but I'll tell you in a few words. Oh, oh, how I've tried to forget it!

MRS. BUSH. Forget what! Look here, what time is it?

(*Mrs. Temple looks at her watch.*)

MRS. TEMPLE. A quarter of nine.

MRS. BUSH. (*excitedly*). Lord, woman, we ain't got no time fur story telling. I've got to hustle!

MRS. TEMPLE. (*hysterically*). You must hear me, you must, you must!

MRS. BUSH. Well, of all things, what *is* the matter with you?

MRS. TEMPLE. Be quiet, just one minute, and let me tell you.

MRS. BUSH. You'd better hurry up.

MRS. TEMPLE. Once . . . I taught a country school in Georgia. I was engaged to Paul Temple . . . I was only nineteen. I had worked hard to make enough to pay for my wedding things . . . it was going to be in the early fall—our wedding. I put my money in the bank. One day, in that bank, I met a man. He helped me. And then I see he wanted his pay for it. He kept on—kept writing to me. He didn't sign his letters, though. I wouldn't answer. I tried to keep away. One night he came to the place where I boarded. The woman where I boarded—she helped him—he bribed her. He came into my room—

MRS. BUSH. The dirty devil!

MRS. TEMPLE. (*continuing her story*). I cried out. There wasn't any one there that cared enough to help me, and you know yourself, Mrs. Bush, what little chance there is for women like us, in the South, to get justice or redress when these things happen!

MRS. BUSH. Sure, honey, I do know!

MRS. TEMPLE. Mother knew—there wasn't any use trying to punish him. She said I'd be the one . . . that would suffer.

MRS. BUSH. You done right . . . and whut your ma told you is the God's truth.

MRS. TEMPLE. I told Paul Temple—the one I was engaged to—the whole story, only I didn't tell him who. I knew he would have tried to kill him, and then they'd have killed him.

MRS. BUSH. (*interrupting*). That wuz good sense.

MRS. TEMPLE. He understood the whole thing—and he married me. He knew why I wouldn't tell him the man's name—not even when—when that man's son was born to me.

MRS. BUSH. You don't mean John?

MRS. TEMPLE. Yes . . . John. And his father. . . .

MRS. BUSH. Oh no . . . no. . . .

MRS. TEMPLE. Yes. (*With a groan.*) Winfield McCallister . . . is John's father, too.

MRS. BUSH. (*clasping her hands excitedly*). My God! My God! (*Whimpering, between sobs.*) Whut kin we do? Just think of my poor, dear chile, May, upstairs there—all dressed up jest lak a bride—'spectin' to git married—and all them people from everywhere—in the parlor—waiting for the seymoaney! Oh, whut kin we tell her . . . whut kin we tell them?

MRS. TEMPLE. (*looking at watch. Gets up, walks up and down excitedly.*) Yes . . . we've got to think and act quickly! We can't tell the world why the children didn't marry . . . and cause a scandal. . . . I'd be ruined!

MRS. BUSH. (*getting irate*). So far as you is consarned . . . I ain't bothered, 'bout your being ruined. May'll be ruined if we don't tell. Why—folks'll all be saying John jilted her, and you can bet your sweet life I won't stand fur that. No siree! I don't keer who it hurts . . . I'm not agoin' see May suffer . . . not ef I kin help it!

MRS. TEMPLE. (*bursting into tears*). Oh! oh! we must do something!

(*Enter Randolph Strong, breathlessly, with mayonnaise dressing from Lyddie Smith's—placing large glass jar of mayonnaise on kitchen table.*)

RANDOLPH STRONG. Good evening Mrs. Temple. I'm a little late, Mrs. Bush, but here's what you sent me for. (*He notices Mrs. Temple in tears.*) My, my, why, what's wrong?

MRS. BUSH. Randolph, my dear boy. . . .

RANDOLPH STRONG. What's the matter? What's happened since I left you awhile ago?

MRS. BUSH. (*slowly and feelingly*). Sump'n . . . sump'n turrible!

RANDOLPH STRONG. Has anything happened to May?

MRS. BUSH. Not only to her—to all of us!

RANDOLPH STRONG. All! Heavens!

MRS. BUSH. Listen, Randolph, and help us, for God's sake! May and John can't get married!

RANDOLPH STRONG. (*turning to Mrs. Temple*). Can't get married! Why?

MRS. TEMPLE. It's a long story. I've told—I've explained everything to Mrs. Bush. She—she understands.

RANDOLPH STRONG. You can trust me. I'm like one of the family. You both know that I have always cared for May.

MRS. BUSH. (*to Mrs. Temple*). Kin I tell him? (*Mrs. Temple silently and tearfully nods her assent.*) May mus' know it too—right away. Let's call her down. May! May! Oh, May! My dear chile come down here a minute— quick—right away! My dear chile . . . my poor chile!

MRS. TEMPLE. What a day! What a day!

MAY'S VOICE. Coming, Ma! (*Enter May Bush, coming downstairs in her wedding gown.*) Am I late? (*Noting Randolph.*) The roses are beautiful. See. (*Points to one in her hair.*)

MRS. BUSH. Randolph . . . Randolph remembered the kind you like, honey.

MAY BUSH. (*to Randolph*). Just like you!

RANDOLPH STRONG. How sweet of you to wear one!

MAY BUSH. (*proudly walking across room toward Mrs. Bush*). How do I look, Ma?

MRS. BUSH. (*tenderly kissing her daughter several times*). Beautiful, my darlin' (*adding softly*), poor chile!

MAY BUSH. (*walking toward and kissing Mrs. Temple*). How do you like me—my other mama?

MRS. TEMPLE. Charming—God protect you, my dear!

MAY BUSH. (*noticing the sad expression on the faces of both mothers*). My, you all look so sad; why so doleful? What is the matter with them, Randolph?

RANDOLPH STRONG. Why . . . I'm wounded, but smiling. The ladies . . .

MRS. BUSH. (*impatiently interrupting*). Oh, children—don't waste this precious time. We've called you together to tell you sump'n . . . (*stuttering*) we've got sump'n to tell you, and we got to tell you right now!

(*Mrs. Bush draws May aside toward Mrs. Temple, hastily and cautiously locking kitchen hall door.*)

MRS. BUSH. (*continuing*). Listen, May. Come here, come here, Randolph, for I feel that both of you are my children. May, you got to be strong—for if ever you needed wits, now's the time to use 'em. May God forgive me—and Mrs. Temple there, both of us—I just got to tell you 'bout it quick—for all them folks are in the parlor and if we don't do something quick, right now, this whole town will be rippin' us to pieces—all of us, you and me—Mrs. Temple—and—and—the las' one of us! There ain't time to tell you the whole story—but—May—my poor chile—I know you kin trus' your own, dear ma that far?

MAY BUSH. (*excitedly*). Yes, Ma, yes, but what is it?

MRS. BUSH. May, you and John can't marry—you jest can't marry!!

MAY BUSH. (*aghast*). Can't marry! Can't marry!

MRS. BUSH. No, never!

MAY BUSH. But why—why!

MRS. BUSH. Your father, and John's father—is—is—

MAY BUSH. You don't mean . . .

MRS. TEMPLE. Yes, May. John's father is your father.

MAY BUSH. (*wrings her hands*). Oh, I'd rather die—I'd rather die than face this. . . .

MRS. BUSH. (*crooning*). I know, honey . . . I know . . . God forgive me . . . God forgive that man. Oh, no . . . I don't want Him to forgive him.

MAY BUSH. Oh why, why did this have to happen to me—oh!! I wish I were dead!

RANDOLPH STRONG. May—don't say that. You mustn't say that.

MAY BUSH. I do. Oh, God—I've kept out of their clutches myself, but now it's through you, Ma, that they've got me anyway. Oh, what's the use . . .

RANDOLPH STRONG. May!

MAY BUSH. The whole world will be pointing at me . . .

MRS. BUSH. Ah, honey, honey, I'll be loving you. . . .

MAY BUSH. I wish I could die right now.

RANDOLPH STRONG. Will you listen to me, now, May?

MAY BUSH. Those people in there—they'll be laughing . . .

(*Knocking is heard.*)

MRS. TEMPLE. It's John. We can't let him come in here now. He mustn't know. . . .

MRS. BUSH. No. We can't let him know or he'll kill his own father. . . .

MRS. TEMPLE. What are you going to do, May?

MRS. BUSH. Yes, May—what are you going to do?

RANDOLPH STRONG. We are going to run away and get married, aren't we, May? Say yes, May—say yes!

MAY BUSH. John . . .

(*The knocking is heard again.*)

MRS. BUSH. Keep it from him. It's the black women that have got to protect their men from the white men by not telling on 'em.

MRS. TEMPLE. God knows that's the truth.

RANDOLPH STRONG. May! Come with me *now!*

MAY BUSH. Randolph—do you want me?

RANDOLPH STRONG. I want you like I've always wanted you.

MAY BUSH. (*shyly*). But—I don't love you.

RANDOLPH STRONG. You think you don't. . . .

MAY BUSH. Do you want me now?

RANDOLPH STRONG. I want you now.

MAY BUSH. Ma, oh Ma!

MRS. BUSH. (*in tears*). Quick, darlin'—tell him.

MAY BUSH. My coat.

MRS. BUSH. I'll get your coat, honey.

MRS. TEMPLE. Here, May, take *my* coat!

MRS. BUSH. What we going to tell John—and all the people?

MAY BUSH. Tell 'em—Oh God, we can't tell 'em the—truth?

RANDOLPH STRONG. Mother Bush—just tell them the bride was stolen by Randolph Strong!

(*Strong puts the coat around her and they go out of the door, leaving the others staring at them.*)

CURTAIN

BLUE-EYED BLACK BOY

C H A R A C T E R S

PAULINE WATERS,	the Mother
REBECCA,	daughter
DR. THOMAS GREY,	fiancé of Rebecca
HESTER GRANT,	Pauline's best friend

Scene: A kitchen in Mrs. Waters's cottage. A stove with food keeping warm and an iron heating, an ironing board in the corner and a table with a lighted oil lamp, two chairs. Door slightly ajar leads to the front room and window opening on to a side street.

Scene Opens: MRS. WATERS *is discoverd seated in a large rocker with her left foot bandaged and resting on a low stool.*

MRS. WATERS. (*Calling to the other room*) Rebecca, come on, your iron is hot now I know.

REBECCA. (*Answers from front room*) I'm coming now ma—(*she enters holding a lacy garment in her hands*) I had to tack these bows on, how you like it now?

MRS. WATERS. (*Scanning the long night dress set off with little pink bows that Rebecca is holding up for inspection*) ugh-hu, it shure is pretty, I don't believe any body ever had as fine a wedding gown in this whole town.

REBECCA. Humph! (*She shrugs her shoulders proudly as she tastes the iron to see if it is hot and then takes it over to the board and begins to press the gown*) That's to be expected aint it—every body in the Baptist Church looks up to us don't they?

MRS. WATERS. Sure they do. I ain't carried myself straight all these years for nothing. Your father was sure one proud man—he is put on a pinnacle.

REBECCA. Well, I sure have tried to walk straight all my life.

MRS. WATERS. Yes, and I'm shore proud—now here you is getting ready to marry a young doctor—My! My! (*Then she suddenly requires saying*) Ouch, I wish he would come on over here to change the dressing on my foot—hope I ain't going to have the lock jaw.

REBECCA. You won't—Tom knows his business (*She tosses her head proudly. She looks over to the stove and goes on:*) Wish Jack would come on home and eat his supper so's I could clean up the dishes.

MRS. WATERS. What time is it?

REBECCA. (*Goes to the middle door and peeps in the next room*) The clock in position to exactly five minutes after seven. He oughter been here a whole hour ago.

MRS. WATERS. I wonder what's keeping him?

REBECCA. Well there's one thing sure and certain, he's not running after girls.

MRS. WATERS. No—he shore dont—just give him a book and he's happy—says he's going to quit running that crane—and learn engineering soons you get married. He's been mighty tied down since your father died—taking care of us.

REBECCA. Every body says he's the smartest and finest looking black boy in the whole town.

MRS. WATERS. Yes he is good looking if he is mine—some of em lay it to his eyes. (*She looks far off thoughtfully.*)

REBECCA. Yes, they do set him off—It's funny he's the only one in our family's got blue eyes though. Pa's was black and yours and mine are black too—It certainly is strange—I wish I'd had em.

MRS. WATERS. Oh, you be satisfied—you're pretty enough. Hush, there's the doctor's buggy stopping now—go let him in. (*Rebecca goes to the door while Mrs. Waters bends over grunting and touching her foot. The doctor enters bag in hand with Rebecca*)

DR. GREY. Well how's my patient feeling—better I know.

MRS. WATERS. Now don't you be kidding me doctor—my foots been paining me terrible—I'm scared to death I'm going to have the lock jaw. For God's sake don't let me—(*Rebecca places chair for him near her mother.*)

DR. GREY. (*Unwinds the bandage, looks at foot and opens his bag*). Fine, it's doing fine—you'll have to keep off of it for a week more and then you'll be all right.

MRS. WATERS. Can't walk on it for a week?

DR. GREY. Not unless you want to die of blood poisoning—lock jaw I mean! (*He touches the foot with iodine and puts on new bandage*) That was an old rusty nail you stuck in your foot—a pretty close call. (*He looks lovingly at Rebecca.*)

MRS. WATERS. Well I'm tickled to have such a good doctor for my new son.

DR. GREY. You bet. (*Then thoughtfully*) I saw some mightly rough looking hoodlums gathering on the streets as I came in—looks like there might have been trouble some where.

REBECCA. Oh, they're always having a squabble on the streets—you get used to em—and you will too after a while—

MRS. WATERS. Yes, there's always something stirring everyday—I just go on and on and don't pay em no mind myself.

DR. GREY. (*Patting the foot tenderly*) Now that's all right. You keep off of it—hear me. Or I won't vouch for the outcome.

MRS. WATERS. It's so sore—I can't stand up even if I was a kind to—See who's that at the back door Rebecca (*She peeps out*)

REBECCA. (*Goes to the door and cracks it*) Who's there?

HESTER. Me—me, its Hester—Hester Grant. Lemme in. (*Rebecca opens the door and* HESTER *comes panting in. She looks around as if hating to speak before the others then blurts out.*) Pauline—Its Jack—your son Jack has been rested—rested and put in jail.

MRS. WATERS. Rested?

REBECCA. Good Lord.

DR. GREY. What for?

HESTER. (*Moving about restlessly*) They say he done brushed against a white woman on the street. They had er argument and she hollowed out he's attacked her—a crew of white men come up and started beating on him and the policeman, when he was coming home from work—dragged him to the jail house.

MRS. WATERS. My God. My God—it ain't so—he ain't brushed up against no lady, my boy ain't. He's, he's a gentleman, that what he is.

HESTER. (*Still moving about restlessly—she hadn't thought—she had something else to say*) And, and Pauline—that ain't the worst—that ain't the worst—they, they say there's gointer be a lynching tonight—they gointer break open the jail and string him up! (*She finished desperately*)

MRS. WATERS. String him up—my son—they can't do that—not to my son—not him!

DR. GREY. (*Excitedly*) I'll drive over and see the judge—he'll do somthing to stop it.

HESTER. (*Sarcastically*) Him—not him—he's a lyncher his own self—Don't put no trust in him—Ain't he done let em lynch six niggers in the last year jes gone—him! (*She scoffed again.*)

REBECCA. (*Wringing her hands*) We got to do something—(*Goes up to Tom*) do you know anybody else—anybody at all who could save him?

MRS. WATERS. Wait, wait—I know what'll do—I don't care what it costs (*To Rebecca*) Fly in yonder (*pointing to the next room*) and get me that little tin box out of the left hand side of the tray in my trunk—hurry—fly (*Rebecca hurries out, while Dr. Grey and Hester look on in wonderment*) Lynch my son—my son (*she yells out to Rebecca in next room*) Got it—you got it?

REBECCA. (*From next room*) Yes ma—I got it (*She hurries in with a small tin box in her hand and hands it to her mother.*)

MRS. WATERS. (*Feverishly tossing the odd bits of jewelry in the box, finally coming up with a small ring. She turns to Dr. Grey.*) Here Tom take this, run jump in your horse and buggy and fly over to Governor Tinkhem's house and don't let nobody—nobody stop you. Just give him the ring and say, Pauline sent this, she says they going to lynch her son born 21 years ago, mind you say twenty one years ago—then say—listen close—look in his eyes—and you'll save him.

DR. GREY. (*Listens in amazement while grasping the small ring in his hand and hastens towards the door saying*) Don't worry I'll put it in his hand and tell him what you said—just as quick as my horse can make it. (*When he leaves the room Rebecca and Hester look at Pauline with open mouths in astonishment.*)

HESTER. (*Starting as if from a dream*) Well, well, well I don't git what you mean, but I reckon you knows what you is doing. (*She and Rebecca watch Dr. Grey from the front window as he drove away.*)

MRS. WATERS. I sholy do!

REBECCA. (*Comes over and throws her arms around her mother's neck*) Mother what does it all mean. Can you really save him?

MRS. WATERS. (*Confidently*) Wait and see—I'll tell you more about it after a while. Don't ask me now.

HESTER. (*Going over to the window*) I hope he'll get over to the Governor's in time. (*Looking out*) Ump! There goes a bunch of men with guns now and here comes another all slouched over and pushing on the same way.

REBECCA. (*Joining her at the window with bated breath*). And look! Look! Here comes wagons full (*the rumble of wagon wheels is heard*) See em Hester, all piled in with their guns too—

MRS. WATERS. (*Her lips moving in prayer, her head turned deliberately away from the window sighing deeply now and then.*)

HESTER. Do Lord! Do Lord! Help us this night.

REBECCA. (*With trembling voice*) Hussies. Look at them men on horses! (*Horses' hooves are heard in the street outside. Rebecca crying lightly.*)

HESTER. Jesus! Jesus! Please come down and help us this night.

REBECCA. (*Running over to her mother and flinging her arms about her neck*). Oh mother, mother what will we do—do you hear em—do you hear all them men on horses and wagons going up to the jail? Poor brother— poor boy.

MRS. WATERS. Trust in God daughter—I've got faith in him, faith in—in the Governor—he won't fail—(*She continues to move her lips in prayer. Rebecca rushes back to the window as new sounds of wagon wheels are heard.*)

HESTER. (*At window*) Still coming!

REBECCA. Why don't Tom come back, why don't he hurry?

HESTER. Hush chile! He ain't had time yet.

MRS. WATERS. (*Breaks out in audible prayer*) Lord Jesus, I know I've sinned against your holy law, but you did forgive me and let me hold up my head again. Help me again dear Jesus—help me to save my innocent

child—him who never done no wrong—save him Lord—Let his father—
(*She stops and looks around at the two women, then cautious*) you understand all, I mean sweet Jesus—come down and rise with this wild mob
tonight—pour your love into their wicked hearts—Lord, Lord, hear my
prayer.

HESTER. (*At window*) Do Lord—hear.

MRS. WATERS. (*Restlessly looking toward the others*) Any sign of Tom
yet—

REBECCA. No ma—I don't see him no where yet

HESTER. Give him time—

MRS. WATERS. Time! Time! It'll be too late reckly—too late—she sobs (*Her
head lifted listening*) What that?

HESTER. (*Peers out and listens*) What?

MRS. WATERS. The sound of many feet I hear.

REBECCA. (*Looks out interestingly*) I see em—wait, wait—Ma! Ma! (*hysterically*) It's the state troops—the Guards—It's the Guards Ma—they're
coming—Look Miss Hester!

HESTER. They sure is Jesus—Sure as I'm born—them military—theys
come—come to save, save him.

REBECCA. And yonders Tom at the gate—he's coming.

DR. GREY. (*Rushes in, as the others look at him in amazement.*) He saved
Miss Waters, saved! Did the Governor send the troops?

END

Mary P. Burrill

(1884–1946)

Mary P. Burrill just before her retirement from Dunbar High School. (*Courtesy of Dunbar High School, Washington, D.C.*)

THE SEPTEMBER 1919 ISSUE OF *Birth Control Review*, a monthly periodical advocating birth control rights of women, featured a special issue on "The Negroes' Need for Birth Control, as Seen by Themselves." In this issue Mary P. Burrill contributed her play *They That Sit in Darkness*, along with a short story by her close friend Angelina Weld Grimké. *They That Sit in Darkness* was one of two published plays written by Burrill. The other, *Aftermath*, was published the same year in another periodical, the *Liberator*. *Aftermath* was produced by the New York Krigwa Players, where it appeared in the David Belasco Little Theatre Tournament in 1928. *They That Sit in Darkness* was produced by smaller groups in the New York area. Although these are her only two available plays, she was known to have written others.

Born and raised in Washington, D.C., Burrill graduated in 1901 from the famous M Street School, later Dunbar High. When her family moved to Boston, Burrill attended Emerson College of Oratory, which later became Emerson College, and received a diploma in 1904. She returned to Emerson in 1929, and earned her Bachelor of Literary Interpretation (BLI). While at Emerson, Burrill revised *They That Sit in Darkness* and retitled it *Unto the Third and Fourth Generations*. The play was published in the 1930 *Emersonian* yearbook and was awarded "Best Junior Play of the Year."

Burrill had an outstanding reputation as a teacher and as a director for numerous dramatic productions throughout the Washington, D.C. area. Burrill spent most of her career at Dunbar High where she taught English, speech, and dramatics. According to Burrill's colleague, Mary Hundley:

> In dramatics, Miss Mary P. Burrill gave many years of outstanding service in the training of speech and acting. . . . Students from underprivileged homes, whose color barred them from the usual cultural contacts, found themselves developing in speech, posture, and poise. At one period, Miss Burrill persuaded Walter L. Smith, principal, to introduce a daily program of posture drill at the beginning of each class period throughout the school![1]

During Burrill's years at Dunbar, she inspired many young students to write plays and try their hand at directing. She encouraged Willis Richardson, one of her prize students, to write plays. Richardson went on to become the first black dramatist on Broadway with *The Chip Woman's Fortune*. Her inspiration also prompted her student May Miller to write *Pandora's Box*, which won Miller a fifty-cent cash prize as well as the honor of being published in *School's Progress* magazine in 1914. So well respected was Burrill that upon her retirement, the Dunbar Class of 1945 dedicated their yearbook to her.

During the 1920s, Burrill became known throughout the district for her productions of Maeterlinck's *The Blue Bird* and J. M. Barrie's *Quality Street*. Her annual presentation of "The Other Wise Men" at Howard University drew large crowds from around the city. Burrill also served as director of the School of Expression, which was a part of the Washington, D.C., Conservatory of Music, headed by Harriet Gibbs Marshall. As director from 1907 to 1911, she taught elocution, public speaking, and dramatics. Upon her retirement in 1944, Burrill moved to New York City. She died on March 13, 1946.

NOTES

1. Hundley, Mary Gibson, *The Dunbar Story 1870–1955*. (New York: Vantage Press, 1965), p. 133.

AFFTERMATH

Time: The present
Place: The Thornton cabin in South Carolina.

It is late afternoon of a cool day in early spring. A soft afterglow pours in at the little window of the Thornton cabin. The light falls on MILLIE, *a slender brown girl of sixteen, who stands near the window ironing. She wears a black dress and a big gingham apron. A clothes-horse weighted down with freshly ironed garments is nearby. In the rear there is a door leading out to the road. To the left, another door leading into the other room of the cabin. To the right there is a great stone hearth blackened by age. A Bible rests on the mantel over the hearth. An old armchair and a small table on which is a kerosene lamp are near the hearth. In the center of the room sits a well-scrubbed kitchen table and a substantial wooden chair. In front of the hearth, in a low rocking chair drawn close to the smouldering wood fire, sits* MAM SUE *busily sewing. The many colors in the old patchwork quilt that she is mending, together with the faded red of the bandanna on her head, contrast strangely with her black dress. Mam Sue is very old. Her ebony face is seamed with wrinkles; and in her bleared, watery eyes there is a world-old sorrow. A service flag containing one star hangs in the little window of the cabin.*

MAM SUE. (*crooning the old melody*).

O, yes, yonder comes mah Lawd,
  He is comin' dis way
Wid his sword in his han'
  O, yes, yonder comes—

(*A burning log falls apart, and Mam Sue suddenly stops singing and gazes intently at the fire. She speaks in deep mysterious tones to Millie, who has finished her task and has come to the hearth to put up her irons.*)
See dat log dah, Millie? De one fallin' tuh de side dah wid de big flame lappin' 'round hit? Dat means big doin's 'round heah tonight!

MILLIE. (*with a start*) Oh, Mam Sue, don' you go proph'sying no mo'! You seen big doin's in dat fire de night befo' them w'ite devuls come in heah an' tuk'n po' dad out and bu'nt him!

MAM SUE. (*calmly*) No, Millie, Ah didn' see no big doin's dat night—Ah see'd *evul* doin's an' Ah tole yo' po' daddy to keep erway f'om town de nex' day wid his cotton. Ah jes knowed dat he wuz gwine to git in a row wid dem w'ite debbils—but he wou'd'n lis'n tuh his ole mammy—De good Lawd sen' me dese warnin's in dis fiah, jes lak He sen' His messiges in de fiah to Moses. Yo' chillun bettah lis'n to—

MILLIE. (*nervously*) Oh, Mam Sue, you skeers me when you talks erbout seein' all them things in de fire—

MAM SUE. Yuh gits skeered cause yuh don' put yo' trus' in de good Lawd! He kin tek keer o' yuh no mattuh whut com'!

MILLIE. (*bitterly*). Sometimes I thinks that Gawd's done fu'got us po' cullud people. Gawd didn' tek no keer o' po' dad and *he* put *his* trus' in Him! He uster set evah night by dis fire at dis here table and read his Bible an' pray—but jes look whut happen' to dad! That don' look like Gawd wuz tekin' keer—

MAM SUE. (*sharply*). Heish yo' mouf, Millie! Ah ain't a-gwine to 'ave dat sinner-talk 'roun' hyeah! (*Derisively*.) Gawd don' tek no keer o' yuh? Ain't yuh bin prayin' night an' mawnin' fo' Gawd to sen' yo' brudder back f'om de war 'live an' whole? An' ain't yuh git dat lettah no longer'n yistiddy sayin' dat de fightin's all done stopp't an' dat de blessid Lawd's done brung yo' brudder thoo all dem battuls live an' whole? Don' dat look lak de Lawd's done 'membered yuh?

MILLIE. (*thoughtfully*). I reckon youse right, Mam Sue. But ef anything had a-happen' to John I wuz'n evah goin' to pray no mo'!

(*Millie goes to the clothes-horse and folds the garments and lays them carefully into a large basket. Mam Sue falls again to her crooning.*)

MAM SUE.

O, yes, yonder comes mah Lawd,
    He's comin' dis way-a.

MILLIE. Lonnie's so late gittin' home tonight; I guess I'd bettah tek Mis' Hart's wash home tonight myse'f.

MAM SUE. Yas, Lonnie's mighty late. Ah reckons you'd bettah slip erlon' wid hit. (*Millie gets her hat from the adjoining room and is about to leave with the basket when Mam Sue calls significantly.*) Millie?

MILLIE. Yas, Mam Sue.

MAM SUE. (*firmly*) Don' you' fu'git to drap dat lettah fu' John in the Pos' Awfus ez yuh goes by. Whah's de lettah?

MILLIE. (*reluctantly*). But, Mam Sue, please don' lets—

(*A knock is heard. Millie opens the door and* REVEREND LUKE MOSEBY *enters. Moseby is a wiry little old man with a black, kindly face, and bright, searching eyes; his woolly hair and beard are snow-white. He is dressed in a rusty black suit with a coat of clerical cut that comes to his knees. In one hand he carries a large Bible, and in the other, a stout walking stick.*)

MILLIE. Good evenin', Brother Moseby, come right in.

REV. MOSEBY. Good eben', Millie. Good eben', Mam Sue. I jes drap't in to see ef you-all is still trus'in' de good Lawd an'—

MAM SUE. Lor', Brudder Moseby, ain't Ah bin trus'n' de good Lawd nigh onter dese eighty yeah! Whut fu' yuh think Ah's gwine to quit w'en Ah'm in sight o' de Promis' Lan'? Millie, fetch Brudder Moseby dat cheer.

MOSEBY. (*drawing his chair to the fire*). Dat's right, Mam Sue, you jes a-keep on trus'n' an' prayin' an evah thing's gwine to come aw-right. (*Observing that Millie is about to leave.*) Don' lemme 'tain yuh, Millie, but whut's all dis good news wese bin heahin' 'bout yo' brudder John? Dey say he's done won some kind o' medal ober dah in France?

MILLIE. (*brightening up*). Oh, yes, we got a lettah day befo' yestiddy f'om John tellin' us all erbout it. He's won de War Cross! He fought off twenty Germuns all erlone an' saved his whole comp'ny an' the gret French Gen'rul come an' pinned de medal on him, *hisse'f!*

MOSEBY. De Lawd bles' his soul! Ah know'd dat boy wud mek good!

MILLIE. (*excited by the glory of it all*). An' he's been to Paris, an' the fines' people stopp't him when they seen his medal, an' shook his han' an' smiled at him—an' he kin go evahwhere, an' dey ain't nobody all the time a-lookin' down on him, an' a-sneerin' at him 'cause he's black; but evah-where they's jes gran' to him! An' he sez it's the firs' time evah in his life he's felt lak a real, sho-nuf man!

MOSEBY. Well, honey, don't de Holy Book say, "De fust shill be las' and de las' shill be fust"?

MAM SUE. (*fervently*). Dat hit do! An' de Holy Book ain't nebber tole no lie!

MOSEBY. Folks ober in Char'ston is sayin' dat some sojers is gwine to lan' dah today or tomorrer. Ah reckons day'll all be comin' 'long soon now dat de war's done stopp't.

MILLIE. I jes hates the thought of John comin' home an' hearin' 'bout dad!

MOSEBY. (*in astonishment*). Whut! Yuh mean to say yuh ain't 'rite him 'bout yo' daddy, yit?

MAM SUE. Dat she ain't! Millie mus' 'ave huh way! She 'lowed huh brudder ough'n be tole, an' dat huh could keep on writin' to him jes lak huh dad wuz livin'—Millie allus done de writin'—An' Ah lets huh 'ave huh way—

MOSEBY. (*shaking his head in disapproval*). Yuh mean tuh say—

MILLIE. (*pleadingly*). But, Brother Moseby, I couldn't write John no bad news w'ilst he wuz way over there by hisse'f. He had 'nuf to worry him with death a-starin' him in the face evah day!

MAM SUE. Yas, Brudder Moseby, Millie's bin carryin' on dem lies in huh lettahs fu' de las' six months; but today Ah jes sez to huh—Dis war done stopp't now, an' John he gwine to be comin' home soon, an' he ain't agwine to come hyeah an' fin' me wid no lie on mah soul! An' Ah med huh set down an' tell him de whole truf. She's gwine out to pos' dat lettah dis minute.

MOSEBY. (*still disapproving*). No good nebber come—

(*The door is pushed violently open, and* LONNIE, *a sturdy black boy of eighteen rushes in breathlessly.*)

LONNIE. Mam Sue! Millie! Whut'da yuh think? John's come home!

MILLIE. (*speechless with astonishment*). John? Home? Where's he at?

MAM SUE. (*incredulously*). Whut yuh sayin'? John done come home? Bles' de Lawd! Bles' de Lawd! Millie, didn' Ah tell yuh sumpin wuz gwine tuh happen?

LONNIE. (*excitedly*). I wuz sweepin' up de sto' jes befo' leavin' an' de phone rung—it wuz John—he wuz at Char'ston—jes landid! His comp'ny's waitin' to git de ten o'clock train fu' Camp Reed, whah dey's goin' to be mustered out.

MOSEBY. But how's he gwine to get erway?

LONNIE. Oh, good evenin', Brother Moseby, Ise jes so 'cited I didn't see yuh—Why his Cap'n done give him leave to run over heah 'tell de train's ready. He ought tuh be heah now 'cause it's mos' two hours sence he wuz talkin'—

MAM SUE. Whuffo yuh so long comin' home an' tellin' us?

LONNIE. (*hesitatingly*). I did start right out but when I git to Sherley's corner I seen a whole lot of them w'ite hoodlums hangin' 'round de feed sto'—I jes felt like dey wuz jes waitin' dah to start sumpin, so I dodged 'em by tekin' de long way home.

MILLIE. Po' Lonnie! He's allus dodgin' po' w'ite trash!

LONNIE. (*sullenly*). Well, yuh see whut dad got by not dodgin' 'em.

MOSEBY. (*rising to go*) Ah mus' be steppin' 'long now. Ah got to stop in to see ole man Hawkins; he's mighty sick. Ah'll drap in on mah way back fu' a word o' prayer wid John.

MAM SUE. Lonnie, yu'd bettah run erlon' as Brudder Moseby go an' tote dat wash tuh Mis' Ha't. An' drap in Mis' Hawkins' sto' an' git some soap an' starch; an' Ah reckons yu'd bettah bring me a bottle o' linimint—dis ole pain done come back in mah knee. (*To Moseby.*) Good eben, Brudder Moseby.

MOSEBY. Good eben, Mam Sue; Good eben, Millie, an' Gawd bles' yuh.

LONNIE. (*as he is leaving*). Tell John I'll git back fo' he leaves.

(*Lonnie and Moseby leave. Millie closes the door behind them and then goes to the window and looks out anxiously.*)

MILLIE. (*musingly*). Po' John! Po' John! (*Turning to Mam Sue.*) Mam Sue?

MAM SUE. Yas, Millie.

MILLIE. (*hesitatingly*). Who's goin' to tell John 'bout dad?

MAM SUE. (*realizing for the first time that the task must fall to someone*). Dunno. Ah reckons yu'd bettah.

MILLIE. (*going to Mam Sue and kneeling softly at her side*). Mam Sue, don' let's tell him now! He's got only a li'l hour to spen' with us—an' it's the firs' time fu' so long! John loved daddy so! Let 'im be happy jes a li'l longer—we kin tell 'im the truth when he comes back fu' good. Please, Mam Sue!

MAM SUE. (*softened by Millie's pleading*). Honey chile, John gwine to be askin' for his daddy fust thing—dey ain't no way—

MILLIE. (*gaining courage*). Oh, yes, 'tis! We kin tell 'im dad's gone to town—anything, jes so's he kin spen' these few lil'l minutes in peace! I'll fix the Bible jes like dad's been in an' been a-readin' in it! He won't know no bettah!

(*Millie takes the Bible from the mantel and opening it at random lays it on the table; she draws the old armchair close to the table as her father had been wont to do every evening when he read his Bible.*)

MAM SUE. (*shaking her head doubtfully*). Ah ain't much on actin' dis lie, Millie.

(*The soft afterglow fades and the little cabin is filled with shadows. Millie goes again to the window and peers out. Mam Sue falls again to her crooning.*)

MAM SUE. (*crooning*).

O, yes, yonder comes mah Lawd,
  He's comin' dis way
Wid his sword in his han'—

(*To Millie.*) Millie, bettah light de lamp; it's gittin' dark.—

He's gwine ter hew dem sinners down
  Right lebbal to de groun'
Oh, yes, yonder comes mah Lawd—

(*As Millie is lighting the lamp, whistling is heard in the distance. Millie listens intently, then rushes to the window. The whistling comes nearer; it rings out clear and familiar—"Though the boys are far away, they dream of home"!*)

MILLIE. (*excitedly*). That's him! That's John, Mam Sue!

(*Millie rushes out of doors. The voices of JOHN and Millie are heard from without in greetings. Presently, John and Millie enter the cabin. John is tall and straight—a good soldier and a strong man. He wears the uniform of a private in the American Army. One hand is clasped in both of Millie's. In the other, he carries an old fashioned valise. The War Cross is pinned on his breast. On his sleeve three chevrons tell mutely of wounds suffered in the cause of freedom. His brown face is aglow with life and the joy of homecoming.*)

JOHN. (*eagerly*). Where's Dad? Where's Mam Sue?

MAM SUE. (*hobbling painfully to meet him*). Heah's ole Mam Sue! (*John takes her tenderly in his arms.*) Bles' yo' heart, chile, bles' yo' heart! Tuh think dat de good Lawd's done lemme live to see dis day!

JOHN. Dear old Mam Sue! Gee, but I'm glad to see you an' Millie again!

MAM SUE. Didn' Ah say dat yuh wuz comin' back hyeah?

JOHN. (*smiling*). Same old Mam Sue with huh faith an' huh prayers! But where's dad? (*He glances toward the open Bible.*) He's been in from de field, ain't he?

MILLIE. (*without lifting her eyes*). Yes, he's come in but he had to go out ag'in—to Sherley's feed sto'.

JOHN. (*reaching for his cap that he has tossed upon the table*). That ain't far. I've jes a few minutes so I'd bettah run down there an' hunt him up. Won't he be surprised!

MILLIE. (*confused*). No—no, John—I fu'got; he ain't gone to Sherley's, he's gont to town.

JOHN. (*disappointed*). To town? I hope he'll git in befo' I'm leavin'. There's no tellin' how long they'll keep me at Camp Reed. Where's Lonnie?

MAM SUE. Lonnie's done gone to Mis' Ha't's wid de wash. He'll be back to-reckly

MILLIE. (*admiring the medal on his breast*). An' this is the medal? Tell us all erbout it, John.

JOHN. Oh, Sis, it's an awful story—wait 'til I git back fu' good. Let's see whut I've got in dis bag fu' you. (*He places the worn valise on the table and opens it. He takes out a bright-colored dress pattern.*) That's fu' you, Millie, and quit wearin' them black clothes.

(*Millie takes the silk and hugs it eagerly to her breast, suddenly there sweeps into her mind the realization that she cannot wear it, and the silk falls to the floor.*)

MILLIE. (*trying to be brave*). Oh, John, it's jes lovely! (*As she shows it to Mam Sue.*) Look, Mam Sue!

JOHN. (*flourishing a bright shawl*). An' this is fu' Mam Sue. Mam Sue'll be so gay!

MAM SUE. (*admiring the gift*). Who'd evah b'lieved dat yo' ole Mam Sue would live to be wearin' clo'es whut huh gran'chile done brung huh f'om Eu'ope!

JOHN. Never you mind, Mam Sue, one of these days I'm goin' to tek you an' Millie over there, so's you kin breathe free jes once befo' yuh die.

MAM SUE. It's got tuh be soon, 'cause dis ole body's mos' wo'e out; an' de good Lawd's gwine to be callin' me to pay mah debt 'fo' long.

JOHN. (*showing some handkerchiefs, with gay borders*). These are fu' Lonnie. (*He next takes out a tiny box that might contain a bit of jewelry.*) An' this is fu' Dad. Sum'pin he's been wantin' fu' years. I ain't goin' to open it 'till he comes.

(*Millie walks into the shadows and furtively wipes a tear from her eyes.*)

JOHN. (*taking two army pistols from his bag and placing them on the table*). An' these las' are fu' *youahs truly*.

MILLIE. (*looking at them, fearfully*). Oh, John, are them youahs?

JOHN. One of 'em's mine; the other's my Lieutenant's. I've been cleanin' it fu' him. Don' tech 'em—'cause mine's loaded.

MILLIE. (*still looking at them in fearful wonder*). Did they learn yuh how to shoot 'em?

JOHN. Yep, an' I kin evah mo' pick 'em off!

MILLIE. (*reproachfully*). Oh, John!

JOHN. Nevah you worry, li'l Sis, John's nevah goin' to use 'em 'less it's right fu' him to. (*He places the pistols on the mantel—on the very spot where the Bible has lain.*) My! but it's good to be home! I've been erway only two years but it seems like two cent'ries. All that life ovah there seems like some awful dream!

MAM SUE. (*fervently*). Ah know it do! Many's de day yo' ole Mam Sue set in dis cheer an' prayed fu' yuh.

JOHN. Lots of times, too, in the trenches when I wuz dog-tired, an' sick, an' achin' wid the cold I uster say: well, if we're sufferin' all this for the oppressed, like they tell us, then Mam Sue, an' Dad, an' Millie come in on that—they'll git some good ou'n it if I don't! An' I'd shet my eyes an' fu'git the cold, an' the pain, an' them old guns spittin' death all 'round us; an' see you folks settin' here by this fire—Mam Sue, noddin, an' singin'; Dad a spellin' out his Bible—(*He glances toward the open book.*) Let's see whut he's been readin'—(*John takes up the Bible and reads the first passage upon which his eye falls.*) "But I say unto you, love your enemies, bless them that curse you, an' do good to them that hate you"—(*He lets the Bible fall to the table.*) That ain't the dope they been feedin' us soljers on! 'Love your enemies!' It's been—git a good aim at 'em, an' let huh go!

MAM SUE. (*surprised*). Honey, Ah hates to hyeah yuh talkin' lak dat! It sound lak yuh done fu'git yuh Gawd!

JOHN. No, Mam Sue, I ain't fu'got God, but I've quit thinkin' that prayers kin do ever'thing. I've seen a whole lot sence I've been erway from here. I've seen some men go into battle with a curse on their lips, and I've seen them same men come back with never a scratch; an' I've seen men whut read their Bibles befo' battle, an' prayed to live, left dead on the field. Yes, Mam Sue, I've seen a heap an' I've done a tall lot o' thinkin' sence I've been erway from here. An' I b'lieve it's jes like this—beyon' a certain point prayers ain't no good! The Lawd does jes so much for you, then it's up to you to do the res' fu' yourse'f. The Lawd's done His part when He's done give me strength an' courage; I got tuh do the res' fu' myse'f!

MAM SUE. (*shaking her head*). Ah don' lak dat kin' o' talk—it don' 'bode no good!

(*The door opens and Lonnie enters with packages. He slips the bolt across the door.*)

JOHN. (*rushing to Lonnie and seizing his hand*). Hello, Lonnie, ole man!

LONNIE. Hello, John. Gee, but Ah'm glad tuh see yuh!

JOHN. Boy, you should 'ave been with me! It would 'ave taken some of the skeeriness out o' yuh, an' done yuh a worl' o' good.

LONNIE. (*ignoring John's remark*). Here's the soap an' starch, Millie.

MAM SUE. Has yuh brung mah linimint?

LONNIE. Yassum, it's in de packige.

MILLIE. (*unwrapping the package*). No, it ain't, Lonnie.

LONNIE. Mis' Hawkins give it tuh me. Ah mus' a lef' it on de counter. Ah'll git it w'en Ah goes to de train wid John.

MILLIE. (*showing him the handkerchief*). See whut John done brought you! An' look on de mantel! (*Pointing to the pistols.*)

LONNIE. (*drawing back in fear as he glances at the pistols*). You'd bettah hide them things! No cullud man bettah be seen wid dem things down heah!

JOHN. That's all right, Lonnie, nevah you fear. I'm goin' to keep 'em an' I ain't a-goin' to hide 'em either. See them (*pointing to the wound chevrons on his arm*), well, when I got them wounds, I let out all the rabbit-blood 'at wuz in me! (*Defiantly.*) Ef I kin be trusted with a gun in France, I kin be trusted with one in South Car'lina.

MAM SUE. (*sensing trouble*). Millie, you'd bettah fix some suppah fu' John.

JOHN. (*looking at his watch*). I don' want a thing. I've got to be leavin' in a little while. I'm 'fraid I'm goin' to miss dad after all.

(*The knob of the door is turned as though someone is trying to enter. Then there is a loud knock on the door.*)

JOHN. (*excitedly*). That's Dad! Don't tell him I'm here!

(*John tips hurriedly into the adjoining room. Lonnie unbolts the door and* MRS. ELEN HAWKINS *enters.*)

MRS. HAWKINS. Lonnie fu'got de liniment so I thought I bettah run ovah wid hit, 'cause when Mam Sue sen' fu' dis stuff she sho' needs hit. Brudder Moseby's been tellin' me dat John's done come home.

JOHN. (*coming from his hiding place and trying to conceal his disappointment*). Yes, I'm here. Good evenin', Mis' Hawkins. Glad to see you.

MRS. HAWKINS. (*shaking hands with John*). Well, lan' sakes alive! Ef it ain't John sho'nuf! An' ain't he lookin' gran'! Jes look at dat medal a-shining' on his coat! Put on yuh cap, boy, an' lemme see how yuh look!

JOHN. Sure! (*John puts on his overseas cap and, smiling, stands at attention a few paces off, while Mam Sue, Lonnie, and Millie form an admiring circle around him.*)

MRS. HAWKINS. Now don' he sholy look gran'! I knows yo' sistah, an' gran'-mammy's proud o' yuh! (*A note of sadness creeps into her voice.*) Ef only yuh po' daddy had a-lived to see dis day!

(*John looks at her in amazement. Millie and Mam Sue stand transfixed with terror over the sudden betrayal.*)

JOHN. (*looking from one to the other and repeating her words as though he can scarcely realize their meaning*). 'Ef your po' daddy had lived—' (*To Millie.*) Whut does this mean?

(*Millie sinks sobbing into the chair at the table and buries her face in her hands.*)

MRS. HAWKINS. Lor', Millie, I thought you'd tole him!

(*Bewildered by the catastrophe that she has precipitated, Selena Hawkins slips out of the cabin.*)

JOHN. (*shaking Millie almost roughly*). Come, Millie, have you been lyin' to me? Is Dad gone?

MILLIE. (*through her sobs*). I jes hated to tell you—you wuz so far erway—

JOHN. (*nervously*). Come, Millie, for God's sake don' keep me in this

su'pense! I'm a brave soldier—I kin stan' it—did he suffer much? Wuz he
sick long?

MILLIE. He wuzn't sick no time—them w'ite devuls come in heah an'
dragged him—

JOHN. (*desperately*). My God! You mean they lynched dad?

MILLIE. (*sobbing piteously*). They burnt him down by the big gum tree!

JOHN. (*desperately*). Whut fu,' Millie? What fu'?

MILLIE. He got in a row wid ole Mister Withrow 'bout the price of cotton—
an' he called dad a liar an' struck him—an' dad he up an' struck him
back—

JOHN. (*brokenly*). Didn' they try him? Didn' they give him a chance? Whut'd
the Sheriff do? An' the Gov-nur?

MILLIE. (*through her sobs*). They didn't do nothin'.

JOHN. Oh, God! Oh, God! (*Then recovering from the first bitter anguish and
speaking.*) So they've come into ouah home, have they! (*He strides over
to Lonnie and seizes him by the collar.*) An' whut wuz you doin' when
them hounds come in here after dad?

LONNIE. (*hopelessly*). They wuz so many of 'em come an' git 'im—whut
could Ah do?

JOHN. Do? You could 'ave fought 'em like a man!

MAM SUE. (*pleadingly*). Don't be too hard on 'im, John, wese ain't got no
gun 'round heah!

JOHN. Then he should 'ave burnt their damn kennels ovah their heads! Who
was it leadin' em?

MILLIE. Old man Withrow and the Sherley boys, they started it all.

(*Gradually assuming the look of a man who has determined to do some
terrible work that must be done, John walks deliberately toward the mantel
where the revolvers are lying.*)

JOHN. (*bitterly*). I've been helpin' the w'ite man git his freedom, I reckon
I'd bettah try now to get my own!

MAM SUE. (*terrified*). Whut yuh gwine ter do?

JOHN. (*with bitterness growing in his voice*). I'm sick o' these w'ite folks
doin's—we're 'fine, trus'worthy feller citizuns' when they're handin' us
out guns, an' Liberty Bonds, an' chuckin' us off to die; but we ain't a
damn thing when it comes to handin' us the rights we done fought an'
bled fu'! I'm sick o' this sort o' life—an' I'm goin' to put an' end to it!

MILLIE. (*rushing to the mantel, and covering the revolvers with her
hands*).Oh, no, no, John! Mam Sue. John's gwine to kill hisse'f!

MAM SUE. (*piteously*). Oh, mah honey, don' yuh go do nothin' to bring sin
on yo' soul! Pray to de good Lawd to tek all dis fiery feelin' out'n yo'
heart! Wait 'tel Brudder Moseby come back—he's gwine to pray—

JOHN. (*his speech growing more impassioned and bitter*). This ain't no time
fu' preachers or prayers! You mean to tell me I mus' let them w'ite devuls
send me miles erway to suffer an' be shot up fu' the freedom of people I

ain't nevah seen, while they're burnin' an' killin' my folks here at home! To Hell with 'em!

(*He pushes Millie aside, and seizing the revolvers, thrusts the loaded one into his pocket and begins deliberately to load the other.*)

MILLIE. (*throwing her arms about his neck*). Oh, John, they'll kill yuh!

JOHN. (*defiantly*). Whut ef they do! I ain't skeered o' none of 'em! I've faced worse guns than any sneakin' hounds kin show me! To Hell with 'em! (*He thrusts the revolver that he has just loaded into Lonnie's hands.*) Take this, an' come on here, boy, an' we'll see what Withrow an' his gang have got to say!

(*Followed by Lonnie, who is bewildered and speechless, John rushes out of the cabin and disappears in the gathering darkness.*)

CURTAIN

THEY THAT SIT IN DARKNESS

A One-Act Play of Negro Life

CHARACTERS

MALINDA JASPER,	the mother
LINDY, MILES, ALOYSIUS, MARY ELLEN, JIMMIE,	
JOHN HENRY, a week-old infant	her children
ELIZABETH SHAW,	a visiting nurse

The action passes in a small country town in the
South in our own day.

Scene: It is late afternoon of a day in September. The room which does a three-fold duty as kitchen, dining room, and living room for the Jasper family is dingy and disorderly. Great black patches as though from smoke are on the low ceilings and the walls. To the right is a door leading into a bedroom. In the opposite wall another door leads into a somewhat larger room that serves as bedroom for six Jasper children. In the rear wall a door opens into a large yard. A window is placed to the left of the door while against the wall to the right there stands an old, battered cow-hide trunk. The furniture which is poor and dilapidated, consists of a table in the center of the room, a cupboard containing a few broken cups and plates, a rocker, and two or three plain chairs with broken backs and uncertain legs. Against the wall to the left there is a kitchen stove on which sit a tea-kettle and a wash-boiler. Near the window placed upon stools are two large laundry tubs. Through open window and door one gets a glimpse of snowy garments waving and glistening in the sun. MALINDA JASPER, *a frail, tired-looking woman of thirty-eight, and* LINDY, *her seventeen year-old daughter, are bending over the tubs swirling their hands in the water to make sure that their task is completed. From the yard come the constant cries of children at play.*

MRS. JASPER. (*Straightening up painfully from the tubs.*) Lor', Lindy, how my side do hurt! But thank goodnis, dis job's done! (*She sinks exhausted into the rocker.*) Run git me one them tablits de doctor lef' fo' dis pain! (*Lindy hurries into the adjoining room and returns with the medicine.*)

MRS. JASPER. (*Shaking her head mournfully.*) Dis ole pain goin' be takin' me 'way f'om heah one o' dese days!

LINDY. (*Looking at her in concern.*) See, Ma, I tole yuh not to be doin' all this wuk! Whut's Mis 'Liz'beth goin' er say when she comes heah this evenin' an' fine out you done all this wuk after she tole yuh pertic'lar yestiddy that she wuz'n goin' let yuh out'n bed 'fo' three weeks—an' here 't'ain't been a week sence baby wuz bawn!

MRS. JASPER. Ah ain't keerin' 'bout whut Mis' 'Liz'beth say! Easy nuf, Lindy, fo' dese nurses to give dey advice—dey ain't got no seben chillern to clothe an' feed—but when dis washin' git back Ah kin nevah ketch up!

LINDY. (*Reprovingly.*) But I could 'a done it all mys'f.

MRS. JASPER. An' been all day an' night doin' it—an' miss gittin' you'se'f off in de mawnin' tuh Tuskegee—no indeedy!

LINDY. (*Hesitatingly.*) P'rhaps I oughtn' be goin' erway an' leavin' yuh wid all dis washin' to do ever' week, an' de chillern to look after—an' the baby an' all. Daddy he gits home so late he cain't be no help.

MRS. JASPER. (*Wearily*). Nebber you mind, Lindy, Ah'm going be gittin' aw-right bime-by. Ah ain't a-goin' be stan'in' in de way yo' gittin' dis edicashun. Yo' chance don' come, Lindy, an' Ah wants ter see yuh tek it! Yuh been a good chile, Lindy, an' Ah wants ter see yuh git mo'e out'n life dan Ah gits. Dem three yeah at Tuskegee warn't seem long.

LINDY. (*Her face brightening up.*) Yassum, an' ef Mister Huff, the sup'inten'ent meks me county teacher lak he sez he'll do when I git back, I kin do lots mo'e fo' you an' the chillern!

(*The cry of a week-old infant comes from the adjoining room.*)

MRS. JASPER. Dar now! Ah'm mighty glad he didn' wake up 'tel we git dis washin' done! Ah reckon he's hongry. Ain't Miles come back wid de milk yet? He's been gawn mos' 'en hour—see ef he's took dat guitar wid 'im.

LINDY. (*Going to the door and looking out.*) I doan see it nowheres so I reckon he's got it.

MRS. JASPER. Den Gawd knows when we'll see 'im! Lak es not he's some'airs settin' by de road thumpin' dem strings—dat boy 'ud play ef me or you wuz dyin'! Ah doan know whut's goin' come o' 'im—he's just so lazy en shif'lis!

LINDY. Doan yuh go werrin' 'bout Miles, Ma. He'll be aw-right ef he kin only learn music an' do whut he likes. (*The cry of the infant becomes insistent.*) No, Ma, you set still—I'll git his bottle an' 'tend to him. (*She goes into the bedroom.*)

(*The shrieks of the children in the yard grow louder. A shrill cry of anger and pain rises above the other voices, and* MARY ELLEN, *age six, appears crying at the door.*)

MARY ELLEN. (*Holding her head.*) Ma! Ma! Mek Aloysius b'have hisse'f! He hit me on de haid wid all his might!

MRS. JASPER. (*Rushing to the door.*) Aloysius! Yuh Aloysius! It warn't do yuh no good ef Ah 'ave to come out'n dere to yuh! John Henry, git down f'om dat tree, 'fo yuh have dem clo'es in de durt! Yo' chillern 'nuf to werry me to death!

(*As Lindy returns with the baby's empty bottle,* MILES *enters the rear door. He is a good-natured but shiftless looking boy of sixteen. A milk pail is swinging on his arm, leaving his hands free to strum a guitar.*)

LINDY. Have yuh brought the milk, Miles? An' the bread?

MILES. (*Setting down the milk pail.*) Nup! Mister Jackson say yuh cain't have no milk, an' no nothin' 'tel de bill's paid.

MRS. JASPER. Den Gawd knows we'll starve, 'cause Ah see'd yo' daddy give de doctor ebery cent o' his wages las' week. An' dey warn't be no mo'e money comin' in 'tel Ah kin git dis wash out to de Redmon's.

LINDY. Well, baby's gawn back to sleep now, and p'rhaps Miss 'Liz'beth will bring some milk fo' de baby when she come in lak she did yestiddy—but they ain't nothing heah fo' de other chillern.

(*The shrieks of the children at play in the yard grow louder.*)

ALOYSIUS. (*Calling from without.*) Ma! Ma! John Henry done pull' down de clo'es line!

MRS. JASPER. (*Rushing again to the door.*) Come in heah! Ever' single one o' yuh! Miles, run fix 'em up an' see ef any o' 'em got in de durt!

(*The Jasper children, four in number, a crest-fallen, pathetic looking little group—heads unkempt, ragged, undersized, under-fed, file in terrified.*)

JOHN HENRY. (*Terror-stricken.*) It warn't me, Ma, it was Aloysius!

MRS. JASPER. Heish yo' mouf'! March yo'se'f ever' one o' yuh an' go to baid!

MARY ELLEN. (*Timidly.*) We's ain't had no suppah.

MRS. JASPER. An' whut's mo'e, yuh ain't goin' git no suppah 'tel yuh larns to b'have yo'se'f!

ALOYSIUS. (*In a grumbling tone.*) Cain't fool me—Ah heerd Lindy say dey ain't no suppah fo' us!

(*Calling to the children as they disappear in the room to the left.*)

MRS. JASPER. Ef Ah heahs one soun' Ah'm comin' in dere an' slap yuh into de middle o' nex' week! (*As she sinks again exhausted into the rocker.*) Them chillern's goan ter be de death o' me yit!

MILES. (*Appearing at the door.*) De clo'es ain't dirty. I fo'git to tell yuh—I stopp't by Sam Jones an' he say he'll be 'round fo' Lindy's trunk 'bout sun-down.

MRS. JASPER. Ah reckons yu'd bettah git yo' clo'es an' pack up 'cause it warn't be long fo' sun-down.

LINDY. (*Dragging the old trunk to the center of the room.*) I ain't a-goin' less'n you git bettah, Ma. Yuh look right sick to me!

(*As Lindy is speaking* MISS ELIZABETH SHAW *in the regulation dress of a visiting nurse, carrying a small black bag, appears at the rear door.*)

MISS SHAW. (*Looking in consternation at Mrs. Jasper.*) Malinda Jasper! What are you doing out of bed! You don't mean to say that you have washed all those clothes that I see in the yard?

MRS. JASPER. Yassum, me an' Lindy done 'em.

MISS SHAW. (*Provoked.*) And you look completely exhausted! Come you must get right to bed!

MRS. JASPER. (*Leaning her head wearily against the back of the rocker.*) Lemme res' myse'f jes a minute—Ah'll be goin' 'long to-rectly.

MISS SHAW. It's a wonder in your condition that you didn't die standing right at those tubs! I don't mean to scare you but—

MRS. JASPER. (*With extreme weariness.*) Lor', Mis' 'Liz'beth, it ain't *dyin'* Ah'm skeer't o', its *livin'*—wid all dese chillern to look out fo'. We ain't no Elijahs, Mis' 'Lis'beth, dey ain't no ravens flyin' 'roun' heah drappin' us food. All we gits, we has to git by wukin' hard! But thanks be to Gawd a light's dawnin'! My Lindy's gittin' off to Tuskegee to school tomorrer, Mis' 'Liz'beth!

MISS SHAW. (*Surprised.*) I didn't know that Lindy was thinking about going away to school.

MRS. JASPER. Thinkin' 'bout it! Lindy ain't been thinkin' an' dreamin' 'bout nothin' else sence Booker Washin'ton talked to de farmers down youder at Shady Grove some ten yeah ergo. Did yo' know Booker Washin'ton, Mis' 'Liz'beth?

MISS SHAW. I saw him once a long time ago in my home town in Massachusetts. He was a great man.

MRS. JASPER. Dat he wuz! Ah kin see him now—him an' Lindy, jes a teeny slip o' gal—after de speakin' wuz ovah down dere at Shady Grove, a-standin' under de magnolias wid de sun a-pou'in' through de trees on 'em—an' he wid his hand on my li'l Lindy's haid lak he wuz givin' huh a blessin', an' a-sayin': "When yuh gits big, li'l gal, yuh mus' come to Tuskegee an' larn, so's yuh kin come back heah an' he'p dese po' folks!" He's daid an' in his grave but Lindy ain't nevah fo'git dem words.

MISS SHAW. Just think of it! And ten years ago! How glad I am that her dream is coming true. Won't it cost you quite a bit?

MRS. JASPER. Lor', Lindy 'ud nevah git dere ef we had to sen' huh! Some dem rich folks up yonder in yo' part de world is sen'in' huh.

LINDY. (*Entering with her arms laden with things for her trunk.*) Good evenin', Mis' 'Liz'beth.

MISS SHAW. Well, Lindy, I've just heard of your good fortune. How splendid it is! But what will the baby do without you! How is he this afternoon?

LINDY. He's right smart, Mis' 'Liz'beth. I been rubbing his leg lack you showed me. Do yuh think it'll evah grow ez long ez the other'n?

MISS SHAW. I fear, Lindy, those little withered limbs seldom do; but with care it will grow much stronger. I have brought him some milk—there in my bag. Be careful to modify it exactly as I showed you, and give what is left to the other children.

LINDY. (*Preparing to fix the milk.*) Yes Mis' 'Liz'beth.

MISS SHAW. (*Nodding at Lindy.*) What *will you do*, Malinda, when she goes? You will have to stop working so hard. Just see how exhausted you are from this heavy work!

MRS. JASPER. Lor', Mis' 'Liz'beth, Ah'll be awright to-reckly. Ah did de same thing after my li'l Tom was bawn, an' when Aloysius wuz bawn Ah git up de nex' day—de wuk had to be done.

MISS SHAW. (*Very gravely.*) But you must not think that you are as strong now as you were then. I heard the doctor tell you very definitely that this baby had left your heart *weaker than ever*, and that you *must* give up this laundry work.

MRS. JASPER. (*Pleadingly.*) 'Deed, Mis' 'Liz'beth, we needs dis money whut wid all dese chillern, an' de sicknis' an' fune'ul 'spenses of li'l Tom an' Selena—dem's de chillern whut come 'tween John Henry an' dis las' baby. At'er dem bills wuz paid heah come Pinkie's trouble.

MISS SHAW. Pinkie?

MRS. JASPER. (*Sadly.*) Yuh nevah seed Pinkie 'cause she lef' 'fo' yuh come heah. She come 'tween Miles an' Aloysius—she warn't right in de haid— she wuked ovah tuh Bu'nett's place—Ah aint nevah been much on my gals wukin' round dese white men but Pinkie *mus'* go; an' fus thing we know Bu'nett got huh in trouble.

MISS SHAW. Poor, poor girl! What did you do to the Burnett man?

MRS. JASPER. (*With deep feeling.*) Lor', Mis' 'Liz'beth, cullud folks cain't do nothin' to white folks down heah! Huh Dad went on sumpin awful wid huh ever' day, an' one mawnin' we woked up and Pinkie an' huh baby wuz gawn! We ain't nevah heerd f'om huh tuh dis day—(*she closes her eyes as if to shut out the memory of Pinkie's sorrow.*) Me an' Jim 'as allus put ouah tru's in de Lawd, an' we wants tuh raise up dese chillern to be good, hones' men an' women but we has tuh wuk so hard to give 'em de li'l dey gits dat we ain't got no time tuh look at'er dey sperrits. When Jim go out to wuk—chillern's sleepin'; when he comes in late at night—chillern's sleepin'. When Ah git through scrubbin' at dem tubs all Ah kin do is set in dis cheer an' nod—Ah doan wants tuh see no chillern! Ef it warn't fo' Lindy—huh got a mighty nice way wid 'em—Gawd he'p 'em!

MISS SHAW. Well, Malinda, you have certainly your share of trouble!

MRS. JASPER. (*Shaking her head wearily.*) Ah wonder whut sin we done that Gawd punish me an' Jim lak dis!

MISS SHAW. (*Gently.*) God is not punishing you, Malinda, you are punishing yourselves by having children every year. Take this last baby—you knew that with your weak heart that you should never have had it and yet—

MRS. JASPER. But whut kin Ah do—de chillern *come!*

MISS SHAW. You must be careful!

MRS. JASPER. *Be keerful!* Dat's all you nu'ses say! You an' de one whut come when Tom wuz bawn, an' Selena! Ah been keerful all Ah knows how but whut's it got me—ten chillern, eight livin' an' two daid! You got'a be tellin' me sumpin' better'n dat, Mis' Liz'beth!

MISS SHAW. (*Fervently.*) I wish to God it were lawful for me to do so! My heart goes out to you poor people that sit in darkness, having, year after year, children that you are physically too weak to bring into the world—children that you are unable not only to educate but even to clothe and feed. Malinda, when I took my oath as nurse, I swore to abide by the laws of the State, and the law forbids my telling you what you have a right to know!

MRS. JASPER. (*With the tears trickling from her closed eyes.*) Ah ain't blamin' you, Mis' 'Liz'beth, but—

MISS SHAW. Come, come, Malinda, you must not give away like this. You are worn out—come, you must get to bed.

LINDY. (*Entering with more things for her trunk.*) I'm glad yuh gittin' huh to bed, Mis' 'Liz'beth, I been tryin' to all day.

MRS. JASPER. (*As she walks unsteadily toward her room.*) Lindy, honey, git yo' trunk pack't. Thank Gawd yo' chance done come! Give dat (*Nodding toward the partially filled bottle of milk.*) to de chillern. Mis' 'Liz'beth say dey kin have it.

LINDY. All right, Ma. Mis' 'Liz'beth, ef you needs me jes call.

(*Malinda and the nurse enter the bedroom. Lindy is left packing her trunk. Miles can be heard from without strumming upon his guitar.*)

MARY ELLEN. (*Poking her head out of the door to the children's room.*) Lindy, Lindy, whut wuz dat ma say we all kin have?

LINDY. Some milk—it ain't much.

(*The children bound into the room. Mary Ellen, first at the table, seizes the bottle and lifts it to her lips.*)

ALOYSIUS. (*Snatching the bottle from Mary Ellen.*) Yuh got 'a be las', 'cause Mis' 'Liz'beth say we mus'n' nebber eat or drink at'er yuh! Did'n' she, Lindy?

LINDY. (*As Mary Ellen begins to cry.*) Ef yo' all git to fussin' I ain't goan to bring yuh nothin' when I comes back!

MARY ELLEN. (*As the children crowd about Lindy.*) Whut yuh goan 'a bring us, Lindy?

LINDY. (*As she puts her things carefully into her trunk.*) When I comes back I'm goan to bring yuh all some pretty readin' books, an' some clo'es so I kin tek yuh to school ever' day where yuh kin learn to read 'em!

JOHN HENRY. (*Clapping his hands.*) Is we all goin', Lindy? Miles too?

LINDY. Yes indeedy! An' whut's mo'e I'm goan 'a git Miles a fine new guitar an' let him learn music. An' some day ever' body'll be playin' an' singin' his songs!

ALOYSIUS. (*Glowing with excitement.*) Some day he might have his own band! Might'n' he, Lindy? Lak dat big white one whut come fru heah f'om 'Lanta! Ole Miles'll come struttin' down de road.

(*Aloysius seizes the broom, and in spite of the handicap of bow legs, gives a superb imitation of a drum-major leading his band.*)

LINDY. (*Watching Ayolsius' antics.*) An' I'm goin' tuh have Aloysius' li'l legs straightened. (*As the children roll in merriment.*) 'Sh! 'sh! Mus'n' mek no noise 'cause Ma ain't well! An' in de evenin' we'll have a real set-down-to-de table suppah—Dad he won't have to wuk so hard so he kin git home early—an' after suppah we all kin set 'round de fiah lak dey do ovah to Lawyer Hope's an' tell stories an' play games—

(*The children, radiant as though these dreams were all realities, huddle closer about Lindy who, packing done, now sits enthroned upon her battered trunk.*)

LINDY. 'Sh—sh! Wuz that Mis' 'Liz'beth callin'? (*They listen intently but can hear nothing save the sweet, plaintive notes of an old Spiritual that Miles is playing upon his guitar.*) Then we'll git some fine Sunday clo'es, an' a hoss an' wagun, an' when Sunday come we'll all climb in an' ride to Shady Grove to Meetin'—an' we'll set under de trees in de shade an' learn 'bout li'l Joseph an' his many-cullud coat; an' li'l Samu'l whut de Lawd called while he wuz sleepin'; an' de li'l baby whut wuz bawn in de stable an' wuz lots poor'n me an' you. An' on Sunday evenin' we'll—

MISS SHAW. (*Appearing at the bedroom door and speaking hurriedly.*) Send the children to bed quickly, Lindy, I need you.

(*The children run into their room.*)

ALOYSIUS. (*Wistfully, at the door.*) Ef we's good, Lindy, let us git up when Sam Jones come an' see de trunk go?

LINDY. (*Quickly.*) Mebbe—hurry up!

MISS SHAW. (*Very seriously.*) Lindy, your mother's condition has grown suddenly very, very serious. The exertion of today is beginning to tell on her heart. Bring me some boiling water immediately for my hypodermic. (*Calling from the rear door.*) Miles, Miles! Run to the Hope's as fast as you can and ask them to telephone for the doctor—your mother is very ill. Tell him the nurse says it is urgent!

(*Miss Elizabeth hurries into the bedroom, followed soon after by Lindy with the water. In a few minutes the sobbing of Lindy can be heard, and the nurse re-enters the kitchen. She leans against the frame of the rear door as though exhausted and stares out into the yard at the clothes fluttering like white spirits in the gathering dusk. Then sighing deeply, she puts on her bonnet and cape and turns to go.*)

MILES. (*Rushing in breathlessly, with his guitar under his arm.*) De Hopes ain't—

MISS SHAW. (*Placing her hand tenderly on his shoulder.*) Never mind, now, Miles, your mother is dead.

MILES. (*His guitar crashing to the floor.*) Dead!

MISS SHAW. Yes, and you must help Lindy all you can. I would not leave but I have a case up the road that I must see tonight. I'll be back tomorrow. (*As Miles walks with bowed head toward his mother's room.*) Come, Miles, you had better bring in the clothes before it gets dark.

(*As Miles follows her out Lindy enters the kitchen. The light has gone from her face for she knows that the path now stretching before her and the other children will be darker even than the way that they have already known.*)

MILES. (*Awkwardly, as he struggles in with the hamper piled high with the snowy clothes.*) Anything mo' Ah kin do, Lindy?

LINDY. (*As she sits on the edge of her trunk and stares in a dazed, hopeless way at the floor.*) I reckon yu'd bettah walk up de road a piece to meet Dad an' hurry him erlong. An' stop in de Redmon's an' tell 'em dey cain't have de wash tomorrer 'cause—(*Gulping back her tears,*) 'cause Ma's dead; but I'll git 'em out myself jes ez soon ez I kin. An', Miles, leave word fo' Sam Jones 'at he need'n' come fo' de trunk.

THE END

Zora Neale Hurston

(1891–1960)

Zora Neale Hurston during her years at Howard University. (*Courtesy of Sheen Educational Foundation*)

Zora Neale Hurston, possibly taken during the late 1930s. (*Courtesy Moorland-Spingarn, Howard University*)

Sometimes, I feel discriminated against, but it does not make me angry. It merely astonishes me. How can any deny themselves the pleasure of my company? It's beyond me.[1]

AT AN EARLY AGE, Zora Neale Hurston's mother told her to "jump at de sun," and Hurston spent her life doing just that. She attended Howard University from 1919 to 1924, where she developed her talents as a writer. In 1928, she became the first black to graduate from Barnard College in New York City, where she received a baccalaureate degree in anthropology. Following her college years, Hurston gradually became the most prolific and widely published black female writer of her era. Between 1920 and 1950 she wrote four novels, two books of folklore, her autobiography, over fifty short stories and essays, and close to twenty plays and musical revues. She was a recipient of a Rosenwald and two Guggenheim Fellowships. Hailed as the most important collector of Afro-American folklore, Hurston's body of works about ordinary people were inspired by her experiences in Eatonville, Florida, the all-black town in which she was born.

Like her contemporary, Shirley Graham, Hurston pursued a professional career in the theatre for many years, but has received little attention for her contributions as playwright and producer. After leaving Florida, at an early age, her first job was with a Gilbert and Sullivan troupe as a maid and wardrobe girl. She traveled with the troupe as far as Baltimore, Maryland. There she enrolled in Morgan Academy (the high school division of Morgan College). While at Morgan, she was persuaded by May Miller to attend Howard so she could study with Alain Locke and become involved in theatre and writing.

In 1925, Hurston's *Color Struck* (possibly her first play) placed second in the *Opportunity* awards for best plays, while another, *Spears*, received honorable mention. In 1927 *Ebony and Topaz* published *The First One*, a play based on the biblical character Noah and his family.

Between 1930 and 1935, Hurston became preoccupied with making a name for herself in the theatre. She wrote over twelve plays during this period. In 1930, she collaborated with Langston Hughes on a three-act comedy, *Mule Bone*. Hurston and Hughes's friendship was destroyed during this time, and as a result the play was never produced and only the third act has ever been published. Hurston's efforts were then spent trying to produce musical revues. Her first big opportunity to have her work seen was with the September 1931 Broadway musical, *Fast and Furious*, a revue in two acts and thirty-seven scenes. Hurston was one of nine writers for the show, which also included Tim Moore and Jackie "Moms" Mabley. Hurston made her Broadway debut as an actress with "Moms" Mabley as a cheerleader during this revue. Unfortunately, the show was panned by the

New York critics. Hurston's next theatrical venture was with her own revue, *Jungle Scandals*, which also proved to be a disappointment.

Hurston's *The Great Day* (1931)—also revised and retitled *From Sun to
Sun* and later called *Singing Steel*—was considered a big success, since it
brought her name to the attention of theatre-going audiences, but it gen-
erated very little income. Centered around a day in the life of a railroad
work camp, the musical revue consisted of Bahamian dances, conjure ceremonies, club scenes, work songs, and children's games. Hurston became ob-
sessed during the next three years with producing *The Great Day*. With
this authentic work of Negro life and music, she felt that she would be able
to build a Negro Theatre. The revue had several performances in New
York, Florida, and other cities around the country, but by 1934 Hurston realized the difficulty in trying to eke out a living in the theatre as a black
playwright and producer. While the black community received Hurston as
a literary author, there was a reluctance to support her theatrical endeavors. Rejections by Bethune-Cookman College and Fisk University of her
applications to head their theatre programs proved to be a disappointment
for Hurston. Financially desperate, she resumed fiction writing after a
nearly six-year hiatus.

Her return to fiction writing, however, did not diminish her interest in
the theatre. During the fall of 1935, Hurston was hired by the New York
Negro Unit of the Federal Theatre Project (FTP) as a "drama coach." Her
hopes of having her play *The Fiery Chariot* produced by the FTP never materialized. John Houseman, director of the Negro Unit, was excited about
the prospect of using a play by Hurston for one of their productions. In his
autobiography, *Run-Through*, he notes:

> For a few days I thought I had found a solution in a new play by Zorah [sic]
> Hurston, our most talented writer on the project, who had come up with a Ne-
> gro *Lysistrata* updated and located in a Florida fishing community, where the
> men's wives refused them intercourse until they won their fight with the canning
> company for a living wage. It scandalized both the Left and Right by its salti-
> ness.[2]

From 1939 to 1940 Hurston was hired to organize a drama program at
North Carolina College for Negroes in Durham. During this period, Hur-
ston met Pulitzer Prize playwright Paul Green (*In Abraham's Bosom*).
Green was with the drama department at the University of North Carolina–
Chapel Hill. The two discussed collaborating on a play entitled *John de
Conqueror*, but the work never materialized. From 1941 to 1942 she worked
for Paramount Studios as a story consultant, where she tried to interest the
industry in making films based on her novels.

One of Hurston's last known playwriting efforts was a collaboration with
Dorothy Waring, a white woman, on the musical comedy *Polk County*. The
production was scheduled to premiere on Broadway during the fall of 1944,

but various problems prevented its opening. Returning to Florida during the late 1940s, Hurston died on October 29, 1960.

NOTES

1. Hurston, Zora, "I Love Myself When I Am Laughing . . . And Then Again When I Am Looking Mean and Impressive." From *How It Feels to Be Colored Me* (Old Westbury, New York: The Feminist Press, 1979).
2. Houseman, John, *Run-Through* (New York: A Touchstone Book, 1980), p. 205.

THE FIRST ONE

A Play in One Act

P E R S O N S

NOAH, His Wife, Their Sons: SHEM, JAPHETH, HAM;
EVE, Ham's Wife; the Sons' wives and children (6
or 7).

Time: Three Years after the Flood
Place: Valley of Ararat

SETTING: *Morning in the Valley of Ararat. The
Mountain is in the near distance. Its lower slopes
grassy with grazing herds. The very blue sky beyond that. These together form the background. On
the left downstage is a brown tent. A few shrubs
are scattered here and there over the stage indicat-
ing the temporary camp. A rude altar is built center stage. A Shepherd's crook, a goat skin water
bottle, a staff and other evidences of nomadic life
lie about the entrance to the tent. To the right
stretches a plain clad with bright flowers. Several
sheep or goat skins are spread about on the ground
upon which the people kneel or sit whenever
necessary.*

ACTION: *Curtain rises on an empty stage. It is
dawn. A great stillness, but immediately* NOAH *enters from the tent and ties back the flap. He is clad
in loose fitting dingy robe tied about the waist with
a strip of goat hide. Stooped shoulders, flowing
beard. He gazes about him. His gaze takes in the
entire stage.*

NOAH. (*fervently*) Thou hast restored the Earth, Jehovah, it is good. (*Turns to the tent.*) My sons! Come, deck the altar for the sacrifices to Jehovah. It is the third year of our coming to this valley to give thanks offering to Jehovah that he spared us.

(*Enter* JAPHETH *bearing a haunch of meat and* SHEM *with another. The wife of Noah and those of Shem and Japheth follow laying on sheaves of grain and fruit [dates and figs]. They are all middle-aged and clad in dingy garments.*)

NOAH. And where is Ham—son of my old age? Why does he not come with his wife and son to the sacrifice?

MRS. NOAH. He arose before the light and went. (*She shades her eyes with one hand and points toward the plain with the other.*) His wife, as ever, went with him.

SHEM. (*impatiently*) This is the third year that we have come here to this Valley to commemorate our delivery from the flood. Ham knows the sacrifice is made always at sunrise. See! (*He points to rising sun.*) He should be here.

NOAH. (*lifts his hand in a gesture of reproval*) We shall wait. The sweet singer, the child of my loins after old age had come upon me is warm to my heart—let us wait.

(*There is off-stage, right, the twanging of a rude stringed instrument and laughter. HAM, his wife and son come dancing on down-stage right. He is in his early twenties. He is dressed in a very white goat-skin with a wreath of shiny green leaves about his head. He has the rude instrument in his hands and strikes it. His wife is clad in a short blue garment with a girdle of shells. She has a wreath of scarlet flowers about her head. She has black hair, is small, young and lithe. She wears anklets and wristlets of the same red flowers. Their son about three years old wears nothing but a broad band of leaves and flowers about his middle. They caper and prance to the altar. Ham's wife and son bear flowers. A bird is perched on Ham's shoulder.*)

NOAH. (*extends his arms in greeting*) My son, thou art late. But the sunlight comes with thee. (*Ham gives bird to Mrs. Noah, then embraces Noah.*)

HAM. (*rests his head for a moment on Noah's shoulder*) We arose early and went out on the plain to make ready for the burnt offering before Jehovah.

MRS. SHEM. (*tersely*) But you bring nothing.

HAM. See thou! We bring flowers and music to offer up. I shall dance before Jehovah and sing joyfully upon the harp that I made of the thews of rams. (*He proudly displays the instrument and strums once or twice.*)

MRS. SHEM. (*clapping her hands to her ears*) Oh, Peace! Have we not enough of thy bawling and prancing all during the year? Shem and Japheth work always in the fields and vineyards, while you do naught but tend the flock and sing!

MRS. JAPHETH. (*looks contemptuously at both Ham and Noah*) Still, thou art beloved of thy father . . . he gives thee all his vineyards for thy singing, but Japheth must work hard for his fields.

MRS. SHEM. And Shem—

NOAH. (*angrily*) Peace! Peace! Are lust and strife *again* loose upon the Earth? Jehovah might have destroyed us all. Am I not Lord of the world? May I not bestow where I will? Besides, the world is great. Did I not give food, and plenty to the thousands upon thousands that the waters licked up? Surely there is abundance for us and our seed forever. Peace! Let us to the sacrifice.

(*Noah goes to the heaped up altar. Ham exits to the tent hurriedly and returns with a torch and hands it to Noah who applies it to the altar. He kneels at the altar and the others kneel in a semi-circle behind him at a little distance. Noah makes certain ritualistic gestures and chants*) "Oh Mighty Jehovah, who created the Heaven and the firmaments thereof, the Sun and Moon, the stars, the Earth and all else besides—

OTHERS. I am here

    I am here, O, Jehovah

    I am here   This is thy Kingdom, and I am here

    (*A deep silence falls for a moment.*)

NOAH. Jehovah, who saw evil in the hearts of men, who opened upon them the windows of Heaven and loosed the rain upon them—And the fountains of the great deep were broken up—

OTHERS. (*repeat chant*)

NOAH. Jehovah who dried up the floods and drove the waters of the sea again to the deeps—who met Noah in the Vale of Ararat and made covenant with Noah, His servant, that no more would he smite the Earth—And Seed time and Harvest, Cold and Heat, Summer and Winter, day and night shall not cease forever, and set His rainbow as a sign.

NOAH AND OTHERS. We are here O Jehovah

    We are here

    We are here

    This is Thy Kingdom

    And we are here.

(*Noah arises, makes obeisance to the smoking altar, then turns and blesses the others.*)

NOAH. Noah alone, whom the Lord found worthy; Noah whom He made lord of the Earth, blesses you and your seed forever. (*At a gesture from him all arise. The women take the meat from the altar and carry it into the tent.*) Eat, drink and make a joyful noise before Him. For He destroyed the Earth, but spared us. (*Women re-enter with bits of roast meat—all take some and eat. All are seated on the skins.*)

MRS. NOAH. (*feelingly*) Yes, three years ago, all was water, *water*, WATER! The deeps howled as one beast to another. (*She shudders.*) In my sleep, even now, I am in that Ark again being borne here, there on the great bosom.

MRS. HAM. (*wide-eyed*) And the dead! Floating, floating all about us—We were one little speck of life in a world of death! (*The bone slips from her hand.*) And there, close beside the Ark, close with her face upturned as if begging for shelter—my *mother!* (*She weeps, Ham comforts her.*)

MRS. SHEM. (*eating vigorously*) She would not repent. Thou art as thy mother was—a seeker after beauty of raiment and laughter. God is just. She would not repent.

MRS. HAM. But the unrepentant are no less loved. And why must Jehovah hate beauty?

NOAH. Speak no more of the waters. Oh, the strength of the waters! The voices and the death of it! Let us have the juice of the grape to make us forget. Where once was death in this Valley there is now life abundant of beast and herbs. (*He waves towards the scenery.*) Jehovah meets us here. Dance! Be glad! Bring wine! Ham smite thy harp of ram's thews and sing!

(*Mrs. Noah gathers all the children and exits to the tent. Shem, Japheth, their wives and children eat vigorously. Mrs. Ham exits, left. Ham plays on his harp and capers about singing. Mrs. Ham re-enters with goatskin of wine and a bone cup. She crosses to where Noah reclines on a large skin. She kneels and offers it to him. He takes the cup—she pours for him. Ham sings—*)

HAM.

"I am as a young ram in the Spring
Or a young male goat
The hills are beneath my feet
And the young grass.
Love rises in me like the flood
And ewes gather round me for food."

(*His wife joins in the dancing. Noah cries "Pour" and Mrs. Ham hurries to fill his cup again. Ham joins others on the skins. The others have horns suspended from their girdles. Mrs. Ham fills them all. Noah cries "pour" again and she returns to him. She turns to fill the others' cups.*)

NOAH. (*rising drunkenly*) Pour again, Eve, and Ham sing on and dance and drink—drown out the waters of the flood if you can. (*His tongue grows thick. Eve fills his cup again. He reels drunkenly toward the tent door, slopping the liquor out of the cup as he walks.*) Drink wine, forget water—it means death, *death!* And bodies floating, face up! (*He stares horrified about himself and creeps stealthily into the tent, but sprawls just inside the door so that his feet are visible. There is silence for a moment, the others are still eating. They snatch tid-bits from each other.*)

JAPHETH. (*shoves his wife*) Fruit and herbs, woman! (*He thrusts her impatiently forward with his foot. She exits left.*)

SHEM. (*to his wife*) More wine!

MRS. SHEM. (*irritated*) See you not that there is plenty still in the bottle? (*He seizes it and pours. Ham snatches it away and pours. Shem tries to get it back but Ham prevents him. Re-enter Mrs. Japheth with figs and apples. Everybody grabs. Ham and Shem grab for the same one, Ham gets it).*

MRS. SHEM. (*significantly*) Thus he seizes all else that he desires. Noah would make him lord of the Earth because he sings and capers. (*Ham is laughing drunkenly and pelting Mrs. Shem with fruit skins and withered flowers that litter the ground. This infuriates her.*)

NOAH. (*calls from inside the tent*) Eve, wine, quickly! I'm sinking down in the WATER! Come drown the WATER with wine.

(*Eve exits to him with the bottle. Ham arises drunkenly and starts toward the tent door.*)

HAM. (*thickly*) I go to pull our father out of the water, or to drown with him in it. (*Ham is trying to sing and dance.*) "I am as a young goat in the sp-sp-sp-. (*He exits to the tent laughing. Shem and Japheth sprawl out in the skins. The wives are showing signs of surfeit. Ham is heard laughing raucously inside the tent. He re-enters still laughing.*)

HAM. (*in the tent door*) Our Father has stripped himself, showing all his wrinkles. Ha! Ha! He's as no young goat in the spring. Ha! Ha! (*Still laughing, he reels over to the altar and sinks down behind it still laughing.*) The old Ram, Ha! Ha! Ha! He has had no spring for years! Ha! Ha! (*He subsides into slumber. Mrs. Shem looks about her exultantly.*)

MRS. SHEM. Ha! The young goat has fallen into a pit! (*She shakes her husband.*) Shem! Shem! Rise up and become owner of Noah's vineyards as well as his flocks! (*Shem kicks weakly at her.*) Shem! Fool! Arise! Thou art thy father's first born. (*She pulls him protesting to his feet.*) Do stand up and regain thy birthright from (*she points to the altar*) that dancer who plays on his harp of ram thews, and decks his brow with bay leaves. Come!

SHEM. (*brightens*) How?

HIS WIFE. Did he not go into the tent and come away laughing at thy father's nakedness? Oh (*she beats her breast*) that I should live to see a father so mocked and shamed by his son to whom he has given all his vineyards! (*She seizes a large skin from the ground.*) Take this and cover him and tell him of the wickedness of thy brother.

MRS. JAPHETH. (*arising takes hold of the skin also*) No, my husband shall also help to cover Noah, our father. Did I not also hear? Think your Shem and his seed shall possess both flocks and vineyard while Japheth and his seed have only the fields? (*She arouses Japheth, he stands.*)

SHEM. He shall share—

MRS. SHEM. (*impatiently*) Then go in (*the women release the skin to the men*) quickly, lest he wake sober, then will he not believe one word against Ham who needs only to smile to please him. (*The men lay the skin across their shoulders and back over to the tent and cover Noah. They motion to leave him.*)

MRS. SHEM. Go back, fools, and wake him. You have done but half.

(*They turn and enter the tent and both shake Noah. He sits up and rubs his eyes. Mrs. Shem and Mrs. Japheth commence to weep ostentatiously*).

NOAH. (*peevishly*) Why do you disturb me, and why do the women weep? I thought all sorrow and all cause for weeping was washed away by the flood. (*He is about to lie down again but the men hold him up.*)

SHEM. Hear, father, thy age has been scoffed, and thy nakedness made a thing of shame here in the midst of the feasting where all might know— thou the Lord of all under Heaven, hast been mocked.

MRS. SHEM. And we weep in shame, that thou our father should have thy nakedness uncovered before us.

NOAH. (*struggling drunkenly to his feet*) Who, *who* has done this thing?

MRS. SHEM. (*timidly crosses and kneels before Noah*) We fear to tell thee, lord, lest thy love for the doer of this iniquity should be so much greater than the shame, that thou should slay us for telling thee.

NOAH. (*swaying drunkenly*) Say it, woman, shall the lord of the Earth be mocked? Shall his nakedness be uncovered and he be shamed before his family?

SHEM. Shall the one who has done this thing hold part of thy goods after thee? How wilt thou deal with them? Thou hast been wickedly shamed.

NOAH. No, he shall have no part in my goods—his goods shall be parcelled out among the others.

MRS. SHEM. Thou art wise, father, thou art just!

NOAH. He shall be accursed. His skin shall be black! Black as the nights, when the waters brooded over the Earth!

(*Enter Mrs. Noah from tent, pauses by Noah.*)

MRS. NOAH. (*catches him by the arm*) Cease! Whom dost thou curse?

NOAH. (*shaking his arm free. The others also look awed and terrified and also move to stop him. All rush to him. Mrs. Noah attempts to stop his mouth with her hand. He shakes his head to free his lips and goes in a drunken fury*) Black! He and his seed forever. He shall serve his brothers and they shall rule over him—Ah—Ah—. (*He sinks again to the ground. There is a loud burst of drunken laughter from behind the altar.*)

HAM. Ha! Ha! I am as a young ram—Ha! Ha!

MRS. NOAH. (*to Mrs. Shem*) Whom cursed Noah?

MRS. SHEM. Ham—Ham mocked his age. Ham uncovered his nakedness, and Noah grew wrathful and cursed him. Black! He could not mean *black*. It is enough that he should lose his vineyards. (*There is absolute silence for a while. Then realization comes to all. Mrs. Noah rushes in the tent to her husband, shaking him violently.*)

MRS. NOAH. (*voice from out of the tent*) Noah! Arise! Thou art no lord of the Earth, but a drunkard. Thou hast cursed my son. Oh water, Shem! Japheth! Cold water to drive out the wine. Noah! (*She sobs.*) Thou must awake and unsay thy curse. Thou must! (*She is sobbing and rousing him. Shem and Japheth seize a skin bottle from the ground by the skin door and dash off right. Mrs. Noah wails and the other women join in. They beat their breasts. Enter Eve through the tent. She looks puzzled.*)

MRS. HAM. Why do you wail? Are all not happy today?

MRS. NOAH. (*pityingly*) Come, Eve. Thou art but a child, a heavy load awaits thee. (*Eve turns and squats beside her mother-in-law.*)

EVE. (*carressing Mrs. Noah*) Perhaps the wine is too new. Why do you shake our father?

MRS. NOAH. Not the wine of grapes, but the wine of sorrow bestirs me thus. Turn thy comely face to the wall, Eve. Noah has cursed thy husband and his seed forever to be black, and to serve his brothers and they shall rule over him. (*Re-enter the men with the water bottle running. Mrs. Noah seizes it and pours it in his face. He stirs.*) See, I must awaken him that he may unspeak the curse before it be too late.

EVE. But Noah is drunk—surely Jehovah hears not a drunken curse. Noah would not curse Ham if he knew. Jehovah knows Noah loves Ham more than all. (*She rushes upon Noah and shakes him violently.*) Oh, awake thou (*she shrieks*) and uncurse thy curse. (*All are trying to rouse Noah. He sits, opens his eyes wide and looks about him. Mrs. Noah carresses him.*)

MRS. NOAH. Awake, my lord, and unsay thy curse.

NOAH. I am awake, but I know of no curse. Whom did I curse?

MRS. NOAH AND EVE. Ham, lord of the Earth. (*He rises quickly to his feet and looks bewildered about.*)

JAPHETH. (*falls at his feet*) Our father, and lord of all under Heaven, you cursed away his vineyards, but we do not desire them. You cursed him to be black—he and his seed forever, and that his seed shall be our servants forever, but we desire not their service. Unsay it all.

NOAH. (*rushes down stage to the footlights, center. He beats his breast and bows his head to the ground.*) Oh, that I had come alive out of my mother's loins! Why did not the waters of the flood bear me back to the deeps! Oh Ham, my son!

EVE. (*rushing down to him*) Unspeak the Curse! Unspeak the Curse!

NOAH. (*in prayerful attitude*) Jehovah, by our covenant in this Valley, record not my curses on my beloved Ham. Show me once again the sign of covenant—the rainbow over the Vale of Ararat.

SHEM. (*strikes his wife*) It was thou, covetous woman, that has brought this upon us.

MRS. SHEM. (*weeping*) Yes, I wanted the vineyards for thee, Shem, because at night as thou slept on my breast I heard thee sob for them. I heard thee murmur "Vineyards" in thy dreams.

NOAH. Shem's wife is but a woman.

MRS. NOAH. How rash thou art, to curse unknowing in thy cups the son of thy loins.

NOAH. Did not Jehovah repent after he had destroyed the world? Did He not make all flesh? Their evils as well as their good? Why did He not with

His flood of waters wash out the evil from men's hearts, and spare the creatures He had made, or else destroy us all, *all?* For in sparing one, He has preserved all the wickedness that He creates abundantly, but punishes terribly. No, He destroyed them because vile as they were it was His handiwork, and it shamed and reproached Him night and day. He could not bear to look upon the thing He had done, so He destroyed them.

MRS. NOAH. Thou canst not question.

NOAH. (*weeping*) Where is my son?

SHEM. (*pointing*) Asleep behind the altar.

NOAH. If Jehovah keeps not the covenant this time, if he spare not my weakness, then I pray that Ham's heart remains asleep forever.

MRS. SHEM. (*beseeching*) O Lord of the Earth, let his punishment be mine. We coveted his vineyards, but the curse is too awful for him. He is drunk like you—save him, Father Noah.

NOAH. (*exultantly*) Ah, the rainbow! The promise! Jehovah will meet me! He will set His sign in the Heavens! Shem hold thou my right hand and Japheth bear up my left arm.

(*Noah approaches the altar and kneels. The two men raise his hands aloft.*)

Our Jehovah who carried us into the ark—

SONS. Victory, O Jehovah! The Sign.

OTHERS. (*beating their breasts*) This is Thy Kingdom and we are here.

NOAH. Who saved us from the Man of the Waters.

SONS. Victory, O Jehovah! The Sign.

OTHERS. We belong to Thee, Jehovah, we belong to Thee.

(*There is a sudden, loud raucous laugh from behind the altar. Ham sings brokenly, "I am a young ram in the Spring."*)

NOAH. (*hopefully*) Look! Look! To the mountain—do ye see colors appear?

MRS. NOAH. None but what our hearts paint for us—ah, false hope.

NOAH. Does the sign appear, I seem to see a faint color just above the mountain. (*Another laugh from Ham.*)

EVE. None, none yet. (*Beats her breast violently, speaks rapidly.*) Jehovah, we belong to *Thee*, we belong to *Thee*.

MRS. NOAH AND EVE. Great Jehovah! Hear us. We are here in Thy Valley. We who belong to Thee!

(*Ham slowly rises. He stands and walks around the altar to join the others, and they see that he is black. They shrink back terrified. He is laughing happily. Eve approaches him timidly as he advances around the end of the altar. She touches his hand, then his face. She begins kissing him.*)

HAM. Why do you all pray and weep?

EVE. Look at thy hands, thy feet. Thou art cursed black by thy Father. (*She exits weeping left.*)

HAM. (*gazing horrified at his hands*) Black! (*He appears stupefied. All shrink away from him as if they feared his touch. He appproaches each in turn. He is amazed. He lays his hand upon Shem.*)

SHEM. (*shrinking*) Away! Touch me not!

HAM. (*approaches his mother. She does not repel him but averts her face.*) Why does my mother turn away?

MRS. NOAH. So that my baby may not see the flood that hath broken the windows of my soul and loosed the fountains of my heart.

(*There is a great clamor off stage and Eve re-enters left with her boy in her arms weeping and all the other children in pursuit jeering and pelting him with things. The child is also black. Ham looks at his child and falls at Noah's feet.*)

HAM. (*beseeching in agony*) Why Noah, my father and lord of the Earth, why?

NOAH. (*sternly*) Arise, Ham. Thou art black. Arise and go out from among us that we may see thy face no more, lest by lingering the curse of thy blackness come upon all my seed forever.

HAM. (*grasps his father's knees. Noah repels him sternly, pointing away right. Eve steps up to Ham and raises him with her hand. She displays both anger and scorn.*)

EVE. Ham, my husband, Noah is right. Let us go before you awake and learn to despise your father and your God. Come away Ham, beloved, come with me, where thou canst never see these faces again, where never thy soft eyes can harden by looking too oft upon the fruit of their error, where never thy happy voice can learn to weep. Come with me to where the sun shines forever, to the end of the Earth, beloved the sunlight of all my years. (*She kisses his mouth and forehead. She crosses to door of tent and picks up a water bottle. Ham looks dazedly about him. His eyes light on the harp and he smilingly picks it up and takes his place beside Eve.*)

HAM. (*lightly cynical to all*) Oh, remain with your flocks and fields and vineyards, to covet, to sweat, to die and know no peace. I go to the sun. (*He exits right across the plain with his wife and child trudging beside him. After he is off-stage comes the strumming of the harp and Ham's voice happily singing: "I am as a young ram in the Spring." It grows fainter and fainter until it is heard no more. The sun is low in the west. Noah sits looking tragically stern. All are ghastly calm. Mrs. Noah kneels upon the altar facing the mountain and she sobs continually.*

We belong to Thee, O Jehovah
We belong to Thee.
She keeps repeating this to a slow curtain).

CURTAIN

COLOR STRUCK

A Play in Four Scenes

PERSONS

JOHN,	a light brown-skinned man
EMMALINE,	a black woman
WESLEY,	a boy who plays an accordion
EMMALINE'S DAUGHTER,	a very white girl
EFFIE,	a mulatto girl

A RAILWAY CONDUCTOR
A DOCTOR
Several who play mouth organs, guitars, banjos.
Dancers, passengers, etc.

Time: Twenty years ago and present.
Place: A Southern City.

SETTING: *Early night. The inside of a "Jim Crow" railway coach. The car is parallel to the footlights. The seats on the down stage side of the coach are omitted. There are the luggage racks above the seats. The windows are all open. There are exits in each end of the car—right and left.*

ACTION: *Before the curtain goes up there is the sound of a locomotive whistle and a stopping engine, loud laughter, many people speaking at once, good-natured shrieks, strumming of stringed instruments, etc. The ascending curtain discovers a happy lot of Negroes boarding the train dressed in the gaudy, tawdry best of 1900. They are mostly in couples—each couple bearing a covered-over market basket which the men hastily deposit in the racks as they scramble for seats. There is a little*

*friendly pushing and shoving. One pair just miss a
seat three times, much to the enjoyment of the
crowd. Many "plug" silk hats are in evidence, also
sun-flowers in button holes. The women are showily
dressed in the manner of the time, and quite conscious of their finery. A few seats remain unoc-
cupied.*

(Enter EFFIE *(left) above, with a basket.)*

ONE OF THE MEN. (*standing, lifting his "plug" in a grand manner*) Howdy
do, Miss Effie, you'se lookin' jes lak a rose. (*Effie blushes and is confused. She looks up and down for a seat.*) Fack is, if you wuzn't walkin'
long, ah'd think you *wuz* a rose—(*he looks timidly behind her and the
others laugh*). Looka here, where's Sam at?

EFFIE. (*tossing her head haughtily*) I don't know an' I don't keer.

THE MAN. (*visibly relieved*) Then lemme scorch you to a seat. (*He takes her
basket and leads her to a seat center of the car, puts the basket in the rack
and seats himself beside her with his hat at a rakish angle.*)

MAN. (*sliding his arm along the back of the seat*) How come Sam ain't
heah—y'll on a bust?

EFFIE. (*angrily*) A man dat don't buy me nothin tuh put in *mah* basket,
ain't goin' wid *me* tuh no cake walk. (*The hand on the seat touches her
shoulder and she thrusts it away*) Take yo' arms from 'round me, Dinky!
Gwan hug yo' Ada!

MAN. (*in mock indignation*) Do you think I'd look at Ada when Ah got a
chance tuh be wid you? Ah always wuz sweet on you, but you let ole Mullet-head Sam cut me out.

ANOTHER MAN. (*with head out of the window*) Just look at de darkies coming! (*With head inside coach.*) Hey, Dinky! Heah come Ada wid a great
big basket.

(*Dinky jumps up from beside Effie and rushes to exit right. In a moment
they re-enter and take a seat near entrance. Everyone in coach laughs.
Dinky's girl turns and calls back to Effie.*)

GIRL. Where's Sam, Effie?

EFFIE. Lawd knows, Ada.

GIRL. Lawd a mussy! Who you gointer walk de cake wid?

EFFIE. Nobody, Ah reckon. John and Emma gointer win it nohow. They's
the bestest cake-walkers in dis state.

ADA. You'se better than Emma any day in de week. Cose Sam cain't walk
lake John. (*She stands up and scans the coach.*) Looka heah, ain't John
an' Emma going? They ain't on heah!

(*The locomotive bell begins to ring.*)

EFFIE. Mah Gawd, s'pose dey got left!

MAN. (*with head out of window*) Heah they come, nip and tuck—whoo-ee!

They'se gonna make it! (*He waves excitedly.*) Come on Jawn! (*Everybody crowds the windows, encouraging them by gesture and calls. As the whistle blows twice, and the train begins to move, they enter panting and laughing at left. The only seat left is the one directly in front of Effie.*)

DINKY. (*standing*) Don't y'all skeer us no mo' lake dat! There couldn't be no cake walk thout y'all. Dem shad-mouf St. Augustine coons would win dat cake and we would have tuh kill 'em all bodaciously.

JOHN. It was Emmaline nearly made us get left. She says I wuz smiling at Effie on the street car and she had to get off and wait for another one.

EMMA. (*removing the hatpins from her hat, turns furiously upon him*) You wuz grinning at her and she wuz grinning back jes lake a ole chessy cat!

JOHN. (*positively*) I wuzn't.

EMMA. (*about to place her hat in rack*) You wuz. I seen you looking jes lake a possum.

JOHN. I wuzn't. I never gits a chance tuh smile at nobody—you won't let me.

EMMA. Jes the same every time you sees a yaller face, you *takes* a chance. (*They sit down in peeved silence for a moment.*)

DINKY. Ada, les we all sample de basket. I bet you got huckleberry pie.

ADA. No I aint, I got peach an' tater pies, but we aint gonna tetch a thing tell we gits tuh de hall.

DINKY. (*mock alarm*) Naw, don't do dat! It's all right tuh save the fried chicken, but pies is *always* et on trains.

ADA. Aw shet up! (*He struggles with her for a kiss. She slaps him but finally yields.*)

JOHN. (*looking behind him*) Hellow, Effie, where's Sam?

EFFIE. Deed, I don't know.

JOHN. Y'all on a bust?

EMMA. None ah yo' bizness, you got enough tuh mind yo'own self. Turn 'round!

(*She puts up a pouting mouth and he snatches a kiss. She laughs just as he kisses her again and there is a resounding smack which causes the crowd to laugh. And cries of "Oh you kid!" "Salty dog!"*)

(*Enter conductor left calling tickets cheerfully and laughing at the general merriment.*)

CONDUCTOR. I hope somebody from Jacksonville wins this cake.

JOHN. You live in the "Big Jack?"

CONDUCTOR. Sure do. And I wanta taste a piece of that cake on the way back tonight.

JOHN. Jes rest easy—them Augustiners ain't gonna smell it. (*Turns to Emma.*) Is they, baby?

EMMA. Not if Ah kin help it.

(*Somebody with a guitar sings: "Ho babe, mah honey taint no lie."*)

(*The conductor takes up tickets, passes on and exits right.*)

WESLEY. Look heah, you cake walkers—y'all oughter git up and limber up yo' joints. I heard them folks over to St. Augustine been oiling up wid goose-grease, and over to Ocala they been rubbing down in snake oil.

A WOMAN'S VOICE. You better shut up, Wesley, you just joined de church last month. Somebody's going to tell the pastor on you.

WESLEY. Tell it, tell it, take it up and smell it. Come on out you John and Emma and Effie, and limber up.

JOHN. Naw, we don't wanta do our walking steps—nobody won't wanta see them when we step out at the hall. But we kin do something else just to warm ourselves up.

(*Wesley begins to play "Goo Goo Eyes" on his accordion, the other instruments come in one by one and John and Emma step into the aisle and "parade" up and down the aisle—Emma holding up her skirt, showing the lace on her petticoats. They two-step back to their seat amid much applause.*)

WESLEY. Come on out, Effie! Sam aint heah so you got to hold up his side too. Step on out. (*There is a murmur of applause as she steps into the aisle. Wesley strikes up "I'm gointer live anyhow till I die." It is played quite spiritedly as Effie swings into the pas-me-la—*)

WESLEY. (*in ecstasy*) Hot stuff I reckon! Hot stuff I reckon! (*The musicians are stamping. Great enthusiasm. Some clap time with hands and feet. She hurls herself into a modified Hoochy Koochy, and finishes up with an ecstatic yell.*)

(*There is a babble of talk and laughter and exultation.*)

JOHN. (*applauding loudly*) If dat Effie can't step nobody can.

EMMA. Course you'd say so cause it's her. Everything she do is pretty to you.

JOHN. (*caressing her*) Now don't say that, Honey. Dancing is dancing no matter who is doing it. But nobody can hold a candle to you in nothing.

(*Some men are heard tuning up—getting pitch to sing. Four of them crowd together in one seat and begin the chorus of "Daisies Won't Tell." John and Emma grow quite affectionate.*)

JOHN. (*kisses her*) Emma, what makes you always picking a fuss with me over some yaller girl. What makes you so jealous, nohow? I don't do nothing.

(*She clings to him, but he turns slightly away. The train whistle blows, there is a slackening of speed. Passengers begin to take down baskets from their racks.*)

EMMA. John! John, don't you want me to love you, honey?

JOHN. (*turns and kisses her slowly*) Yes, I want you to love me, you know I do. But I don't like to be accused o' ever light colored girl in the world. It hurts my feeling. I don't want to be jealous like you are.

(*Enter at right Conductor, crying "St. Augustine, St. Augustine." He exits left. The crowd has congregated at the two exits, pushing good-naturedly and joking. All except John and Emma. They are still seated with their arms about each other.*)

EMMA. (*sadly*) Then you don't want my love, John, cause I can't help mah-self from being jealous. I loves you so hard, John, and jealous love is the only kind I got.

(*John kisses her very feelingly.*)

EMMA. Just for myself alone is the only way I knows how to love.

(*They are standing in the aisle with their arms about each other as the curtain falls.*)

SCENE II

Setting: A weather-board hall. A large room with the joists bare. The place has been divided by a curtain of sheets stretched and a rope across from left to right. From behind the curtain there are occasional sounds of laughter, a note or two on a stringed instrument or accordion. General stir. That is the dance hall. The front is the ante-room where the refreshments are being served. A "plank" seat runs all around the hall, along the walls. The lights are kerosene lamps with reflectors. They are fixed to the wall. The lunch-baskets are under the seat. There is a table on either side upstage with a woman behind each. At one, ice cream is sold, at the other, roasted peanuts and large red-and-white sticks of peppermint candy.

People come in by twos and three, laughing, joking, horse-plays, gauch-ily flowered dresses, small waists, bulging hips and busts, hats worn far back on the head, etc. People from Ocala greet others from Palatka, Jacksonville, St. Augustine, etc.

Some find seats in the ante-room, others pass on into the main hall.

Enter the Jacksonville delegation, laughing, pushing proudly.

DINKY. Here we is, folks—here we *is*. Gointer take dat cake on back tuh Jacksonville where it belongs.

MAN. Gwan! Whut wid you mullet-head Jacksonville Coons know whut to do wid a cake. It's gointer stay right here in Augustine where de *good* cake walkers grow.

DINKY. Taint no 'Walkers' never walked till John and Emmaline prance out—you mighty come a tootin'.

(*Great laughing and joshing as more people come in. John and Emma are encouraged, urged on to win.*

EMMA. Let's we git a seat, John, and set down.

JOHN. Sho will—nice one right over there.

(*They push over to wall seat, place basket underneath, and sit. Newcomers shake hands with them and urge them on to win.*)

(*Enter JOE CLARKE and a small group. He is a rotund, expansive man with a liberal watch chain and charm.*)

DINKY. (*slapping Clarke on the back*) If you don't go 'way from here! Lawdy, if it aint Joe.

CLARKE. (*jovially*) Ah thought you had done forgot us people in Eatonville since you been living up her? in Jacksonville.

DINKY. Course Ah aint. (*Turning.*) Looka heah folks! Joe Clarke oughta be made chairman uh dis meetin'—Ah mean Past Great-Grand Master of Ceremonies, him being the onliest mayor of de onliest colored town in de state.

GENERAL CHORUS. Yeah, let him be—thass fine, etc.

DINKY. (*setting his hat at a new angle and throwing out his chest*) And *Ah'll* scorch him to the platform. Ahem!

(*Sprinkling of laughter as Joe Clarke is escorted into next room by Dinky.*)

(*The musicians are arriving one by one during this time. A guitar, accordion, mouth organ, banjo, etc. Soon there is a rapping for order heard inside and the voice of Joe Clarke.*)

JOE CLARKE. Git yo' partners one an' all for de gran' march! Git yo' partners, gent-mens!

A MAN. (*drawing basket from under bench*) Let's we all eat first.

(*John and Emma go buy ice-cream. They coquettishly eat from each other's spoons.* OLD MAN LIZZIMORE *crosses to Effie and removes his hat and bows with a great flourish.*)

LIZZIMORE. Sam ain't here t'night, is he, Effie?

EFFIE. (*embarrassed*) Naw suh, he aint.

LIZZ. Well, you like chicken? (*Extends arm to her.*) Take a wing!

(*He struts her up to the table amid the laughter of the house. He wears no collar.*)

JOHN. (*squeezes Emma's hand*) You certainly is a ever loving mamma–when you aint mad.

EMMA. (*smiles sheepishly*) You oughtn't to make me mad then.

JOHN. Ah don't make you! You makes yo'self mad, den blame it on me. Ah keep on tellin' you Ah don't love nobody but you. Ah knows heaps uh half-white girls Ah could git ef Ah wanted to. But (*he squeezes her hard again*) Ah jus' wants *you!* You know what they say! De darker de berry, de sweeter de taste!

EMMA. (*pretending to pout*) Oh, you tries to run over me an' keep it under de cover, but Ah won't let yuh. (*Both laugh.*) Les' we eat our basket!

JOHN. All right. (*He pulls the basket out and she removes the table cloth. They set the basket on their knees and begin to eat fried chicken.*)

MALE VOICE. Les' everybody eat—motion's done carried. (*Everybody begins to open baskets. All have fried chicken. Very good humor prevails. Delicacies are swapped from one basket to the other. John and Emma offer the man next them some supper. He takes a chicken leg. Effie crosses to John and Emma with two pieces of pie on a plate.*)

EFFIE. Y'll have a piece uh mah blueberry pie—it's might nice! (*She proffers it with a timid smile to Emma who "freezes" up instantly.*)

EMMA. Naw! We don't want no pie. We got cocoanut layer-cake.

JOHN. Ah—Ah think ah'd choose a piece uh pie, Effie. (*He takes it.*) Will you set down an' have a snack wid us? (*He slides over to make room.*)

EFFIE. (*nervously*) Ah, naw, Ah got to run on back to mah basket, but ah thought maybe y'll mout' want tuh taste mah pie. (*She turns to go.*)

JOHN. Thank you, Effie. It's mighty good, too. (*He eats it. Effie crosses to her seat. Emma glares at her for a minute, then turns disgustedly away from the basket. John catches her shoulder and faces her around.*)

JOHN. (*pleadingly*) Honey, be nice. Don't act lak dat!

EMMA. (*jerking free*) Naw, you done ruint mah appetite now, carryin' on wid dat punkin-colored ole gal.

JOHN. Whut kin Ah do? If you had a acted polite Ah wouldn't a had nothin' to say.

EMMA. Naw, youse jus' hog-wile ovah her cause she's half-white! No matter whut Ah say, you keep carryin' on wid her. Act polite? Naw Ah aint gonna be deceitful an' bust mah gizzard fuh nobody! Let her keep her dirty ole pie ovah there where she is!

JOHN. (*looking around to see if they are overheard*) Sh-sh! Honey, you mustn't talk so loud.

EMMA. (*louder*) Ah-Ah aint gonna bite mah tongue! If she don't like it she can lump it. Mah back is broad—(*John tries to cover her mouth with his hand*). She calls herself a big cigar, but *I* kin smoke her!

(*The people are laughing and talking for the most part and pay no attention. Effie is laughing and talking to those around her and does not hear the tirade. The eating is over and everyone is going behind the curtain. John and Emma put away their basket like the others, and sit glum. Voice of Master-of-ceremonies can be heard from beyond curtain announcing the pas-me-la contest. The contestants, mostly girls, take the floor. There is no music except the clapping of hands and the shouts of "Parse-me-lah" in time with the hand-clapping. At the end Master announces winner. Shadows seen on curtain.*)

MASTER. Mathilda Clarke is winner—if she will step forward she will receive a beautiful wook fascinator. (*The girl goes up and receives it with great hand-clapping and good humor.*) And now since the roosters is crowin' foah midnight, an' most of us got to git up an' go to work tomorrow, The Great Cake Walk will begin. Ah wants de floor cleared, cause de representatives of de several cities will be announced an' we wants 'em to take de floor as their names is called. Den we wants 'em to do a gran' promenade roun' de hall. An' they will then commence to walk fuh de biggest cake ever baked in dis state. Ten dozen eggs—ten pounds of flour— ten pounds of butter, and so on and so forth. Now then—(*he strikes a pose*) for St. Augustine—Miss Lucy Taylor, Mr. Ned Coles.

(*They step out amid applause and stand before stage.*)

For Daytona—

Miss Janie Bradley, Enoch Nixon

(*Same business.*)
For Ocala—
Miss Docia Boger, Mr. Oscar Clarke
(*Same business.*)
For Palatka—
Miss Maggie Lemmons, Mr. Senator Lewis
(*Same business.*)
And for Jacksonville the most popular "walkers" in de state—
Miss Emmaline Beazeley, Mr. John Turner.
(*Tremendous applause. John rises and offers his arm grandiloquently to Emma.*)
EMMA. (*pleadingly, and clutching his coat.*) John let's we all don't go in there with all them. Let's we all go on home.
JOHN. (*amazed*) Why, Emma?
EMMA. Cause, cause all them girls is going to pulling and hauling on you, and—
JOHN. (*impatiently*) Shucks! Come on. Don't you hear the people clapping for us and calling our names? Come on!
(*He tries to pull her up—she tries to drag him back.*)
Come on, Emma! Taint no sense in your acting like this. The band is playing for us. Hear 'em? (*He moves feet in a dance step.*)
EMMA. Naw, John, Ah'm skeered. I loves you—I—.
(*He tries to break away from her. She is holding on fiercely.*)
JOHN. I got to go! I been practising almost a year—I—we done come all the way down here. I can walk the cake, Emma—we got to—I got to go in! (*He looks into her face and sees her tremendous fear.*) What you skeered about?
EMMA. (*hopefully*) You won't go it—You'll come on go home with me all by ourselves. Come on John. I can't, I just can't go in there and see all them girls—Effie hanging after you—.
JOHN. I got to go in—(*he removes her hand from his coat*)—whether you come with me or not.
EMMA. Oh—them yaller wenches! How I hate 'em! They gets everything they wants—.
VOICE INSIDE. We are waiting for the couple from Jacksonville—Jacksonville! Where is the couple from—.
(*Wesley parts the curtain and looks out.*)
WESLEY. Here they is out here spooning! You all can't even hear your names called. Come on John and Emma.
JOHN. Coming. (*He dashes inside. Wesley stands looking at Emma in surprise.*)
WESLEY. What's the matter, Emma? You and John spatting again? (*He goes back inside.*)
EMMA. (*calmly bitter*) He went and left me. If we is spatting we done had our last one. (*She stands and clenches her fists.*) Ah, mah God! He's in

there with her—Oh, them half whites, they gets everything, they gets everything everybody else wants! The men, the jobs—everything! The whole world is got a sign on it. Wanted: Light colored. Us blacks was made for cobble stones. (*She muffles a cry and sinks limp upon the seat.*)

VOICE INSIDE. Miss Effie Jones will walk for Jacksonville with Mr. John Turner in place of Miss Emmaline Beazeley.

S C E N E   I I I — D A N C E   H A L L

(*Emma springs to her feet and flings the curtains wide open. She stands staring at the gay scene for a moment defiantly, then creeps over to a seat along the wall and shrinks into the spanish Moss, motionless.*)

(*Dance hall decorated with palmetto leaves and Spanish Moss—a flag or two. Orchestra consists of guitar, mandolin, banjo, accordion, church organ and drum.*)

MASTER. (*on platform*) Couples take yo' places! When de music starts, gentlemen parade yo' ladies once round de hall, den de walk begins. (*The music begins. Four men come out from behind the platform bearing a huge chocolate cake. The couples are "prancing" in their tracks. The men lead off the procession with the cake—the contestants make a grand slam around the hall.*)

MASTER. Couples to de floor! Stan' back, ladies an' gentlemen—give 'em plenty room.

(*Music changes to "Way Down in Georgia." Orchestra sings. Effie takes the arm that John offers her and they parade to the other end of the hall. She takes her place. John goes back upstage to the platform, takes off his silk hat in a graceful sweep as he bows deeply to Effie. She lifts her skirts and curtsies to the floor. Both smile broadly. They advance toward each other, meet midway, then, arm in arm, begin to "strut." John falters as he faces her, but recovers promptly and is perfection in his style. (Seven to nine minutes to curtain. Fervor of spectators grows until all are taking part in some way—either hand-clapping or singing the words. At curtain they have reached frenzy.*)

QUICK CURTAIN
(*It stays down a few seconds to indicate ending of contest and goes up again on John and Effie being declared winners by judges.*)

MASTER. (*on platform, with John and Effie on the floor before him*) By unanimous decision de cake goes to de couple from Jacksonville!

(*Great enthusiasm. The cake is set down in the center of the floor and the winning couple parade around it arm in arm. John and Effie circle the cake happily and triumphantly. The other contestants, and then the entire assembly fall in behind and circle the cake, singing and clapping. The festivities continue. The Jacksonville quartet step upon the platform and sing a verse and chorus of "Daisies won't tell." Cries of "Hurrah for Jacksonville! Glory for the big town," "Hurrah for Big Jack.")*

MAN. (*seeing Emma*) You're from Jacksonville, aint you? (*He whirls her around and around.*) Aint you happy? Whoopee! (*He releases her and she drops upon a seat. She buries her face in the moss.*)

(Quartet begins on chorus again. People are departing, laughing, humming, with quartet cheering. John, the cake, and Effie being borne away in triumph.)

S C E N E   I V

Time: present. The interior of a one-room shack in an alley. There is a small window in the rear wall upstage left. There is an enlarged crayon drawing of a man and woman—man sitting cross-legged, woman standing with her hand on his shoulder. A center table, red cover, a low, cheap rocker, two straight chairs, a small kitchen stove at left with a wood-box beside it, a water-bucket on a stand close by. A hand towel and a wash basin. A shelf of dishes above this. There is an ordinary oil lamp on the center table but it is not lighted when the curtain goes up. Some light enters through the window and falls on the woman seated in the low rocker. The door is center right. A cheap bed is against the upstage wall. Someone is on the bed but is lying so that the back is toward the audience.

Action: As the curtain rises, the woman is seen rocking to and fro in the low rocker. A dead silence except for the sound of the rocker and an occasional groan from the bed. Once a faint voice says "water" and the woman in the rocker arises and carries the tin dipper to the bed.

WOMAN. No mo' right away—Doctor says not too much. (*Returns dipper to pail.—Pause.*) You got right much fever—I better go git the doctor agin.

(There comes a knocking at the door and she stands still for a moment, listening. It comes again and she goes to door but does not open it.)

WOMAN. Who's that?

VOICE OUTSIDE. Does Emma Beasely live here?

EMMA. Yeah—(*pause*)—who is it?

VOICE. It's me—John Turner.

EMMA. (*puts hands eagerly on the fastening*) John? did you say John Turner?

VOICE. Yes, Emma, it's me.

(*The door is opened and the man steps inside.*)

EMMA. John! Your hand (*she feels for it and touches it*). John flesh and blood.

JOHN. (*laughing awkwardly*) It's me all right, old girl. Just as bright as a basket of chips. Make a light quick so I can see how you look. I'm crazy to see you. Twenty years is a long time to wait, Emma.

EMMA. (*nervously*) Oh, let's we all just sit in the dark awhile. (*Apologetically.*) I wasn't expecting nobody and my house aint picked up. Sit down. (*She draws up the chair. She sits in rocker.*)

JOHN. Just to think! Emma! Me and Emma sitting down side by each. Know how I found you?

EMMA. (*dully*) Naw. How?

JOHN. (*brightly*) Soon's I got in town I hunted up Wesley and he told me how to find you. That's who I come to see, you!

EMMA. Where you been all these years, up North somewheres? Nobody round here could find out where you got to.

JOHN. Yes, up North. Philadelphia.

EMMA. Married yet?

JOHN. Oh yes, seventeen years ago. But my wife is dead now and so I came as soon as it was decent to find *you*. I wants to marry you. I couldn't die happy if I didn't. Couldn't get over you—couldn't forget. Forget me, Emma?

EMMA. Naw, John. How could I?

JOHN. (*leans over impulsively to catch her hand*) Oh, Emma, I love you so much. Strike a light honey so I can see you—see if you changed much. You was such a handsome girl!

EMMA. We don't exactly need no light, do we, John, tuh jus' set an' talk?

JOHN. Yes, we do, Honey. Gwan, make a light. Ah wanna see you.

(*There is a silence.*)

EMMA. Bet you' wife wuz some high-yaller dickty-doo.

JOHN. Naw she wasn't neither. She was jus' as much like you as Ah could get her. Make a light an' Ah'll show you her pictcher. Shucks, ah gotta look at mah old sweetheart. (*He strikes a match and holds it up between their faces and they look intently at each other over it until it burns out.*) You aint changed none atall, Emma, jus' as pretty as a speckled pup yet.

EMMA. (*lighter*) Go long, John! (*Short pause*) 'member how you useter bring me magnolias?

JOHN. Do I? Gee, you was sweet! 'Member how Ah useter pull mah necktie loose so you could tie it back for me? Emma, Ah can't see to mah soul how we lived all this time, way from one another. 'Member how you useter make out mah ears had done run down and you useter screw 'em up agin for me? (*They laugh.*)

EMMA. Yeah, Ah useter think you wuz gointer be mah husban' then—but you let dat ole—

JOHN. Ah aint gonna let you alibi on me lak dat. Light dat lamp! You cain't look me in de eye and say no such. (*He strikes another match and lights*

the lamp.) Course, ah don't wanta look too bossy, but ah b'lieve you got
to marry me tuh git rid of me. That is, if you aint married.

EMMA. Naw, Ah aint. (*She turns the lamp down.*)

JOHN. (*looking about the room*) Not so good, Emma. But wait till you see
dat little place in Philly! Got a little "Rolls-Rough," too—gointer teach
you to drive it, too.

EMMA. Ah been havin' a hard time, John, an' Ah lost you—oh, aint nothin'
been right for me! Ah aint never been happy.

(*John takes both of her hands in his.*)

JOHN. You gointer be happy now, Emma. Cause Ah'm gointer make you.
Gee Whiz! Ah aint but forty-two and you aint forty yet—we got plenty
time. (*There is a groan from the bed.*) Gee, what's that?

EMMA. (*ill at ease.*) Thass mah chile. She's sick. Reckon ah bettah see 'bout
her.

JOHN. You got a chile? Gee, that great! Ah always wanted one, but didn't
have no luck. Now we kin start off with a family. Girl or boy?

EMMA. (*slowly*) A girl. Comin' tuh see me agin soon, John?

JOHN. Comin' agin? Ah aint gone yet! We aint talked, you aint kissed me
an' nothin', and you aint showed me our girl. (*Another groan, more pro-
longed.*) She must be pretty sick—let's see. (*He turns in his chair and
Emma rushes over to the bed and covers the girl securely, tucking her
long hair under the covers, too—before he arises. He goes over to the bed
and looks down into her face. She is mulatto. Turns to Emma teasingly.*)
Talkin' 'bout *me* liking high-yallers—*yo* husband musta been pretty near
white.

EMMA. (*slowly*) Ah, never wuz married, John.

JOHN. It's all right, Emma. (*Kisses her warmly.*) Everything is going to be
O.K. (*Turning back to the bed.*) Our child looks pretty sick, but she's
pretty. (*Feels her forehead and cheek.*) Think she oughter have a doctor.

EMMA. Ah done had one. Course Ah cain't git no specialist an' nothin' lak
dat. (*She looks about the room and his gaze follows hers.*) Ah aint got a
whole lot lak you. Nobody don't git rich in no white-folks' kitchen, nor in
de washtub. You know Ah aint no school-teacher an' nothin' lak dat.

(*John puts his arm about her.*)

JOHN. It's all right, Emma. But our daughter is bad off—run out an' git a
doctor—she needs one. Ah'd go if Ah knowed where to find one—you kin
git one the quickest—hurry, Emma.

EMMA. (*looks from John to her daughter and back again.*) She'll be all
right, Ah reckon, for a while. John, you love me—you really want me sho'
nuff?

JOHN. Sure Ah do—think Ah'd come all de way down here for nothin'? Ah
wants to marry agin.

EMMA. Soon, John?

JOHN. Real soon.

EMMA. Ah wuz jus' thinkin', mah folks is away now on a little trip—be
home day after tomorrow—we could git married tomorrow.

JOHN. All right. Now run on after the doctor—we must look after our girl. Gee, she's got a full suit of hair! Glad you didn't let her chop it off. (*Looks away from bed and sees Emma standing still.*)

JOHN. Emma, run on after the doctor, honey. (*She goes to the bed and again tucks the long braids of hair in, which are again pouring over the side of the bed by the feverish tossing of the girl.*) What's our daughter's name?

EMMA. Lou Lillian. (*She returns to the rocker uneasily and sits rocking jerkily. He returns to his seat and turns up the light.*)

JOHN. Gee, we're going to be happy—we gointer make up for all them twenty years (*another groan*). Emma, git up an' gwan git dat doctor. You done forgot Ah'm de boss uh dis family now—gwan, while Ah'm here to watch her whilst you're gone. Ah got to git back to mah stoppin'-place after a while.

EMMA. You go git one, John.

JOHN. Whilst Ah'm blunderin' round tryin' to find one, she'll be gettin' worse. She sounds pretty bad—(*takes out his wallet and hands her a bill*)—get a taxi if necessary. Hurry!

EMMA. (*does not take the money, but tucks her arms and hair in again, and gives the girl a drink*) Reckon Ah better go git a doctor. Don't want nothin' to happen to *her*. After you left, Ah useter have such a hurtin' in heah (*touches bosom*) till she come an' eased it some.

JOHN. Here, take some money and get a good doctor. There must be some good colored ones around here now.

EMMA. (*scornfully*) I wouldn't let one of 'em tend my cat if I had one! But let's we don't start a fuss.

(*John caresses her again. When he raises his head he notices the picture on the wall and crosses over to it with her—his arm still about her.*)

JOHN. Why, that's you and me!

EMMA. Yes, I never could part with that. You coming tomorrow morning, John, and we're gointer get married, aint we? Then we can talk over everything.

JOHN. Sure, but I aint gone yet. I don't see how come we can't make all our arrangements now.

(*Groans from bed and feeble movement.*)

Good lord, Emma, go get that doctor!

(*Emma stares at the girl and the bed and seizes a hat from a nail on the wall. She prepares to go but looks from John to bed and back again. She fumbles about the table and lowers the lamp. Goes to door and opens it. John offers the wallet. She refuses it.*)

EMMA. Doctor right around the corner. Guess I'll leave the door open so she can get some air. She won't need nothing while I'm gone, John.

(*She crosses and tucks the girl in securely and rushes out, looking backward and pushing the door wide open as she exits. John sits in the chair beside the table. Looks about him—shakes his head. The girl on the bed groans, "water," "so hot." John looks about him excitedly. Gives her a drink. Feels her forehead. Takes a clean handkerchief from his pocket and wets it and places it upon her forehead. She raises her hand to the cool object. Enter Emma running. When she sees John at the bed she is full of fury. She rushes over and jerks his shoulder around. They face each other.)*

EMMA. I knowed it! (*She strikes him.*) A half white skin. (*She rushes at him again. John staggers back and catches her hands.*)

JOHN. Emma!

EMMA. (*struggles to free her hands*) Let me go so I can kill you. Come sneaking in here like a pole cat!

JOHN. (*slowly, after a long pause*) So this is the woman I've been wearing over my heart like a rose for twenty years! She so despises her own skin that she can't believe any one else could love it!

(*Emma writhes to free herself.*)

JOHN. Twenty years! Twenty years of adoration, of hunger, of worship! (*On the verge of tears he crosses to door and exits quietly, closing the door after him.*)

(*Emma remains standing, looking dully about as if she is half asleep. There comes a knocking at the door. She rushes to open it. It is the doctor. White. She does not step aside so that he can enter.*)

DOCTOR. Well, shall I come in?

EMMA. (*stepping aside and laughing a little*) That's right, doctor, come in.

(*Doctor crosses to bed with professional air. Looks at the girl, feels the pulse and draws up the sheet over the face. He turns to her.*)

DOCTOR. Why didn't you come sooner. I told you to let me know of the least change in her condition.

EMMA. (*flatly*) I did come—I went for the doctor.

DOCTOR. Yes, but you waited. An hour more or less is mighty important sometimes. Why didn't you come?

EMMA. (*passes hand over face*) Couldn't see.

(*Doctor looks at her curiously, then sympathetically takes out a small box of pills, and hands them to her.*) Here, you're worn out. Take one of these every hour and try to get some sleep. (*He departs.*)

(*She puts the pill-box on the table, takes up the low rocking chair and places it by the head of the bed. She seats herself and rocks monotonously and stares out of the door. A dry sob now and then. The wind from the open door blows out the lamp and she is seen by the little light from the window rocking in an even, monotonous gait, and sobbing.*)

Eulalie Spence

(1894–1981)

Eulalie Spence during the early 1940s. (*Courtesy of Patricia Hart*)

Eulalie Spence around the time she won the Crisis Playwriting Award in 1927. (*Courtesy of Patricia Hart*)

> I have seen plays written by our Negro writers with this caption: To Be Read, Not Played!
>   A play to be read! Why not the song to be read not sung, and the canvas to be described, not painted! To every art its form, thank God! And to the play, the technique that belongs to it.[1]

EULALIE SPENCE WAS ONE of the more experienced female playwrights prior to the 1950s. She graduated from New York City's Wadleigh High School and the New York Training School for Teachers, then received a B.A. from New York University in 1937 and an M.A. from Teachers College, Columbia University, in 1939. While at Columbia, Spence studied playwriting with such professors as Hughes Hatcher and Estelle H. Davis. Spence began her teaching career with the New York public school system in 1918. She taught elocution, English, and dramatics at Eastern District High School, Brooklyn, from 1927 until her retirement in 1958.

Born June 11, 1894, Spence migrated to the United States in 1902 from the island of Nevis, West Indies, with her parents and four of five sisters. (Another sister would be born in the United States.) At the turn of the century, her father, a sugar planter, had lost his entire crop to a hurricane and came to America to seek employment. In an unpublished 1973 interview located in the Hatch-Billops Collection, Spence recalled the difficulty her father had obtaining work because he was West Indian. She grew up realizing that West Indians, particularly those with some basic education, were not popular in this country. It wasn't until later in life that Spence realized she had grown up poor and unfortunate. Spence's mother instilled in her daughters a strong sense of pride, making them aware that they were important individuals regardless of how little they possessed materially.

Eulalie Spence was "prim, proper and ultracorrect in her speech and dress, yes—but she was gentle, generous and loving and the backbone of a family of seven girls."[2] Inspired by her mother, who often read stories to the girls, she developed an interest in writing. In the same 1973 interview, Spence spoke of her father as being a very quiet man who left most decisions up to her mother when it came to the seven girls. She indicated that perhaps the female characters in her plays were very strong personalities as compared with the weak male figures because of her upbringing. However, she did not consciously intend for the characters to appear as such.

In 1926, Spence's *Foreign Mail*—possibly her first play—placed second in the *Crisis* competition for playwriting. But the year 1927 was a coup for her. She won the *Opportunity* second place award for *The Hunch* and one half of third place for *The Starter*. That same year, W. E. B. DuBois entered *Foreign Mail* as well as *Fool's Errand* in the David Belasco Little Theatre Tournament. *Fool's Errand* won the Samuel French $200 prize and both plays had the distinction of being published by French. Two of Spence's sisters, Doralyne and Olga, performed in her plays. In fact, Spence coached her sister Doralyne when she took over Rose McClendon's role in *Abraham's Bosom* at the Cherry Lane during the 1920s.

A member of DuBois's Krigwa Players from 1926 until the group's demise two years later, Spence respected the activist, but the two had major disagreements. DuBois attempted on many occasions to persuade her to use her excellent writing skills for propaganda. Spence emphasized that her rationale for avoiding propaganda issues was that she knew nothing about lynchings, rapes, nor the blatant racial injustices in this country. As a West Indian, she claimed, these issues were not a part of her background. Spence was also adamant in her belief that a play could not depend on propaganda for success. She was a "folk dramatist," who wrote for fun and entertainment.

Despite their differences, DuBois and the Krigwa Players presented a third play by Spence, *Her*, as part of their second season in 1927 at the 135th Street New York Public Library. *Her*, a ghost play, is an interesting piece centered around a foreigner who attempted to find happiness in a strange country. Spence is perhaps speaking of her own family, particularly of her father's alienation in the United States. *Her* also illustrates Spence's use of the strong female character and the weak male. While Martha is a dominating woman, she is also very loyal to her invalid husband, John. When the play was produced, Spence's sister Doralyne played the role of *Her*.

Because of her teaching responsibilities, as well as heading the Drama Club at Eastern District High, Spence did not have a great deal of time to meet the many writers of the Harlem Renaissance. She often corresponded with Alain Locke at Howard, and it is possible that she and Zora Neale Hurston crossed paths since both were active with the Krigwa Players.

Of the fourteen plays written by Spence, six are known to have been published and at least seven produced. Spence primarily wrote comedies with the exception of *Her* (1927), *La Divina Pastora* (1929) and *Undertow* (1929). Her only full-length play, *The Whipping* (1932), was optioned by Paramount Studios, but was never made into a movie. Spence died March 7, 1981, in Pennsylvania.

NOTES

1. Eulalie Spence, "A Criticism of the Negro Drama," *Opportunity* (June 28, 1928), p. 180.
2. Letter dated January 20, 1988 to Kathy A. Perkins from Patricia Hart, niece of Spence.

UNDERTOW

PERSONS IN THE PLAY

DAN,   the man
HATTIE,   the man's wife
CHARLEY,   their son
CLEM,   the other woman
MRS. WILKES,   a lodger

Time: About 8 o'clock one winter's night.

Scene: Harlem. The dining room in Hattie's private house. It is a cheerful room, never sunny, but well furnished and spotless from shining floor to snowy linen. The supper dishes have been cleared away, but the table is still set for one who did not appear. Double doors opening upon the hall are at center back. At right there is a door leading to the kitchen. At the left there are two windows facing the street.

At Rise: HATTIE *is sitting at the head of the table frowning heavily at the place of the one who did not appear. She drums impatiently with her fingers for a few seconds then pushing her chair back with more violence than grace, rises. Hattie's dark face is hard and cold. She has a disconcerting smile—a little contempt and a great deal of distrust. Her body is short and spreads freely in every direction. Her dark dress is covered by an apron which makes her look somewhat clumsy.* CHARLEY, *dressed in an overcoat and hat of the latest mode bursts noisily into the room. He is a slender fellow, about the same complexion as his mother, but possessing none of her strength of character. His good-looking face is weak, with a suggestion of stubbornness about it. His manner is arrogant and somewhat insolent)*
CHARLEY. Ah'm off, Ma.
HATTIE. So Ah see.

CHARLEY. (*his glance falls on the table*) Say, Ma—Gee whiz! Ain't Dad bin home fer supper yet?

HATTIE. (*shortly*) No.

CHARLEY. (*with a low whistle*) Dat's funny, he ain't never stayed out befo' has he?

HATTIE. Not sence Ah married him—'cept—

CHARLEY. (*curiously*) 'Cept whut, Ma?

HATTIE. 'Cept wunce 'fo yuh was born.

CHARLEY. (*with an uproarious laugh*) An' the old man ain't tried it sence! Reckon yuh fixed him, didn't yuh, Ma! (*he sits down beside the table and laughs once more*)

HATTIE. (*sharply*) Ah ain't trained yuh half's as well's Ah's trained yo' Dad. (*she resumes her seat*) Ah shoulda made yuh stay in school fer one thing.

CHARLEY. Yuh had mo' sense Ma! If yuh'd a bossed me lak yuh's bossed Dad, Ah'd runned away long 'fo now.

HATTIE. Thar ain't no danger uh Dan runnin' off. He ain't got de nerve. Sides, nobuddy'd want him.

CHARLEY. Now doan' fool yuhself, Ma! An easy simp lak Dad'd be snapped up soon 'nuff ef he ever got it intuh his head dat he could do sech a thing.

HATTIE. Dan's a fool, but he knows which side his bread's buttered on.

CHARLEY. (*giving his thigh a loud slap*) Holy smoke!

HATTIE. (*irritably*) Whut's eatin' yuh?

CHARLEY. Nuthin.

HATTIE. (*impatiently*) Never mind lyin'! Whut's on yuh mind?

CHARLEY. Oh, nuthin'! Ah jes' thought er sumpth'n dat's all. Say, Ma—

HATTIE. Well?

CHARLEY. Ah gotta have five bucks ter-night,—Need'em bad.

HATTIE. It doan do no harm tuh need 'em. Thar's a plenty things Ah's wanted dat Ah ain't never got.

CHARLEY. (*roughly*) Where the devil do yuh think Ah kin git it, ef Ah doan ask yuh?

HATTIE. Yuh might wuk 'cassionally. Dan ain't bin home a day dese twenty-five years.

CHARLEY. (*with a sneer*) An' yuh's jes' done callin' him a fool, ain't yuh? The guys in mah crowd doan do no work see? We lives by our brains.

HATTIE. Not by exercisin' 'em, Lawd knows!

CHARLEY. How come yuh think we hits de Number ev'y week? Brain work!

HATTIE. Ef yuh hits so often whut yuh allus comin' ter me 'bout money fer?

CHARLEY. Ef dat ain't lak a woman! It takes money ter make money!

HATTIE. Charley, yuh's gotta cut out dis gamblin'. Ah ain't goin' give yuh no mo' money.

CHARLEY. (*insolently*) Yuh think Ah'm Dad, doan' yuh? Well, Ah ain't! Ah wish ter Gawd Ah knew whut yuh's got over on him. No free man would er stood yuh naggin' all dese years.

HATTIE. (*coldly*) Dem whut can't stan' fer mah ways knows whut dey kin do.

CHARLEY. Wouldn't 'sprise me none ef Dad has walked off—

HATTIE. (*quickly*) Whut makes yuh think so?

CHARLEY. Reckon yu'd like tuh know, wouldn't yuh?

HATTIE. 'Tain't likely whut yuh could say's wurth five dollars tuh hear.

CHARLEY. Whut Ah seen wouldn't ah bin wuth nuthin' las' week, but sence Dad ain't showed up, fer supper, it's wuth a damn sight mo'. Yuh'd never guess whut Ah seen him doin' one night las' week up on Lenox Avenue.

HATTIE. Well, yuh might's well say it. Yuh kin have dat five, but lemme tell yuh dat yuh'll be de loser, later, if yuh's lied tuh me.

CHARLEY. Whut Ah's gotta lie fer? (*he stretches his hand across the table, palm upturned*) Hand it over, Ma. (*Hattie takes a bill, from her stocking and puts it on the table, beside her. She places her closed fist upon the money. Charley frowns and draws his hand back*)

HATTIE. Ah ain't never refused tuh pay fer whut Ah gits.

CHARLEY. Oh, all right. Here goes. Me an' Nat Walker was strollin' up Lenox Avenue one night las' week 'bout half past six. Right ahead uh me Ah seen Dad. He was walkin' 'long, slow ez usual wid his head bent, not seein' nobuddy. All uv a sudden, a woman comin' down de Avenue, went up tuh him an' stops him. He looked up kinda dazed like an' stared at her lak he'd seen a ghost. She jes' shook him by de arm an' laughed. By dat time, we come along side an' Ah got a good look at her. She warn't young an' she warn't old. But she looked—well—Ah jes' doan know how she did look—all laughin' an' happy an' tears in her eyes. Ah didn't look at her much fer starin' at Dad. He looked—all shaken up—an' scared like—Not scared like neither fer Ah seen him smile at her, after a minute. He ain't never smiled lak that befo'—not's Ah kin remember. Nat said—"Reckin yuh Dad's met an' ole gal 'er his"—But Ah only laughed—Struck me kinda funny—that! Dad meetin' an 'ole flame uh his—Ah meant tuh ask Dad 'bout her but it went clean outa mah head. (*he reaches once more for the money. This time he takes it easily, enough. Hattie has forgotten it*)

HATTIE. (*after a pause*) Was she tall?

CHARLEY. Kinda. Plenty taller'n you. (*he rises and takes his hat from the table*)

HATTIE. (*after a pause*) Light?

CHARLEY. So—So,—lighter'n you. (*he moves toward the door*)

HATTIE. Pretty?

CHARLEY. Mebbe. She warn't no chicken—but she was good tuh look at. Tain't no use mopin', Ma. Dad ain't de fus' husban' tuh take dinner wid his girl friend. Funny, though his never doin' it befo'. Well, s'long!

(*He goes out and the door slams noisily. Hattie rouses up at that and starts clearing the table. She has just left the room with the last handful of dishes when the hall door is opened quietly and DAN enters. He is a dark*) *man of medium height, slender of build. He looks a little stooped. There is a beaten look about his face—a tired, patient look. He takes off his overcoat and still stands there hesitating. Hattie re-enters, frowns darkly but does not speak. She places a scarf upon the table and a little silver-plated basket from the sideboard)*

DAN. (*dropping his coat and hat upon a chair*) Sorry, Ah'm late, Hattie. (*she does not answer*) Ah ain't had no supper. Reckon Ah'll get it an' eat in de kitchen.

HATTIE. (*icily*) Reckon yuh'll hang dat coat an' hat in de hall whar dey belongs.

DAN. (*apologetically*) Sure. Dunno how Ah come tuh ferget. (*He goes out with his clothes and returns almost immediately. He looks timidly at Hattie, then passes on toward the kitchen door*)

HATTIE. (*fiercely*) Keep outa dat kitchen!

DAN. But Ah'm hungry, Hattie. Ah ain't had nuthin' tuh eat.

HATTIE. Whar yuh bin, dat yur ain't had nuthin 'tuh eat? (*Dan doesn't answer*) Yuh kain't say, kin yuh?

DAN. Ah went tuh see a friend uh mine.

HATTIE. Half past six ain't callin' hours! (*Dan looks unhappily at the floor*) Less'n yuh's asked ter dine!

DAN. It was important! Ah had tuh go.

HATTIE. Had tuh go whar? Yuh ain't said whar yuh's bin. (*Dan does not answer*) An yuh ain't got no intention uh saying, has yuh?

(*Dan does not answer. He moves once more toward the kitchen*)

HATTIE. (*in a shrill voice*) Yuh keep outa thar! Keep outa mah kitchen! Ah kep yuh supper till eight o'clock. Yuh didn' come, an Ah's throwed it out!

DAN. Ah'll fix sumpth'n else. Ah doan want much.

HATTIE. Yuh ain't goin' messin' in mah kitchen! Yuh's hidin' sumpth'n, Dan Peters, and Ah's gwine fine it out 'fo' long. Yuh ain't gonna throw no dust in mah eyes no second time—not ef Ah knows it!

DAN. All right, Ah doan' want no fuss, Hattie. Ah'll go out an' git sumpth'n.

HATTIE. Yuh kin fix de furnace 'fo' yuh go. Ah's got 'nuff tuh do runnin' a lodgin' house, 'thout fixin' fires day an' night.

DAN. Charley was home. Yuh coulda asked Charley tuh do it.

HATTIE. Charley doan' never fix no furnace. It's yo' job when yuh's home an' Ah ain't got no reason tuh wish it on Charley.

DAN. Ah'll fix it when Ah gits back. Ah'm hungry, now an' Ah's gwine tuh git sumpth'n tuh eat.

(*He goes out. Hattie listens for the click of the iron gate, then hurries to the window and peers after him. The door is opened softly and a little brown woman sidles in. Her eyes rove constantly always seeking—seeking. Hattie turns around and glares fiercely at her*)

HATTIE. What yuh want?

MRS. WILKES. (*startled slightly at the grimness of the other's voice*) Ah declare, Mis' Peters, yuh sho' does look put out! Anything de matter?

HATTIE. (*shortly*) Did yuh come down here tuh tell me dat?

MRS. WILKES. (*with an uneasy laugh*) C'ose not, Mis' Peters! . . . It's pretty cold upstairs. Ah s'pose de fire's goin' ez usual?

HATTIE. Yes.

MRS. WILKES. It's gettin' colder, Ah reckon. (*Hattie does not answer*) It's warmer down here. As Ah always tells Mr. Wilkes, gimme a parlor floor an' basement any time. Ef thar's any heat goin' yuh's sure tuh git it— Co'se, Ah ain't complainin', Mis' Peters—

HATTIE. H'm!

MRS. WILKES. See Mr. Peters got home pretty late tuh-night, didn he? (*Hattie answers only with a venomous glance*) Thar's a man with reg'lar habits. Ah often tells Mr. Wilkes dat Ah wish tuh goodness he was a home lovin' man lak Mr. Peters. . . . Well, reckon Ah'll be gwine up again' seein' ez yuh's got comp'ny.

HATTIE. (*with a puzzled frown*) Comp'ny?

MRS. WILKES. Thar's a lady tuh see yuh. She's upstairs settin' in de parlor.

HATTIE. Who let her in?

MRS. WILKES. Mr. Wilkes did. He seen her on de stoop. She was jes' gwine tuh ring de bell when Mr. Wilkes come up wid his key. She ask tuh see Mis' Peters an' he tole her tuh set in de parlor. Ef thar's ever a stupid man it sure is mah husban'. 'Stead uh goin' down an tellin' yuh, 'er hollerin' tuh yuh, 'er sendin' her on down, he comes up-stairs an' tells *me* ter go down an' tell yuh. He'd oughta sent her down de basement do' fust place.

HATTIE. Send her down, will yuh? Some fine day, Ah 'spec we'll be cleaned out, ef yuh all's gwine let strangers in de house that 'a way.

MRS. WILKES. (*with a little cough*) Thought yuh might want tuh see her in de parlor. Ah reckon she ain't no thief, not judgin' from her looks.

HATTIE. H'h! Whut she look lak?

MRS. WILKES. She's tall—but not too tall.

HATTIE. (*forcing her stiffening lips to move*) Light?

MRS. WILKES. Lighter'n yuh an' me—

HATTIE. (*with a supreme effort*) Pretty?

MRS. WILKES. Well, yuh knows her all right! She ain't never bin here befo' ez Ah knows—but yuh knows her frum de way yuh's 'scribed her. Well, 'slong! Ah'll send her down. (*she opens the hall door*) B'r! (*she shivers*) Dis hall cert'nly is cold!

(*The door closes after her. For a moment Hattie looks bewildered. But only for a moment. With a sudden harsh laugh she rips the apron from about her waist and pushes it quickly into the side-board drawer. She goes up to the mirror over the mantle, but one look at herself is all that she can bear. As she turns sharply away the door opens and CLEM enters. In one glance Hattie's burning eyes take in the tall, well-dressed figure. The graying hair, the youthful face. If Clem's glance is less piercing, it is nevertheless just as comprehensive*)

CLEM. (*softly*) It's bin a long time, Hattie. (*Hattie opens her lips to speak, but she doesn't. She sits, rather heavily, and continues to stare at Clem*) Ah doan' wonder yuh's 'sprised Hattie. (*She hesitates and then drawing up a chair facing Hattie, she too, sits.*) Ah know yuh's waitin' tuh hear whut brought me . . . It's a long story, Hattie. (*at that, Hattie moves impatiently*)

HATTIE. Yuh kin start—at de end—

CLEM. At de end?

HATTIE. At de end. Whut yuh come fer? Yuh's come ter git sumpth'n—Is it—Dan?

CLEM. (*leaning back in her chair with a sigh*) De same ole Hattie! De years ain't changed yuh, none.

HATTIE. (*with a bitter laugh*) An' de years ain't changed *you*, none.

CLEM. Yes. Ah reckon they has, Hattie, Ah's suffered a-plenty.

HATTIE. (*with a curl of her lip*) An' yuh think dat yuh's de only one?

CLEM. Oh no! Ah kin see yuh's not bin over happy, Hattie, an' Ah knows dat Dan ain't bin happy.

HATTIE. Whut reason yuh got ter bring up all dis talk 'bout suff'rin'? Yuh bin seein' Dan agin', ain't yuh?

CLEM. Yes. Ah met him jes' by accident one night las' week.

HATTIE. An' yuh's bin seein' him sence?

CLEM. Yes, ev'y night. Ah's bein' gwine down town ter meet him 'roun six o'clock an' Ah's ride home wid him in de "L."

HATTIE. An' tuh-night yuh had him out tuh dinner. (*Hattie's voice has a deadly calm*)

CLEM. No. Tuh-night Ah couldn' go tuh meet him. Ah was called away on business. Ah ain't seen him tuh-night.

HATTIE. Did he know yuh was comin' here?

CLEM. No.

HATTIE. Why'nt yuh tell him, yuh was comin'.

CLEM. He wouldn' 'er let me come.

HATTIE. Well, say whut yuh's come fer, an' go. It ain't easy settin' here an' listenin' tuh yuh talkin' 'bout Dan.

CLEM. (*abruptly*) Yuh's almost driv' him crazy. An' yuh said yuh loved him. (*Hattie's fingers clench slowly*)

HATTIE. Whar'd yuh go to? Whar you bin all dese years?

CLEM. South—Virginia, whar I come frum.

HATTIE. H'm!

CLEM. Ef Ah'd knowed yuh was gwine tuh be unkind tuh him, Ah'd never let him go! Dan ain't knowed a day's happiness sence Ah went away.

HATTIE. He—he tole yuh dat?

CLEM. Yes! Ah kin fergive yuh fer takin' him 'way frum me—an' de way yuh done it—but it ain't easy fergivin' yuh fer makin' him suffer.

HATTIE. An' dat's whut yuh's come here tuh tell me?

CLEM. (*passionately*) Dan's dyin' here, right under yo' eyes, an' yo' doan see it. He's dyin' fer kindness—He's dyin' frum hard wuk. He's dyin' frum de want uv love. Ah could allus read him lak a book. He won't talk 'gainst yuh, Hattie, but Ah kin see it all in de way he looks—in de way he looks at me. (*Clem dabs at her eyes with her handkerchief*)

HATTIE. Go on. (*she marvels at her own quietness*)

CLEM. (*accusingly*) He's shabby—all uv him—hat an' shoes an coat. Ef he had one suit fer ev'y five dat yuh son has, he'd be pretty well dressed.

HATTIE. (*slowly*) Yuh fergit, Charley is Dan's son ez well ez mine.

CLEM. An' yuh's set him 'gainst his dad. He sides with yuh ev'y time, doan' he?

HATTIE. (*with a faint sneer*) Did yuh read dat too, in de way Dan—looked—at yuh?

CLEM. Ef yuh had a brought Charley up diff'rent yuh mighta held on tuh Dan. 'Stead uh dat, yuh's brought him up tuh look down on him.

HATTIE. (*she is breathing heavily, her voice comes thick and choked*) Is yuh tru? (*rises*)

CLEM. Yuh doan' need Dan an yo' son doan' need him. Well, sence yuh ain't got no use fer him, Ah's gwine take him frum yuh, Hattie. Now yuh knows why Ah's come. (*she rises also and looks down at Hattie, much to the latter's disadvantage*)

HATTIE. (*forcing the words out, as though each one pains her*) Funny—how—thoughtful yuh's got sence Ah's las' seen yuh. Yuh come inta mah house twenty years ago as a frien'—an' yuh took Dan when Ah hadn't bin married ter him a year. Yuh didn' give no 'nouncement den 'bout whut yuh was gwine ter do. Yuh jes' took him—an' me expectin' tuh be de mother uv his chile. Gawd! (*a deep shudder runs through her body*) But now—dat yuh's got mo' stylish—mo' lady-like in yuh ways yuh come tuh tell me ve'y politely, dat yuh's gwine tuh take him agin. Is it mah blessin' yuh's waitin' fer? Yuh doan' need no permission.

CLEM. Yuh, yuh doan' un'erstan'—Yuh never did un'erstan' Hattie.

HATTIE. Mebbe not. Some things is hard tuh un'erstan'.

CLEM. Co'se Dan an' me could go off tergether, 'thout yuh permission. Yuh knows dat well 'nuff. It's bein' done ev'y day. But we doan' want ter go lak dat.

HATTIE. Yuh mean Dan doan' want ter go that 'a-way!

CLEM. Yuh's wrong, Hattie. Dan ain't thinkin' 'er nuthin' 'er nobuddy but me. He's fer quittin' an' never sayin' a word tuh yuh but jes' goin' off, me an' him together. But Ah ain't gwine tuh go lak dat. Dis time it's gotta be diff'rent.

HATTIE. Diff'rent—how?

CLEM. Hattie, Ah wants yuh tuh free Dan. Yuh owes it tuh him. He ain't never bin free sence he's knowed yuh. Will yuh free him?

HATTIE. Free him—how?

CLEM. Give him a divo'ce.

HATTIE. A divo'ce—tuh marry you?

CLEM. (*pleadingly*) Yes. 'Taint lak yuh loved him Hattie. Ef yuh loved him Ah couldn' ask yuh. But yuh only holds onta him tru spite—Yuh hates him, mebbe—Yuh treats him lak yuh does.

HATTIE. Yuh knows Ah kain't keep him ef he wants tuh go. Reckon Ah knows it, too. Well, ef he wants tuh go he kin go.

CLEM. (*with an exclamation of relief*) Thank Gawd! Ah didn' think yuh'd do it, Hattie.

HATTIE. Yuh coulda spared yuhself de trubble comin' here—an jes' gone off. It woulda bin more lak yuh.

CLEM. But—but—how? Yuh'd have ter know 'bout de devo'ce, Hattie.

HATTIE. Devo'ce? Ah ain't said nuthin' 'bout gettin' no devo'ce!

CLEM. But—but—yuh—Ah thought—Whut yuh mean, Hattie?

HATTIE. Yuh didn' need no devo'ce de fust time, did yuh?

CLEM. (*biting her lips to keep back the tears*) Dat—Dat was diff'rent.

HATTIE. Ah doan' see it.

CLEM. Well, it was. It's gotta be a divo'ce dis time.

HATTIE. Ah see Dan's morals has improved some sence *you* went away.

CLEM. It ain't Dan whut's holdin' out fer devo'ce—It's—it's me.

HATTIE. (*Hattie's laugh has a bitter edge*) Den it's yo' morals dat's bin im-provin'—Well, dey could stan' improvin' a-plenty. (*the fierce edge returns suddenly to her voice*) Yuh's wastin' yo' time an' mine an Dan's! 'Bout let-tin' him go—He coulda gone all dese years—Ah warn't holdin' him back! He'd gone too, ef he'd knowed whar to find yuh. Ah knowed ef he ever found yuh, he'd leave me. Well, he didn' find yuh tell now. But long's Ah's got breaf tuh breathe, Ah ain't gwine say "Yes!" 'bout no divo'ce. Ef he kin git one 'thout me, let him git it! Yuh hear me? Now ef yuh's tru, yuh better get outa here. Ah ain't 'sponsible' fer whut Ah says frum now on!

CLEM. Hattie, 'fore Gawd, yuh's hard!

HATTIE. Ah was soft 'nuff, when yuh fust stepped on me. Ef Ah's hard now, 'tis yo' fault!

CLEM. Hattie—Ah ain't tole yuh de real reason why Ah wants dat di'voce— (*a note of despair has crept into her voice*)

HATTIE. No? Well, Ah ain't in'trested none.

CLEM. Still Ah wants yuh tuh hear! It's sumpthin' dat Ah ain't tole Dan. (*The door is opened quietly and Dan enters. He starts—looks fearfully from Clem to Hattie and then back again to Clem*) Come in, Dan. Ah hope yuh doan' mind ma comin' tuh see Hattie. Ah jes' had tuh come.

DAN. (*swallowing painfully*) It won' do no good. (*Hattie is gazing at him curiously*)

CLEM. Mebbe not, but Ah had tuh come.

DAN. Ah'm sorry, Hattie. We—we—(*he turns away as if ashamed*)

CLEM. Hattie knows ev'ything Dan. Ah's tole her. (*Dan turns toward her*)

DAN. Clem, whut was yuh sayin' when Ah come on in? Ah heard yuh—

CLEM. (*embarrassed*) Ah didn' want tuh tell yuh—lak dis—

DAN. (*gently*) We kain't go back now, Clem. Sence we's in de middle we's gotta git tru, somehow.

CLEM. (*turning from him to Hattie*) Ah didn' mean tuh beg, 'less'n Ah had tuh—

HATTIE. (*coldly*) Yuh doan' have tuh—

CLEM. Ef 'twas only me—but it ain't. It's fer mah Lucy,—Dan's chile (*there is a terrible silence*) Dan's chile—Ah didn' tell yuh, Hattie, an' Ah didn' tell Dan. Whut woulda bin de use? She's a woman now an' good—an' pretty. She thinks her dad died when she was a baby an' she thinks—she thinks—Ah'm a good woman. She's proud uh me. (*as if unconscious of Hattie's presence, Dan grips Clem's hands. They look at each other*)

HATTIE. (*as if to herself. She seems to be trying to get it all quite clear*) She thinks yuh's a good woman! An' dat's why yuh expects me tuh give Dan a divo'ce.

CLEM. (*eagerly*) Yes, Yes! Yuh see, doan' yuh?

HATTIE. Yes, Ah see. Gawd, ef dat ain't funny! She thinks yuh's a good woman. (*she laughs loudly,—hysterically*) Oh, my Gawd!

DAN. (*sharply*) Hattie!

HATTIE. (*ignoring him*) Tell me mo'—'bout dis—dis new relation, uh Dan's.

CLEM. Ah's wuked hard tuh git her de chances Ah didn' have. She's bin tuh school—she's got an' eddication. An' now she's goin' tuh git married tuh a fine feller whut'll be able tuh take care uv her. Now yuh see dat Ah kain't jes' go off wid Dan. It's got tuh be proper—a divo'ce an' all. Yuh see, doan' yuh, Hattie?

HATTIE. (*nodding*) Mother an' daughter—double weddin'.

CLEM. (*anxiously*) An yuh'll do it, Hattie? Gawd'll bless yuh, Hattie.

HATTIE. (*derisively*) How come *you's* passin' on blessins? Yuh knows a lot, doan' yuh 'bout blessins? Wonder ef yuh knows ez much 'bout curses?

CLEM. Now, Hattie—

HATTIE. (*darkly*) Yuh doan know nuthin' much 'bout curses, does yuh? Well, yuh's cursed, Clem Jackson! Cursed! Yuh's allus bin cursed sence de day yuh cast yuh eyes on Dan!

DAN. (*harshly*) Hattie, yuh ain't got no call tuh go on lak dat.

HATTIE. (*who does not seem to hear him*) Dan was cursed when he set eyes on yuh. An' Ah was cursed when Ah took yuh fer a frien'.

CLEM. (*hurriedly*) Ah'm goin', Hattie! Ah see yuh ain't gwine give in.

HATTIE. Whut's yuh hurry? Yuh better hear whut Ah's gwine tuh say . . . Curses. Yes, we's all bin cursed, Clem. Mah Charley's cursed an' yo' Lucy—too bad.

CLEM. (*angrily*) Doan' yuh call mah Lucy's name 'long uv yours.

HATTIE. (*with a sneer*) Too bad. Wonder how she'll feel when she hears whut a good woman yuh is?

CLEM. (*shrinking as if from a blow*) Whut? Yuh—yuh wouldn'—yuh wouldn'—

HATTIE. Wouldn'—wouldn'—(*she laughs again—crazily*) Sure, Ah'll fine her! Ef it takes de rest uh mah life, Ah'll fine her. It's too good—tuh keep. How she'll stare when she knows her ma was a prostitute an' her dad—

DAN. (*hoarsely*) Damn yuh, Hattie! Doan yuh say no mo'.

HATTIE. Ah'll tell her all—all—leavin' out nuthin'.

CLEM. (*pleading as if for life*) Yuh couldn', Hattie! Yuh couldn'! Hattie—Hattie—

HATTIE. How she play me false—when Ah trusted her—an' how she lie tuh me—How she ruin' mah life—an' come on back tuh take de leavin's once more—

DAN. Doan yuh say no mo, Hattie!

HATTIE. Yuh'd shut mah mouf' wouldn' yuh? How? How—

DAN. Let's go, Clem. Let's go—

HATTIE. (*shrilly*) G'wan. Is Ah keepin' yuh? Take yuh street walker back whar she come frum. Yuh kin give Lucy mah regahds. Tell her dat a frien's gwine call on her—real soon—an' ole frien' uv her ma's.

DAN. (*with a cry of rage, grips Hattie by the shoulder and shakes her*) Yoh'll shut yo' mouf, Hattie. Promise, 'er fo' Gawd-A-Mighty.

HATTIE. (*scornfully*) How yuh's thinkin' 'er shuttin' mah mouf, Dan Peters?

DAN. Yuh'll keep 'way frum Lucy. Yuh'll promise not tuh say nuthin' 'bout Clem. (*Dan shakes her again roughly*)

HATTIE. (*her speech broken with little gasping cries*) Never! An' yuh kain't make me! Ah'll tell her 'bout dis good woman! Dis thief! Dis dirty minded whore! (*without a word, Dan grips her by the throat and forces her back—back against the table. Her arms claw awkwardly and then drop to her sides. Clem utters a low cry and springs upon Dan, tearing wildly at his fingers.*)

CLEM. Dan! Leggo! Leggo, fer Gawd's sake! Dan! (*with a violent movement of disgust he thrusts Hattie from him. She falls heavily from the chair, her head striking the marble base of the mantle—an ugly sound. She lies very still. Dan looks at her stupidly. Clem throws her arms about his neck, sobbing hysterically*) Dan! Dan! Yuh come near killin' her!

DAN. (*breathing heavily*) Ah'd a done it too, ef yuh hadn't bin thar.

CLEM. (*stooping over Hattie*) She hit her head an awful crack!

DAN. Hattie's head's harder'n mos'. Come on, Clem. We kain't stay here, now. She'll be comin' to, 'fo' long! An raisin' de roof.

CLEM. (*who is still peering at Hattie*) Dan, thar's blood comin' out de corner uv her mouf.

DAN. She'll be waggin' it again' fo' yuh knows it.

CLEM. (*going up to Dan and putting her hand on his shoulder*) Dan, Ah wish yuh hadn't done it! 'Twon' do no good!

DAN. Ah couldn' stan' it no longer. Ah clean los' mah head when she call yuh—whut she did.

CLEM. Yes, Ah know. Poor Danny boy! Ah doan see how yuh's stood it all dese years.

DAN. (*putting his arms about her*) Ah was allus thinkin' uv yuh, Clem. Yuh shouldn' 'a lef' me behin'. Yuh'd oughta tole me whar tuh fine yuh. Yuh shoulda tole me 'bout Lucy.

CLEM. Yes, Ah see dat now. But yuh b'longed tuh Hattie 'n Ah thought—

DAN. Ah never b'longed tuh Hattie. (*he kisses her*) Let's go, Clem. (*she draws away from him*) Why, whut's wrong?

CLEM. Ah's gotta think uh Lucy.

DAN. Lucy?

CLEM. Yes, Lucy. She's yo' chile Dan, an' she doan' know—'bout us.

DAN. An' me—Whut 'bout me, an you—Clem—Clem—

CLEM. Ah you musn'. Then thar's Hattie. Yuh's gotta think uv Hattie— (*they both turn and look at the figure huddled there on the floor*) Dan, we'd better try'n bring her to. Get some water, Dan.

DAN. Ah won't touch her!

CLEM. It ain't human leavin' her lak dat. Help me lif' her, Dan. She'll catch her death uh cold on dat flo'! (*very unwillingly Dan assists. Together he and Clem get Hattie into a chair. Her head lolls persistently to one side. Clem rubs her hands*) Lak ice! Why, Dan, her fingers all stiff! An'—an' Dan! Feel her pulse! Dan!

(*She draws back terrified. Hattie's body, unsupported, sags awkwardly against the table. Dan quickly seizes her hands, feeling her pulse. He tilts her head backward, looks into her face—feels her heart, then straightens up—his face distorted, his eyes blank.*)

CLEM. (*in a whisper*) Dan—she ain't—dead?

DAN. Dead. (*he looks down at his hands in horror*)

CLEM. (*wildly*) Dan! Whut'll we do! Whut'll we do!

DAN. Yuh'll go back tuh Lucy. She needs yuh.

CLEM. You needs me mo', Dan!

DAN. Yuh kain't help none! Ah doan stan' no chance—reckon Ah owes it tuh Lucy tuh send yuh back tuh her. Ah ain't never had de chance tuh do nuthin' fer her—but dis.

CLEM. Ah kain't go, Dan! Doan' mek me. (*her body is wracked with sobs*)

DAN. (*taking her in his arms and kissing her*) We's gotta think 'bout Lucy—We's brung each other bad luck, Clem. Hattie was right.

CLEM. But Ah loved yuh Dan, an' yuh loved me.

DAN. Ah ain't never loved nobuddy else.

CLEM. Whut'll dey do tuh yuh Dan? Dey won't kill yuh? (*she clings tightly to him*) Will dey, Dan?

DAN. Co'se not, Honey! Reckon Ah'll git twenty—er fifteen years—mebbe ten—(*he buttons her coat and draws her firmly toward the door*)

CLEM. Ten years! (*she wrings her hands with a low moaning cry*)

DAN. Ah'll spend 'em all dreamin' 'bout yuh, Clem, an'—an' Lucy! Yuh musn' grieve, Honey. Go, now, fer Gawd's sake! Ah hears sombuddy comin' down! (*He pushes her out, forcibly. And then the door is shut. The outer door slams. Dan listens for the click of the gate. Finally he turns and looks down at Hattie*) Ah'm sorry, Hattie! 'Fore Gawd, Ah didn' mean tuh do it!

CURTAIN

FOOL'S ERRAND

PERSONS OF THE PLAY

CASSIE,	a busy-body
SISTER WILLIAMS,	the minister's wife
DOUG,	father of Maza
PARSON WILLIAMS	
MAZA,	daughter of Doug
JUD,	a suitor of Maza
FREDDIE,	another suitor
MOM,	mother of Maza

BRETHREN AND SISTERS OF THE CHURCH COUNCIL.

Scene: The living-room of a cabin in an unprogressive Negro settlement. There is an old folding couch, covered with cheap cretonne, and an ugly red plush armchair. Two pine chairs are drawn up about a large, round table in the C. *of the room. On one side of the fireplace at the* L. *is an old rocker—on the other, a large chest of drawers lurching forward in search of a long-lost castor. The rough mantel is strewn with gewgaws—a vase of brilliant paper flowers, cheap photographs, sea shells and a book or two. Beside the ornate kerosene lamp on the center table, lies the family Bible. At the back, we find a small curtainless window and a door leading to the front yard. At the* R. *a door leads into the bedroom.*

Time: A summer evening.

At Rise: AUNT CASSIE, *a shriveled, ugly little woman, is peering stealthily out of the window. At last she draws back and turns to her companion, who is rocking leisurely to and fro.* SISTER WILLIAMS, *the Parson's wife, is a large honey-tongued woman with an enormous brown face.*

SISTER WILLIAMS. Whut's she doin'?

CASSIE. A-standin' by de gate an' a-lookin' down de road jes' lak she's done ev'y night dis week.

SISTER WILLIAMS. An' thar ain't neither uv 'em showed up?

CASSIE. Co'se dey ain't. Ev'y night she puts on dat pink frock an' goes out thar by de gate. She ain't got no mo' shame left, Ah reckon.

SISTER WILLIAMS. She did look mighty nice, as Ah came in.

CASSIE. (*With a sniff*) Sence her ma done git her dat comb, she doan do nothin' but straighten dat hair er hern.

SISTER WILLIAMS. (*With a sorry shake of her head*) Maza's pretty an' she's allus bin sech a right-minded gal, it does seem too bad. Yuh's sure yuh ain't makin' no mistake, Cassie?

CASSIE. (*Positively*) Ah's done tole yuh de truth, Sister Williams. Reckon Ah ain't got no call tuh doubt mah own eyes.

SISTER WILLIAMS. (*After a pause*) No, Ah reckon thar ain't nuthin' wrong wid yuh eyes, Cassie.

CASSIE. Well, Sister Williams, what're we gwine do?

SISTER WILLIAMS. Reckon we'd better wait fer her ma tuh come home. Seems tuh me, dis is sumpth'n fer Maza's ma ter settle. Mary's comin' home mos' any day now, ain't she?

CASSIE. Dat's jes' it. An' ef yuh knows Mary lak Ah thinks yuh does, she won't do nuthin' sens'ble.

SISTER WILLIAMS. Well, but whut kin *we* do? It's up tuh her dad an' ma, ain't it?

CASSIE. (*Triumphantly*) Now yuh's talkin'! An' as her ma ain't here, we'll put it up ter her dad—

SISTER WILLIAMS. (*Stilling her rocker for a moment*) We? Now see here, Cassie—

CASSIE. An' we'll put it tuh him dis ve'y night!

SISTER WILLIAMS. (*Rising*) Yuh'll have tuh 'scuse me, Cassie. Ah's got a Council meetin'. 'Sides, Ah ain't got no call mixin' up wid dis, even ef Ah is de Parson's wife. Doug ain't no church member an' he doan' lak me an' Parson none. Yuh's Maza's aunt, an' sence her ma ain't here, reckon yuh'll have tuh handle dis case yuhself. Ah'd like tuh help yuh, hones', but Ah doan' see how Ah kin.

CASSIE. (*Eagerly*) Ah'll tell yuh how yuh kin help.

SISTER WILLIAMS. (*Curiously*) How?

CASSIE. De Council holds a meetin' at yo' house ter-night, doan' dey!

SISTER WILLIAMS. (*Nodding*) Yes, but—

CASSIE. Have 'em meet here instead. When dey comes send 'em over here.

We'll put it up tuh de Council. Dat's whut it's fer, ain't it? Ef de Council fer Suppreshun uh Vice an' Correckshun uh Sinners ain't gwine tuh handle cases lak dis here, den dey better bust up. De Council oughta make her tell which one uh dem two fellers it is, an' it oughta make him marry her.

SISTER WILLIAMS. (*Looking at Cassie with reluctant admiration*) Yuh's cert'nly got a quick mind, Cassie. Reckon yuh's right, too. Co'se Ah kain't promise, but Ah'll tell Parson Williams whut yuh wants. Ef he says it's all right, Ah'll send de Council over when dey comes tuh mah house. Parson was sayin' only las' night, dat it was high time de Council got tuh dealin' wid some uh dese young folks. Dey's gettin' outer han'—clean outer han'.

CASSIE. (*Spitefully*) It's mah 'pinion dey's bin outer han' a mighty long time. Whut wid de way dey cuts off de little hair Gawd gives 'em, an' den spends all dey's got tuh straighten it out—flyin' in de face uh Gawd, Ah calls it!

SISTER WILLIAMS. (*Whose hair is straightened*) Lawd, dat ain't nothin', Cassie! Why, Parson was tellin' me only las' night, 'bout dis here new case de Council's gwine tuh settle. Give a guess, will yuh?

CASSIE. Reckon it ain't dancin', fer dat's common 'nuff.

SISTER WILLIAMS. No, ma'am! Wouldn't be so bad ef 'twas some uh dis wild dancin', though we doan' hold wid no sech doin's. It's smokin', Cassie! Two gals from de Corners had de low-down nerve tuh smoke cigarettes at our Sunday School picnic!

CASSIE. (*With a gasp*) What're we comin' tuh!

SISTER WILLIAMS. Ef sech doin's keeps on, reckon our young people'll be jes' as brazen's white folks.

CASSIE. Reckon yuh's right, Sister Williams.

SISTER WILLIAMS. Well, Ah'll be runnin' 'long, Cassie. (*Walking lumberously toward the door.*) Reckon Maza's case's mo' impo'tant dan dem gals. But Ah's gotta see whut Parson says.

CASSIE. Ef he says, " Yes," put yuh red light in de winder, so's Ah'll know.

SISTER WILLIAMS. (*Pausing, with her hand on the door knob*) Say, Cassie! 'Case de Council's gwine tuh take up Maza's case, yuh oughta have dem young fellers here.

CASSIE. Dat's so! But how's we gwine git 'em, Sister Williams? Freddie cut Maza dead, at de picnic, an Jud ain't bin here sence.

SISTER WILLIAMS. (*Thoughtfully*) Mebbe Ah could stop by Freddie's house an' git him tuh come. Ask him tuh fetch sumpth'n er other—

CASSIE. (*Quickly*) Camp chairs! We ain't got 'nuff chairs!

SISTER WILLIAMS. (*Admiringly*) Yuh's sho' got some head, Cassie! Sure, Ah'll ask Freddie tuh fetch dem chairs fer me, ef he's home. Reckon he can't refuse, nohow, even ef he doan' want tuh come. But how 'bout Jud? 'Tain't so easy tuh git hold uh Jud.

CASSIE. We's got tuh git him here, somehow. 'Spec' Ah'll think uh some ways—

SISTER WILLIAMS. (*Opening the door quite wide*) Lawd, Cassie! Ef thar ain't Jud now, a-talkin' tuh Maza!

CASSIE. Looks lak de hand er Providence, doan' it, Sister Williams?

SISTER WILLIAMS. 'Deed it does! 'Twon't do no harm tuh keep yuh eyes on him, Cassie. Reckon yuh'd better tell Doug, too, 'fo' de folks come. We doan' want no trubble, Cassie, an' yuh knows Doug ain't allus peaceable. (*With a nod, Sister Williams goes out. Cassie shuts the door, walks quickly to the bedroom door and opens it.*)

CASSIE. Doug! Doug! Douglas Lee!

DOUG. (*With a low growl*) Huh? Whut de hell do yuh want?

CASSIE. Now, Doug, doan' go fer gittin' mad 'fo' yuh has tuh. Ah's gotta see yuh 'bout sumpth'n.

DOUG. (*With another growl*) Close dat do' an' git outa here!

CASSIE. Yuh'd better pull yuhself tergether, Doug! Thar's gwine tuh be a meetin' here ternight.

DOUG. (*With a brutal laugh*) Lak hell thar is! An' who de devil tole yuh dat Ah's goin' tuh stan' fer a meetin' in mah house? Lemme tell yuh dis, sister—ef any psalm-singin' fools comes here ternight, dey's gwine tuh git throwed out!

CASSIE. (*Sharply*) Yuh's drunk Doug!

DOUG. (*Defiantly*) Well? An' what uv it? Ain't yuh seen me drunk 'fo' now?

CASSIE. Yuh's gotta pull yuhself tergether, quick. Thar's trouble, Doug, trubble 'bout Maza.

DOUG. Maza's a good 'nuff gal! Damned ef yuh ain't wuss'n Mary, wid yuh naggin'. Lemme 'lone! Shut dat do'!

CASSIE. Maza's in trubble wid a man, Doug. D'yuh hear, Doug? Maza's in trubble—(*Very quickly she draws back from the door, retreating toward the window. A tall, powerful man lurches out of the bedroom and stands glowering at her with fierce blood-shot eyes. His blue shirt sleeves are rolled high upon his brawny arms; his shirt is open at the neck. He stands there swaying slightly for a moment, then drops heavily upon the couch which rattles and creaks fearfully at his weight.*)

DOUG. Whut's dis yuh's sayin' 'bout Maza? (*He rubs his hand back and forth across his eyes.*)

CASSIE. Maza's in trubble. She's gwine tuh have a baby. (*Doug's hand drops heavily at his side. He only stares and stares at Cassie.*) She's bin makin' de clothes already. Got 'em pretty near all made. Ah seen 'em mahself, jes' by accident in de bottom drawer. (*She jerks her head toward the chest-of-drawers.*) 'Cose Ah ain't natcherly cu'rus, but when Ah seen dat none uh dem drawers was locked, savin' only dat bottom drawer, Ah knowed sumpth'n was wrong. Well, Ah takes out de drawer above, an' looks, an' ef Ah ain't seen a bran' new set uh baby things, mah name ain't Cassie Lee.

DOUG. (*With a sneer*) An' a hell-boun' liar!

CASSIE. (*Angrily*) Ef yuh thinks Ah's lyin' lemme show yuh. (*She runs to the chest-of-drawers and in another second is holding up for Doug's in-spection a baby's dress. With a snarl like that of some wild beast, Doug makes a spring for the little garment and with one motion of his claw-like hands, rends it in two. He throws the pieces on the ground and reels to-ward the street door. Cassie places her back against the door, with the courage of desperation.*) Listen, Doug! 'Tain't no use rowin' ner fightin'. 'Tain't no use killin' Maza an' yuh doan' know nobuddy else tuh kill. More sense tuh find out who's ter blame an' make him marry Maza.

DOUG. Ah'll choke it outer her, by Gawd!

CASSIE. Dat ain't no way uh talkin', Doug! Listen tuh me! Chokin' an' killin' is fool's talk! De Parson's gwine tuh make her tell his name an' he's gwine tuh fix it so she gits married.

DOUG. Ah ain't gwine have no parson buttin' in mah business! Now, git outa mah way or by Gawd—!

CASSIE. (*Rapidly*) Listen, Doug! Ah's jes' seen Sister Williams' red light in de winder. Dat means Parson's comin', an' de Council. Set down, Doug, an' pull yuhself tergether! Yuh bein' drunk shows yuh in a bad light! Ma-za's ma off workin' an' you home loafin' an' on a drunk. Fine example yuh shows Maza! Fine care yuh's took uv her sence her ma's bin off wid dem white folks! What'll yuh say tuh Mary when she gits home, ef yuh ain't let Parson Williams do his dooty by Maza? Reckon yuh ain't so drunk but yuh kin be 'shamed er yuh no 'count ways. (*Very slowly Doug drops back upon the couch. Suddenly he buries his face in his hands. Cassie draws a breath of relief.*) Now yuh jes' set thar, Doug! Ev'ything'll be fixed sure 'nuff! Jes' doan' say nuthin' 'til de time comes. (*She opens the door and calls to* MAZA.) Maza! Reckon dey's got dat ker'sene in! Run down tuh de Corners an' fetch dat can, will yuh? Jud kin help yuh bring it back! (*At the sound of Jud's name, Doug stirs once more and looks up. But Cassie is ready for him.*) Now doan' yuh be doin' nuthin' hasty, Doug. It takes a smart man lak Parson tuh know de rights an' wrongs uv a case lak dis. (*She takes up the torn dress and places it on the table. Doug drops his head once more into his hands with a groan. Cassie opens back the street door and crouching down on the threshold starts rocking to and fro. Fi-nally she begins to sing in a quavering voice.*)

> Camp meetin' in de wilderness,
> Thar's a meetin' here ter-night.
> Doan' let dat sinner hab no res',
> Thar's a meetin' here ter-night.
> Come along
> Thar's a meetin' here ter-night,
> Git yuh ready,
> Thar's a meetin' here ter-night,
> Ah know yuh by yo' daily walk,
> Thar's a meetin' here ter-night.
> Come along—

(*Several voices without join Cassie's. She draws back from the door and the Council for Suppression of Vice and Correction of Sinners enters, headed by* PARSON WILLIAMS. De Lawd be praised, yuh could come, Parson! De Lawd be praised!

PARSON WILLIAMS. (*A veritable giant of a man, amply provided by Nature with the physical and vocal ability to cast out devils—spiritual and otherwise*) Dooty, Sister Cassie! Dooty! (*He looks doubtfully at Doug, who has not moved.*)

CASSIE. Reckon yuh'll want tuh set by de lamp, Parson. (*He seats himself with a large flowing movement, quickly checked by the uncalculated size of the chair. He straightens up and frowns disapprovingly at the Council— three Sisters and two Brothers. A hard, fanatical, relentless look seems in some imperceptible fashion to stamp each face. Here, the gleam of an eye; there, the tight fold of a lip. The Sisters carry palm leaf fans for the night is hot. They are dressed in ill-fitting white frocks and ugly black hats. The men seem uncomfortable in collars and their Sunday best.*) Reckon we kin seat a few on de couch. Sister Williams will be here 'fore long wid de camp chairs.

(*All look at Doug who is hunched there in the middle of the couch. None venture to sit beside him. The women take the rocker, the red plush chair and the seat beside the Parson. The men stand awkwardly by the window. All stare fixedly at Doug, but he does not look up. Suddenly Cassie, who has resumed her seat beside the open door, breaks once more into song. All join in except Parson Williams who is thumbing the pages of the Bible on the table.*)

> Come along,
> Thar's a meetin' here ter-night.
> Git yuh ready,
> Thar's a meetin' here ter-night.
> Ah know yuh by yo' daily walk,
> Thar's a meetin' here ter-night.

(*Now Cassie is drawing to one side, to make room for* MAZA *and* JUD. *They look very much surprised to see the gathering. Maza's astonishment increases as she observes Doug—Doug of all people—sitting there—like that. She turns her beautiful, dark face to Jud with a questioning look. Jud is tall and straight, a bit rough of speech and a bit clumsy but very much in love with Maza and unable to conceal it. Cassie comes forward, takes the kerosene can from Jud and places it in the corner.*)

MAZA. (*Whose soft voice has an intriguing drawl*) Evenin', Parson Williams. Ah didn' know yuh-all was havin' a meetin' here ter-night.

JUD. Evenin', Parson.

PARSON WILLIAMS. Ah, yes! Thar's a meetin' here ter-night.

MAZA. (*With an all-inclusive glance*) Evenin', ev'ybody. (*There are a few very stiff nods. No one speaks. Maza turns doubtfully to Jud. They move toward the door.*) Reckon we ain't wanted here, Jud.

CASSIE. Wait, Maza. Reckon yuh *is* wanted here, too.

MAZA. (*Surprised*) This is Council meetin', ain't it? Ah knows yuh-all doan' want me an' Jud.

PARSON WILLIAMS. (*Gravely*) Yes, daughter, we do want yuh an' we wants Jud, too.

MAZA. Jud? What yuh-all wants me an' Jud fer, Parson? This is Council meetin', ain't it?

PARSON WILLIAMS. It is. An' we needs both uv yuh, here.

JUD. (*Slowly*) Whut yuh wants us ter do, Parson? Maza an' me ain't no help tuh a Council meetin'. Is we, Maza?

MAZA. (*With a faint laugh*) Not's Ah knows uv!

PARSON WILLIAMS. (*Sternly*) Sence yuh pretends ignorance, reckon yuh's got tuh be enlightened.

MAZA. (*Quietly*) Reckon so, Parson. Ah sho doan' know whut yuh's talkin' 'bout. (*The Sisters and Brothers make various clicking and muttering sounds intended to express consternation at such effrontery. Jud glares fiercely at them and clenches his hands. Maza looks slowly around the room as if trying to find a key to the situation. Her eyes linger on Doug— Doug! She frowns quickly then a great light dawns in her eyes. She walks up to her father and places a gentle hand on his shoulder.*) Whut they tryin' tuh do tuh yuh, Dad? Yuh doan' have tuh stan' fer no Council meetin'. Ef Ma ain't stopped yuh swearin' an' drinkin', reckon no Council's gwine tuh help none. Yuh ain't no church member, nohow, so they can't do nuthin' tuh yuh. (*Doug raises his head and looks at her as if he would read her very soul.*)

DOUG. (*Hoarsely*) Maza! (*His hand grips her arm like a vise.*)

MAZA. Yes, Dad.

DOUG. Ef Ah hadn't uh bin drunk, Ah'd knowed she was lyin', long 'fo' now. (*His voice trembles in spite of himself.*) Mah head ain't good an' it kind uh knocked me over. Jes' explain 'bout them clothes an' den Ah's gwine throw de whole damned bunch outa here.

MAZA. Whut clothes yuh's talkin' 'bout, Dad?

DOUG. (*Impatiently*) Them damn baby clothes! Reckon Ah's jes' tore one tuh pieces!

MAZA. Dad! Yuh's talkin' wild! Ah doan' know nothin' 'bout no baby clothes. Who's bin tellin' yuh all dis truck?

DOUG. Cassie tole me 'bout 'em! Cassie knows! Cassie says yuh's hid 'em in dat cupboard!

MAZA. (*Contemptuously*) That's a lie, Dad! Yuh doan' believe it, do yuh? (*Doug's hand drops from her arm.*)

DOUG. (*Huskily*) Ah's seen 'em, Maza. Explain 'bout 'em quick for Gawd's sake! Ah knows yuh ain't no liar, Maza!

MAZA. (*Turning angrily upon Cassie*) Whut yuh bin tellin' Dad 'bout me? Whut yuh mean bringin' Parson Williams here, an' de Council?

CASSIE. (*Vindictively*) Reckon yuh'll know, soon 'nuff! Here comes Sister Williams, now.

(*Sister Williams enters, all out of breath, followed by* FREDDIE *who carries an armful of camp chairs. Freddie is a tall, good-looking youth. At present he is scowling heavily at the room in general. Maza looks at Freddie, then turns away. Jud notices every movement of Maza's. His eyes never leave her for a moment.*)

SISTER WILLIAMS. (*Distributing the chairs*) Thar! Guess we's got 'nuff fer all! Here, Freddie! Straighten dis out fer me! Ah declare dese chairs is an awful trial! (*Freddie makes short work of the chair, then strides toward the door. Sister Williams lays a firm detaining hand upon his arm.*) Not so fast, Freddie. Parson wants yuh tuh stay fer de meetin'.

FREDDIE. (*Looking up in sullen anger*) What fer?

SISTER WILLIAMS. Jes' tuh help out de meetin'. It'll be in a good cause, Freddie. (*She shuts the door tightly and gives the boy a little push toward a chair.*)

FREDDIE. (*Stubbornly*) Ah can't stay. Ah's gotta go somewheres. What you-all wants me fer, anyhow?

PARSON WILLIAMS. (*With nothing short of a roar and a violent thump of the table*) Set down! (*In spite of himself Freddie obeys. Jud obeys. Only Maza continues to look out of the window, without moving. Having succeeded in securing the undivided attention of the company, Parson Williams draws himself up as tall as he can, arranges his spectacles, and continues in carefully measured tones.*) Dis meetin' will now come tuh order! Yuh all knows Sister Cassie. She has served faithfully in dis community fer many years. She has bin a vigilant watchman 'gainst de inroads of sin an' rebellion, 'specially among our young people. Sister Cassie will now place her charge befo' de Council.

CASSIE. (*With a pleased smile*) Parson Williams, Sisters and Brothers an' all concerned! Dis is a mighty se'rus charge Ah's makin'. Maza's ma's bin away nearly two weeks an' Ah's bin stayin' here 'long er Maza an' mah brother, Doug. Ah usta have a pretty high 'pinion uh Maza but de las' few months she's bin diff'rent, somehow. She's bin kinda wild an' upstart in her ways an' she's bin a-playin' fas' an' loose wid two fellers whut doan' amount tuh nothin'! (*There is a concerted movement of protest from Jud and Freddie but their intention is lost before a fierce look from Parson Williams. The Council nod heads in approval of Sister Cassie's words.*) Las' week, at de Sunday School picnic, Ah minded how Freddie Jackson didn' speak tuh Maza, but went galavantin' 'round wid dat tough Daisy Miller from de Corners. An' Ah's minded how Jud Bolton, here, ain't bin 'round fer a week—not till ter-night. Well, puttin' one an' one tergether, Ah commence tuh git kinda suspicious. Well, dis mornin', Ah finds dat de bottom cupboard drawer's locked. Mary ain't one fer lockin' up her things, so Ah pulls out de drawer above tuh see whut's down below. Maza comes in jes' at dat minute an' lights on me real quick. "Whut yuh lookin' fer?" she said. "Yuh's allus spyin' an' huntin'! Yuh ain't got no call lookin' tru dat cupboard. Thar ain't nobuddy would look tru yo' cupboard!" An' wid dat, she slams dat drawer back, an' goes on out, real mad. Well, co'se Ah had tuh see whut was in dat bottom drawer. So Ah takes out de drawer above, an' lo an' behold! Ef Ah doan' see a bran' new set er baby clothes! (*Maza starts and turns quickly around. Cassie returns her look insolently.*) Now ef them clothes ain't Maza's, whose is dey? Maza knew dey was thar, dat's why she took on so when she seen me at dat cupboard. Now ef dis Council, under Parson Williams, does its dooty, it'll make Maza tell who de man is. Reckon we ain't far tuh look, neither. (*She turns deliberately and looks at Jud and Freddie. Wrathful consternation is plainly written on their faces. Each glares at the other and at Cassie. Then like every one else in the room, they turn and look at Maza. She has come quite close to Cassie, now, and is trembling with rage.*)

MAZA. You hateful, evil-minded old hag! You sneak! How dar yuh say such a thing 'bout me! Ah won't have it! Yuh'll take it back! Take it back! (*Cassie shrinks back as if in fear, then recovers her poise.*)

CASSIE. We ain't tryin' tuh harm yuh, Maza. We'll make de feller whut's tuh blame do his dooty by yuh. We's gwine tuh make him marry yuh.

PARSON WILLIAMS. (*Forestalling another outburst from Maza*) Dat will do, Sister Cassie. Yuh's stated yuh case very well, indeed. Very clear tuh all. Now, Maza, are yuh gwine tuh confess or has we got tuh make yuh?

MAZA. (*With angry scorn*) Reckon yuh's got mo' sense, Parson, dan tuh believe dem lies!

PARSON WILLIAMS. (*Patiently*) Now, Maza, we're bein' gentle wid yuh. Yuh doan' need tuh be a-skeered uh nuthin' but de wrath er de Lawd who yuh's sinned against. Which uh dese two fellers is yuh shieldin'?

MAZA. (*Fiercely*) Ah ain't shieldin' nobuddy! Ah ain't got no call tuh shield nobuddy. (*Hot tears of humiliation choke her and she turns away.*)

PARSON WILLIAMS. (*Solemnly*) Let us listen tuh de words uh de prophet, Isaiah. (*He reads from the Bible.*) Wash yuh, make yuh clean; put away de evil of yuh doin's from befo' mah eyes; cease tuh do evil.

THE COUNCIL. Amen! Amen!

PARSON WILLIAMS. Learn tuh do well; seek judgment, relieve de oppressed, judge de fatherless, plead fer de widow.

THE COUNCIL. Glory! Glory! Amen! Amen!

PARSON WILLIAMS. Come now, an' let us reason tergether, saith de Lawd; though yo' sins be as scarlet dey shall be white as snow; though dey be red lak crimson, dey shall be as wool.

THE COUNCIL. (*Singing*)
Have yuh bin tuh Jesus fer de cleansing power?
Are yuh washed in de blood uv de Lamb?
Are yuh garments spotless, are dey white as snow?

Are yuh washed in de blood uv de Lamb?

PARSON WILLIAMS. If yuh be willin' and obedient, yuh shall eat de good uh de land.

THE COUNCIL. De Lawd be praised! Hallelujah!

PARSON WILLIAMS. But if yuh refuse an' rebel yuh shall be devoured wid de sword; fer de mouth uh de Lawd hath spoken it.

THE COUNCIL. Halelujah! Amen! Amen!

PARSON WILLIAMS. Now, daughter, yuh's heard de promise uh Gawd fer forgiveness. Are yuh ready tuh tell de truth an' shame de devil?

MAZA. (*Who is sobbing hysterically*) Ah's tole de truth, Parson! Ah can't tell—no diff'rent! Ah can't tell—no diff'rent!

(*Once more the Council make audible sounds of disapproval.*)

PARSON WILLIAMS. Let us pray! (*All kneel except Doug, Freddie, Jud and Maza.*) Lawd, soften de heart uh dis erring daughter an' bring her back tuh de fold!

THE COUNCIL. Amen! Amen!

PARSON WILLIAMS. Give us a sign Lawd, whereby we kin see de truth an' do yo' will!

THE COUNCIL. Amen! A sign, Lawd! A sign!

PARSON WILLIAMS. Lawd, place yuh han' upon de guilty man! Move his heart! Force him tuh rise! Make him speak!

THE COUNCIL. Amen! Amen! (*In varying degress of shrillness and intensity.*)

PARSON WILLIAMS. Thar's a powerful curse fer them dat defies de Lawd! Ah's chargin' dese sinners fo' de las' time, tuh speak!

THE COUNCIL. (*With an ominous mutter*) A curse! A curse!

(*Like two wild animals straining at the leash, Jud and Freddie eye each other. Jud's teeth are drawn back, his face completely distorted. Freddie's face has a wild look.*)

MAZA. (*Hysterically*) Don't, Parson! Fer Gawd's sake, don't!

PARSON WILLIAMS. (*In a loud, denunciatory tone*) Dey's rewarded me, evil fer good an' hatred fer mah love.

THE COUNCIL. Yes, Lawd! Dat's true!

PARSON WILLIAMS. Set Thou a wicked man over him; an' let Satan stan' at his right han'.

THE COUNCIL. Amen! Amen!

PARSON WILLIAMS. When he shall be judged let him be condemned, an' let his prayer become sin!

THE COUNCIL. Have mercy, Lawd! Have mercy! (*Some of them moan aloud and wring their hands.*)

PARSON WILLIAMS. (*His voice rising ever higher and shriller in a sort of ecstasy*) When yuh's tryin' tuh climb an' de way is rough an' de path is steep, yuh'll stumble an' fall in de bottomless pit. When de dark night comes an' yuh calls on His name, when yuh runs to an' fro a-callin' His name—thar ain' gonna be no answer—thar ain' gonna be no sound.

THE COUNCIL. No sound! Lawd! Lawd!

PARSON WILLIAMS. Then yuh calls some mo' an' yuh begs for help—an' de debbil will mock yuh—de debbil will laugh!

THE COUNCIL. Lawd! True, Lawd! True!

PARSON WILLIAMS. On de heels uh de guilty thar treads a terribul ha'nt—

THE COUNCIL. Save us, Lawd! Save us!

PARSON WILLIAMS. An' de night is dark—an' thar ain't no moon—

THE COUNCIL. Thar ain't no moon!

PARSON WILLIAMS. An' thar ain't no stars—an' yuh looks fer de light—an' thar ain't no light!

THE COUNCIL. Light! Light!

PARSON WILLIAMS. Yuh calls on de Lawd an' thar ain't no sound—an' yuh calls out agin an' de debbil laughs—

(*With a gasping cry Freddie leaps to his feet.*)

FREDDIE. Damn yuh! Doan' yuh say no mo'! Yuh's a debbil! Lemme outa here! (*He leaps toward the door, but Doug is there before him. He grasps the boy by the throat and forces his head backward. The Council scrambles screaming to their feet. It takes all of Parson Williams' strength to tear Doug's fingers from Freddie's throat. Freddie collapses on a chair. Maza runs to him and starts fanning him vigorously with a palm leaf fan. She calls his name again and again.*)

CASSIE. (*Triumphantly*) Jes' whut Ah thought! Jes' whut Ah thought!

PARSON WILLIAMS. (*With the air of a man who has accomplished a difficult task*) De Lawd is good! (*He mops his brow with a large handkerchief.*)

THE COUNCIL. Amen! Amen! Amen!

PARSON WILLIAMS. Every one will be seated! Now dat we knows de guilty man de business uh dis meetin' will go forward!

(*Maza starts and looks up. Freddie has opened his eyes and is looking around in bewilderment. He rubs his bruised throat and remembers. Jud stands there twisting his cap and striving desperately to retain his self-control.*)

JUD. (*Jerkily*) Reckon—Ah kin go—Parson. Yuh doan' need me—now.

MAZA. (*Rushing forward and grasping him by the arm*) Jud! Jud! Yuh doan' believe Parson! Yuh doan' believe whut dey's sayin' 'bout me! Say yuh doan', Jud! Say yuh doan'!

JUD. (*Shakes her off. His hoarse voice breaks oddly with a sob*) Yuh—yuh—Oh, curse yuh, Maza! Curse yuh! (*He turns and runs headlong out of the room. Maza pulls the door open, calling "Jud! Jud!" Very roughly, her father draws her away from the door.*)

DOUG. Reckon yuh kin tie de knot, now, Parson.

(*Freddie staggers to his feet and goes slowly toward Maza*)

FREDDIE. Maza, it's Jud yuh cares 'bout, ain't it? (*She does not answer.*) Dat's funny! Ah mean it's funny Jud's goin'—lak dat—ef he loves yuh.

MAZA. He hates me! He believes 'em!

FREDDIE. Jud's a fool! He oughta know they's all bug-house! Crazy ez loons!

MAZA. Ah ain't gwine let 'em marry us, Freddie! It ain't fair on yuh.

FREDDIE. Ah loves yuh, Maza! Reckon yuh's knowed dat a long time. It ain't dat Ah doan' want tuh marry yuh, Maza, only, Ah ain't got nuthin' much tuh give yuh.

MAZA. Freddie?

FREDDIE. Huh?

MAZA. Freddie—ain't yuh thinkin' that mebbe it's Jud who'd oughta stayed an' married me? Ain't yuh thinkin' dat, Freddie?

FREDDIE. Naw! Ah ain't thinkin' no sech thing! Ah knows dey's all daffy. Ah's thinkin'—is it Jud yuh cares 'bout, Maza?

MAZA. (Sadly) What'd yuh speak out fer, Freddie? Dey mistook whut yuh said.

FREDDIE. (Ruefully) Dunno. Reckon dey got on mah nerves.

DOUG. (Grimly) Well, dat line er talk ain't good fer mah nerves, neither. Yuh kin tie dat knot, Parson, an' doan' waste no time 'bout it.

PARSON WILLIAMS. Right! De Lawd was on our side an' we couldn' make no mistake.

(The door is opened quietly and a short, stout, pleasant-faced little woman enters with a small bag. Every one turns and stares. With a glad cry Maza runs to the newcomer and throws her arms about the latter's neck. The little bag drops to the floor.)

MAZA. Oh, Mom, yuh's come jes' in time! Yuh'll believe me! Oh, Mom, make 'em see dat it's all lies! (Quite unexpectedly she starts crying once more.)

MOM. Thar, honey! Thar! Evenin', Parson. Cassie, Ah reckon yuh an' Doug kin tell me whut's wrong here!

CASSIE. Parson is jes' gwine tuh marry Maza an' Freddie.

MOM. Marry Maza! Whut fer? Yuh'd better talk quick, Cassie.

CASSIE. We's jes' found out dat Maza's gwine tuh have a baby. Here's one er de dresses—(She holds up the torn dress.)

MOM. (Sharply) Whar'd yuh git dis? (She pulls the pieces unceremoniously out of Cassie's hand.)

CASSIE. Outa de bottom cupboard drawer. Ah discovered 'em. Ah knew Maza was a-hidin' 'em, so Ah got Parson—

MOM. (With scathing contempt) Ah see! Reckon yuh's still got yuh meddlin' dirty ways, Cassie. Them things're mine. Ah made 'em an' Ah's de one whut put 'em thar!

ALL. You!

MOM. Yes, an' whut's mo', Ah's de one whut's gwine tuh have dat baby.

ALL. You!

MOM. Ah doan' wonder yuh's all s'prised—me wid a daughter old 'nuff tuh git married. Ef yuh stares any harder, Doug, reckon yuh eyes'll pop out yuh head!

PARSON WILLIAMS. (Angrily) Well, Sister Cassie, seems tuh me yuh's brought us here ter-night on a fool's errand!

THE COUNCIL. Bless mah soul! Did yuh ever! Ah know it's de truth! Kin yuh beat dat! Whut yuh know 'bout dat!

MOM. (*Addressing the Council. With biting sarcasm*) Sorry tuh spile yuh pleasure! Reckon yuh's had a pretty good time, ain't yuh? Oh, yuh needn't trubble 'splainin'! Yuh's done yuh dooty as yuh seen it, Gawd help yuh! (*She looks after them grimly as they file out carrying camp chairs. Sister Cassie and Sister Williams go out first.*)

PARSON WILLIAMS. (*With a noble attempt to regain his composure*) Ah regrets dis occasion, Sister Lee! Regrets it mo' dan Ah kin say!

MOM. Ah knows yuh does, Parson.

PARSON WILLIAMS. Ah hopes dis will make no diff'rence, Sister Lee?

MOM. No diff'rence tuh me, Parson, but a powerful lot tuh some others, Ah'm thinkin'. (*She glances beyond him to where Maza and Freddie are standing. Her glance wanders on to Doug. Doug! She has forgotten Parson Williams. He seems to know it, bows stiffly and goes out. Doug, meeting his wife's glance, turns away as if ashamed.*)

MAZA. Mom?

MOM. Yes, honey?

MAZA. Freddie was willin' tuh marry me. Whut yuh know 'bout that? He didn' believe none uh dem lies 'bout me! (*She links her arm in Freddie's. Freddie grins happily, in appreciation of this tribute.*)

MOM. (*Serenely*) Well, why should he, honey? Freddie ain't no fool, Ah reckon. (*She looks wistfully at Doug and then smiles.*) Wish Ah could say de same 'bout Doug! (*Still Doug stands there unable to look up. Then Freddie and Maza find the door and go out.*) Doug? (*She comes very close and touches his arm.*)

DOUG. (*Bitterly*) Ah knows Ah's a fool, Mary! An ole fool!

MOM. (*With a little laugh that loses its way in her throat*) Well, but whut 'bout me, Doug? (*Doug does not answer. A voice is heard singing without. Mom hurries to the door, opens it and then beckons to Doug, who joins her. Together, they stand in the doorway listening.*)

Ah met mah sister de odder night
   She call me by mah name.
An' jes' as soon's mah back wuz turned
   She scandalize mah name.

Yuh call dat a sister?
   No! No! (*Chant the Council*)
Yuh call dat a sister?
   No! No!

Yuh call dat a sister?
   No! No!
Who'd scandalize mah name!

(*The curtain descends slowly on the last No! No!*)

CURTAIN

HER

A Mystery Play in One Act

PERSONS IN THE PLAY

MARTHA
PETE
JOHN KINNEY
ALICE
SAM

Time: About eight o'clock one rainy night in spring.
Scene: Martha's living room.

(To describe this, we must describe MARTHA—*old, black Martha who takes in washing for some "very old families," who is, herself, always immaculate in her grey dress and white apron. Martha, who takes care of Pete, her husband—crippled and an idler for more than fifteen years—Martha, who irons in the living room—eats there for the accommodation of Pete, and spreads her clothes horse there on rainy days. Martha, who is the oldest tenant in the house—who rents the rooms for John Kinney, and collects the rentals, as well.*

We must also describe old PETE *in his invalid chair—his steel rimmed spectacles and his Bible lying open on his knees.*

No modern living room, this—just Martha's room—with her cheap prints on the walls—religious, every one of them—and her odd tables and cast off chairs—hand-me-downs from the "white folks." All we really need to know about the construction of the room is that a door at back, left, opens upon the hallway.)

MARTHA. (*Picking up some of the clothes from the horse, rolling them into a bundle, and putting them into a pillow case on the chair beside her ironing board.*) They's most as wet as they was when Ah hung'em out. Ef

Reprinted by permission of Patricia C. Hart.

this weather keeps up Ah doan see how Ah's goin' git these clothes out
by Saturday. Weather what's good fer farmers doan help us wash-
wimmen none.

PETE. (*Looking up, surprised*) 'Tain't lak yuh, Martha, complainin! Reckon
yuh back's bad ter-night.

MARTHA. (*Who punctuates her remarks with little emphatic clamps of her
iron*) No wuss'n usual.

PETE. Then somethin's on yuh mind.

MARTHA. Mebbe.

PETE. Yuh wuks too hard, Martha. Ah wish—(*He ends with a sigh*)

MARTHA. (*Looking up, quickly*) What yuh wishin' fer, Pete?

PETE. In them magazines yuh brung home last week there was a piece 'bout
some cripple fellers—how they's learned how ter make money—plenty
money. Ah ain't read nuthin' so mirac'lus in a long time, Martha, an' Ah
got ter thinkin'—Ah might er bin helpin' yuh all these years, ef Ah'd
knowed how.

MARTHA. (*Clamping her electric iron down with alarming energy*) Pete
Alexander, ef yuh ain't got no better sense than ter pick out pieces 'bout
cripples, Ah'm goin' stop bring' home them no 'count books. Now doan
lemme hear no more er that trash.

PETE. (*Humbly*) Ah was only thinkin'—

MARTHA. (*Still irate*) Yuh ain't got no business thinkin'—'bout sech trash.
Yuh's puttin' yourself with these here young fellers what's bin hurt in the
War. It's nigh on fifteen years yuh bin settin' there an' Ah ain't done no
complainin's Ah knows uv.

PETE. (*Proudly*) That ain't no woman lak yuh, Martha, nowhar. Ah knows
it an' Ah thanks Gawd fer yuh, day an' night.

MARTHA. (*Somewhat mollified*) Well, doan lemme hear no more talk 'bout
yuh earnin' money. (*After a few seconds*) Ah ain't slep' good these two
nights, Pete.

PETE. Ah heard yuh movin' long 'bout five this mornin'.

MARTHA. Five! Ah didn' close mah eyes all night.

PETE. (*Anxiously*) What's the mattuh, Martha?

MARTHA. Pete. (*Martha lowers her voice which is pregnant with meaning*)
Ah seen Mr. Kinney this mornin'. He's got some folks fer up above.

PETE. Fer upstairs? (*Pete's voice, like Martha's, has acquired a new note,
not unmixed with dismay.*)

MARTHA. They's ter come ter-night ter see the rooms.

PETE. Ter-night?

MARTHA. Ah'm ter show them 'round—so he said. Reckon ef it keeps on
rainin' they won't come.

PETE. (*Uneasily*) Reckon they won't . . . Martha, did yuh tell him?

MARTHA. Yuh bet Ah tole him. But it didn' do no good, Pete. Nobuddy ain't
goin' change him.

PETE. Ah reckon yuh's right, Martha.

MARTHA. (*Significantly*) 'Lessen it's *Her*.

PETE. Her?

MARTHA. She's kep' me awake these two nights.

PETE. (*Moving restlessly in his chair*) It ain't natural—this talk 'bout Her.

MARTHA. 'Course it ain't natural, but it's *real*. What yuh hears is *real*, ain't it?

PETE. (*Stubbornly*) Ah ain't never heard nothin', Martha.

MARTHA. But they's them what has heard. Yuh knows that, doan yuh?

PETE. So they says, but mah ears jes' good's yours, Martha. Ah ain't never heard nothin'.

MARTHA. (*Scornfully*) Then they ain't so good's yuh thinks, Pete.

PETE. Yuh ain't heard Her in more'n a year—

MARTHA. The place ain't bin rented in more'n a year.

PETE. 'Tain't honest rentin' them rooms after what's happened.

MARTHA. Ah tole Mr. Kinney 's much.

PETE. An' what he said ter that, Martha?

MARTHA. He says ef Ah doan want ter show them rooms ter people, he kin git somebuddy else. 'Course Ah needs the money, little's it is.

PETE. (*Clinging to a forlorn hope*) It's rainin' so hard Ah reckon they won't come ter-night.

MARTHA. Ah 'spec not, 'lessn they wants 'em real bad.

PETE. (*Resentfully*) Ef Mr. Kinney's so set on rentin' them rooms he oughta show'em himself.

MARTHA. (*With one of her energetic swoops on the ironing board*) Him! He ain't bin near them rooms in eighteen years, an' Ah reckon he ain't never goin' up thar!

PETE. Ah reckon not, sence he doan never go higher'n the ground floor.

MARTHA. He's lookin' powerful bad. Looks' though he bin worryin' plenty 'bout somethin.

PETE. (*with a rare chuckle*) Worryin' 'bout how he kin spen' some er that money uv his.

MARTHA. More likely worryin' 'bout Her.

PETE. *Her*? What good'll it do him ter worry 'bout Her, *now*?

MARTHA. Yuh kin call it conscience, or yuh kin call it HER! 'Tis one and the same thing, Ah reckon. But he's worryin' powerful hard. (*A loud peal of the door bell. Martha and Pete exchange glances. Martha puts down her iron*) Ah reckon it's the folks ter see the rooms. (*Pete nods. Martha opens the door. Standing upon the threshold, silent, gaunt, austere, is* JOHN KINNEY. *His yellow face is seamed and somewhat haggard. His eyes are burning with a strange fire. Martha, evidently astonished, just stands there gasping. Pete fumbles for his spectacles, finds them, puts them on— and still no word is spoken*)

JOHN KINNEY. Well, are you going to let me in? (*Such a cold ironic voice with a world of weariness behind it. Martha silently draws back and the visitor enters. Pete recovers his wits a full second before Martha does*)

PETE. Take a seat, suh! 'Tis a bad night, Ah reckon.

MARTHA. (*Placing a chair for John Kinney*) Ah's powerful 'sprised ter see yuh, Mr. Kinney. Ah stared lak Ah'd seen a ghost, sure 'nuff. (*The moment the words are out, Martha recognizes her blunder. Pete looks at her reproachfully. John Kinney, however, merely smiles his little mocking smile*)

JOHN KINNEY. No ghost, this time. (*Takes a seat*) And that brings me to the subject of my visit. I'm expecting a young couple here, this evening. They ought to be here at any minute. (*Looks at his watch*) They wish to see the rooms above.

MARTHA. Yes suh. Yuh's tole me 'bout showin' em.

JOHN KINNEY. Well, I've changed my mind. When they come I'll show them the rooms myself.

MARTHA. Yuh going up *thar*? (*Consternation is plainly written on her face*)

JOHN KINNEY. Yes. If you will give me the keys—

MARTHA. But, good Lawd, suh! Yuh ain't bin up thar goin' on twenty years!

JOHN KINNEY. Then it's time I did go up. The place may need a few repairs.

MARTHA. Yuh did it over last year fer them other folks. They didn' stay more'n a month.

JOHN KINNEY. Ah! To be sure. Well, I'll just take a look around and see for myself. I told Mrs. Smith to bring her husband and meet me here at eight o'clock. Don't let me interrupt your work, Martha. I see you are busy.

MARTHA. (*Returning to her ironing board, reluctantly*) Ah ain't so busy but what Ah kin show them rooms fer yuh, suh. Ah hopes you ain't mad 'count uv what Ah said this mornin'. Ah's allus done mah best 'bout rentin' them rooms.

JOHN KINNEY. Perhaps you have, in the past. But you don't want to do your best *now*. (*Martha is silent*) That, however, is not my real reason for wanting to see those rooms. Looking back over the years, twenty you say—Twenty! I can see what a fool I've been—what a fool you've helped me to be. (*Nothing moves in the room now—not even Martha's iron*) You—with your talk of signs and omens—sound and night alarms. You've filled my mind with superstitious fears. I, who used to laugh at fears! (*An additional sternness creeping into his voice*) Well, you've frightened away my tenants long enough with your gossip and your fancies. I won't say that you've done these things out of malice, but—By God! Some men might!

MARTHA. (*Slowly*) Then—Then yuh doan believe nothin' Ah's ever tole yuh?

JOHN KINNEY. (*Grimly*) I did, once. Now I know they're lies or fancies.

PETE. (*Moved to resentment*) Martha ain't no liar! Ef she says she's heard goins on, she's heard 'em!

JOHN KINNEY. I suppose you've also heard these goings on, as you call them?

PETE. (*Reluctantly*) No. Ah ain't never heard nothin'. But Lawd, Ah ain't got the ears Martha's got. Thar ain't a tenant what's lived up thar that ain't left, 'cause uv *Her.*

JOHN KINNEY. (*With a faint smile*) But *you've* slept—

PETE. (*Stoutly*) Mah ears ain't nowhere ez good's Martha's.

JOHN KINNEY. Nor mine. How is it that in all these years she's never bin back to disturb my slumbers? How do you account for that?

MARTHA. (*Angrily*) Ah ain't no call ter account fer nothin' but what Ah knows 'bout.

JOHN KINNEY. Very good. Now with the best of intention, perhaps, you've frightened away my tenants. The power of suggestion is a greater force than we realize. I can forgive this, but I can't forgive your filling your mind with your fancies. I've come to the conclusion that the only way to wipe the incident clean from my mind—except as we have occasion to remember some unfortunate happening—is to go up there tonight and show Mrs. Smith those rooms myself.

MARTHA. 'Tain't fer me to say yuh shouldn't go up thar. Only Ah doan lak it none. Thar's bin plenty goin' on up thar these two nights. Ah doan lak it none (*with a shake of her head*) Ah reckon it means somethin's going ter happen.

JOHN KINNEY. Something is going to happen. I'm going to brush a thousand cobwebs from my brain. I haven't felt happier about anything in a long time. I ought to have done this years ago instead of avoiding the place.

PETE. Mebbe yuh's right suh. Mebbe yuh's right.

JOHN KINNEY. Of course I'm right. (*Looking at his watch*) Eight on the minute. I hope they don't keep me waiting—Oh, by the way, I may as well tell you good people that I expect to sell this house.

PETE. (*Almost dropping his spectacles in surprise*) Sell this house!

MARTHA. Ef yuhs goin' sell it suh, why yuh wants to bother goin' up thar?

JOHN KINNEY. (*With his one-sided smile*) Just to prove to you that you've been wrong and that I've been as gullible as a child. It's my one chance of being a free man and I'm not going to lose it. (*The door bell rings*) Ah! Here they are. (*Martha opens the door. On the threshold stands* ALICE SMITH, *a good-looking brown girl, and her husband* SAM, *somewhat browner. Alice wears a tricky little felt hat and yellow raincoat. Sam wears—well—brown hat, coat, and shoes, a very trying harmony for one of his complexion*)

ALICE. (*Nodding to Martha, but addressing herself to John Kinney*) Ah reckon we ain't more'n a minute late. (*To Sam*) Sam this' Mr. Kinney. Mr. Kinney this's mah husband, Mr. Sam Smith.

JOHN KINNEY. (*Shaking hands with Sam, a cordiality which surprises Martha*) Glad to meet you. You're certainly on time.

SAM. (*Pleased*) We's colored through an' through, Alice an' me 'sceptin' that we's allus on time. When we says eight, we means eight, not half past nine. (*Sam chuckles as if at a huge joke.*)

JOHN KINNEY. Well, as a man of business I appreciate that. This—(*Waving *his hand in the direction of Pete and Martha*) This is Mrs. Alexander and her husband. (*Nodding in Martha's direction*) Mrs. Alexander usually rents my rooms—shows them to visitors—But I'll show you these myself. Martha, if you'll get me the key—(*Martha dives into an old jug and produces the key. Very slowly she hands it to John Kinney who pockets it.*) (*To the Smiths*) I have a powerful search light (*tapping his coat pocket*) So if you're ready, we'll go up and inspect the rooms. (*Martha and Pete exchange glances. Perhaps the smile on John Kinney's lips is just a shade more mocking than usual as he turns to Martha*) I will stop in on my way down, Martha. There is a little matter I want to see you about. (*In about another second Martha and Pete are left alone. Martha spreads another garment on the board and takes up her iron. Pete looks at her timidly and clears his throat*)

PETE. I reckon he's right 'bout goin' up thar. A man ain't got no right actin' so scared bout nothin' (*Hastily*) Ah mean 'bout—(*His voice dies away under the fierce glare in Martha's eyes*)

MARTHA. Yuh doan need say nothin' more. Yuh' allus bin a disbeliever, Pete, an Ah reckon yuh'll never change 'lessen yuh's give a sign.

PETE. (*Uneasily*) Ah doan need no sign, Martha.

MARTHA. (*Pointing to the Bible on Pete's knees*) Yuh ain't read that thar Book frum cover to cover 'thout comin' cross signs an' wonders a-plenty.

PETE. Sure they's signs. But—

MARTHA. 'Taint *you* Ah'm thinkin'' uv, Pete, nor John Kinney. It's that girl Ah'm thinkin' uv—her an' that young feller. She's got a sweet face. Ah took ter her right off. She ain't a bit older than *she* was when she come here. They ain't goin' have no happiness up thar.

PETE. Ah hope yuh ain't right 'bout that Martha.

MARTHA. Pete Alexander! (*Perhaps Martha's iron as well as her tone causes Pete to draw himself up with a start*) Pete Alexander. Ah ain't never tole a soul 'bout what happen up thar. Yuh knows that.

PETE. Sure. Ah knows that.

MARTHA. Mr. Kinney thinks Ah's tole all them other folks an' that scared 'em way frum here.

PETE. Ah reckon he does.

MARTHA. Well, Ah ain't never tole nobuddy, but Ah'm goin' tell that little gal 'fore she moves up thar. 'Taint fair lettin' 'em move in.

PETE. (*Curiously*) When yuh goin' tell her Martha? Yuh ain't goin' tell her 'fore Mr. Kinney?

MARTHA. Ah doan know. Ah reckon the Lawd'll 'pint the time. (*A knock on the door, and John Kinney and the Smiths come in once more. Perhaps Kinney's face is a bit more pale, but his mocking smile is more pronounced as his eyes encounter Martha's*)

JOHN KINNEY. Everything is quite ship shape, Martha.

ALICE. It's jes' lovely, Gimme large rooms every time. Everything looks nice an' clean, too.

SAM. Ah reckon we'll settle fer them rooms now. How 'bout it, Alice?

ALICE. Sure. We'll pay a deposit right now.

JOHN KINNEY. Half a month, please.

SAM. Right. (*He takes a wallet from his pocket, extracts two bills and hands them to Kinney. Pete glances anxiously at Martha, but the latter is standing downcast, her eyes on the floor. Kinney seats himself at one of the little tables, reaches into an inner pocket, produces a receipt book, then jumps up with an exclamation of annoyance*)

JOHN KINNEY. My wallet! I'm afraid I've dropped it! (*He searches his other pockets feverishly—but the missing wallet is not forthcoming. Everyone looks at him uncomfortably*)

SAM. (*Sympathetically*) That sure is tough!

JOHN KINNEY. (*Angrily*) Tough! There were over five hundred dollars in that wallet! And what's more, I had it when I came in here tonight!

MARTHA. In here!

PETE. (*Echoing Martha's words blankly*) In here!

ALICE. You might uv dropped it in the hall, or upstairs.

JOHN KINNEY. A note-book! I wonder if I could have dropped my wallet then!

SAM. It doan do no harm lookin'. Ah'll go with yuh ef yuh wants.

JOHN KINNEY. (*Sharply*) No, thank you. Wait here a few minutes, if you don't mind. I prefer going alone.

SAM. Sure we'll wait.

ALICE. It's too bad. But yuh'd better look upstairs. Yuh might er dropped it sure 'nuff. (*Kinney goes out, giving the door an angry slam*)

SAM. Ah hope he doan think *we* found his ole wallet. Gee! Five hundred dollars! Bet that guy's got money ter burn.

ALICE. (*With a little laugh*) Bet he doan burn none, though.

MARTHA. (*In a tone of suppressed excitement*) Listen! He'll be back any minute, an' Ah's got somethin' powerful important ter say. (*Paying no heed to the surprised glances of Sam and Alice*) Yuh musn' take them rooms, 'lessen yuh wants ter have more trouble than yuh knows 'bout. They's—they's haunted!

ALICE. (*In a shrill voice*) What's that yuh said?

SAM. Good Lawd!

MARTHA. (*Her voice containing a deadly seriousness*) Haunted! They ain't nobuddy bin able ter live in them rooms longer'n they could git out!

ALICE. (*In a faltering voice*) Yuh ain't jokin'?

MARTHA. Before the good Lawd, Ah's tellin' yuh the truth!

SAM. But—listen here! Ef what yuh says is true—Does this landlor know 'bout what yuh's tellin' us?

MARTHA. He knows alright. Ah reckon he'll tell us ter leave, when he knows Ah's tole yuh. Well, Ah'm thinkin' 'tis time we did quit. Doan yuh think so, Pete?

PETE. (*Loyally*) Ah thinks same's you does, Martha.

ALICE. I can't believe it.

SAM. Nor me. (*Becoming suddenly suspicious*) Say. Yuh ain't tryin' ter
scare us outer them rooms in favor uv somebuddy else, are yuh?

MARTHA. (*Tensely*) Listen. It's nigh on twenty years ago when we first
seen Her. She was one of these here Philippine gals. John Kinney met her
when he was soljerin' in them parts. He was young then, an' handsome.
She was pretty's a picture, with her big, black eyes an' a head uv hair lak
we doan never see no more. An' she had plenty money. Well, John Kinney marries her an 'bout a year later they comes ter New York. He quits
the army, then, an' goes inter real estate. He tole Her he's goin' buy her
a beautiful house—an' he takes her money—she was only a furriner—an'
young. She didn' know no better. But he doan buy the pretty house he
tole her 'bout. He buys this apartment house. That's when she first commence ter see through him. He uster live then in two little rooms back uv
his dingy office. 'Tweren't no place fer the likes uv Her. She pined fer the
country an' the grass and the flowers. She wanted him ter fix up one uv
these floors so's she could have some place ter breathe in. But he figgered
on the rent from them apartments, an' he wouldn't let her have one.

SAM. Gee! What a brute! (*Alice slips her hand into his*)

MARTHA. She uster come here ter collect the rents. Many's the time Ah's
seen her big, black eyes a-swimmin' in tears. She jes' took ter me right
off—An' Pete an me thought the world uv her. We didn't always understan' what she said. She didn' speak no good English lak Pete an' me, but
we could make out she was lonesome an' scared uv New York—scared
too, uv that husban' uv hers. She missed her folks back home powerful
bad. She was jes' a little wild bird, caught an' put in a cage in a dark
room. Well, seems lak John Kinney tole her one time that she could have
the next floor that got vacant. She runs up here ter tell me—jes' laughin'
an' cryin' all together. She uster come here whenever she got a chance—
an' sit here an' plan how she'd fix them rooms. Such funny ideas she had,
too, 'bout fixins—but pretty. Well, 'bout three months later, the folks on
the top floor move away an' she tole John Kinney 'bout her plans. She was
all ready ter move in. (*Martha pauses just long enough to wipe a tear
with the corner of her apron*) If the ole devil didn' up an' tell her he'd
changed his mind. Seems he'd done forgot all about it. He tole her he
needed the money real bad ter pay some bills. Ah ain't never forgot how
she look when she tole me 'bout it. Her heart was nigh breakin', Ah reckon. She tole me that them rooms was hers—an' she was goin' ter move
in. Ah thought she was jes' talkin wild—but she weren't.

ALICE. (*Breathlessly*) What happened?

MARTHA. The next afternoon John Kinney found her up thar hangin' between the parlor an' the bedroom.

ALICE. (*With a little moan*) Oh, my Gawd! She'd—

MARTHA. (*Nodding confirmation*) An' she ain't never moved away from up
thar—jes' lak she said.

SAM. (*Mopping his face with a hand that shakes perceptibly*) Ah reckon they ain't no rooms fer us, Alice.

ALICE. (*In a voice bordering on the hysterical*) Let's go, Sam. Quick 'fore he comes back!

SAM. (*With clarity*) Sure. Ah doan never want ter see nothin' more uv him. Reckon he's still lookin' fer that wallet. (*A loud crash is heard. Everyone starts violently—Pete, so violently that his Bible falls to the floor. A moment of petrified silence*)

MARTHA. It's upstairs!

SAM. Somebuddy fell down! (*He swallows convulsively*)

ALICE. (*Bursting into tears*) Oh, Sam, let's get outer here, quick 'fore somethin' happens!

MARTHA. Ah 'spec somethin' *has* happened. (*To Sam*) Reckon we'd better go up an' see ef Mr. Kinney's hurt.

SAM. (*Drawing back*) Who, me? Yuh ain't talkin' ter me, sister!

ALICE. (*Clinging tightly to his arm*) Doan yuh do it, Sam. Doan leave me!

SAM. Sam Smith ain't never goin' near them rooms no more!

MARTHA. Well, Ah reckon Ah'd better go up an' see what's happened.

SAM. (*Looking his horror at the mere suggestion*) Yuh's crazy, woman. Let me outer here!

MARTHA. Ah reckon Ah'll ask the people downstairs ter go with me.

PETE. (*Anxiously*) Doan yuh go by yuhself, Martha!

MARTHA. (*Reassuringly*) Ah'll jes' step downstairs an' ask Mr. Brown ter go thar with me.

SAM. An, we'll jes hop on downstairs with yuh. This ain't no place fer comfort! (*Alice, who has Sam tightly by the arm, stoops to lift her umbrella which has fallen to the floor. At that moment, Martha, who has opened the door and gone out into the hall, hurries back into the room, shutting the door precipitately behind her. She rushes over to Pete, grasping him by the arm, and giving him a little shake*)

MARTHA. Pete! Pete! yuh wanted a sign! Ah jes seen John Kinney walkin' down the stairs with *Her*! She had him by the hand an' she was laughin'!

(*The curtain starts to descend just as Alice's piercing scream rings through the room*)

THE END

May Miller

(1899–   )

May Miller during the early 1940s. (*Courtesy of May Miller*)

May Miller in 1986. (*Courtesy of May Miller*)

We create only from familiar elements, the possibilities of
which are enhanced by imagination.[1]

MAY MILLER (SULLIVAN) WAS PRESENTED with the 1986 Mister Brown
Award for Excellence in Drama and Poetry by the National Conference of
African American Theatre at Morgan State University in Baltimore, Maryland. (Mr. William Brown was manager of the African Company in New
York, 1816–1823.) Presently hailed as an outstanding poet, Miller is also
recognized as one of the outstanding playwrights of the 1920s and 1930s,
along with Georgia Douglas Johnson and Eulalie Spence. Not only was
Miller a prolific and versatile playwright, but she was the most widely published black female playwright of this period. Of her fifteen plays, nine were
published; many of them were staged at numerous colleges and little theatre groups throughout the country.

Born January 6, 1899, to Kelly and Annie May Miller, she grew up on
Howard University's campus where her father was a prominent professor.
Kelly Miller gained national recognition for his scholarly essays in sociolo-
gy and as an educator. He was also one of the founders of the Moorland-
Spingarn Research Center at Howard. He served as an early influence on
Miller in her aspiration to become a writer.

Miller graduated from the famous Paul Laurence Dunbar High School in
1916, where she studied under playwrights Mary P. Burrill and Angelina
Grimké. It was Mary Burrill who encouraged her to write her first play,
Pandora's Box (1914), while still a student. The play was submitted and
published in the *School Progress* magazine that same year. As a Howard
University student, Miller received further encouragement to write from
such eminent professors as Alain Locke and Montgomery T. Gregory. She
graduated in 1920 at the head of her class with a Bachelor of Arts degree
and during the graduation exercises received the first prize ever awarded
at Howard in playwriting for her one-act play, *Within the Shadow*.

Following graduation, Miller taught speech, drama, and dance at Frederick Douglass High School in Baltimore. It was there that she wrote most
of her plays. Miller joined the Baltimore Krigwa Players and on weekend
trips to Washington, D.C., frequented Georgia Johnson's "S Street Salon."
During the summer months, Miller took playwriting courses at such insti-
tutions as Columbia University. At Columbia, she studied under the well-
known scholar Frederick Koch, who recognized and encouraged her talents.
In 1925 she placed third in the *Opportunity* playwriting contest for *The Bog
Guide*, and received honorable mention in the 1926 contest for *The Cuss'd
Thing*.

May Miller's plays stand out from those of other women writers because
of her diversity. Considered a "folk" dramatist, she also wrote on a variety

of topics which bordered on "propaganda." While most black women chose to utilize an all-black cast, Miller would incorporate white characters to stress a point as in *Stragglers in the Dust* (1930) and *Nails and Thorns* (1933). Miller cleverly dealt with sensitive issues of the times without offending her audience by leaving unanswered such questions as: "Is the body in the Tomb of the Unknown Soldier really that of a black soldier?" or "how bad is lynching in this country?" In *Graven Images* (1929), a play written for eighth graders, Miller explores racial discrimination as seen in the Old Testament. She relied on Numbers 12:1 for the basis of her play: "And Miriam and Aaron spake against Moses because of the Ethiopian woman he had married."

Some of Miller's plays centered on rural blacks, and on both the educated and uneducated black in urban America. As an educator she wrote history plays to educate her students at Douglass High. In 1934, Carter G. Woodson urged Miller and renowned playwright Willis Richardson to collaborate on an anthology dramatizing the lives of black heroes and heroines. In 1935, *Negro History in Thirteen Plays* was published. Miller had three entries in this anthology—*Sojourner Truth*, *Samory*, and *Harriet Tubman*. She also included Georgia Johnson's plays *William and Ellen Craft* and *Frederick Douglass*.

In 1943, Miller wrote her last work—*Freedom's Children on the March*—a dramatic folk ballad with music which was performed at the June commencement exercises at Frederick Douglass. The following year, she retired from the Baltimore school system. Feeling that she no longer had a platform to perform her plays, Miller began concentrating on poetry that same year. She resides in Washington, D.C., where she continues to write poetry.

NOTE

1. May Miller, "The Creative Urge," *Journal of National Association of College Women* (1936).

STRAGGLERS IN THE DUST

C H A R A C T E R S

MAC,	a watchman in the great cemetery
NAN,	a Negro charwoman
LESTER BRADFORD,	a distinguished politician
THE STRAGGLER	
THE GUARD	

Time: Early 1920s

(*When the curtain rises,* NAN, *a slender stoop-shouldered woman of about fifty years, is discovered seated on the steps. She is hunched over with her face resting on her hands, and her elbows on her knees. Beside her is her scrub pail with a rag hanging carelessly over the rim. Nan has clearly forgotten the pail, a symbol of her drudgery, and is lost in reverie as she gazes past the columns to the marble sepulchre and beyond that to the mist that rises from the lazy Potomac. One instinctively thinks of "I dreamed I dwelt in marble halls" and realizes that here is a new interpretation. Softly she begins to hum and slowly the humming grows into these words:*)

> Keep dis in min' an' all'll go right,
> as on yo way you goes,
> Be shore you knows 'bout all you tells,
> But don't tell all you knows.
> (*Refrain*)
> Be shore you knows 'bout all you tells,
> But don't tell all you knows.

As she is lost in her reverie again, the words of the song are no longer intelligible, but the air is held by a soft humming. A shadowy figure that one distinguishes to be that of a young man in his twenties moves slowly across the top lift of the stairway. He peers down intently at the huddled figure of Nan and listens a moment to her song, then tips behind a column from which he looks out again at Nan. The face that one sees clearly now is chalky in its paleness and the eyes seem haunted as they stare vacantly about. The face disappears as MAC, *the watchman, moves steadily toward Nan. Mac is a stout man of about sixty. He wears a double-breasted suit fastened with brass buttons. His blue cap is trimmed with a gold cord. In his hand he swings a regular watchman's clock which he consults as he approaches.*)

MAC. Well, Nan, I guess it's about finishing up you be.

NAN. Yes, Mistah Mac, Ah's just 'bout done. Ah's rubb'd and rubb'd all dat brass bright 'nough to make heavenly crowns.

MAC. To be sure might nice things look nice Nan, but I doubt if I'd be wantin' any brass crown.

NAN. No Ah guess not, Mistah Mac, there's still some of us what's deservin' of better. We done tasted the brass here on earth. God sartinly must be a savin' de gold. (*She sadly shakes her head and stops to pick up the pail.*)

MAC. That's right, Nan, kinda get your things together. It's six thirty and almost closing time.

NAN. Closin' time so soon! Ah hates tuh see it come.

MAC. Hate the time for leaving to come?

NAN. Ah's always kinda had a hankering after graveyards and now—

MAC. Well it's too bad I don't feel that way since I have to spend most of my time here. As for me seven o'clock can't come soon enough to get home.

NAN. Ahh! you see, sah, dat's de difference. Ah ain't got nothin' at home. All Ah got is heah.

MAC. All you got is here?

NAN. Well yuh see, Mistah Mac, Ah ain't nevah had nobody but mah boy, Jim. Dere's nevah been nobody but jus' him and me. An' since he's been heah Ah jus' kinda likes tuh stay neah.

MAC. But I never heard about your son working here. Which one is he?

NAN. Who mah Jim? Ah no he ain't workin'. Fact is Jim ain't neveah liked tuh work much, but now he can't work no more. (*Pointing to the sepulchre*) Dey put him in dat marble box dere aftah dey fin' him on de field. Flanders, Ah think dey calls it.

MAC. (*Looking bewildered*) You mean you lost your Jim in the war, eh?

NAN. Yeah, ain't yuh hear'd dem talkin' 'bout him de uhda day? Dat grand ol' man stand up dere an' tol' how dey call'd an' how Jim lef' me broken hearted tuh go fight for dis country an' den how dem guns got him. An' how dey fin' him finally on dat fiel' in France an' bring him back ober heah an put him in dere. (*She points again to the tomb.*)

MAC. (*In a hestitant manner*) Yes, I heard that, but Nan, they weren't

talking 'bout your Jim. Why they don't even know who that soldier is—
he's unknown. It wasn't about your Jim they were talking.

NAN. Yeah, Ah know some of dem don' know; but Ah knows an' dat man
knows. Didn't he say "Yuh mother dere bow'd in grief.' Ah was hidin' behin' dis very pillow an' Ah heah'd him, but Ah didn' come out cause Ah
know'd dere'd be them dere as wouldn't want Jim tuh stay dere cause he's
cullud.

MAC. But Nan, that's foolish, don't you see—

NAN. Ah done right didn't Ah?

MAC. (*Despairing of making Nan understand*) Yes, I guess you did right
not to say anything. (*The haunted face of the stranger appears from behind the last column. He listens intently unseen by the others and then
disappears again.*)

NAN. Mistah Mac, but you won' tell nobody will ya 'cause Ah don' wan' em
tuh keep movin' him.

MAC. (*As if pacifying a child*) Of course not, Nan.

NAN. Yuh know it's kinda nice dat dey bring all dem wreaths and ribbons
to put on him, but somehow Ah wishes dey had lef' him where he was.

MAC. Well of all ridiculous ideas this is just about the worst.

NAN. (*Misinterpreting*) Ah know it is an Ah am proud when Ah look at this
temple dat's his'n, and see dat soldiers dat's lookin' out for him day an'
night; but den when Ah thinks of Jim an' how he lubbed de woods an' de
fields Ah'm jus' a little sorry. He might had rested bettah ober dere in
France. Dey say de wooden crosses is kinda ugly but dat de big blue sky
ober head guards an' blesses 'em an' den too dose poppies grow between
de rows an' dat wouldn't have been haf bad 'cause Jim liked red. Maybe
it's best as 'tis 'cause ober dere be nobody to watch. (*She sighs as she
stoops to pick up pail again.*)

MAC. Watch, watch for what?

NAN. Dat's right Ah guess dere ain't no need ob no guard ober dere.

MAC. As far as need's concerned we don't need any either.

NAN. O! yes we does. Dere's dat creature wid de ghost like face and empty
eyes what's been haunting dis place for two days. He sartingly needs
watchin'. De first time Ah saw him he couldn't see me for lookin' so hard
at dat tomb.

MAC. I don't think we'll have any more trouble with him. I notified the police and any way he seems to be perfectly harmless.

NAN. Ah'm sartin he's moon-duff but Ah ain't worried non now, 'cause Jim's
got plenty of pertection.

MAC. I'm afraid the moon's got more than one of us, but if you're certain
you're satisfied with that protection you can be leaving now.

NAN. (*Taking her pail and moving through the portal*) Thanks Mistah Mac
an' if yuh be aneedin' me again soon ju' sen' for me cause yuh knows Ah
like tuh come.

MAC. All right, Nan, good-night. (*Mac follows Nan to the left portal and closes it behind her. As he stands there meditatively shaking his head, a tall distinguished looking gray haired man in an elegant dark suit mounts the steps and stands facing pass as he turns. Mac is startled*)

LESTER BRADFORD. I'm very sorry if I startled you.

MAC. It wasn't that exactly but it is an odd feeling to think that you're alone and suddenly face company.

BRADFORD. And, too, it's a little late for visitors isn't it?

MAC. Yes, sir, it is. We close the gates in about fifteen minutes. After dusk there aren't so many that tarry here.

BRADFORD. So I noticed as I came up. I passed only one person—a colored woman.

MAC. That was only Nan. She comes here only once a week to shine the brass.

BRADFORD. But during the day many do visit the tomb, eh? I've been out several times and there were always quite a few.

MAC. Sunday's the day, though when we have a crowd. Sundays there's nothing else much to do but think of the dead. Then hundreds visit the unknown's grave. He seems somehow to belong to each one separately.

BRADFORD. He undoubtedly has had an unexplainable effect on the whole white race.

MAC. No sir, you needn't make it that narrow. Better say on all races. You'd be surprised at the number of Negroes that visit here.

BRADFORD. (*Surprised*) For what? Out of patriotism? (*He smiles at his own irony*).

MAC. No telling how many of them feel like Nan.

BRADFORD. (*Wondering*) Nan?

MAC. That colored woman you met as you came up the hill.

BRADFORD. O yes.

MAC. Do you know she really believes that the unknown is actually her boy, Jim, that she lost in the war.

BRADFORD. But how could she think that?

MAC. She kinda misunderstood some of the speeches she's heard out here— took everything to herself.

BRADFORD. Such a thing has never even crossed my mind. Why that isn't even possible.

MAC. Of course not, Nan's just a poor old colored woman with nothing left but her dreams.

BRADFORD. But if it were—what a terrible joke on America!

MAC. But it can't be. We just naturally hear and experience odd things out here in this land of tombstones. Some of the visitors might surprise you a little. Nan was just talking about some poor half dazed boy who's been hanging around here for two days. Real innocent sort but with his ghost-like face, not the one you'd want for company in a place like this.

BRADFORD. (*Greatly interested and speaking hurriedly*) And where is that boy now?

MAC. Hanging 'round here somewhere I guess but there's no telling just where he is. I could have sworn there was nobody in this place except the guard when I locked the gates last night. Yet the first creature I met this morning was that crazy boy. Really no use trying to put your hands on that kind.

BRADFORD. But that's just why I am here.

MAC. Beg pardon, sir?

BRADFORD. There's no time for mincing matters, I am here because I think the boy may be—may be my—my son.

MAC. I am sorry, sir, I didn't understand, but what makes you think so?

BRADFORD. My son is missing and when I notified the police they told me of your report. I asked to come for him alone.

MAC. But you are not certain.

BRADFORD. The description tallies but they didn't say anything of his condition. Did he seem sick?

MAC. God knows he was white enough.

BRADFORD. (*Nervously*) Yes, yes, it's those attacks. They always leave him like that.

MAC. But this might not be your son.

BRADFORD. But it is, I know it is—and you say he has been wandering here for two days—ever since he left home. Each attack gets worse. (*He hesitates for a moment, then clenches his hands. As he speaks he becomes more and more vehement.*) Each attack gets worse—God when will they end? He'd be better off dead—dead, did you hear me? And I can say that of my only son. (*Bradford starts and listens as a voice is heard singing off stage in a strained uncanny voice.*) I'm afraid you're a bit nervous too.

MAC. O, sir, there he is now. You had better get your nerves steady to meet him. Let's sit here like we've been chatting; we don't want to startle him. You let me talk to him.

BRADFORD. Yes—yes of course.

(*They have just assumed their position on the steps when the unknown enters. Upon close view one notes that the deathlike pallor of his skin is accompanied by a slight tremor of limbs. One realizes that he's a sick man. Bradford rises and starts with outstretched arms toward the boy who apparently does not even see him. Mac pulls him gently but forcefully back in place shaking his head in admonition.*)

STRAGGLER. (*To Mac in a hollow weak voice*) I thought you had gone. Isn't it closing time yet?

MAC. (*Calmly*) Yes just about, but I thought I'd kinda wait for you—thought maybe you'd walk home with me.

STRAGGLER. O no—no I can't go yet—you see I've got to wait for him.

MAC. For your father? Then we can leave now because—

STRAGGLER. No for him—the Nigger.

MAC. What Nigger? No one's coming here this late. I shall close the gates in a few minutes.

STRAGGLER. Locked gates are nothing to him. He comes every evening after you've gone, that's the reason I have to stay here. He's a sly rascal. That guard walks back and forth and never even sees him; he comes so quickly and quietly.

BRADFORD. (*Impatiently*) Who?

STRAGGLER. The Nigger who lives in there.

BRADFORD. Where?

STRAGGLER. In the tomb.

BRADFORD. Nobody but the unknown dead's there.

STRAGGLER. He's dead well enough but he's not unknown. There are at least three if not more that know him.

MAC. It's nobody that knows, they tell me.

STRAGGLER. (*Laughing loud*) I heard that colored woman confess to you. You don't know and—

MAC. Who? Nan? The moon-daft one. She's feebled minded.

STRAGGLER. Maybe she is but she only told you what I've been knowing for months. I didn't know though that he was her son. You see I met him in No man's land. It was just a few minutes after one of those infernal German shells had exploded near me. I was standing there a little dazed when he came to save me—did you hear—to save me, I said. (*He laughs harshly*) He was such a huge black one and it was so easy for him to carry me. We had gone some distance when he missed his gun and went back. A shell got him.

MAC. Poor lad—poor fellow.

STRAGGLER. Lucky lad! Didn't they go right to that spot to get him.

MAC. How would you be knowing that?

STRAGGLER. He told me himself how shocked he was when he saw where they were putting him, because he knew how they felt over here about Niggers.

BRADFORD. But son you said he was dead.

STRAGGLER. Sure he's dead but I've talked to him and even Niggers learn sense after death. He only stays there from evening 'til dawn. The rest of the time he spends at the Capitol. He says it's lots of fun to come back and see what foolish things big men say and do. Isn't it funny they can't change the only thing that counts?

MAC. It's bad to be alisten'ning to that lad.

STRAGGLER. From a black Nigger too who stole my place. (*He becomes violent in his expression*) He caught the shell aimed at me. He holds the tomb meant for me! He sleeps there and leaves me to live on a shell of a man, a shadow tagging after him—me Captain Lester Bradford Jr.—and I can't die.

BRADFORD. Son, you do remember then and you know me?

STRAGGLER. (*He stands for a moment bewildered and then a gleam of intelligence suffuses the empty face.*) Certainly dad.

BRADFORD. You've been away from home two days.

STRAGGLER. (*Surprised*) Two days?

BRADFORD. The folks were getting anxious about you.

STRAGGLER. Mother and Zelma?

BRADFORD. I promised them I'd bring you back with me.

STRAGGLER. All right, I'm ready.

BRADFORD. (*Turning quickly to speak to Mac*) I am sorry if we detained you. Thank you for your trouble. (*He is in the act of drawing a bill from his wallet.*)

STRAGGLER. (*Turning back*) I had almost forgotten those things don't make any difference.

BRADFORD. What things?

STRAGGLER. Name—home—those things.

BRADFORD. Maybe not, son, but it's late. Let's go.

STRAGGLER. (*He stares at tomb as he walks away.*) I can't go now. If I wait this time until he comes I may go in the tomb with him. I've missed for two nights but tonight I'll make it.

BRADFORD. Nobody can get in that tomb. This gentleman is waiting to lock the gates, come let's go home.

STRAGGLER. You don't understand yet. He belongs there and when he comes from the Capitol in the evening the side opens for him. I talked to him this morning when he left and he promised that I can go in with him tonight if I get there when the slab slides for him.

BRADFORD. (*Taking his son's arm forcefully*) Come son.

STRAGGLER. (*Breaking away from his father*) It's time for him to start now. (*As a faint fog horn is heard in the distance.*) Hear that's the signal for him. (*He runs to the top of the steps*)

BRADFORD. (*He goes up the steps after his son.*) I believe I did hear something.

MAC. Only some boat, sir, as she puts into wharf.

STRAGGLER. See there he is. He's standing right on the top of the Capitol dome. Watch him. The light's on him now.

BRADFORD. (*Nodding as if wanting to believe him.*) I see him.

MAC. Surely, sir, 'tis the same statue that's always been there.

STRAGGLER. He's stepping off now. (*In his excitement he puts his arm around his father's shoulders and points with the other hand as if following something.*) Doesn't he stride like a king over the city and they don't even know he's there. Look! See him pause at the water's edge!

BRADFORD. Yes—Yes. I see.

MAC. Indeed, sir, you do not; they're only trying to place the search light from Arlington Tower.

BRADFORD. Didn't he walk the Potomac in a hurry, son?

STRAGGLER. He's coming up the hill now and I must be there. Dad you'll tell the folks where I am, won't you. I'm glad you came because now you understand.

BRADFORD. (*Reluctantly holding his son*) I'm going too, son.

STRAGGLER. No, no, dad, you stay here. He might not let me go in if he sees anybody else.

BRADFORD. But—

STRAGGLER. (*Breaking loose and rushing out to the tomb.*) Bye, dad.

MAC. O, sir, why did you let him loose. (*Starts after boy.*) (*Bradford clutches Mac's arm and holds him firmly.*)

MAC. (*Struggling*) I fear your son is sick, sir. See he has fallen. Let me go to him.

BRADFORD. O no! You might keep him from getting in.

MAC. But there's no place to get in, sir.

BRADFORD. Sh! Sh! There he goes. He's quite all right now. (*He frees Mac who rushes out to the tomb where the boy has fallen. With the aid of the soldier he turns him over and listens to his heart. The guard straightens and removes his hat standing at attention. Mac arises and returns to the top step where Bradford remains standing.*)

MAC. I am sorry sir, but I fear that your son is dead.

BRADFORD. (*Undisturbed*) You mean that he went with the Nigger. Yes, I know, I saw him.

MAC. No, No, sir. Of course I shall have to notify the police but I was wondering if you care to give any directions concerning the body.

BRADFORD. (*Wondering*) Body, what body?

MAC. Your son's body over there.

BRADFORD. You are mistaken; that's not my son's body.

MAC. But you called him son when you were just talking to him.

BRADFORD. O yes! That was my son, but he went in the tomb you know. (*He starts down the steps, turns back and thrusts the same bill in Mac's hand.*) Thank you for your trouble. Good-night. I am sorry if I detained you. (*He goes down the steps and off stage. Mac stands dazed for a moment and then rushes off stage after him. At the tomb the soldier keeps his silent vigil. A boat's whistle calls shrilly in the distance as the curtain falls.*)

THE END

RIDING THE GOAT

PERSONS OF THE PLAY

WILLIAM CARTER,	a young physician
RUTH CHAPMAN	
ANT HETTY,	Ruth's grandmother
CHRISTOPHER COLUMBUS JONES,	the lodge inspector

Scene: The sitting-room of Ant Hetty's home. The action takes place in South Baltimore in a community of draymen.

Time: Six o'clock of a June evening in the early part of the twentieth century.

Scene: The stuffy sitting-room of Ant Hetty's home. In the side right wall down stage, a door leading outside. When the door is open, a white stoop and a few white steps can be seen. In the middle of the left wall is a door leading into the kitchen. The room is furnished with the usual three-piece parlor set upholstered in red plush. Diagonally across the corner, an easel supports a portrait of a heavy-set man. Stretched from the table in the middle of the room to the back of a chair is an ironing board before which ANT HETTY stands ironing. She is a stout dark woman of about sixty. Her gingham house dress is open at the throat and a pair of well worn bedroom slippers are more off her feet than on.

When the curtain rises, she pauses in her ironing of a stiffly starched white dress. She turns the iron upon the board and wetting her finger tests the heat. She sighs, shakes her head, dries her face on the end of her apron, and then taking the iron goes into the kitchen humming. She returns with another iron and continues her work singing "Such a Meetin's Goin' Be Here To-night." When she is half through the second chorus, a knock is heard at the outer door. Ant Hetty calls without stopping her work.

ANT HETTY. Who's there?

CARTER. It's I, Carter.

ANT HETTY. Why don't cha come on in then?

(CARTER *enters with a physician's bag in his hand and a bundle under his arm. He is a slender brown fellow of medium height, neatly dressed in a dark suit. As he enters he takes off his straw hat and mops his brow with a pocket handkerchief.*)

CARTER. Good evening. How're you this time, Ant Hetty?

(*He sits on the sofa and Ant Hetty adjusts the ironing board so that she may see him as she talks.*)

ANT HETTY. Well, son, I guess I can't complain none. Is it hot 'nough fo' you?

CARTER. Too hot with all the work I've had to do.

ANT HETTY. You jest wait, honey, 'til I finishes ironin' this dress an' I'll make you some cool mint water.

CARTER. Thanks.

ANT HETTY. An' the worse is there ain't no change in sight. That wasn't no wet moon that riz las' night. It was there a-shinin' over them roof tops as clear as a whistle—nary a rain ring 'bout it.

CARTER. You can't tell; maybe we'll catch a stray shower.

ANT HETTY. No, I don't b'lieve it. Them stray showers might fool the moon, but they nevah fools Ant Hetty. Sho as it's gonna rain, my feet and limbs begins to trouble me; an' ain't I been standin' on my feet most nigh all day widout ache nor pain? Anyhow who'd want a shower to-day—the day of the parade?

CARTER. I would.

ANT HETTY. (*Turning around abruptly.*) Huh!

CARTER. Nothing.

ANT HETTY. (*She takes the dress off the board and drapes it carefully over the back of a chair. She talks to the dress as she smooths its folds.*) Now you'se already spick and span fo' that perade tonight; ain't cha? (*Looking up, she remembers Carter. She takes the ironing board under her left arm and carries the iron in her right hand. She starts toward the kitchen.*) Wait a minute, son, an' your Ant Hetty'll fix you up. (*She goes into the kitchen.*)

(*Carter stares at the white dress with a frown. He opens the bundle that he brought with him and shakes out his uniform. Holding it at arm's length, he views it with disgust.*)

CARTER. Damn that lodge and all its parades!

(*He throws the costume on the floor as Ant Hetty enters carrying a glass of her concoction. He hastily, almost guiltily, replaces the costume on the sofa.*)

ANT HETTY. Now drink that, honey, 'cause you mus' be tir'd chasin' roun' all day in this heat 'tending niggers. Since you been gran' mastah looks lak folks tryin' to outdo one 'nother callin' you.

CARTER. And before I joined the lodge, the same people wouldn't even consider me. (*He takes the proffered glass.*) Thanks.

ANT HETTY. (*Sitting in the rocker and watching Carter as he drinks.*) What was you doin' down in Haw Street so lon' befo' perade time?

CARTER. I had a call down the street and I dropped in thinking maybe Ruth would be home early to-day.

ANT HETTY. Yes, Ruth'll be alon' in a little while now. But Lawd, who's sick in our street now?

CARTER. Mrs. Riles called me to see Mr. Ike.

ANT HETTY. I 'clare ev'ry time that nigger gets tir'd of workin' he gits 'nother spell of rheumatics.

CARTER. Ant Hetty!

ANT HETTY. It's the truf. Lon' time ago I tol' Mary Riles that there wasn't nothin' the mattah wid Ike but laziness, an' she knows it.

CARTER. But he is sick.

ANT HETTY. 'Course he's sick. He's made hisself sick a-thinkin' so. Ain't he been arguin' wid hisself fo' twenty years' til now even him is convinced he's dyin'?

CARTER. But it's not so easy to convince a doctor.

ANT HETTY. Yes 'tis. Don't I remember ten years ago Mary Riles come runnin' in here. Me an' Mistah Chapman was settin' at the dinner table. She was a-weepin' an' sobbin' out that the doctor said Ike couldn't live 'nother week. I says to her then, "Mary Riles, you dry them tears. Ike'll bury the three of us." There was my Sam a-settin' there as strong as 'n ox; ain't he gone now an' Ike's a-livin' on? Too bad though he can't march in that perade to-day.

CARTER. It's too hot for parades.

ANT HETTY. That you, the gran' mastah, a-talkin' 'bout it's too hot fo' perades?

CARTER. The heat's enough without having to wear that heavy regalia.

ANT HETTY. But it's only round the block that you has to go. Jest think of all the folks from Frémont to Green Street that'll be standin' on the corners to see the candidates in review!

CARTER. (*Bitterly.*) How interesting for me!

ANT HETTY. Yes, you know Sara Blake's boy, James, jest turned eighteen an' that reformed scape-goat of a husban' of Rachel Lee's is both 'mong the candidates.

CARTER. Plague the candidates and their parade! I'm getting tired of all this useless thumping over cobblestones. Work all day, and parade all night. I can be just as good a doctor to them outside the lodge as in it.

ANT HETTY. Sh! son, be careful there. Of course, you'se talkin' to your Ant Hetty, but there's them that wouldn't understan'. The gran' 'xalted ruler of the United Order of Moabites can't afford to talk thata way.

CARTER. No, I guess not. All in the line of duty.

ANT HETTY. Now ain't that jest lak a man atalkin' 'bout duty an' there's fifty others wantin' your place. A woman ought to have it; she'd know a good thing.

CARTER. Any woman who'd want it is welcome to the trouble.

ANT HETTY. Oh, there's plenty. I ustah hear my poor dead Sam talk 'bout a woman who hid in a closet at her husban's lodge meeting an' heard an' saw all the 'nitiation. Nobody knew that she was there; but jes' as they was 'bout to leave, she sneezed an' they opens the closet an' there she was.

CARTER. (*Laughing.*) What did they do to her?

ANT HETTY. They give her her choice—she could jine the lodge or die.

CARTER. Which did she take?

ANT HETTY. She went aridin' the goat, of course.

CARTER. (*Rising and taking his bag.*) It must have been funny. I wish I could have seen that performance. (*He starts to roll the uniform to make a bundle.*) Ant Hetty, I guess I had better not wait for Ruth. I have a call to make on Frémont Avenue and I'll be back this way later.

ANT HETTY. All right; but why you gotta tote that uniform up an' down the street to get it all messed up?

CARTER. (*Quickly dropping the uniform.*) Thanks. I hated to have to bring it with me, but I feared that I could not get uptown again. (*Laughing as he pauses in the doorway.*) And, Ant Hetty, be sure to take good care of the grand regalia of the grand exalted ruler of the United Order of Moabites. (*He goes out.*)

ANT HETTY. (*Following Carter to the door.*) I wonder why he was laffin', the young upstart!

(*Ant Hetty goes to the sofa and smooths the rumpled uniform. She straightens the chairs, carefully arranges the much fondled white dress over her arm and starts toward the kitchen. RUTH enters. She is a tall, well developed brown girl of about eighteen. Her smoothly brushed hair and the pretty checked gingham she wears bespeak personal care.*)

RUTH. Hello, grandma!

ANT HETTY. (*Pausing at the kitchen door.*) How'd you make out this time, child?

RUTH. Very well. I rode down though; I was too tired to walk.

ANT HETTY. Did you meet Doctor Carter?

RUTH. (*A little excited.*) No. Was he here?

ANT HETTY. Jes' lef' the minute befo' you come in. He lef' that uniform an' I guess he'll be back.

RUTH. (*Talking rapidly as if to change the subject.*) Grandma, you should have looked in the sewing room today. You know the Framinghams on Charles Street, don't you?

ANT HETTY. (*Coming back into the room to listen.*) Now listen, who you'se askin'! 'Course I do; ain't them the folks Mary Riles works fo'?

RUTH. Well, the Framingham girl marries next week.

ANT HETTY. You don't say so!

RUTH. Yes, and we finished her wedding clothes to-day—every stitch by hand. I'm so tired now that I can't see anything but ruffles, tucks, and laces. I think I'll lie down a little. (*She starts toward the door.*)

ANT HETTY. (*Shocked.*) You ain't got no time to sleep an' eat an' see the parade too.

RUTH. It's too hot for parades.

ANT HETTY. (*Looking at Ruth closely.*) I've heard that 'nough fo' one day. You young ones gits me. You'se too pert fo' your years. There's Doctor Carter now agettin' too high an' mighty fo' parades, says he's tir'd of useless marchin'. Did you evah hear the lak of it?

RUTH. I don't blame him.

ANT HETTY. Huh!

RUTH. No, mam, I don't see any sense in all that parading either.

ANT HETTY. O Lawd! an' did I evah think I'd live to hear Sam Chapman's granddaughter talk lak that!

RUTH. But, grandma, what sense is there in it?

ANT HETTY. What would your grandpap's funeral've been without his lodges?

RUTH. I don't know; I hardly remember it.

ANT HETTY. The peradin' of his brothers wid their swords ashinin' an' their plumes awavin' was a gran' sight.

RUTH. Yes, mam.

ANT HETTY. But the brightest spot in the whole affair was when they lit them candles 'round the coffin an' the gran' mastah stood at the head ahittin' Sam wid his sword yellin' "Rise, Brother Chapman, an' jine the order of departed Moabites." They beat on him so lon' an' I was alookin' so close I thought I seen Sam move under them dim lights.

RUTH. Yes, mam, I am sure that was a grand funeral.

ANT HETTY. 'Course there was them as called him a habitual jiner, but I didn't mind. They was only jealous of that turnout, cause Sam was a member of three lodges an' nary a one failed to show up on his big day.

RUTH. But I can't see that that made any difference to him then.

ANT HETTY. I didn't 'spect you to see. But, child, you'd better hurry an' learn that you gotta see lak some other folks sees if you wanta git alon'! Take Doctor Carter now. He needn't 'spect to get too uppish fo' the lodge an' still come down hopin' to 'tend these folks.

RUTH. But, grandma, they need him so.

ANT HETTY. 'Course they does but they won't have him.

RUTH. What will they do then?

ANT HETTY. Jes' what they done befo' he come. That good ol' white doctor is still livin' an' I guess he's got a few mo' of them pills.

RUTH. Yes, and just a few more of us will die.

ANT HETTY. Well, what diff'rence do that make? Ain't people been dyin' since there was folks?

RUTH. It's all right if it can't be helped, but Doctor Carter can cure them and wants to.

ANT HETTY. If he's so set on helpin' his folks why don't he act lak it? Instid he laffs at our peradin'—I know.

RUTH. Grandma, why are you so anxious about the parade?

ANT HETTY. Ain't your Ant Sara's Jim marchin' wid the candidates ? It seems lak ev'ryone's got somebody an' me widout a frazzlin' soul in the line.

RUTH. I don't understand why you would worry.

ANT HETTY. It was so diffrent when your grandpap was livin'; I had somethin' to watch fo' then. Since he died I been out of it. Then recently I been thinkin', "Here's Ruthie growed up wid a nice doctor an' he gran' mastah." I could hold my haid higher 'n the res'. Now he's 'bout to spoil it all, an' you aidin' an' abettin' him in it.

RUTH. It's not exactly that, grandma.

ANT HETTY. You know, sometimes I wishes you had liked Chris.

RUTH. Please, grandma, don't start that again.

ANT HETTY. 'Course I thinks Doctor's all right in some ways but the educated chaps always manages to think a little diff'rent. I guess that's where the trouble comes wid you—them sisters at that convent kinda educated you 'way from me.

RUTH. Grandma, I'm not away from you in any way, but I just can't marry Chris. (*Her voice breaks.*)

ANT HETTY. There now. honey, I didn't mean fo' you to git all riz up 'bout it. You'se tired. Set down a minute an' res' while I fixes you a bite to eat. (*Ant Hetty goes to the kitchen. A knock is heard at the outer door. Ruth walks wearily over and opens the door. JONES enters. He is a very dark, stockily built fellow of about twenty-three. He wears the uniform of the order, the long-tail, double-breasted coat with bright brass buttons. The badges of the order decorate his breast. His helmet-like hat is decorated with a finely curled white ostrich feather. As he enters, he grins broadly.*)

RUTH. Hello, Chris! Coming in?

JONES. I guess mebbe I kin fin' time to tell some of my good friends hello; but 'course this is the busy day an' I ain't got much time—me bein' made the gran' inspector fo' the lodge.

RUTH. (*With an effort.*) Isn't that lovely!

ANT HETTY. (*Entering from kitchen.*) Christopher Columbus Jones, they ain't gone an' made you lodge inspector, has they?

JONES. (*Proudly drawing himself up.*) Yes, mam, that's jest what they done.

ANT HETTY. You know I always tol' your ma when she give you that gran' an' mighty name that you was gonna be a great man some day. If your ma had only lived to see this day!

JONES. (*Complacently.*) Yes, 'tis too bad she can't see me, ain't it? What's the mattah, Ruth, you ain't sayin' nothin'?

RUTH. Your uniform does look nice.

ANT HETTY. It sho does but you wouldn't go doublin' it up an throwin' it all roun', would you? (*She looks significantly at Carter's rumpled suit but*

Jones is busy surveying himself in the mirror which hangs on the back wall.)

JONES. No, Ant Hetty, 'course not. When my pa give me this suit, it was such a decent suit that I jest keeps it decent.

ANT HETTY. Your pappy bein' the richest drayman down this way, I bet he could give you many a suit.

JONES. Yes, he is rich; but I does take good care of this suit. 'Course I'm not talkin' 'bout nobody, but there is them that is high in the order what don't look haf so good.

RUTH. Many of them haven't the time you have, Chris, because most of them are working since they have no rich fathers.

JONES. Yes, that's too bad, but they oughta fin' time.

ANT HETTY. We that stands an' watches you pass knows who's keerful an' who ain't. (*Sniffing toward the kitchen.*) That my baby's dinner burnin'? (*She goes into the kitchen.*)

JONES. I thinks mebbe the lodge oughta stan' an' watch itself in perade sometime, then it might reward them as deserves it.

RUTH. Who is unrewarded now, Chris?

JONES. Nobody perticular. 'Course lodge inspector is a mighty good job, but I don't see why I couldn't be gran' mastah same as some nigger from the outside. I'm jest as fittin' as that doctor chap.

RUTH. Then you aren't satisfied?

JONES. I'm proud all right of this job, but I'd be prouder of that one. Mebbe if I was gran' mastah you'd like me a little better.

RUTH. Chris, I do like you. Haven't we been friends since we were kids?

JONES. You remember how we ustah race scrubbin' the front stoop? You always made yourn whiter'n mine an' got through sooner.

RUTH. You never did like to work.

JONES. Is that the reason you ain't lovin' me?

RUTH. No, I can't say it's that.

JONES. You'se right, 'taint that. You ustah be my gal 'til you went up on Vine Street to that there place wid the high wall 'roun' it. Since then, you ain't been yourself—wantin' something new all the time.

RUTH. No, Chris, I haven't been the same.

JONES. Turned me down wid all them ol' things, huh.

RUTH. I told you I am still your friend.

JONES. Frien'! I don't want you fo' no frien' when that doctor fella's got you fo' a sweetheart. But don't think I'm givin' you up so easy. Remember how I ustah fight all the gang in Haw Street fo' you? I'm grown a little but I ain't changed much. (*He starts toward the door. Ruth starts after him.*)

RUTH. Chris, come back a minute.

JONES. What'cha want?

RUTH. What did you mean by that?

JONES. Nothin'.

RUTH. Oh, yes, you did, too.

JONES. Well, do you think I'm gonna let any fella step in an' take the job that oughta be mine an' my gal to boot an' not raise my hand to stop it?

RUTH. What are you going to do?

JONES. Don't think doctors can't make no mistakes an' just remember Christopher Columbus Jones is watchin' him. (*He goes out the front door. Ruth stands in the doorway looking down the street. Ant Hetty enters from the kitchen.*)

ANT HETTY. I 'clare wid all these hindrances nobody kin get a bite. Come now, Ruthie, 'cause I know you're most nigh starved to death.

RUTH. (*Standing in the doorway.*) No'm, I'm not so hungry now.

ANT HETTY. Chris take your appetite?

RUTH. No'm.

ANT HETTY. But you does lak him a little, don't you, honey?

RUTH. Yes, mam, of course, I do.

ANT HETTY. That's right. Jest remember you'll please your granny. Chris is a right nice boy even if he won't work; but Lawd, he don't have to wid his pappy stablin' five horses an' buggies an' everythin'.

RUTH. Chris is all right.

ANT HETTY. Much better 'n some uppish niggers I knows wid new fangled ideas. Now Doctor Carter—

RUTH. (*Turning back into the room.*) Sh! here he comes.

ANT HETTY. Talk 'bout the devil!

CARTER. (*Standing in the open door.*) Here I am, back again, Ant Hetty. Hello, Ruth!

RUTH. Hello, Doctor!

ANT HETTY. Anybody out yit?

CARTER. A few folks dressed in white are sitting on their stoops.

ANT HETTY. I know'd it. I was atellin' Sara this mornin' as how them folks 'ud have on everythin' but the kitchen stove. (*She goes toward the kitchen door.*) Ruthie, don't forgit your dinner. I'm gonna dress.

RUTH. No'm.

CARTER. What's the matter, Ruth? You haven't much to say to-day.

RUTH. Nothing.

CARTER. I know better than that.

RUTH. It's nothing much, Doctor Carter—

CARTER. How many more times shall I tell you to drop the "Doctor"?

RUTH. I remember, but you're so different from the rest of the men I know.

CARTER. Tell me about that later. Right now I want to know what is troubling you. (*He pushes his uniform in the corner of the sofa and sits down.*)

RUTH. (*Sitting in a chair near the sofa.*) Are you—are you going to give up the lodge?

CARTER. Why do you ask?

RUTH. Grandma said you were talking doubtful about it.

CARTER. Oh, Ruth, I am sick of all that foolishness. From the day I put on that little white apron and rode a bony gray mare around the block, I've been hating it, and I'm just about through with all of it.

RUTH. They don't think it's foolishness.

CARTER. They've got to be taught.

RUTH. But not in that way.

CARTER. Why?

RUTH. Because I know them better than you do. If you leave their lodge now, they won't have you attend them; even grandma wouldn't and she's no member.

CARTER. Well, if that's the way they feel, let them cut me. I guess I can manage to get along.

RUTH. But they will suffer for it.

CARTER. Which will be their own fault. They ought to suffer.

RUTH. But aren't they your people?

CARTER. Of course, they are, but not even for my people am I going to don that regalia again. (*He grabs the uniform, looks at it a minute in disgust and drops it in a heap on the floor.*)

RUTH. Don't say that! There are too many waiting for you to take just that attitude.

CARTER. Maybe, but let's forget them. (*He goes over to Ruth's chair and takes her hand to help her rise.*) Come here, I want to say something to you.

RUTH. (*Standing beside him and nervously measuring heights with her hand.*) In these new shoes, I'm as tall as you are—not quite so big though.

CARTER. Bigger in some ways. I guess that's why I care so much.

RUTH. Do you mean that?

CARTER. Surely. Why?

RUTH. Wouldn't you do almost anything for a person you liked that way?

CARTER. You know I would.

RUTH. (*Slipping her hand on his coat coaxingly.*) Well, march to-day—just today, please.

CARTER. (*Looking away.*) That's another matter.

RUTH. Then you didn't mean what you said?

CARTER. Certainly I did. I'll always mean that part.

RUTH. But you won't march?

CARTER. Ruth, I am tired. I've been working all day in this heat and heaven knows when I will collect some of those bills.

RUTH. And if you don't stay in the lodge, they may never pay you.

CARTER. Consider it then my contribution to charity.

RUTH. You have definitely decided?

CARTER. Yes, and I wish you wouldn't say anything more about it.

RUTH. I can't help feeling that you're unwise.

CARTER. Since you are so crazy about parading, it's really a pity you can't march yourself.

RUTH. William!

CARTER. Excuse me, Ruth. I'd better be going. I'm talking all kinds of ways. Good-by, Ruth. (*He takes his bag from the table and goes toward the door hurriedly.*)

RUTH. Good-by! (*Starting after him.*) William!

(*Ant Hetty appears in the kitchen doorway with her white dress on. She is struggling with the many hooks and eyes. Ruth turns abruptly away from the door.*)

ANT HETTY. Fix this, Ruthie. (*Ruth goes to her grandmother and fastens the hooks.*) Doctor Carter gone?

RUTH. (*Slyly kicking Carter's uniform under the sofa.*) Yes, mam.

ANT HETTY. It's gittin' late, an' me not dressed yit. I leaned out the window upstairs an' heard them callin' the line together. Them folks'll be havin' a monkey an' parrot time, an' I'll be missin' it. Have you ate yit?

RUTH. No'm.

ANT HETTY. (*Going back to the kitchen.*) Well, hurry.

RUTH. Yes, mam.

(*She hears a bugle call, goes to the door and looks out. She comes back into the room, views herself in the mirror a minute. Hastily she goes to the sofa, reaches under it and pulls out the suit. Without taking off her dress she dons the costume which is like Jones' except for a bright golden plume on the hat and a large black mask. She views herself in the mirror and goes out as Ant Hetty calls from the kitchen.*)

ANT HETTY. Ruthie, Ruthie, how many mo' times has I got to call you? (*Entering the room fully dressed.*) I 'clare that gal's gone on. (*She rushes to the door and meets Carter entering.*) Ain't you gone yit?

CARTER. I had. Where's Ruth?

ANT HETTY. She always sets on the Riles' stoop; the steps is higher an' you can see better. I guess she's there. Why?

CARTER. Nothing particularly. I just wanted to tell her something. (*He looks for his uniform on the sofa.*)

ANT HETTY. Why don't you hurry an' git in line? You'se late already.

CARTER. I want my uniform; I thought I left it here.

ANT HETTY. You taken it wid you when you left befo', didn't you?

CARTER. No, I left it right here. (*He looks nervously under the couch. The strains of "Maryland, My Maryland" are heard.*) Oh, well, it's too late now. I could never fall in in time.

ANT HETTY. (*Harshly.*) You didn't mean to go in the first place.

CARTER. Yes, I did.

ANT HETTY. But you said as how it was too warm fo' parades.

CARTER. I did, but I have changed my mind about that and a number of other things.

ANT HETTY. You sho'lly had me upset 'cause I was athinkin' you was giving up the lodge an' everythin'. I'm sartinly glad to fin' you'se still got good sense. (*The strains of the music are heard again. Ant Hetty opens the street door wide and sits in the doorway. Carter looks from the window.*) I won't make the corner now. I guess I kin see jest as well from the stoop mebbe. You'd better set here wid me.

CARTER. No, I don't think it wise to be seen. I'm here and not here.

ANT HETTY. You'll have to tell them that you was called on a mattah of life an' death.

CARTER. All right, Ant Hetty, I guess I shall have to depend on you to help me tell it. (*The strains of music grow louder and there is silence for a minute as both Ant Hetty and Carter watch intently.*)

ANT HETTY. Doctor, ain't they gran'? In the twilight, they looks jest lak 'n army acomin' on. Look undah that lamppost 'cross the street. See Linda Dodd?

CARTER. Who?

ANT HETTY. Her wid the new silk parasol an' no rain in sight.

CARTER. Uh-huh!

ANT HETTY. Watch her bowin' an' scrapin' to ev'rybody jest ahopin' some-body'll ask fo' Lew.

CARTER. Which one do you call Lew? (*The music is very near.*)

ANT HETTY. That's Lew—the fella what's leadin' the ban'. I 'clare I don't know when that nigger prances mos'—when he's leadin' that ban' in per-ades or shoutin' in church on Sundays. (*They continue to look intently.*)

ANT HETTY. Doctor, look! Who's leading them Candidates?

CARTER. Only my assistant could ride for me, and that isn't he, for he's very fat. (*Pressing closer to the window.*) That's my outfit, too—mask and all!

ANT HETTY. If I didn't see you asettin' right there, I'd vow it was you. Even got that sway of yourn. (*The strains of music become fainter.*)

CARTER. Of all odd things ! How did any one get my uniform? I would have sworn that I left it right here. I wonder if I could have taken the bundle out and lost it in my hurry; but who in creation had nerve enough to wear it?

ANT HETTY. Some low-down rascal wid the nerve of Judas.

CARTER. (*Starting toward the table and reaching for his hat.*) I'm going to find out.

ANT HETTY. Wait a minute. They're disbandin' at the corner. Well, will you look at Sara Blake! She's gone to cryin' on her James' neck. An' there's Rachel Lee jest makin' a fool of herself over that no-count man. (*In dis-gust she comes into the room but goes to the window.*) I 'clare Chris jest keeps tryin' to talk to that scapegoat in your outfit. The rascal's sho in a hurry an' he's haided this way.

CARTER. (*Grasping his hat.*) Well, I'll meet him.

ANT HETTY. (*Suddenly turning away from the window, she grasps Carter's arm, and almost drags him into the kitchen.*) Now we'll fin' out somethin' 'bout this rascal.

(*As Ant Hetty closes the kitchen door, Ruth dashes in and locks the outer door. She is panting breathlessly, but without pausing she tears off the mask and helmet and undresses rapidly. A knock is heard at the outer door. She rolls the regalia together and opening the kitchen door tosses it in without looking. She opens the door for Jones who enters sword in hand.*)

JONES. (*Breathlessly.*) Where's gran' mastah?

RUTH. (*Nervously.*) Grand Master! What made you think that he was here?

JONES. You ain't foolin' Christopher Columbus Jones. I seen the one what marched in that perade come in here aracin' an' I believes you was the one.

RUTH. I—the grand master!

JONES. What'cha call yourself adoin'? Tryin' to save him—huh. You ain't bided your time right 'cause all us knowed how that doctor fella's been gittin' tir'd of us an' we's been watchin' him. When I goes back an' tells them what you done fo' him he better make hisself scarce in this neighborhood.

RUTH. But, Chris, what can you tell them?

JONES. Tell 'em that I knows the doctor got you to march fo' him in our line.

RUTH. You would tell them that!

JONES. Ruth, you oughta be 'shamed of yourself agoin' back on your own folks fo' some outside nigger. (*The kitchen door opens and Carter, dressed in the uniform, hat in hand, stands in the doorway almost overshadowing Ant Hetty who is behind him. Ruth and Jones stare at him stupidly.*)

CARTER. Good evening, inspector. Didn't our parade move along smoothly?

JONES. (*With an effort.*) Yes, sah, yes, sah, it sho did.

CARTER. Ant Hetty said she enjoyed it a great deal. What did your friends think of it?

JONES. I ain't seen my friends, but I guess I got time to speak to 'em an' ax how the new inspector done. Well, folks, I guess I'll be movin' 'lon'.

RUTH. Don't forget to tell them how grand I thought you looked.

JONES. All right. Bye, folks.

ANT HETTY. Good-by, Chris. (*She follows Jones to the door and closes it after him.*) Ruthie, how'd you evah do it?

RUTH. (*Sitting on the couch and sighing with relief.*) I don't know.

ANT HETTY. Well, you sartinly saved the doctor's skin 'cause there's mo' lak Chris jest waitin' to give him the devil up Sixth Street.

CARTER. But, Ruth, how did you ever carry it through?

RUTH. I couldn't have if you hadn't put on the suit and come in at just the right moment.

CARTER. I confess that I was a little alarmed when I came back and couldn't find that suit.

RUTH. Then you did change your mind? (*She goes toward Carter and starts to embrace him.*) Oh, Doctor—William!

ANT HETTY. There, now, ain't you got no respect fo' my presence. (*Chuckling.*) Go on, Doctor, when a gal does that much fo' a man, he oughta hug her. (*She starts toward the door.*)

RUTH. Where're you going, grandma?

ANT HETTY. Jest keep your shirt on, Miss, I'm goin'. I got to talk to Mary Riles 'bout the perade. (*Calling from the doorway.*) Lawd, child, I knows you mus' be faint wid hunger. You go right out in that kitchen an' eat 'cause nobody's fixin' to lose you. (*She goes out the front door.*)

RUTH. Yes, mam. (*Sinking on sofa exhausted.*) I'm so glad that's over.

CARTER. (*Standing before her.*) Ruth, I don't know what to say.

RUTH. Please don't let's talk about it at all. I tremble every time I think of what I did.

CARTER. (*Stooping and placing his helmet on her head.*) Very well, grand master, just as you command. (*As the curtain falls he kneels before Ruth in mock salute.*)

CURTAIN

CHRISTOPHE'S DAUGHTERS

CHARACTERS

ATHÉNAIRE } daughters of King Henry Christophe
AMÉTHISTE }
QUEEN MARIE-LOUISE,   wife of the King
BARON VASTEY, tutor to Prince Victor and
        devoted friend of the King
JEAN, nephew and chief aide of Duke Richard
MARIE,   a house servant
A SOLDIER

Time: 1820.
Place: Milot, Haiti.

SCENE: *The Grand Salon of Sans Souci, the Palace of Henry Christophe.*

The room is a very pretentious one, done in the ornate style of Louis XIV. Rich tapestries are draped over doorways and windows. Gilded chairs and divans are placed here and there. A massive throne chair on a small dais is center back, and mid stage to the left a French door leads to the balcony.

In the distance, the constant rumbling of drums is heard. Faraway shouts of an assembling mob and occasional shots sound over the valley. It is twilight. Dark shadows play in the rich hangings, and fall aslant the throne chair in which AMÉTHISTE, *the older daughter of* HENRY CRISTOPHE, *is seated. She is a young woman of dark complexion and straight body, but she is sitting bent over, with her hands cupping her chin. She glances solicitously from time to time at her young sister standing at the balcony door.*

Reprinted by permission of the author.

AMÉTHISTE. It's getting dark, Athénaire. Come off the balcony and draw the portieres.

ATHÉNAIRE. I think I am less afraid when I stand here and watch. At least I shall see them when they come.

AMÉTHISTE. Seeing will not help.

ATHÉNAIRE. Nor will drawing the portieres. You hear and I hear. From the hillsides and all down the valley they're shouting, "Down with the King! Long live Independenoe!" The horrid drums are carrying it and the peasants are singing it. Listen! (*They are silent for a second, and the cries and drum beats sound louder.*) As it grows darker, it grows worse. (*She covers her ears with her hands but does not change her position.*)

AMÉTHISTE. Once I thought I heard a voice cry, "The King is dead." I wouldn't listen; I came in.

ATHÉNAIRE. But he is not dead. God will not let him die; will He? Haiti needs him so much.

AMÉTHISTE. Haiti needs him, but Haiti needed Toussaint L'Ouverture, and the people let France take him.

ATHÉNAIRE. Once I heard our father say, "Toussaint, the Tiger, and I—we dreamt so much and have done so little."

AMÉTHISTE. But he has done much. Under him, Haiti has grown rich. A merchant marine floats in the harbor. We export now, besides sugar more coffee, cocoa, and cotton than the people ever dreamed of. We buy with produce and are paid in gold. They ought to look to the chateaux throughout the kingdom, to this palace and the citadel, La Ferriere, and see that their king's dreams are not idle. They should have pride, but they haven't. Maybe some day they will understand and be sorry.

ATHÉNAIRE. Today is the one that matters and today they hate him. All day long in little groups they have been stealing down the road to Cap Henry to join the rebels. Most of the house servants have gone, too. Only Marie waits in the dining hall. Even the soldiers he reviewed this morning and to whom he gave gold have slinked away. Why, why, I ask myself again and again.

AMÉTHISTE. Because the politicians are corrupt and stir up rebellion. The mulattoes hate a black king. They call work slavery. The landlords hate justice, and the people, who themselves benefit by labor, are lazy. There is no hope for anything different. Our father, the King, works alone. He says that to be great is to be lonely; to be magnificent is to have men hate you.

ATHÉNAIRE. But he was not magnificent this morning and still they hate him. When he came down from the balcony, dragging his poor paralyzed legs to mount his horse before the army, it was pathetic. They should have loved him for his courage, but when he fell in the mud, I heard someone jeer. I didn't wait to see them carry him in. I fled from the balcony into my chamber and wept. (*She covers her face with her hands as if to shut out the memory.*)

AMÉTHISTE. It is well that he did not see the tears when he sent for you. Tears, he says, are not becoming to princesses.

ATHÉNAIRE. Oh, sister, I hate being a princess.

AMÉTHISTE. Hush, Athénaire, you must not be a traitor, too.

ATHÉNAIRE. (*Walking back and forth.*) I cannot stand it any longer. Our father lying in there, still on his couch while we sit waiting—waiting.

AMÉTHISTE. Impatience is useless.

ATHÉNAIRE. How can one be anything else, not knowing why we wait, for what we wait? And all the time, it grows later.

AMÉTHISTE. Late enough for tea; isn't it?

ATHÉNAIRE. Let Marie spread it here. I want to stay here where I can see and hear.

(*Athénaire turns back to the window. Améthiste pulls the bell cord. There is no response. She tugs again at the bell cord.*)

AMÉTHISTE. Marie, Marie! (*There is still no answer.*)

ATHÉNAIRE. She was in the dining hall when I passed through a few minutes earlier. She must be there.

AMÉTHISTE. (*Going to the door and calling impatiently.*) Marie! Marie!

(*A young black woman creeps in from the right. She is wrapped in a gaily-colored shawl and carries a bundle behind her, which she attempts to hide by standing near the wall.*)

MARIE. (*Bowing.*) You called me, Princess?

AMÉTHISTE. Yes. I want tea spread here in the salon. (*Marie stands gazing blankly at Améthiste.*) Did you understand, Marie? I want tea served in this chamber.

MARIE. There be no time, Princess.

AMÉTHISTE. (*Growing impatient.*) Time for what? I asked for tea.

MARIE. I know, Princess, but there is time lost in the brewing of tea, and time is precious.

ATHÉNAIRE. (*Turning suddenly from the window.*) You speak strangely, today, Marie. (*Marie drops her head and shifts guiltily from foot to foot, but says nothing.*)

AMÉTHISTE. (*Seating herself in the throne chair.*) Come here, Marie. (*Marie approaches slowly, almost sullenly. As she walks away from the wall, the bundle is in full view.*) What is that bundle for? Why do you wrap yourself in a shawl? Are you cold?

MARIE. No, Princess, but the road to my home in the hills is long, and I carry food and clothes.

ATHÉNAIRE. So you're going, too. You're a deserter like all the others.

AMÉTHISTE. A traitor, Marie, who came to serve a king, and sneaks away when he has need of you. You are not fit to have looked on his face.

MARIE. No, Princess, I love my king. He was ever good to me. But my Claude, he has gone, and where he is, I must go.

AMÉTHISTE. Claude has gone and you must follow; is that it? Well, I order you to put down the bundle and take off the shawl. You shall learn a lesson of loyalty.

MARIE. (*Dropping her bundle and throwing herself at Améthiste's feet.*) Oh, Princess, do not hold me here. Me—I want to live. I can't love my Claude dead. I go back to the plantation, I see my mother again, I don't want to die. (*She crosses herself.*)

ATHÉNAIRE. And you must die if you stay here?

MARIE. Claude, he said that I must leave before nightfall.

ATHÉNAIRE. Why?

MARIE. Because Duke Richard comes then with men to burn the castle and take the King. Claude said when the drums beat, they start burning the chateaux in the Plaine du Nord. I heard the drums. Now they march here and I must leave.

AMÉTHISTE. You shall not leave. You shall remain here to greet them when they come.

MARIE. No, no, Princess, not me. I am not a king's daughter to stay here and die. I am only Marie, a girl from the hills, and I love life.

ATHÉNAIRE. She is right, Sister. Every girl is not supposed to die like a princess. Let her go back to her hills, her mother, and her Claude. Why should she stay?

MARIE. Oh, Princess Athénaire, may the Mother Mary protect you. (*She crosses herself.*)

AMÉTHISTE. The Mother Mary always protects those who are faithful to their trusts, Marie. She does not like traitors.

MARIE. (*Drawing from her bosom a charm.*) But this charm protects the hill girls when the Mother no longer will.

AMÉTHISTE. Not only a traitor, but a heathen also. (*Reaching for the charm.*) Here, give it to me.

MARIE. (*Tucking the charm back in its hiding place.*) Oh, no, Princess, I keep this though you make me stay to die.

AMÉTHISTE. How many times have I told you that those charms of the witch doctors are evil? You don't love your God. You still worship snakes.

MARIE. No, no, Princess, I believe in all of them. I love God, but I fear the snakes.

ATHÉNAIRE. Sister, let her keep her charm and her Claude. She will never understand. It brings no comfort to have her stay when her heart goes.

AMÉTHISTE. Go, and may we never see you again. (*Marie rises hastily from her knees and grasps her bundle in eager hands.*)

MARIE. May the Holy Mother protect both of you—both of you. (*Crossing herself, she stumbles out the room, bowing continually.*)

ATHÉNAIRE. Shall we go to our father and tell him what she has said?

AMÉTHISTE. I think he knows already. Word came early yesterday morning that the St. Marc troops had left Ennery. They reached Cap Henry this morning. As Marie says, they are probably waiting only until nightfall to march on us.

ATHÉNAIRE. Is that the reason Victor was sent with Doctor Stewart to Cap Henry to the English friends? Only Baron Vastey and our mother remain with our father.

AMÉTHISTE. The Prince must be safe.

ATHÉNAIRE. But they keep us here. King's daughters matter little. I don't understand why we can't flee with our father to safety up to the citadel. We could take the secret passage and reach there before nightfall.

AMÉTHISTE. We can't do that because our father is still the king and kings don't run away.

ATHÉNAIRE. So we have to stay here and wait for them to take the palace. But what will they do to our sick father—to us?

AMÉTHISTE. I don't know. We can expect anything with Duke Richard leading the rebels. You know how he hates our father. He has never forgotten that out father sent him, with many criminals, to work on the citadel for three months.

ATHÉNAIRE. Our father was powerful then, and now, it's Richard's turn.

AMÉTHISTE. (*Going to the window.*) Somewhere down there, he's talking to our men, promising them money and free rum to drive out their king. Our father called him a dirty yellow soul, and he's worse than that.

ATHÉNAIRE. Do you think Jean's with him?

AMÉTHISTE. I don't know. He's weak and spineless; he follows the Duke.

ATHÉNAIRE. But he is his nephew and chief-aide, and he has to go where the Duke goes.

AMÉTHISTE. It is well that all the traitors be together. I don't understand why God made them. Even for his own son he made a Judas. I should never have given him breath. May the Mother forgive my hatred.

ATHÉNAIRE. But I don't hate Jean.

AMÉTHISTE. He's a traitor to his king and you must hate him.

ATHÉNAIRE. And God help me, I don't.

AMÉTHISTE. Marie said she couldn't love her Claude dead, and living, you must not love Jean. Even now, the Duke and your Jean are burning the chateaux as Marie said they would. Look!

ATHÉNAIRE. (*Standing beside her sister and speaking with horror in her voice.*) The beautiful chateaux!

AMÉTHISTE. Only a rose glow and a heap of gray ashes to mark the end of all that loveliness. Do you remember the happy summers there?

ATHÉNAIRE. I loved our childhood. I shall never forget it—not even when the troops take us—not even when I am . . . (*Athénaire throws herself in the throne chair, weeping disconsolately.*)

AMÉTHISTE. One should not weep for the beauty of things past nor for the fear of things to come.

ATHÉNAIRE. Sister, I am no better than Marie of the hills. I don't want to be captured. I, too, love life.

AMÉTHISTE. Sh! I hear someone.

ATHÉNAIRE. Are the soldiers come so soon?

(*She shudders but restrains her tears.* BARON VASTEY *appears at the door to the right. He is a small emaciated black man, dressed in the elaborate regalia of Christophe's court.*)

B. VASTEY. (*Bowing.*) I bring a message from the King. The chateaux are aflame. He orders me to escort the princesses to safety. There is yet time for the secret passage.

AMÉTHISTE. Does the King agree to leave with us?

B. VASTEY. No, Princess.

ATHÉNAIRE. And Queen Marie-Louise?

B. VASTEY. The Queen remains with the King.

AMÉTHISTE. And I remain, too.

ATHÉNAIRE. But Sister, our father thought it best that we should go.

AMÉTHISTE. Our father is considerate to give us a chance to make our own decisions. Nevertheless, Christophe's daughters can no more run away than Christophe himself.

ATHÉNAIRE. But it would not be running away. The King, with his family, merely moves to safety until the rebellion is ended.

AMÉTHISTE. Our father cares nothing for safety without honor. (*Turning to Baron Vastey.*) Baron, will you say to the King—? Better still, I shall go talk with him myself. Will he see me?

B. VASTEY. I think it would please the King to see you, Princess. (*Baron Vastey bows and goes out.*)

AMÉTHISTE. (*Pausing at the door and looking at Athénaire.*) Will you go, too?

ATHÉNAIRE. I shall wait here for word of your conference. I should be more than useless there. My weakness would be little comfort to him.

AMÉTHISTE. As you will, Athénaire.

(*Améthiste goes out. Athénaire stands watching the red gleam brighten the sky. The door to the left opens cautiously. The head and shoulders of* JEAN *can be seen. He is a young mulatto with downcast, shifty eyes. His costume is that of the regular army.*)

JEAN. (*Cautiously.*) Athénaire! Athénaire!

(*Athénaire wheels hastily from the window.*)

JEAN. Have they gone? I have been outside waiting long to speak with you alone.

ATHÉNAIRE. Yes, Jean, I am alone. The King's family seems much alone anyhow. Everyone has deserted, including the servants. But why have you come back?

JEAN. (*Breathless.*) I have hastened here ahead of the troops to save you.

ATHÉNAIRE. It's too late, Jean. I can't be saved.

JEAN. Why? You have only to go with me. Jean's betrothed is safe with the soldiers.

ATHÉNAIRE. I am not your betrothed. Moreover, I can't desert my family. It is safety for all or for none.

JEAN. You will not be deserting. You will be helping your family if you will only listen to me.

ATHÉNAIRE. I am listening, Jean.

JEAN. Do you love me?

ATHÉNAIRE. Yes, Jean. Always shall I love you.

JEAN. Do you trust me?

ATHÉNAIRE. That's another matter. I am loyal to my father, the King, and therefore, I cannot trust you. You belong to Duke Richard's party.

JEAN. But all parties will be one if I succeed.

ATHÉNAIRE. Did Duke Richard send you to bargain with the King through me?

JEAN. No, I am here because I love you and want to bring peace out of this confusion.

ATHÉNAIRE. And how do you hope to do that?

JEAN. I have a plan.

ATHÉNAIRE. Duke Richard's plan?

JEAN. Duke Richard doesn't even know where I am. I left without his knowledge.

ATHÉNAIRE. And what is the plan?

JEAN. There are still men in the army who love your father, and there are those, of course, who follow my uncle. They are marching now over the road from Cap Henry. In a little while they will be in the courtyard below. You shall stand with me at the palace gate and I shall cry aloud to the men as they march in, "Look! the happy union of King Christophe's daughter and Duke Richard's nephew. The rebellion is over." All groups will be satisfied. The men want peace and we shall bring it. The King and the Duke will be reconciled.

ATHÉNAIRE. And what will Duke Richard gain?

JEAN. Only a return to the good grace of your father. With that he will be content.

ATHÉNAIRE. And if my father will not receive him?

JEAN. He will. You shall see.

ATHÉNAIRE. (*Starting toward the door.*) I shall go to my father and ask his consent.

JEAN. (*Putting out his arm to hold her.*) There is no time for that. He doesn't know how the men feel. He may not be able to understand how well the plan will work.

ATHÉNAIRE. Are you so certain then?

JEAN. Yes.

ATHÉNAIRE. Certain that the rebels will be quieted?

JEAN. Yes, if only you will come with me in time.

ATHÉNAIRE. Certain, too, that my father will still be King and that we shall live on here at Sans Souci?

JEAN. (*Uneasily.*) Yes.

ATHÉNAIRE. But why must I go and why now? Can't you meet the troops and tell them I have promised my hand?

JEAN. They will not believe. They must see. It will make you happy to know that you have restored peace for your father and his people.

ATHÉNAIRE. (*As if dreaming of a great accomplishment.*) I shall restore peace. I shall save my father. I shall make the people happy. (*Turning toward Jean.*) Very well, Jean, I shall go with you.

JEAN. (*Grasping Athénaire's hands.*) You shall always be—(*As he speaks, a loud report shatters the quiet of the room.*)

ATHÉNAIRE. What was that?

JEAN. Probably a stray shot of a soldier who has arrived early in the court-yard.

ATHÉNAIRE. No, it seemed nearer.

JEAN. (*Impatiently.*) We waste time.

ATHÉNAIRE. I shall go see. (*She breaks from his clasp as two Soldiers enter.*)

1ST SOLDIER. I am sorry, sir. I heard a shot and Duke Richard's orders were to see you back safely.

JEAN. That is quite all right. You may wait in the courtyard. (*The two Soldiers leave.*)

ATHÉNAIRE. (*Angrily.*) So Duke Richard did send you?

JEAN. I came myself.

ATHÉNAIRE. (*Firmly.*) He sent you.

JEAN. (*Faltering.*) Well, only because he hoped for peace.

ATHÉNAIRE. No, only because he hoped the union of the King's daughter and his nephew could ease the guilty conscience of the men who still nurse some little respect for their majesty. I see through his dirty little scheme now.

JEAN. It's not a dirty little scheme. It was a good idea. He said our union would end the rebellion.

ATHÉNAIRE. Certainly, end the rebellion and bring him undivided support. For that end he used you, and you would use me.

JEAN. But it isn't a matter of using.

ATHÉNAIRE. I could weep for my own stupidity. To think I believed you!

JEAN. But I do love you.

ATHÉNAIRE. You know nothing of love. Go back with your guard to your uncle and tell him Princess Athénaire is still the daughter of King Christophe.

JEAN. You mean—

ATHÉNAIRE. I mean that you had better go.

JEAN. Then you will not hear me—

ATHÉNAIRE. There is nothing more to hear.

(*She turns away from her suitor. Crestfallen, he goes out. Forgetful of the shot, she sinks on the divan, looking blankly at the door through which Jean has gone. Améthiste enters with bowed head, carrying in her arms a large sheet and two poles. She bolts the door on the left.*)

AMÉTHISTE. (*In a dry, far-away voice.*) Athénaire, our father, the King, is dead.

ATHÉNAIRE. (*Startled from her dreaming.*) Dead! Our father dead! The shot—

AMÉTHISTE. Yes, he sent the golden bullet through his brain. He could not do less.

ATHÉNAIRE. It's too horrible—Our father dead!

AMÉTHISTE. It's best that way.

ATHÉNAIRE. Best with nothing left—nothing. (*She bursts into wild weeping.*)

AMÉTHISTE. There is no time for tears. We have work to do. Already the looters may have heard. They're yelling below. We must get the body out. His body must not be mutilated. (*Shaking Athénaire who continues to weep.*) Do you hear me, Athénaire? His body must not be mutilated.

ATHÉNAIRE. I hear, Sister. What shall I do?

AMÉTHISTE. We make the stretchers. Our mother and Baron Vastey prepare the body.

ATHÉNAIRE. Then what?

AMÉTHISTE. We may have time to take him through the secret passage to the citadel. We could hide him there.

ATHÉNAIRE. Yes, we must reach the citadel. They must not have him.

(*She takes an end of the sheet from Améthiste and begins tying the ends to the poles. Silently, they work. Athénaire sobs, but works diligently. The cries below grow louder, louder. There is an imperative knock on the door to the left.*)

AMÉTHISTE. So soon the word has travelled.

JEAN. (*Calling from outside.*) Athénaire! Athénaire!

ATHÉNAIRE. That's only Jean. He has been here.

AMÉTHISTE. This evening?

ATHÉNAIRE. Yes, while you were out. He has probably come back to tell me again that he loves me.

AMÉTHISTE. We shall let him in.

ATHÉNAIRE. But I don't want to see him again.

AMÉTHISTE. (*Thoughtfully.*) You must see him again. A man could hold that mob.

ATHÉNAIRE. Jean couldn't.

AMÉTHISTE. Tell him to bribe the men. (*Reaching in her bosom.*) Here are jewels and gold. Our mother said use them. I shall go back to the others while you speak with Jean.

(*Athénaire takes the valuables. Améthiste takes the stretchers amd goes off to the right. Athénaire goes to the door to the left.*)

ATHÉNAIRE. (*In a hushed voice.*) Jean?

JEAN. Yes, let me talk to you. (*Athénaire opens the door.*) Athénaire, I had to come back.

ATHÉNAIRE. Well?

JEAN. The rioters gather below. It is not safe here. Come with me.

ATHÉNAIRE. That's impossible.

JEAN. You need not go to Duke Richard. I can't leave you here to the mercy of that mob. Just let me take you to safety.

ATHÉNAIRE. If you would have me safe, take these jewels and coins and scatter them among the rioters. Only hold them off a while.

JEAN. But Athénaire—

ATHÉNAIRE. That's the only thing you can do for me now. Will you? (*She extends her hands filled with coins and jewels.*)

JEAN. (*Taking the valuables.*) Yes. Is that all you have to say, Athénaire?

ATHÉNAIRE. That's all, Jean.

(*Jean looks once more at Athénaire, then, turns and goes out. Athénaire bolts the door and leans heavily against it. Améthiste calls in a hushed voice from the next room.*)

AMÉTHISTE. Athénaire, are you alone?

ATHÉNAIRE. Alone, Sister.

(QUEEN MARIE-LOUISE, *Vastey and Améthiste stagger into the room, bearing the stretchers weighted down with Christophe's heavy body. They put down their burden and go to the throne chair. Athénaire joins them. Silently bracing themselves against the heavy structure, they push it slowly out from the wall. Choking back hysterical sobs, Athénaire joins the procession, taking an end of the stretcher from the hand of Vastey. The group moves slowly through the opening, carrying their burden. After they have disappeared, the half-choked sobs of Athénaire can be heard. Then they are drowned by loud cries from below. "Down with the King! Long live independence!"*)

THE CURTAIN FALLS

HARRIET TUBMAN

C H A R A C T E R S

HARRIET TUBMAN
HENRY ROSS,   her brother
CATHERINE,   his sweetheart
SANDY
SABENA
THOMAS,   a white overseer
EDWARD,   another white overseer
FUGITIVE SLAVES

Place: Eastern Shore, Maryland.
Time: About the Middle of the Nineteenth Century.

SCENE: *A neck of marsh land on Eastern Shore, Maryland.*

When the curtain rises, the gray mask of twilight hangs over the swamp. Dark shadows play among the tall, straggly trees and touch threateningly the young Negro Girl and Fellow seated on a fallen log. Only the disconsolate sobbing of the girl breaks the awful stillness. The Fellow puts his arm about the Girl's shaking shoulders. She clings to him hysterically.

HENRY. Come on, Cath'rine, thar ain't no use n' yo' breakin' yo'self up lak that. Ain't Ah tole you Ah'm comin' back to git you?

CATHERINE. (*In a tear-choked voice*) You can't git back.

HENRY. Ain't Harriet comin' back wid ev'ry slave town 'twixt heah an' Canada off'ring forty thousand dollars foh huh?

CATHERINE. But the Lord leads Harriet. She says she talks wid God.

HENRY. An' why can't the Lord lead me? Ah'm Harriet's brother, an' besides Ah love you. Ah won't neber close mah eyes in peace, Ah won't neber dream no sweet dreams, even in Canada, 'til Ah gits you 'way from heah. Freedom won't be nothin' without you.

CATHERINE. Ah knows, but Ah'm scared. Mas'r Charles am so mean!

HENRY. Well, it ain't too late. You can still make up yo' mind to go wid us. Harriet'll take you.

CATHERINE. Ah gis Harriet wouldn't mind. She's jes lak a angel. Ah don' know no other slave what's got free an' come back all the way from Canada nine or ten times to git others free—an' wid 'em watchin' foh huh, too.

HENRY. Harriet say when she first crossed the line an' knowed she was free, she made up huh mind that, God helpin' huh, she'd come back to Maryland an' make huh folks free, too.

CATHERINE. She really ought'n be a-comin' at this time though—wid Mas'r Charles so mad at huh. He jes' put up a new reward for huh yistiddy.

HENRY. She had to come now, if she was a-comin' a-tall. She send word through that this was the bes' time foh huh an' the friends what helps huh 'lon' the way. 'Sides that, if we starts foh freedom tonight, being'st it's Saturday, no advertisements kin be sent on Sunday. That'll put us one day 'head o' 'em. That's the way Harriet figures.

CATHERINE. Ah jes' pray no trouble come up.

HENRY. Ain't no trouble Harriet can't beat. You needn't be scared to come wid us.

CATHERINE. No, you'd neber git 'way wid me in the band. The other Mas'rs on the Eastern Sho' is kinda lazy, but Mas'r Charles's still mad 'bout Joe runnin' 'way wid Harriet the las' time she came down. Thar ain't no way in the worl' he'd let another slave o' his'n git to Canada no time soon. If Ah went now, he'd git out the bloodhounds, cover the roads, an' drag the Ches'peake, too; then he'd catch all o' you.

HENRY. But he didn' catch Joe.

CATHERINE. But look at them advertisements he's put up all ovah the county—fifteen hundred dollars, they say, he's off'red, an all 'spenses clar an' clean foh his body in Eastern Jail.

HENRY. An' Joe safe in Canada, laffin' at him. An' we'll laff, too, when we git thar.

CATHERINE. No, Henry, Ah ain't goin' this time, 'cause Ah knows you'll be safer widout me. Ah didn' mean to cry that-a-way. Mah head sees clar; it's jes' mah heart that hates to hab you lebe me behin'.

HENRY. An' what 'bout Sandy?

CATHERINE. Don' you worry none 'bout him. Ah kin manage him.

HENRY. But 'spose Mistah Charles beat you, an' make you marry him?

CATHERINE. They kin marry me to him, but ain't no way in the worl' they kin make me hab him. Ah'm gonna watch an' wait ev'ry day, 'til the time Harriet send you back foh me.

HENRY. An' Ah'll come. You know Ah'll come; don' you?

(*Catherine nods her head vigorously, as if keeping back the tears. Henry draws her in his arms, kisses her fiercely, and rushes off the stage without looking back. Catherine stares after him as if stunned; then covering her face with her hands, gives vent to her grief. Upon hearing footsteps, she jumps up guiltily and wipes her eyes. She looks around fearfully.* SANDY, *a mulatto youth, has entered. He is carrying a swinging lantern, from which a dim light flickers.*)

SANDY. Hello, Cath'rine.

CATHERINE. Oh, it's you, Sandy. Mah heart was in mah mouth, Ah was that scared when you come tippin' up.

SANDY. What was you doin' down heah, all by yo'self?

CATHERINE. Nothin' much. Ah jes' sat down a-thinkin', an' fust thing Ah knowed, it was late.

SANDY. What was you thinkin' 'bout to make you so sad? You looks lak you bin cryin'.

CATHERINE. Ev'rythin' looks so sad an' dreary-lak, it make me wanta cry.

SANDY. It is kinda lonesome-lak. This ain't no place foh you, no way. Sho you ain't seen no one?

CATHERINE. No. Why?

SANDY. Thar ain't no tellin' who's 'bout. Them scalawags, lak Mistah John's niggers, might be galavantin'.

CATHERINE. Sandy, you do talk so foolish.

SANDY. That ain't so foolish neither. Up in the kitchen, they talk 'bout how one o' Mistah John's bucks lak you. Who is he?

CATHERINE. They's jes' talkin'. They don' know nothin'.

SANDY. Well, all Ah got to say is: You bettah git some good sense in yo' head, 'cause Mas'r Charles ain't neber gonna let you marry none o' Mistah John's niggers. He hates 'em all, 'cause Harriet come o' that pascel.

CATHERINE. What's the mattah wid Harriet? You talk lak you don' think she's a good woman.

SANDY. Ah ain't got nothin' to say foh, nor 'gin huh, but Mas'r Charles has. An' he say he ain't gonna let no black wench steal his niggers an' git 'way wid it.

CATHERINE. What's he gonna do 'bout that, wid huh 'way up in Canada?

SANDY. She ain't in no Canada. She's—(*He pauses, as if regretting his revelation.*)

CATHERINE. What you say 'bout Harriet?

SANDY. (*Guardedly*) Oh, don' let's talk 'bout huh. (*He sits beside Catherine on the log.*) Let's talk 'bout you an' me.

CATHERINE. What 'bout you an' me?

SANDY. Mas'r Charles say he's gonna give you to me.

CATHERINE. He ain't said that foh really?

SANDY. Sho, and what you got agin' it?

CATHERINE. But Ah don' love you.

SANDY. Why don' you? Ah love you. What's the mattah wid me?

CATHERINE. Nothin', only you don' dream the dreams Ah dream. You's jes' as happy bein' a slave as Ah'd be bein' free. You don' neber hab no thought of freedom.

SANDY. Ah don'; don' Ah! Ah gis' you won't min' marryin' me when you finds Ah'm rich.

CATHERINE. (*Throwing back her head in laughter.*) You rich, Sandy! That's funny.

SANDY. It ain't so funny as you think. (*Catherine continues laughing.*) You laff if you wants to, but Ah'll show you. This time, tomorrow, I'll hab 'nough money to buy bofe o' us free.

CATHERINE. You mus' be a-thinkin' the angel Gabriel's gonna drap a bag o' gold at yo' feet.

SANDY. Gabriel ain't got nothin' to do wid this. But money's money, an' what Ah'm tellin' you is that you kin be free widout bloodhounds on yo' tracks, if you marries me.

CATHERINE. Jes' the same, Ah do want to know who's givin' 'way that much money foh nothin'.

SANDY. It ain't foh nothin'. Mas'r Charles ain't partin' wid his money foh nothin'. Ah has to do somethin' foh it.

CATHERINE. What?

SANDY. You ain't gonna lak it, Ah gis; but we don' owe nothin' to Mistah John's niggers, an' if we kin git free, we oughtta; ought'n we?

CATHERINE. (*Catherine's voice definitely becomes conciliatory.*) Sho. What you gonna do foh it?

SANDY. Ain't you seen the notices? Mas'r Charles, hisself's gonna give me 'nough money foh bofe you an' me to go 'way from heah an' be free.

CATHERINE. You mean them notices 'bout Harriet? How kin you catch huh? The bloodhounds ain't been quick 'nough foh huh. She's slippery lak oil.

SANDY. Yeah, but she ain't planned good, this time; she's trapped huhself. She come ovah the road this evenin'. They did'n see huh then, but they knows she come. An' they ain't worried none, 'cause they knows she can't git out. Ev'ry road is watched an' them men ain't gonna see dollars slip through their han's that easy—an' she can't go t'other way.

CATHERINE. Which other way?

SANDY. By the Eastern Branch. She can't make it; the tide's high an' she couldn't git 'way from this end, wid all the boats locked up.

CATHERINE. But the boats rides free, an' thar ain't no one heah to roun' 'em up. Mas'r Charles an' them others is down the road.

SANDY. Thar's me. Ah got to do somethin' foh mah money. You see, if them runaways finds the roads is watched, an' goes foh the boats, they'll be locked tight in the boat-house, wid the key in mah pocket.

CATHERINE. An' standin' on the sho' waitin' to start foh freedom, Mas'r Charles an' t'others'll catch 'em—huh?

SANDY. No. Mas'r Charles say they ain't really a-thinkin' 'bout the watah way. He jes' hab me tie up the boats so as to make sho. What they's really gonna do is go by the back road. Mas'r Charles know; the folks in the kitchen done tole him. Already, he's done sent Mistah Eddie an' Mistah Thomas an' the res' o' the bosses down the road.

CATHERINE. Has they guns?

SANDY. Yeah.

CATHERINE. An' do you think they'd really shoot them folks?

SANDY. Sho. Lawd! heah Ah'm talkin' to you, an' it mos' dark. You go on back to the house. It ain't safe foh you heah. Ah'll see you when Ah comes back.

CATHERINE. Awright.

(*She rises and starts off the other way, as Sandy goes off the stage to the left. Cautiously, she returns. It is growing darker and darker.* SABENA, *an old woman, approaches. She is singing softly, as if to herself.*

SABENA. (*Singing.*)

> Moses, go down in Egypt,
> 'Til ole Pharaoh let me go;
> Hadn't been foh Adam's fall,
> Shouldn't hab to die atall.
> Moses, go down in Egypt,
> 'Til ole Pharaoh let me go,

CATHERINE. (*Calling gently.*) Sabena, Sabena!

SABENA. Huh?

CATHERINE. Whar's Harriet? .

SABENA. Canada, ain't she?

CATHERINE. No, Sabena. You knows bettah'n that, You got to tell me.

SABENA. Tell you what?

CATHERINE. Whar Harriet is.

SABENA. You's one o' Mistah Charley's niggers, an' Ah ain't trustin' none o' 'em, They ain't no good. (*She starts singing again.*)

CATHERINE. (*Grasping her arm.*) Lissen, Sabena, you gotta lissen to me.

SABENA. Gotta?

CATHERINE. You love Harriet, don'cha?

SABENA. What you got to do wid that?

CATHERINE. Ah love Henry. You knows that. Ah don' want him nar Harriet, neither, to git caught, an' they's trappin' 'em.

SABENA. But you ain't trappin' me.

CATHERINE. Ah ain't tryin' to trap you. Ah want to save Harriet—an' Henry.

SABENA. Sho, you do.

CATHERINE. Then, you ain't gonna tell me?

SABENA. You foun' out that much; now fin' out the res'. (*She shakes Catherine's hand from her arm.*)

CATHERINE. Neber min'. Ah'll fin' huh, mahself. She musta stop past to see huh mammy an' pappy. Ah'll go thar. Thar ain't no time to waste; but if Henry comes this way, you'd bettah tell him to wait foh me.

(*Catherine runs rapidly off the stage to the left. One by one, the* SLAVES, *some men, some women, enter. They are carrying lanterns; and as they steal in to join the assembled band, they are crooning softly*):

> Oh, Freedom! Oh, Freedom!
> Oh, Freedom, ovah me, ovah me.
> Rather than to be a slave,
> Ah'd be burried in mah grave,
> An' go on to mah Lawd an' be free.

(HARRIET TUBMAN *comes cautiously in. Henry is at her side. The men and women fall on their knees and kiss her dress.*)

HARRIET. Git up off o' yo' knees; we's got to be startin', an' the way is long, Ah tell you. Once started, you gotta go on or die—thar ain't gonna be no turnin' back.

(*The Slaves groan softly.*)

HENRY. How far we goin'?

HARRIET. Ah takes mah people clar off to Canada. Ah can't trus' Uncle Sam wid 'em.

HENRY. Even if they's trailin' us?

HARRIET. Always they's trailin' you—clar to the line an' back. They was watchin' foh me today, but they ain't caught me. We's the fools an' they's the wise men; but Ah warn't fool 'nough to go down the high road in the broad daylight.

HENRY. Was they watchin' the road?

HARRIET. Sho, but Ah always knows when thar is danger near me. 'Pears lak mah heart go flutter, flutter, an' they may say, "Peace! peace!" as much as they lak; Ah knows it's gwine to be war.

HENRY. If they was watchin' the road, they's on to us.

HARRIET. Ah ain't scared one jot. Ah always trust the Lawd. Ah says to him, "Ah don' know whar to go, or what to do, but Ah 'spects you to lead me." An' he always do. Now, them what trusts wid me, kin follow; the res' kin stay heah. We takes the back road.

(*The Slaves say "Amen!" in chorus. Some groan softly. Harriet starts off stage. Sabena comes forward and grasps Harriet's arm.*)

SABENA. Harriet, you got to be careful down heah, an' go kinda slow.

HARRIET. John saw the city, didn' he? Well, what did he see? Twelve gates—three o' them gates was on the North, three o' 'em was on the East, three o' 'em was on the West; but thar was three o' 'em on the South, too. An' Ah reckon if they kill me down heah, Ah'll git into one o' them gates, don'cha?

SABENA. But we don' want you to walk right into them rascals' hands.

HARRIET. Ain't we takin' the back road? Why you so het up?

SABENA. A gal was heah a-talkin'.

HARRIET. What gal?

SABENA. One o' Mistah Charley's gals.

HENRY. (*Eagerly.*) Which one, Sabena? Not Cath'rine?

SABENA. Yeah, the one that say she loves you.

HENRY. What'd she say?

SABENA. Somethin' 'bout you waitin' heah foh huh. She only went as far as Ben's an' Ritty's, a-lookin' foh Harriet. She say thar's trouble foh Harriet.

HARRIET. Trouble or no trouble—thar's two things Ah got a right to, an' they is death an' liberty. One or t'other, Ah mean to have. No one will take me back into slavery alive. Ah'll fight foh mah liberty, an' when the time come foh me to go, the Lawd'll let'em kill me.

HENRY. But Harriet, if Cath'rine say that Ah'm waitin', she'll be back 'mos' anytime now

HARRIET. Well, Ah can't wait on no scattah-brain gal.

HENRY. But she ain't scattah-brain; she loves me.

HARRIET. (*Pausing.*) She loves you, huh? Does you love huh?

HENRY. So much, Harriet, that Ah'd come back from Canada ten times, lak you done, jes' to git huh free.

HARRIET. Then we's waitin'. Ah trusts the sense o' a man in love, 'cause God speaks in him then.

(*The Slaves say, "Amen" softly. They sing softly*):

> Aroun' him are ten thousan' angels,
> Always ready to 'bey comman';
> They is always hov'rin' 'roun' you,
> 'Til you reach the hebbenly lan'.
> Dark an' thorny is the desert.
> Through the pilgrim make his ways;
> Yet beyon' this field o' sorrow,
> Lies the fields of endless days.

HARRIET. Hush! Ah hear someone!

(*The Slaves disappear into the shadows. Catherine rushes on the stage exhausted. She looks madly around. Henry calls to her softly.*)

HENRY. Cath'rine, Cath'rine, what's the mattah?

CATHERINE. (*Panting.*) Henry, tell Harriet she can't take none o' the roads.

HARRIET. (*Stepping forth.*) What's that?

CATHERINE. (*Clutching Harriet's arm.*) Harriet, they's watchin' ev'ry road an' path. You can't git out. You'd bettah hide.

HARRIET. Me stay heah! Ah'll git out. We'll take the rivah.

CATHERINE. They's locked up the boats.

HARRIET. Jesus walked the watah, an Ah've waded many a stream.

HENRY. You can't wade this one; the tide's high. We'd be washed down lak Pharaoh's army. Cath'rine, how you know the boats is locked up?

CATHERINE. Sandy's lockin' 'em up. But you all's got to git 'way from heah. He'll be 'long in a minute. Ah come that away, an' he was 'mos' nigh finished.

HENRY. Orn'ry nigger! We'll knock down the do' an' take them boats.

HARRIET. An' hab ev'ryone heah the noise, an' come down on our heads at once, huh?

CATHERINE. But you can't git 'em no other way, Sandy's got the key.

HARRIET. He ain't got to keep it. Didn' you say he was a-comin' this way?

CATHERINE. He's jes' down to the boathouse. He'll be heah any minute.

HARRIET. Well, we'll git that key, if Ah hab to take it.

HENRY. No. If Cath'rine call him, he'd come to huh. He laks huh.

HARRIET. That's good. Now Cath'rine, if you would kinda git him to stop a minute when he come alon' . . .

CATHERINE. Ah could. Ah know Ah could. But you bettah hurry an' don' let him see you. Ah'll call to him an' see if he's started back.

HARRIET. No. We can't take no chances. You walk on down the road an' meet him, while we git things a bit straight. When you come back wid him, sing loud 'nough foh us to heah you comin'.

CATHERINE. Awright, an' we'll stop neah this heah big log.

HENRY. Then we'll 'ten' to the res'. (*Catherine goes off stage to the left.*)

HARRIET. We oughtta tie him up so as he can't git to the road; but whar kin we fin' rope this time o' night?

SABENA. To tie one o' Mistah Charley's limbs o' Satan, you kin hab this frum 'roun' mah bundle.

ANOTHER SLAVE. An' mine, too. Thar ain't no place in no boat foh all these trappin's, no how.

HARRIET. (*Taking the rope as the Slaves untie their bundles.*) Now, Henry, when they stops heah, you, an' two o' them others, grab him from behin'.

SABENA. An jes' hopes that gal o' Mistah Charley's ain't trickin' us.

HENRY. Sabena, you's plumb crazy. Thar ain't no way in the worl' foh Cath'rine to be trickin' me.

SABENA. You know, young gals lak money, an' thar's men when thar ain't money.

HARRIET. An' money an' men ain't nothin' widout freedom. Heah, Henry, take the rope.

SABENA. Ah only hopes you won't hab to wish you could string up the gal, too.

HARRIET. Hush yo' squabblin'; we ain't got no time foh that. Ah think Ah heah some singin' now. Git back in them shadows—out o' the clearin'.

(*The Slaves go to the back of the stage and crouch low. In the distance, growing nearer and nearer, comes Catherine's voice. She is singing "GO DOWN, MOSES." Sandy and Catherine enter.*)

SANDY. Why you sing that ole song?

CATHERINE. Ah lak it; don' you? It makes me think o' goin' 'way from heah.

SANDY. This time tomorrow, you kin be goin' if you says so. An' it won't be no foolin', neither, lak them folks tonight.

CATHERINE. Whar you think they is by now?

SANDY. They ain't come this way, so Ah gis' they got stopped on the road.

CATHERINE. An' if they does come heah, they can't git nowhar, huh—(*She stops and speaks distinctly.*) wid the key safe an' soun' in yo' hip pocket?

SANDY. That they can't!

(*Two Men grab him quickly from behind. Henry goes rapidly through his pockets and finds the key.*)

HENRY. Ah got it—Ah got it!

SANDY. (*Struggling.*) Turn me loose. Mas'r Charles'll kill you, if you take that.

HARRIET. Shet up, shet up, you Judas o' yo' own people. You oughtta burn in torment. Tie him up.

(*The Men begin to tie his hands and feet. He attempts to scream. They clap their hands over his mouth.*)

SANDY. (*Struggling and trying to shout at Catherine*) You two-faced devil! Ah'll tell Mas'r Charles, an' he'll break ev'ry bone in yo' dirty, lyin' body.

HARRIET. Shet up! Ah hates to lebe you livin' anyhow. If you yells out thar once mo', Ah'll choke the breath out o' yo' worthless body wid mah bare han's.

CATHERINE. He's right. Mas'r'll kill me, when he know it. You gotta take me wid you.

HARRIET. Sho! An' you ain't thinkin' Ah'd be a-leavin' no smart gal lak you behin'.

HENRY. Cath'rine, you's goin', too! Then, when we git to Canada, we kin git married lak real folks.

HARRIET. Hush yo' nonsense, Henry, Thar ain't no time foh that now—it'll keep 'til we git thar. You stay heah, an' finish tyin' him up, an' keep his mouth shet while we git to the rivah. You kin catch up. Come on, folks, you's boun' foh Canaan.

(*Harriet leads the little procession off stage to the left. Henry ties Sandy and drags him behind the log, stuffing a rag, from Sabena's bundle, into his mouth.*)

HENRY. Wid yo' mouth shet, maybe you kin think a li'l. An' jes' remember when you gits yo' reward foh tellin' on yo' own folks, that Ah got Cath-'rine.

(*Henry goes off stage. Sandy rolls and struggles, groaning. Finally, he gets the gag out of his mouth. He calls weakly, at frst, then louder.*)

SANDY. Mas'r Charles! Mas'r Charles! Mas'r Charles! (EDWARD enters.)

EDWARD. Hello! hello! Did someone call?

SANDY. It's me. (*Edward holds his lantern high.*)

EDWARD. Where? Where the devil are you?

SANDY. (*Weakly.*) Heah. Heah, behin' the log.

EDWARD. Well, I'll be damned. What the devil are you doin' here?

SANDY. They tied me.

EDWARD. Who tied you?

SANDY. Harriet an' them.

EDWARD. They ain't been this way, have they? The men're watchin' for 'em down the road. They plan to come that way.

SANDY. They's gone.

EDWARD. Gone where?

SANDY. To the rivah.

EDWARD. They can't git away. Mistah Charles said the boats was locked up.

SANDY. Ah did lock 'em up, but they taken the key.

EDWARD. I oughtta hang you—lettin' 'em git that key. Mistah Charles is gonna raise the devil. (*He works roughly at Sandy's bonds*)

SANDY. (*Half sobbing.*) They beat me—they beat me an' taken the key.

EDWARD. (*Roughly.*) Shut up, an' git out of these ropes. We can beat 'em yet. (THOMAS *enters from the left.*)

THOMAS. Who's there?

EDWARD. That you, Tom?

THOMAS. Yeah. Who's on the river?

EDWARD. On the river? Have they made the river?

THOMAS. Jes' pushed off. Who was it?

EDWARD. That Harriet, I guess, an' another pascel of niggers gittin' away.

THOMAS. Damn it! A minute sooner, an' I'd had 'em. Did you catch one of 'em?

EDWARD. No. It's only Sandy. They tied him up.

THOMAS. Mistah Charles left him to watch the river-stretch, 'cause he said nobody was comin' that way. I tried to tell him; but, no, he believed the niggers, an' they said "the back road."

EDWARD. Didn' you shoot?

THOMAS. Mistah Charles kept my gun for a fellow down the road. He was that certain. 'Sides, I warn't sure 'twas them. I called but they didn' answer.

EDWARD. Can't we follow 'em?

THOMAS. Not a chance. They're 'bout midstream by now. 'Sides, they musta cut ev'ry damned boat, 'cause the rest are ridin' wild on this high tide.

EDWARD. They got the key from this nigger.

THOMAS. Mistah Charles's gonna sell you down the river.

SANDY. They beat me! They beat me an' taken the key!

EDWARD. Shut up, you blubberin' fool, an' git back to the house. (*Sandy goes off still tugging at the ropes on one arm.*)

THOMAS. That black witch works like magic.

EDWARD. Yeah, damn it—slippin' out like that, with forty thousand dollars on her head. (*Slowly they start off stage together as the*

CURTAIN FALLS)

Marita Bonner

(1899–1971)

Marita Bonner about 1928. (*Courtesy of The Crisis Publication*)

Why do they see a colored woman only as a gross collection of desires, all uncontrolled, reaching out for the Apollos and the Quasimodos with avid indiscrimination?[1]

IN 1964, PLAYWRIGHT ADRIENNE KENNEDY was awarded an Obie for her surrealistic play *Funnyhouse of a Negro* (1962). This play commanded attention primarily because Kennedy deviated from the realistic style of writing that was prevalent among black writers. She would eventually adapt this surrealistic style of writing for many of her works. Although Kennedy's work was considered revolutionary for a black, Marita Bonner had embraced this same style of writing almost thirty-five years earlier with her play *The Purple Flower* (1928).

While Bonner's period as a playwright was brief, her three known plays—*The Purple Flower*, *Exit: An Illusion* (1929), and *The Pot Maker* (1927)—are significant because she dared to divert from the realistic pattern that was expected of the early black dramatists. She is credited with having written another play, *Muddled Dream*, which unfortunately cannot be located.

Marita Bonner was born in Boston in 1899 and educated at Brookline High School, where she excelled in music and German. She entered Radcliffe College in 1918 and, while there, had the opportunity to study creative writing under Professor Charles Townsend Copeland. Upon graduation from Radcliffe in 1922 with an A.B., Bonner taught in West Virginia and then in Washington, D.C., at Armstrong High School.

While in Washington, D.C., Bonner attended Georgia Johnson's famous S Street gatherings and became a member of the Krigwa Players. It was during this period that Bonner's first work, "The Hands—A Story," was published in the August 1925 edition of *Opportunity*. Following this entry, Bonner became a regular contributor to *Opportunity* and *Crisis* magazine with her short stories, essays, reviews, and plays until 1941.

It was her friend Georgia Douglas Johnson who encouraged Bonner to attempt playwriting. Her first play, *The Pot Maker*, with its rural and simple setting, shows the strong influence of Johnson. Her second piece, *The Purple Flower*, goes totally beyond the realistic mode with its allegorical characters and setting. The play examines the black man's struggle for freedom in a racist society. Her last known extant play, *Exit: An Illusion*, explores the revenge of a jealous lover. The message in the play, however, goes much deeper:

Exit: An Illusion, gives the reader a feeling of urgency and deals with the problem of acceptance within the black community. Although on the surface a naturalistic drama about a jealous lover's revenge, it ultimately appears to be about

Buddy's destruction of Dot through his permanent suspicion and hatred of the white side of her mixed ancestry.[2]

There is no evidence that any of Bonner's plays were ever produced despite the fact that *The Purple Flower* won the 1927 Crisis award for best play. According to speculation, Bonner's plays were never staged because of their demanding technical requirements, particularly compared to the other plays written at the time.

In 1930 Bonner married William Almy Occomy. The couple moved to Chicago where they raised three children. Bonner died in 1971.

NOTES

1. Marita Bonner, "On Being Young—A Woman—And Colored," *Crisis*, December 31, 1925.

2. Joyce Flynn, "Marita Bonner," in *Afro-American Writers from the Harlem Renaissance to 1940*, ed. Trudier Harris, Vol. 51 (Detroit: Gale Research Company, 1987), p. 51.

THE PURPLE FLOWER

CHARACTERS

Sundry White Devils (They must be artful little things with soft wide eyes such as you would expect to find in an angel. Soft hair that flops around their horns. Their horns glow red all the time—now with blood—now with eternal fire—now with deceit—now with unholy desire. They have bones tied carefully across their tails to make them seem less like tails and more like mere decorations. They are artful little things full of artful movements and artful tricks. They are artful dancers too. You are amazed at their adroitness. Their steps are intricate. You almost lose your head following them. Sometimes they dance as if they were men—with dignity—erect. Sometimes they dance as if they were snakes. They are artful dancers on the Thin-Skin-of-Civilization.)

The Us's (They can be as white as the White Devils, as brown as the earth, as black as the center of a poppy. They may look as if they were something or nothing.)

Time: The Middle-of-Things-as-They-Are. (Which means the End-of-Things for some of the characters and the Beginning-of-Things for others.)

Place: Might be here, there or anywhere—or even nowhere.

SETTING: *The stage is divided horizontally into two sections, upper and lower, by a thin board. The main action takes place on the upper stage. The light is never quite clear on the lower stage; but it is bright enough for you to perceive that sometimes the action that takes place on the upper stage is duplicated on the lower. Sometimes the actors on the upper stage get too vociferous—too violent— and they crack through the boards and they lie twisted and curled in mounds. There are any number of mounds there, all twisted and broken. You look at them and you are not quite sure whether you see something or nothing; but you see by a curve that there might lie a human body. There is thrust out a white hand—a yellow one—one brown—a black. The Skin-of-Civilization must be very thin. A thought can drop you through it.*

Scene: An open plain. It is bounded distantly on one side by Nowhere and faced by a high hill—Somewhere.

Argument: The White Devils live on the side of the hill. Somewhere. On top of the hill grows the purple Flower-of-Life-at-Its-Fullest. This flower is as tall as a pine and stands alone on top of the hill. The Us's live in the valley that lies between Nowhere and Somewhere and spend their time trying to devise means of getting up the hill. The White Devils live all over the sides of the hill and try every trick, known and unknown, to keep the Us's from getting to the hill. For if the Us's get up the hill, the Flower-of-Life-at-Its-Fullest will shed some of its perfume and then there they will be Somehwere with the White Devils. The Us's started out by merely asking permission to go up. They tilled the valley, they cultivated it and made it as beautiful as it is. They built roads and houses even for the White Devils. They let them build the houses and then they were knocked back down into the valley.

Scene: When the curtain rises, the evening sun is shining bravely on the valley and hillside alike.
The Us's *are having a siesta beside a brook that runs down the Middle of the valley. As usual they rest with their backs toward Nowhere and their faces toward Somewhere. The* WHITE DEVILS *are seen in the distance on the hillside. As you see them, a song is borne faintly to your ears from the hillside. The White Devils are saying:*

> You stay where you are!
> We don't want you up here!
> If you come you'll be on par
> With all we hold dear.
> So stay—stay—stay—
> Yes stay where you are!

The song rolls full across the valley.

A LITTLE RUNTY US. Hear that, don't you?

ANOTHER US. (*lolling over on his back and chewing a piece of grass*) I ain't studying 'bout them devils. When I get ready to go up that hill—I'm going! (*He rolls over on his side and exposes a slender brown body to the sun.*) Right now, I'm going to sleep. (*And he forthwith snores.*)

OLD LADY. (*an old dark brown lady who has been lying down rises suddenly to her knees in the foreground. She gazes toward the hillside*) I'll never live to see the face of that flower! God knows I worked hard to get Somewhere though. I've washed the shirt off of every one of them White Devils' backs!

A YOUNG US. And you got a slap in the face for doing it.

OLD LADY. But that's what the Leader told us to do. "Work," he said. "Show them you know how." As if two hundred years of slavery had not showed them!

ANOTHER YOUNG US. Work doesn't do it. The Us who work for the White Devils get pushed in the face—down off of Somewhere every night. They don't even sleep up there.

OLD LADY. Something's got to be done though! The Us ain't got no business to sleep while the sun is shining. They'd ought to be up and working before the White Devils get to some other tricks.

YOUNG US. You just said work did not do you any good! What's the need of working if it doesn't get you anywhere? What's the use of boring around in the same hole like a worm? Making the hole bigger to stay in?

(*There comes up the road a clatter of feet and four figures, a middle-aged well-browned man, a lighter-browned middle-aged woman, a medium light brown girl, beautiful as a browned peach, and a slender, tall, bronzy brown youth who walks with his head high. He touches the ground with his feet as if it were a velvet rug and not sunbaked, jagged rocks.*)

OLD LADY. (*addressing the Older Man*) Evenin', Average. I was just saying we ain't never going to make that hill.

AVERAGE. The Us will if they get the right leaders.

THE MIDDLE-AGED WOMAN—CORNERSTONE. Leaders! Leaders! They've had good ones looks like to me.

AVERAGE. But they ain't led us anywhere!

CORNERSTONE. But that is not their fault! If one of them gets up and says, "Do this," one of the Us will sneak up behind him and knock him down and stand up and holler, "Do that," and then he himself gets knocked down and we still sit in the valley and knock down and drag out!

A YOUNG US. (*aside*) Yeah! Drag Us out, but not White Devils.

OLD LADY. It's the truth, Cornerstone. They say they going to meet this evening to talk about what we ought to do.

AVERAGE. What is the need of so much talking?

CORNERSTONE. Better than not talking! Somebody might say something after while.

THE YOUNG GIRL—SWEET. (*who just came up*) I want to talk too!

AVERAGE. What can you talk about?

SWEET. Things! Something, father!

THE YOUNG MAN—FINEST BLOOD. I'll speak too.

AVERAGE. Oh you all make me tired! Talk—talk—talk—talk! And the flower is still up on the hillside!

OLD LADY. Yes and the White Devils are still talking about keeping the Us away from it, too.

(*A drum begins to beat in the distance. All the Us stand up and shake off their sleep. The drummer, a short, black, determined-looking Us, appears around the bushes beating the drum with strong, vigorous jabs that make the whole valley echo and re-echo with rhythm. Some of the Us begin to dance in time to the music.*)

AVERAGE. Look at that! Dancing!! The Us will never learn to be sensible!

CORNERSTONE. They dance well! Well!!

(*The Us all congregate at the center front. Almost naturally, the Young Us range on one side, the old Us on the other. Cornerstone sits her plump brown self comforably in the center of the stage. An old Us tottering with age and blind comes toward her.*)

OLD US. What's it this time, chillun? Is it day yet? Can you see the road to that flower?

AVERAGE. Oh you know we ain't going to get up there! No use worrying!

CORNERSTONE. No it's not day! It is still dark. It is night.

(*For the sun has gone and purple blackness has lain across the Valley. Somehow, though, you can see the shape of the flower on top of Somewhere. Lights twinkle on the hill.*)

OLD US. (*speaking as if to himself*) I'm blind from working—building for the White Devils in the heat of the noon-day sun and I'm weary!

CORNERSTONE. Lean against me so they won't crowd you.

(*An old man rises in the back of the ranks; his beard reaches down to his knees but he springs upright. He speaks.*)

OLD MAN. I want to tell you all something! The Us can't get up the road unless we work! We want to hew and dig and toil!

A YOUNG US. You had better sit down before someone knocks you down! They told us that when your beard was sprouting.

CORNERSTONE. (*to youth*). Do not be so stupid! Speak as if you had respect for that beard!

ANOTHER YOUNG US. We have! But we get tired of hearing "you must work" when we know the old Us built practically every inch of that hill and are yet Nowhere.

FIRST YOUNG US. Yes, all they got was a rush down the hill—not a chance to take a step up!

CORNERSTONE. It was not time then.

OLD MAN. (*on the back row*) Here comes a Young Us who has been reading in the books! Here comes a Young Us who has been reading in the books! He'll tell us what the books say about getting Somewhere.

(*A Young Man pushes through the crowd. As soon as he reaches the center front, he throws a bundle of books.*)

YOUNG MAN. I'm through! I do not need these things! They're no good!

OLD MAN. (*pushes up from the back and stands beside him*) You're through! Ain t you been reading in the books how to get Somewhere? Why don't you tell us how to get there?

YOUNG MAN. I'm through I tell you! There isn't anything in one of these books that tells Black Us how to get around White Devils.

OLD MAN. (*softly—sadly*) I thought the books would tell us how!

YOUNG MAN. No! The White Devils wrote the books themselves. You know they aren't going to put anything like that in there!

YET ANOTHER OLD MAN. (*throwing back his head and calling into the air*) Lord! Why don't you come by here and tell us how to get Somewhere?

A YOUNG MAN (*who had been idly chewing grass*) Aw, you ought to know by now that isn't the way to talk to God!

OLD MAN. It ain't! It ain't! It ain't! It ain't! Ain't I been talking to God just like that for seventy years? Three score and ten years—Amen!

THE GRASS CHEWER. Yes! Three score and ten years you been telling God to tell you what to do. Telling Him! And three score and ten years you been wearing your spine double sitting on the rocks in the valley too.

OLD US. He is all powerful! He will move in his own time!

YOUNG US. Well, if He is all powerful, God does not need you to tell Him what to do.

OLD US. Well, what's the need of me talkin' to Him then?

YOUNG US. Don't talk so much to Him! He might want to talk to you but you do so much yelling in His ears that He can't tell you anything.

(*There is a commotion in the back stage. Sweet comes running to Cornerstone crying.*)

SWEET. Oh—oo—!

CORNERSTONE. What is it, Sweet?

SWEET. There's a White Devil sitting in the bushes in the dark over there! There's a White Devil sitting in the bushes over in the dark! And when I walked by—he pinched me!

FINEST BLOOD. (*catching a rock*) Where is he, sister? (*He starts toward the bushes.*)

CORNERSTONE. (*screaming*) Don't go after him son! They will kill you if you hurt him!

FINEST BLOOD. I don't care if they do. Let them. I'd be out of this hole then!

AVERAGE. Listen to that young fool! Better stay safe and sound where he is! At least he got somewhere to eat and somewhere to lay his head.

FINEST BLOOD. Yes I can lay my head on the rocks of Nowhere.

(*Up the center of the stage toils a new figure of a square-set middle-aged Us. He walks heavily for in each hand he carries a heavy bag. As soon as he reaches the center front he throws the bags down groaning as he does so.*)

AN OLD MAN. 'Smatter with you? Ain't them bags full of gold.

THE NEWCOMER. Yes, they are full of gold!

OLD MAN. Well why ain't you smiling then? Them White Devils can't have anything no better!

THE NEWCOMER. Yes they have! They have Somewhere! I tried to do what they said. I brought them money, but when I brought it to them they would not sell me even a spoonful of dirt from Somewhere! I'm through!

CORNERSTONE. Don't be through. The gold counts for something. It must!
(*An Old Woman cries aloud in a quavering voice from the back.*)

OLD LADY. Last night I had a dream.

A YOUNG US. Dreams? Excuse me! I know I'm going now! Dreams!

OLD LADY. I dreamed that I saw a White Devil cut in six pieces—head here (*pointing*), body here—one leg here—one there—an arm here—an arm there.

AN OLD MAN. Thank God! It's time then!

AVERAGE. Time for what? Time to eat? Sure ain't time to get Somewhere!

OLD MAN. (*walking forward*) It's time! It's time! Bring me an iron pot!

YOUNG US. Aw don't try any conjuring!

OLD MAN. (*louder*) Bring me a pot of iron. Get the pot from the fire in the valley.

CORNERSTONE. Get him the pot! (*Someone brings it up immediately.*)

OLD MAN. (*walking toward pot slowly*) Old Us! Do you hear me. Old Us that are here do you hear me?

ALL THE OLD US. (*cry in chorus*) Yes, Lord! We hear you! We hear you!

OLD MAN. (*crying louder and louder*) Old Us! Old Us! Old Us that are gone, Old Us that are dust do you hear me?
(*His voice sounds strangely through the valley. Somewhere you think you hear—as if mouthed by ten million mouths through rocks and dust—"Yes—Lord!—We hear you! We hear you"!*)
And you hear me—give me a handful of dust! Give me a handful of dust! Dig down to the depths of the things you have made! The things you formed with your hands and give me a handful of dust!
(*An Old Woman tottering with the weakness of old age crosses the stage and going to the pot, throws a handful of dust in. Just before she sits down again she throws back her head and shakes her cane in the air and laughs so that the entire valley echoes.*)

A YOUNG US. What's the trouble! Choking on the dust?

OLD WOMAN. No, child! Rejoicing!

YOUNG US. Rejoicing over a handful of dust?

OLD WOMAN. Yes. A handful of dust! Thanking God I could do something if it was nothing but make a handful of dust!

YOUNG US. Well dust isn't much!

OLD MAN. (*at the pot*) Yes, it isn't much! You are dust yourself; but so is she. Like everything else, though, dust can be little or much, according to where it is.

(The Young Us who spoke subsides. He subsides so completely that he crashes through the Thin-Skin-of-Civilization. Several of his group go too. They were thinking.)

OLD MAN. *(at the pot)* Bring me books! Bring me books!

YOUNG US. *(who threw books down)* Take all these! I'll light the fire with them.

OLD MAN. No, put them in the pot. *(Young Us does so.)* Bring me gold!

THE MAN OF THE GOLD BAGS. Here take this! It is just as well. Stew it up and make teething rings!! *(He pours it into the pot.)*

OLD MAN. Now bring me blood! Blood from the eyes, the ears, the whole body! Drain it off and bring me blood! *(No one speaks or moves.)* Now bring me blood! Blood from the eyes, the ears, the whole body! Drain it off! Bring me blood!! *(No one speaks or moves.)* Ah hah, hah! I knew it! Not one of you willing to pour his blood in the pot!

YOUNG US *(facetiously)* How you going to pour your own blood in there? You got to be pretty far gone to let your blood run in there. Somebody else would have to do the pouring.

OLD MAN. I mean red blood. Not yellow blood, thank you.

FINEST BLOOD. *(suddenly)* Take my blood! *(He walks toward the pot.)*

CORNERSTONE. O no! Not my boy! Take me instead!

OLD MAN. Cornerstone we cannot stand without you!

AN OLD WOMAN. What you need blood for? What you doing anyhow? You ain't told us nothing yet. What's going on in that pot?

OLD MAN. I'm doing as I was told to do.

A YOUNG US. Who told you to do anything?

OLD MAN. God. I'm His servant.

YOUNG US. *(who spoke before)* God? I haven't heard God tell you anything.

OLD MAN. You couldn't hear. He told it to me alone.

OLD WOMAN. I believe you. Don't pay any attention to that simpleton! What God told you to do?

OLD MAN. He told me take a handful of dust—dust from which all things came and put it in a hard iron pot. Put it in a hard iron pot. Things shape best in hard molds!! Put in books that Men learn by. Gold that Men live by. Blood that lets Men live.

YOUNG US. What you supposed to be shaping? A man?

OLD US. I'm the servant. I can do nothing. If I do this, God will shape a new man Himself.

YOUNG MAN. What's the things in the pot for?

OLD MAN. To show I can do what I'm told.

OLD WOMAN. Why does He want blood?

OLD MAN. You got to give blood! Blood has to be let for births, to give life.

OLD WOMAN. So the dust wasn't just nothing? Thank God!

YOUTH. Then the books were not just paper leaves? Thank God!

THE MAN OF THE GOLD BAGS. Can the gold mean something?

OLD MAN. Now I need the blood.

FINEST BLOOD. I told you you could take mine.

OLD MAN. Yours!

FINEST BLOOD. Where else could you get it? The New Man must be born. The night is already dark. We cannot stay here forever. Where else could blood come from?

OLD MAN. Think child. When God asked a faithful servant once to do sacrifice, even his only child, where did God put the real meat for sacrifice when the servant had the knife upon the son's throat?!

OLD US. (*in a chorus*)

In the bushes, Lord!
In the bushes, Lord!
Jehovah put the ram
In the bushes!

CORNERSTONE. I understand!

FINEST BLOOD. What do you mean?

CORNERSTONE. Where were you going a little while ago? Where were you going when your sister cried out?

FINEST BLOOD. To the bushes! You want me to get the White Devil? (*He seizes the piece of rock and stands to his feet.*)

OLD MAN. No! No! Not that way. The White Devils are full of tricks. You must go differently. Bring him gifts and offer them to him.

FINEST BLOOD. What have I to give for a gift?

OLD MAN. There are the pipes of Pan that every Us is born with. Play on that. Soothe him—lure him—make him yearn for the pipe. Even a White Devil will soften at music. He'll come out, and he only comes to try to get the pipe from you.

FINEST BLOOD. And when he comes out, I'm to kill him in the dark before he sees me? That's a White Devil trick!

OLD MAN. An Old Us will never tell you to play White Devil's games! No! Do not kill him in the dark. Get him out of the bushes and say to him: "White Devil, God is using me for His instrument. You think that it is I who play on this pipe! You think that is I who play upon this pipe so that you cannot stay in your bushes. So that you must come out of your bushes. But it is not I who play. It is not I, it is God who plays through me—to you. Will you hear what He says? Will you hear? He says it is almost day, White Devil. The night is far gone. A New Man must be born for the New Day. Blood is needed for birth. Blood is needed for the birth. Come out, White Devil. It may be your blood—it may be mine—but blood must be taken during the night to be given at the birth. It may be my blood—it may be your blood—but everything has been given. The Us toiled to give dust for the body, books to guide the body, gold to clothe the body. Now they need blood for birth so the New Man can live. You have taken blood. You must give blood. Come out! Give it." And then fight him!

FINEST BLOOD. I'll go! And if I kill him?

OLD MAN. Blood will be given!

FINEST BLOOD. And if he kills me?

OLD MAN. Blood will be given!

FINEST BLOOD. Can there be no other way—cannot this cup pass?

OLD MAN. No other way. It cannot pass. They always take blood. They built up half their land on our bones. They ripened crops of cotton, watering them with our blood. Finest Blood, this is God's decree: "You take blood—you give blood. Full measure—flooding full—over—over!"

FINEST BLOOD. I'll go. (*He goes quickly into the shadow. Far off soon you can hear him—his voice lifted, young, sweet, brave and strong.*) White Devil! God speaks to you through me!—Hear Him!—Him! You have taken blood: there can be no other way. You will have to give blood! Blood!

(*All the Us listen. All the valley listens. Nowhere listens. All the White Devils listen. Somewhere listens. Let the curtain close leaving all the Us, the White Devils, Nowhere, Somewhere, listening, listening. Is it time?*)

EXIT: AN ILLUSION

A One-Act Play

FOREWORD

(Which presents the setting, the characters, and the argument)
The room you are in is mixed.
It is mixed.
There are ragged chairs with sorry sagging ragged bottoms.—There are
lace curtains with sorry ragged holes—but all over the chairs are scattered
clothes, mostly lingerie of the creamiest, laciest, richest, pastel-crepe vari-
ety.
Everything is mixed.
Dishes are pushed back on the table. They may be yesterday's dishes or
they may be today's. But dishes are pushed back and the tablecloth is rum-
pled back. A pair of red kid pumps are on the edge of the table. Your eyes
skip from the scarlet omen of their owner's hasty death—omen, if the bot-
tom still holds in superstition—
Shoes mixed with dishes on the table.
Newspapers, pillows, shoes and stockings are scattered across the floor,
making a path straight to an exquisite dressing-table of the variety type.
This stands at the extreme right of the stage.
There is a window at right back—nearly at the center—through which
you see snow falling. Directly beside the window there is a door which must
lead into an inner hall. It is not stout enough to be an outer door. It is the
brownish sort of nondescript door that shuts a cheap flat off from the rest of
the world.
On the left side of the room is an open couch-bed. The sheets and blankets
depend almost to the floor in uneven jags. Easily, then, you can see the fig-
ure of a woman lying there. Her hair which is a light brown—lies with a
thick waving around her head. Her face—thin—is almost as pale as the
sheets. She is sleeping with an arm hung over the side of the bed. Even
though she keeps tossing and twitching as if she would come awake, she
holds her arm over the side.

Down on the floor on the same side, lying so that her arm falls across him—there is a man. A part of his face shows against the bed-clothes and you can see he is blackly brown with the thin high-poised features that mark a "keen black man."

You can see at a glance that his slender body is cast for high things. High things. High things of the soul if the soul is fully living—high things of the flesh if the soul is fully dead.

He is BUDDY.

The girl is DOT.

You are in their flat.   They are most assuredly not brother and sister. Neither are they man and wife.

The room is mixed.

—Dot suddenly leans over the side toward Buddy. You wonder how she awakens so easily.

DOT. Well Buddy I got a date. I got to get gone. Buddy! Buddy! (*She leans over further and shakes him.*)

BUDDY. Hunh—hunh? What say, Dot? (*He wakes up.*) What say Dot? (*He yawns.*) Uh-uh! Guess I was sleep. What say?

DOT. I say I got a date, Buddy.

BUDDY. (*fully awake at once*) Date? Where you think you're going keeping a date sick as a dog and with the snow on the ground! (*He looks toward the window.*) Snowing now! Where you think you're going?

DOT. I got a date I tell you!

BUDDY. An' I tell you you ain't going to keep it!

DOT. Aw cut that stuff! How long since you thought you could tell me when to go and when to come! Store that stuff!

BUDDY. I ain't storing nothing! You ain't going, I say.

DOT. Aw Buddy I been knowing the guy all my life! Played with him when I's a kid! Been on parties with him since I been going around!

BUDDY. Aw don't try that old friend stuff! What's his name?

DOT. Exit.

BUDDY. Exit? Exit! Where'd he get that! off the inside of a theayter door? Exit! Exit! What's his other name or is that the onliest one he got?

DOT. Mann. Exit Mann. That's his name. Yeah—(*She hesitates and seems to be uncertain.*)

BUDDY. Well it sure is a rotten name! Must be hiding from the cops behind it!

(*Dot takes this opportunity to rise from her couch. The filmy night garments cling to her almost as closely as her flesh. You see she is not curved. You see she is flat where she should curve, sunken where she should be flat. You wish she would lie down again but she gets up—almost falls back— takes hold of the back of the chair and passes across the room to the dressing table.*)

BUDDY. Look at you! 'Bout to fall down! You better lay down again.

(*Dot has begun to brush her hair before the dressing table. She brushes rapidly with strokes that grow vigorous as if each one made some new strength start up in her.*)

DOT. Aw let me alone! I'm going out!

(*Buddy sits on the floor and watches her. She rouges her cheeks and paints her lips and begins to powder heavily with white powder.*)

BUDDY. You ain't fixin' to go out passing are you?

DOT. Aw don't ask so many fool questions!

BUDDY. (*growing angry*) Don't get too smart! Guess there's something after all in what the fellers been saying 'bout you anyhow.

DOT. What your nigger friends been saying now?

BUDDY. Nigger friends? You're a nigger yourself for all your white hide!

DOT. (*shrugging*) I may not be—You'd never know!

BUDDY. Aw shut up! You'd like to think ya was white! You'd have never lived with niggers if you'd a been all white and had a crack at a white man!

(*Dot starts to speak—changes her mind—and paints her lips again.*)

BUDDY. (*after a second's silence*) Take some of that stuff off!

DOT. I can't! Mann likes a woman like me to paint up so I'll flash out above the crowd.

BUDDY. Mann! what's Mann got to do with the way you look! Look here you! You been running 'round with this fellow Mann? (*He plunges to his feet and lunges toward her.*) Is he the white feller they been seeing you out with for the past three months?

DOT. They? What they? Some more of your—!

BUDDY. Don't call them niggers again you half-white—(*Dot catches him by the shoulder and pushes him away.—She selects a piece of clothes out of a drawer.*)

DOT. I told you in the beginning I been knowing this guy all my life! Been out with him!

BUDDY. Is he white?

DOT. I don't know!

BUDDY. You don't know! Where'd you meet him?

DOT. Aw for God sake shut up and let me alone! I never met him! This is the last time I'm going to tell you I been knowing him all my life!

BUDDY. Naw I ain't lettin' you alone! Naw I ain't letting you alone! This is the guy the fellers been telling me about! This is the guy! Ol' lop-sided lanky white thing! Been hanging around you at all the cafes and dances and on the streets all the time I'm out of the city! I'm out of the city— working to keep you—you hanging around with some no count white trash! So no count he got to come in nigger places, to nigger parties and then when he gets there—can't even speak to none of them. Ain't said a word to nobody the fellers say! Ain't said a word! Just settin' 'round— settin' 'round—looking at you—hanging around you—dancin' with you! He better not show hisself 'round here while I'm here!

DOT. He can't never come when you're here.

BUDDY. You right he can't come here. Can't never come! He better be afraid of me.

DOT. He ain't afraid of you. He's afraid of your love for me.

BUDDY. (*laughing shortly*) Aw for crap sake! My love! He ain't afraid of my love! He's afraid of my fist! (*Dot does not seem to hear him now. She talks to herself—"It's almost time! It's almost time!" Buddy hears her the second she speaks.*) Almost time for what?

DOT. Him to come!

BUDDY. Who?

DOT. Exit!

BUDDY. (*cursing*) He ain't coming here! He ain't coming here! I'll knock his head clean off his shoulders if he comes here!

DOT. He's coming!

BUDDY. I'll kill you 'fore he gets here and then kill him when he comes!

DOT. Aw Buddy—don't take on so! If you love me he can't come in between your love and come to me!

(*Buddy curses until his veins are swollen—packed full of the poison of the curses.*)

BUDDY. Damn you! Damn you! Trying to throw this "your love" stuff out to cam'flage and hide behind. I tol' you when we were fussing before you went to sleep that I didn't believe you when you said everybody was lying on you! You said everybody was lying and you was tellin' the truth! Say you ain't never been with other men! Naw I don't love you! (*He breaks off and rushes to a drawer and snatches out a mean, ugly, blue-black, short pistol.*)

DOT. (*screaming and overturning her chair*) Aw Buddy—Buddy don't! You love me!

BUDDY. Shut up!! (*He lifts the gun as if he were going to bring it down—raking her with fire the length of her body. He stops-*) 'Naw I don't love you! Half-white rat!

DOT. (*crawling to her knees away from him*) Then he's got to come! I got to go with him!

BUDDY. Yas he's got to come! And when he comes I'll fix you both! Get up! (*He prods her with his foot.*) Get up! Get up and dress to go out before your Exit is here! Exit! Exit! I'll Exit him when I get through with you!

(*Dot completes her powdering then she suddenly reaches her hat down from a hook above the table. It is a smart black turban. It is black crepe and is wound and wound around. She snatches up a sealskin coat that has been lying on another chair and begins to put it on.*)

BUDDY. You must be foolish! What you putting the coat on over the nightclothes for?

DOT. I ain't got time to put no more on.

BUDDY. Aw yes you got time, sister! Put on all you want! I ain't going to run you off before he gets here! You ain't going 'till your Exit comes!

DOT. This is all I need—all I need! I'm ready.

BUDDY. You're ready—where's your friend? Can't go without him!

DOT. He's here! (*She points.*) There he is.

(*And close behind Buddy you see a man standing. He is half in the shadow. All you can see is a dark overcoat, a dark felt hat. You cannot see his face for his back is turned. You wonder how he came there. You wonder if perhaps he has not been there all the while.*)

BUDDY. (*starting back as he sees the man*) You're a regular sneak, ain't you! Ain't enough to sneak in and take a man's girl while he's out workin'! Got to sneak in his house! Sneak in on him when he's minding his business!

(*The man does not move or answer. Dot's color is bright. Her eyes glow in the semi-shadow. The lights in the room seem dimmer somehow. Dot is breathing so that the fur mounts and slides—mounts and slides on her bosom. She keeps wetting her lips as if they were drying out. She starts across the floor toward him but pauses and draws back almost at once.*)

BUDDY. (*still talking to the man*) Turn around and say something! Turn around and say something! They say all you do is hang around niggers' places and keep a still tongue! (*To Dot:*) Go on over! Go on up to your Exit. Go on so you can go off the way I am sending you off. Go off like you lived! lying in some man's arms—then lying to me. (*As if to himself*) That's the way to die anyhow: jus' like you lived!

DOT. (*rubbing a hand across her face*) Buddy! (*gasping*) Buddy! Say you love me! I don't want to go! I don't want to go with him!

(*Buddy's answer is an inarticulate wild roar: "Get on to him! Get on over to him! With a scream and a quick run Dot crosses the little space and as quickly the man opens his arms and draws her to him without turning around.*)

DOT. (*crying smothered against the coat as if she were far away*) Buddy— Buddy—Buddy! Do you love me? Say you love me before I go!

(*As she cries out the man begins to walk toward the back door. Buddy curses and fires at the same time. A stray shot strikes the light. It goes out. Buddy scratches a match and you see the man standing in the doorway— about to cross the threshold. His back is still turned but as you look he slowly begins to turn around.*)

BUDDY. Mann? Mann!! Dot! Dot!

(*At that the man turns fully and you see Dot laid limp—hung limp—silent. Above her, showing in the match light between the overcoat and the felt hat are the hollow eyes and fleshless cheeks of Death. But almost at once the light flares back. You see the room as it was at first. Dot on her couch with her arms hanging over the side—Buddy lying beside the couch. The red shoes on the table.*)

DOT. (*struggling awake*) Buddy! (*You can hear a rattling in her throat. A loud rattling. The rattling of breath soon to cease.*) Buddy!!! Buddy!! Aw God, he can't hear me!—Buddy, do you love me? Say you love me 'fore I go! Aw—ah—ah—!"*

(*The rattling is loud—loud. It stops on a high note. She stretches rigid and is still. The room is quiet an instant. You think you hear the rattling, though.*)

BUDDY. (*striving in his sleep*) Exit!! Mann!! Exit! (*He pauses—then cries aloud:*) You lied! Naw I don't love you! (*He cries so loudly that he comes fully awake and sits up swiftly.*) Say Dot—I had a—! Dot! Dot!! Oh my God! (*He touches her.*) My Dot! (*And he leans over her and begins to cry like a small boy.*) Oh Dot! I love you! I love you!

CURTAIN

Shirley Graham

(1896–1977)

Shirley Graham during the early 1940s. (*Courtesy of the Schomburg Center*)

> Gradually, I believe I can break through the barriers.
> And this is the only hope for real development of the Ne-
> gro in the theatre. Some one of us must be in a position
> of authority. Until that happens we get no plays produced
> and most of our acting is turned into burlesque.[1]

THE MANY CONTRIBUTIONS OF Shirley Graham have on the whole been ne-
glected in the annals of American theatre history. Graham was one of few
black women, prior to the 1950s, to actively pursue a career in professional
theatre as a playwright, composer, designer, and director. The fact that
only one play and one musical composition authored by her have been published to date testifies to the neglect that her work suffers.

Shirley Lola Graham (née Lola Bell Graham) was born November 11,
1896, to the Reverend David Graham and Etta Bell Graham. Her minister
father changed jobs frequently and as a result Graham lived in parsonages
all over the United States. The play *I Gotta Home* is clearly based on her
childhood experiences. After graduation from Lewis and Clark High School
in Spokane, Washington, Graham attended business school. In 1921 she
married Shadrach T. McCanns. They had two sons, Robert and David. After her divorce from McCanns, she went to Paris to study music at the
Sorbonne.

In Paris, Graham met numerous Africans who taught her the music of
various African countries. Upon returning to the United States in the late
1920s, she furthered her studies in music at Howard University. From 1929
to 1931, she headed the music department at Morgan State College in Baltimore. Recognizing that a degree would open up opportunities in academia
and enable her to better support her sons, Graham enrolled at Oberlin College in Ohio during the fall of 1931 to work on her A.B. degree in the music
conservatory. While a student at Oberlin, Graham's opera *Tom-Tom* was
produced during the spring of 1932 at the Cleveland Stadium in Cleveland,
Ohio, before a crowd of 25,000. An opera in three acts, *Tom-Tom* traces African music to the United States. The work is significant because it was the
first all-black opera to be produced on a professional level in America. In
addition to its performance at the Cleveland Stadium, *Tom-Tom* was also
aired over NBC radio and received favorable reviews. Unfortunately, this
was the first and last production of the opera, although Graham attempted
for several years to restage it.

Conclusive evidence suggests that *Tom-Tom* had a major impact in the
changing of American theatre. Following fast on the heels of this opera
were numerous shows with "jungle themes," such as *Voo-Doo MacBeth*,
Haiti, *Swing Mikado*, and an opera version of *The Emperor Jones*.

After the success of *Tom-Tom*, Graham returned to Oberlin to complete
her studies and received her A.B. and M.A. degrees by 1935. Her master's

thesis was on "The Survival of Africanism in Modern Music." Upon graduating from Oberlin, Graham accepted a position as head of the Fine Arts Department at Tennessee A.&I. State College in Nashville. Graham wrote a number of articles on the influence of African music in western culture.

In 1936 she was asked to head the struggling Chicago Negro Unit of the Federal Theatre Project (FTP) where she remained until 1938. While director of the unit, Graham elevated the nearly defunct group to a level of national recognition and importance with the musical adaptation of Charlotte Chopenning's *Little Black Sambo* and her company's production of *The Swing Mikado*. During her two years with the company, Graham designed, wrote, composed musical scores and organized classes, in addition to fulfilling her role as an administrator. Her outstanding achievements with the FTP were brought to the attention of Yale University where she was awarded a Rosenwald Fellowship in creative writing. While at Yale, from 1938 to 1940, Graham wrote three plays, all of which explored class, social, or racial issues: *Dust to Earth, I Gotta Home,* and *It's Morning.* She also wrote a radio comedy, *Track Thirteen*, which takes a look at train porters and their superstitions. *Track Thirteen* was produced by Yale over WICC Radio in New Haven in 1940.

After leaving Yale, Graham secured a position as director of a YWCA theatre group in Indianapolis, where she staged various operas by well-known composers. She was then appointed to a YWCA-USO camp at Fort Huachuca in Arizona, where her interest in the arts was eclipsed by an interest in civil rights activism that grew out of her experiences on the base. She observed the blatant discrimination against the black soldiers there, and was compelled to speak out against these conditions. She was dismissed from the camp in 1942 and moved to New York to become a field secretary for the NAACP. Simultaneously, Graham began writing biographies about black heroes, as well as attempting to promote the production of her plays. From 1944 to 1975, Graham wrote twelve biographies and one novel. In 1960 she became the founding editor of *Freedomways* magazine.

When Shirley Graham married W. E. B. DuBois in 1951, her remaining aspirations for a professional career in the theatre came to an abrupt end. That was the same year that DuBois was indicted for his activism in the world peace movement. From this period until her death, Graham spent her life supporting DuBois's cause and working to vindicate his name. On March 27, 1977, Shirley Graham died at the age of 80 in Peking, China.

Among Graham's many plays, only one was ever published, but they were all produced. Her works were presented by such colleges and theatre groups as Yale University, Karamu Theatre in Cleveland, Goodman Theatre in Akron, Ohio, Florida A.&M. College, and Oberlin College.

NOTE

1. W. E. B. DuBois Manuscript Collection, Letter to Dr. W. E. B. DuBois dated September 8, 1938.

IT'S MORNING

A One-Act Play in Two Scenes

Note: The dialect in "It's Morning" is not uniform. It is not intended to be. Many African languages express different meanings by changes in pitch and volumn. The most primitive of American Negroes indicate slight changes in meaning by changing vowel sounds. Also, the old type of Negro preachers used a biblical mode of expression which cannot be expressed in dialect. The song used in Scene II, "Ah want Jesus to walk wid me," is one of the oldest of the Spirituals. As are most of these older songs, it is in the minor mode. Music for the other lyrics is original and harmonizes with the theme of the play.

                                                           S.G.

CHARACTERS

CISSIE,	a Slave Woman
MILLIE,	her fourteen-year-old daughter
PETE,	her ten-year-old son
GRANNIE LOU,	the oldest slave on the plantation, considered a little crazy
ROSE, PHOEBE, AUNT SUE,	slave women
CRIPPLE JAKE,	the banjo player
UNCLE DAVE,	slave preacher from Green's plantation
SOLDIER,	a white Union soldier

Other slaves, men and women, singers, small military band

Reprinted by permission of David G. DuBois.

Place: A Remote Plantation in the Deep South
Time: The last day in December, 1862
Early in the morning of January 1, 1863

SCENE I

Place: Interior of Cissie's cabin.

Time: Nearly noon on the last day in December, 1862.

Scene: Bright morning sunshine streams through the open door and frameless window in the back of a rather large, sparsely furnished room. The walls are crudely plastered with old newspapers, but through the knotholes and cracks come bits of light, pointing up the strings of bright red peppers hanging near the fire, and reflecting in the piece of broken mirror above the hearth. The left wall is almost taken up by the wide, open fireplace in which burn heaps of pine cones. Pots and pans are on the hearth and over the flames an iron kettle hangs. On the shelf above sit an oil-lamp, and odds and ends of heavy dishes, while dried herbs hang from a nail. Fishing poles are in a corner of the room; a fishnet is draped along the wall. There are split-bottom chairs, a bench before the fire, a bare table down front left.

When the curtain rises, a slave is discovered just outside the open door, chopping wood and singing as he works. He swings his ax in long, even strokes, beating out the rhythm of his song. Beyond him and through the window may be seen a field of dead, dried cottonstalks, standing naked in the sunshine. A few women are at work, digging up stalks or turning the earth. Within the room GRANNIE LOU is bending over the fire and stirring the kettle with a long-handled spoon. She is shrunken and frail as a withered leaf. Her face is very black and wrinkled, her hands are bony and twisted. The bandana fastened about her head fits tight and smooth as a skull-cap, but it is a pleasing bit of bright color as she moves about. Between her toothless gums is stuck a lighted corn-cob pipe. She is humming to herself—a soft accompaniment to the woodchopper's song.

MAN. (Singing)
Don' min' wo'kin' from sun tuh sun
  Dis mawnin',
Don' min' wolkin' from sun tuh sun
  Dis mawnin',
Don' min' wo'kin' from sun tuh sun
Jus so Ah gets mah wo'k all done,
  Dis mawnin'.

Wen' tuh da ribbah tuh wade across,
  Dis mawnin',
Wen' tuh da ribbah tuh wade across,
  Dis mawnin',
Wen' tuh da ribbah tuh wade across,
Ribbah so deep Ah had tuh grab me a hoss,
  Dis mawnin'.

Grabbed a donkey didn't hab no hair,
  Dis mawnin',
Grabbed a donkey didn't hab no hair,
  Dis mawnin',
Grabbed a donkey didn't hab no hair,
When Ah come to Ah wasn't dere,
  Dis mawnin'.

(*There is the sound of laughter. The slave tosses his ax to one side and waves his hand to someone in the field. As he does so he sees something that catches and holds his attention. With his eyes still rivited, he stoops and absent-mindedly begins piling the wood in his arms. Now, he pauses and, sticking his head in the cabin, gives a quick look around. The old woman does not notice him and he says nothing. Then, as if anxious to get away, he piles the wood high in his arms and goes right. He gives a troubled look over his shoulder as he passes the window. Hardly has he disappeared when through the window may be seen* ROSE *and* PHOEBE, *whispering excitedly and watching someone approach. Upon the head of the taller woman is balanced a water pail. Both fall silent as* CISSIE *appears in the doorway, clinging there a moment, as if for support. They watch her grope her way across the floor to the table where she drops into a chair and leans forward, one hand hiding her face, the other hanging listlessly at her side. Her motionless figure casts a long shadow across the floor and somehow this shadow seems to spread and widen, blotting out the sunshine in the room. The old woman stops her humming, takes her pipe from her mouth, and gives Cissie a long, piercing look. Then without a word, she turns back to the fire.*

The two women hesitate in the doorway. Rose swings the pail of water from her head, sets it just inside the door and asks anxiously)
ROSE. Has yo'all heared da word, Cissie?
CISSIE. (*dully*) Yes. . . . Dey's gwine in da mawnin'.
PHOEBE. (*choking back a cry*) Jesus! Jesus! In da mawnin'!
ROSE. (*comes downstage and clasps her hands*)
            Oh, Lawd,
Look down an' see dis po' woman,
Bowed in huh grief an' woe,
He'p huh bear dis hebby cross,
An' make huh meek an' 'umble

Tuh dye will.

(*During Rose's prayer,* AUNT SUE *appears at the threshold. She is older than the three women. Her ample frame in the clean cotton dress fills the doorway, her great bosom trembles with suppressed emotion and her kindly face is filled with sympathy as she stands listening. She waits until Rose is silent.*)

AUNT SUE. (*entering*)
Hit kain't be true, an' yet Ah knows it am,
Ole missie wouldn't touch a bite o' food,
She cry all day an' wish fuh massa Charles.
Dat man give huh no peace,
He say he will hab Millie gal,
Else tu'n us out tuh starve—an' missie, too.

PHOEBE. He'd do it kase he's cruel an' hard,
He's lak a beast dat's scented fresh, young meat,
He's old—He'll suck huh blood lak damp
swamp ting. (*She shudders*)

AUNT SUE. His jowls hang down lak empty 'tatah sacks,
An' 'bacca juice falls drippin' f'om his mouth,
Leavin' a trail o' slime whar he has passed.

(*Cissie has sat motionless while the others talked. Now, she drops her hand from her face. Her eyes stare straight ahead. She speaks as if from a distance, with difficulty, still looking with horror upon a picture etched on her brain.*)

CISSIE. Ah seed him lick his lips an' smile an' grin,
Ole missie beg him wait till cotton bust,
An' promise him da best bales in da lot.
He say he wait no mo'. . . . He want da gal.
Ah seed his hands . . . dey touch huh golden breast,
She war so scared, she couldn't run . . .
An' den she scream . . . an' missie tell huh go.
Ah heared him laf . . . an' spit upon da floah!

(*Cissie pulls herself to her feet and, as if weights are fastened to her limbs, drags across the floor toward the inner room. Outside is heard a girl's voice singing.*)

GIRL. Oh, see dat sun,
See how he run,
Don' yo' ebber let 'em catch yo',
Wid yo' wo'k undone.
Oh, see dat sun,
See how he run,
Don' yo' ebber let 'em catch yo'
Wid yo' wo'k undone,

(*Cissie disappears in the gloom of the other room.*)

ADDED VOICES. (*outside*) Oh! Ah'm a gonna shine,

Lawd, Ah'm a gonna shine.

AUNT SUE. (*shaking her head and looking after Cissie*)
Cissie uster sing lak dat—
Jes' lak huh gal.

PHOEBE. ⎫
        ⎬ (*astonished*) Cissie! Sing?
ROSE. ⎭

AUNT SUE. Yes, Cissie! she war beautiful!
Black as a berry an' lovely as da night,
Slender an' swift as a young colt—
She nevah walk, jes' prance an' run
    about da place.
Ah seen da buckra eyin' huh—an' she jes' laf.
Den come a day when she war very still,
Ah donno why, till one night seen huh slippin'
trough da shadows lak a hounded coon
crawls tuh his hole to lick his bleedin' wounds.

ROSE. Dey say dat she war proud, an' dat da
ovahseer swear he'd break huh will.

AUNT SUE. (*bitterly*) He did . . . An' when he'd come along da row
She tremble lak a leaf, an' once she fall
down cryin' at his feet. He laf, an' kick
huh wid his foot, not hard, but lak you'd kick
a bitch dat's large wid puppy, out of yo' path.
(*A deep sigh from the three women.*)

ROSE. Huh Millie's lak a flower,
She watch huh day an' night,
An' now . . .

PHOEBE. She know dat Millie's singin' days am gone—

AUNT SUE. Yes, an' huh dancin', too . . .
Po' lil gal—She'll mos' wish she war dead.

ROSE. An' Peter—Spite of he small an' weak,
He take to round da bargain out complete.

PHOEBE. Mussy Jesus! He'p us, Lawd!
(*The prayer is interrupted by Grannie dropping her spoon on the hearth with a loud clatter. The women give a start. They had forgotten her presence. Grannie breaks into high-pitched, crazy laughter.*)

GRANNIE. He! He! He! Ha! Ha!

PHOEBE. Mek huh stop! Somebody'll hyear.

ROSE. What's da mattah, grannie,
Why yo' all laf?

GRANNIE. (*mocking*) Mussy Jesus! Mussy Jesus!
(*She snickers while the women gasp.*)
Day don' hab tuh go, Ah tells yo',
Day don' hab tuh go!

AUNT SUE.   Let huh talk.

We allus calls huh crazy, but who knows?
Maybe da Voodoo wo'k dat way, maybe she
bile up sompin' dat kin help.
(*Gently to the old woman*)
What is it, grannie, what dey kin do?
Might dey bof run away?

GRANNIE. (*in a cracked, singsong voice*)
Da ribbah's high, da rains dat fall las' week,
Make all da ma'shes tick wid mud an' deep.

AUNT SUE. Den what? . . . Why yo' all laf?
Hit's Cissie's chillun dat's been sole down ribbah.
Millie, huh gal, an' Pete, huh lil boy.

PHOEBE. Aw, Antie, why yo' askin' po' ole Lou?

GRANNIE. (*Sharply to Phoebe*) Shut yo' mouf!
Ah ain't so ole dat Ah don' member.
(*Turning to the others*)
Ain't Ah nebbah tole yo' bout dat 'oman
long time gone? Dey say she straight from jungles
in da far off Af'ica. . . . She nevah say.
Dat war a 'oman—straight lak tree, an' tall,
Swift as a lion an' strong as any ox.
Da sugah cane went down fo' huh big knife,
Lak cottonstalks under da fierces' hail—
No man could walk wid huh . . . An' sing!
She uster sing out in da fields . . .
Da niggahs wo'k dem days . . . When Ah war young.

(*Her voice dies away in a mumble of reminiscence. She turns back to her pots, forgetting her audience, forgetting the present, lost in the happy memories of her youth. Cissie may be seen standing just within the doorway of the inner room. The women do not see her. Now they turn away from Grannie in disgust.*)

PHOEBE.   Humph!
Ah tought yo' gonna tell us sompin' we
kin do to he'p po' Cissie an' huh gal,
An' all yo'all comes talkin' bout is some
cane-choppin' heathen dat kin sing.
Gwan! Anybody kin sing!

GRANNIE. (*facing about angrily*)
Ain't Ah tol' yo' shut yo' fat mouf, yo'?
Dat 'oman dar do mo' den sing! Lissen—
(*She gesticulates with her pipe. Cissie presses forward listening intently.*)
She hab tree sons, dey black an' tall lak she,
An' one day news comes dat dey sole huh sons down
ribbah . . . . . . Dey brings good price.
She say dey nebbah go. Da white folks laf,

but niggahs dassent laf—dey see huh face.
She don' say no'tin' mo', but go away,
An' early in da mawnin' call huh boys,
An' when dey come, she tell 'em to stan' close,
An' watch da sun come up out ob da hills.
Dey sort ob smile at huh an' look,
An' den dat 'oman lift huh big cane knife,
She cry out sompin' in a wild, strange voice,
An' wid one sweep she cut off all dey heads,
Dey roll down at huh feet—All tree ob dem.

(*The women give a gasp! It is Grannie's moment of triumph. She holds it. Then, with a shrug of her shoulders and a toothless grin, she turns back to her pots. Outside the girl's voice comes nearer. The women's heads bow, but in the background Cissie remains standing as if spellbound.*)

GIRL. Oh! see dat sun,
  See how he run,
  Don' yo ebbah let' em catch yo',
  Wid yo' wo'k undone,
  Oh! Ah'm a-gonna shine,
  Lawd, Ah'm a-gonna shine.

(*The song stops as the girl reaches the door. It is* MILLIE. *Her thin dress reveals the beautifully molded lines of young womanhood as she hesitates just outside in the sunshine. She is the color of burnished gold, and in her soft, wavy hair, framing the round face, are glints of copper. Her mouth is full and curves sweetly like a little child's. Her eyes are wide and know no shadows. Now, she puckers her brow anxiously as she sees the three women, silent and bowed. But the silence is broken by Cissie, speaking from where she stands. Her voice is thick and harsh. The women look at each other in consternation. They are wondering how long she has been in the room.*)

CISSIE. Com' hyear, chile.

(*Millie's eyes fill with alarm at her mother's voice.*)

MILLIE. Mammy, mammy, Ah ain't done nottin'.
  Ole missie tell me Ah kin go—
  She say tuh hurry hyear an' look fuh yo'.

(*The girl advances timidly, looking from one woman to the other, noting the strained expressions. Cissie stares at her with awful concentration. Millie stops uncertain.*)

MILLIE.   What's de mattah, mammy?
  What's da mattah wid ever'body today?
  Ole missie, too. She lookin' powerful sad.
  Hav' sompin' awful come to Massa Frank—
  Way at da war?. . . . Why, hyear come Pete!

(PETE, *prancing on his spindly legs, has just entered the cabin. He is grinning widely and brings with him an air of exuberance which relieves the tension and seems to lift some of the shadows in the room. As if to avoid further questions, Cissie walks rapidly to the fireplace and begins to busy herself at the hearth. Millie addresses the boy severely.)*

MILLIE. Hey, what yo'all doin' pussyfootin' off f'om wo'k dis time a day?

PETE. (*cheerfully*) Pussyfootin' yo'self!

(*He whirls on his bare feet*)

No mo' wo'k fuh me today,

Nottin' tuh do but go an' play!

Hoopla! Hoopla!

(*Millie grins in spite of herself. Pete continues.*)

Is dar gwine be a pahty o' sompin'?

Us ain't had no pahty fuh Christmas.

(*Eagerly*) Maybe Massa Frank come back f'om da war!

He sho' giv' us pahties!

(*Cissie's face is hidden as she bends over the hearth. Now, she speaks in a light, high, but slightly muffled voice.*)

CISSIE. No, Massa Frank ain't come back yet,

But us gwine tuh hab a pahty!

(*Pete bounds up with joy. The women show amazement. Cissie turns with a laugh. Her eyes are shining, her voice animated. She is galvanized into action. Each of the next lines is punctuated by some definite, playful motion.*)

CISSIE. Scour out da kettles,

Fill up da pails,

Run tell Cripple Jake to get his banjo down.

Fotch me a chicken,

Heap up da cones,

Ah'm cookin' up a mess o' victuals wid cawnpone.

Go quick! (*She grabs a pail and gives it to Pete, who rushes out.*)

Call Paul! (*She calls after him*)

We'll dance!

Tell all!

(*She gives Millie a playful push out the door. The merry voices of the two may be heard outside.*)

PHOEBE. A pahty!

Cissie, is yo' crazy?

(*Cissie has remained standing near the door looking out after the children. As their happy voices fade, her shoulders sag. She seems to wither and shrink as she stands there, her back to the room. She speaks without turning, all the life gone from her voice.*)

CISSIE. Dey gonna sing an' dance till dey kain't dance

no mo'. Till sleep pulls hebby at dar lids,

An' dey sinks down wid belly full o' joy.

(*Almost in a whisper*)

Happy will be der dreams—der long, long dreams.

ROSE. (*Sudden fear clutching at her throat and thickening her voice.*)

What yo' sayin', Cissie?

What yo'all sayin'?

(*Cissie whirls in the doorway like a wounded animal at bay. Her eyes are blazing. She speaks wildly.*)

CISSIE. Dey ain't gwine, yo' hyear me?

DEY. . . . ain't gwine . . . NEIDDAH!

(*She rushes out the door.*)

GRANNIE. He! He! He! Ha! Ha! Ha!

CURTAIN

SCENE II

Place: Same interior as SCENE I.

Time: The hour just before the dawn of the following day.

Scene: The night of revelry has passed. The room, still bedecked for the party—with its half-emptied pots upon the hearth, table and bench pushed against the wall and piles of dirty dishes scattered about—is like an actress, when the comedy is finished, ghastly beneath her grease paint. A bright, gay cloth is draped at the window, the wooden shutter is closed. Spanish moss, gathered in the swamp, is festooned from the rafters of the unceiled room. When the room is lighter the little red berries of holly may be seen nestling in the thick bed of green bunches. Over the door sprays of mistletoe now droop—tiny, white pearls hanging heavy upon the wilted stems.

When the curtain lifts the room is in deep shadow, lighted only by the fire which has burned down to a few glowing cones. The young folks have gone home, but there remain the older slaves who watch with Cissie for the dawn. For the most part they are huddled together near the fire, but several sit tense, staring into the shadows. CRIPPLE JAKE, *alone in a corner, his rude crutch at his side, holds a banjo in his lap. At intervals he strums it softly. Slightly separated from the group, down front, crouches Cissie. She sits like a graven image, except that from time to time her hand reaches out and touches the blade of the huge cane knife that lies beside her. The women are talking in whispers, glancing at Cissie. Darkness and chill lie like a pall upon the room. A moment passes.*

CISSIE. (*without turning her head*) Look out, Phoebe, see if hit ain't mos' sun-up.

(*The slaves hold their breath and every eye, except Cissie's, follows Phoebe as she goes to the door and opens it. Outside there is only darkness. A sigh of relaxation comes from the group.*)

PHOEBE. No, hit's still dark.

AUNT SUE. (*devoutly*) Tank yo', Jesus!

PHOEBE. (*still looking out, speaks again*) Why, hyear comes somebody! (*Pause*) Hit's Uncle Dave . . . Uncle Dave from way ovah Green's plantation.

(*Several join Phoebe at the door. In a moment an old man enters, walking feebly. His hair is a white halo about a gentle, wrinkled face. He is greeted warmly.*)

VOICES. Howdy, Uncle Dave.

Good mawnin', Uncle Dave.

Come right in.

ROSE. Praise da Lawd! Maybe she'll
listen to yo', Uncle Dave.

PHOEBE. Lawsy mussy! Yo'all ain't come all trough dat black swamp by yo'-self, is yo'?

UNCLE DAVE. (*His voice is rich, and in it sounds the music of deep rivers.*)
Yes, chile,

Ah heared da han' ob God lay hebby on yo',

Ah prayed da master'd get me hyear on time. (*He looks around*)
Whar be da chilluns?

ROSE. (*Pointing towards the other room*) In dar . . . Sleepin'.

ROSE. (*continuing*)

Dey eat dere full an' all us dance an' sing,

An' Cissie, dere, lafs loudes' of us all . . .

Po' lam's, deys plum tuck out, an' so dey
sleepin' sound.

UNCLE DAVE. Thank God! An' Cissie . . . ?

(*The group opens up allowing him to see Cissie who sits unheeding and motionless.*)

PHOEBE. (*loudly*) Hit's all dat black Lou's fault.

(*She is interrupted by several who motion warningly towards the other room.*)

VOICES. Sh-sh-sh-sh-sh!

She'll hyear!

(*Phoebe continues angrily, but in a lower voice.*)

PHOEBE. She put a spell on Cissie,

Shuttin' huh eyes an' stoppin'

up huh ears tuh evahting

dat we kin do an' say.

She gotta evil eye,

Dat's what she got!

UNCLE DAVE.   Dar now, daughtah,

De Lawd takes care ob his own,

Us ain't got no cause tuh fret.

(*A wavering wail comes softly from the banjo. It hangs suspended in the air a moment and Cripple Jake speaks.*)

CRIPPLE JAKE. Ah'm tinkin' bout dis ting—
  Hebbin is a high an' a holy place,
  Da chilluns done no wrong,
  Dyin' will bring 'em joy,
  Da good book say, "Lam's
  In His bosom—safe."
  While Cissie know dat
  Livin's jes a slow decay
  Wid worms gnawin' lak nits
  Into dey heart an' soul.

ROSE. But Cissie kain't . . .

1ST WOMAN. Dey'll beat huh mos' tuh death!

2ND WOMAN. She'll be a mu'deress!

3ND WOMAN. She'll bu'n in hell!

CRIPPLE JAKE. Yes, Cissie, will be lonely—now,
  An' maybe fuh a t'ousand yeahs tuh come.

(*They turn at the unexpected sound of Cissie's voice. It is low and vibrant.*)

CISSIE. But, when da saints ob God go marchin' home
  Mah gal will sing! Wid all da pure, bright stars,
  Tuhgedder wid da mawnin' stars—She'll sing!

(*Cissie's head is lifted and for one moment a strange beauty illumines her black, gaunt face. A soft chord sounds from the banjo, gentle as wings brushing across the strings.*)

UNCLE DAVE. (*Sternly*) We be forgettin' God!
  Didn't He bring Daniel out ob da lion's den,
  An' da Hebrew chillun out da fiery furnace,
  Didn't He open up da Red Sea,
  An' save Jonah from da belly ob da whale?

WOMEN. (*fervently*) Yes, ma Lawd!
  Save us, Jesus.

(*The women begin to rock back and forth, humming softly. Uncle Dave moves down stage to Cissie. He places his hand on her shoulder. She starts violently, but when she sees who it is she sinks back. The light has faded from her face.*)

WOMAN. (*Singing, with humming accompaniment.*)
  Ah want Jesus tuh walk wid me,
  Ah want Jesus tuh walk wid me,
  All along mah hebbenly journey,
  Ah want Jesus tuh walk wid me.
  In mah sorrow, walk wid me,
  In mah sorrow, walk wid me,
  When mah hea't wid'in is breakin',
  Ah want Jesus tuh walk wid me.
(*The singing sinks to a hum*)

UNCLE DAVE. Kain't yo' trus' de Lawd, daughtah? Hit's al wid Him. Yo' kain' stain yo' han's wid da blood ob yo' own chilluns.

CISSIE. (*wearily*) Ah tought da time is come. Dat man comin' fuh 'em at sun-sup.

UNCLE DAVE. (*fallen on his knees*)
          Oh, Lawd! Our Lawd!
  Sittin' on yo' great white throne,
  Wid da stars a crown o' beauty fur
    yo' haid,
  An' de earth a mighty footstool fur
    yo' feet,

  Lean down ovah da ramparts of Heb-
    bin' dis mawnin',
  An' see us 'umble sinners kneelin'
    hyear.
  We been prayin' so long,
  We been singin' so . . .

VOICE. Open the door! Open the door!

CISSIE. Da man! He's come!

(*Cissie clutches the knife, but does not yet rise. The slaves watch her terrified. Two men spring forward to hold the door. A woman cautiously cracks the shutter and peeps out. She jerks back and speaks with surprise.*)

WOMAN. Hit's a soldier!

VOICES. Soldiers?

(*The slaves spring up, perplexed, crowd to the window trying to see. The men are uncertain whether or not to hold the door. The pounding becomes more purposeful. The door is giving way. Cissie rises swiftly. This new excitement means nothing to her. The time has come. Knife in hand, she slips unnoticed into the inner room. Just as she disappears, the outer door gives way admitting a white soldier. He is hardly more than a boy. His face is pale with emotion and, though he wears a torn and dusty blue uniform, he stands there poised like some radiant messenger of glad tidings. Behind him the sky is turning rosy with the dawn. He points upward, his voice exalting:*)

SOLDIER. Look! Look, the day has come!
  The day for which we fought.
  Stilled for a moment are the guns
  And from the fallow earth do rise
  The souls of those who fell
  That they might see you go forth
  Free to greet this Dawn!

(*The eager black folks gather round him at the door, questioning, their faces lifted.*)

VOICES. Free? Free?

SOLDIER. Free! Do you understand?
  You're free! No longer slaves.
  Loud sound the bugles and the drums,
  The mighty armies march—
  For this day sets you free!

(*From the outside is heard the sound of a galloping horse. It draws rapidly nearer. There is the sound of pawing feet just outside the door. The horse neighs and in a moment comes loud knocking on the door.*)

(*While the soldier has been speaking from the distance, borne upon the fresh, morning breeze, comes spirited, marching music.*)

UNCLE DAVE. (*He falls upon his knees and lifts his hands towards the rising sun.*)

Thank God! Oh! Thank—

(*His words are cut short by a scream of terror coming from the inner room. Like puppets fastened on a single string, the black folks give a startled jerk and then freeze motionless. Outside the music draws nearer while from the room backs little Pete, his mouth still distended with his scream, his eyes dilated. There is a moment of tense waiting and Cissie comes through the door, walking slowly and deliberately. In her arms is the lifeless body of Millie, her head fallen back. Cissie advances into the room towards the soldier, her face a deeply chiseled mask in ebony, with set, unseeing eyes.*)

CISSIE.   Yo' come too late.
Mah gal is dead! Da boy yo' didn't wan' no how,
He's wo'thless in da fields—he is too weak.
But huh. . . . (*She extends the soft body*)
See how huh red blood falls hyear in da sun,
Hit's warm an' pure. . . . Come, dip yo' han's in it
She will not shrink away—Huh teahs will nevah
Choke huh song nor will huh limbs grow hebby
wid dispair.   Mah gal is dead!

(*Everyone has crouched back except the young soldier, who stands as if paralyzed, his face turning white. Now, he finds his voice.*)

SOLDIER. My God! My God! What? What . . .

UNCLE DAVE. (*speaking from his knees*)
Cissie! Cissie, dis—dis ain't da man.
Dis am a Yankee soldier, come tuh tell us
Dat we's. . . .

(*The old man cannot finish. The word chokes in his throat. He buries his face in his hands. Outside a chorus of happy, singing voices is swelling, forming a joyous obligato to the music of the band.*

VOICES. (*Singing*)
Free, Free, Free
   Ah'm free, lil chillun,
Free! Free!

Free! Free! Free!
   Oh! Da sun ob God
Does sot us free dis mawnin'!

(*Through the door behind Cissie has come Grannie Lou. She stumbles, rubbing her sleep-heavy eyes and shaking her shriveled frame. She sees Cissie facing the white man and her clouded brain can take in only one meaning for the scene.*)

SOLDIER. (*speaking gently to Cissie*)

Do you hear them?

You're no longer a slave! You—

(*He is stopped by a burst of wild, loud laughter from Grannie, who points her skinny finger at the limp body.*)

GRANNIE. He! He! He! Ha! Ha! Ha!

Ah tole yo'. . . . She don' hab tuh go!

He! He! He!

(*Several women rush to Grannie, soothing her as they would a child. Only bewilderment shows in Cissie's face, but the boy soldier's poise is completely shattered. Flinging up his hand to shut out the sight, vainly trying to stop his ears, he rushes out into the morning sunshine. Two or three men follow him. Gradually Grannie is quieted. They lead her back into the sleeping room. Little Pete has buried his face in Aunt Sue's deep bosom. He is still shaking, but makes no sound. The women have dropped to their knees. They rock their bodies and give an occasional moan.*)

(*Cissie walks to the door, her inert burden clasped to her breast. For a moment she stands in the bright sunshine, gazing out. The music has gradually diminished into the distance and now may be heard only faintly. The dew-drenched earth is sweet, bathed in the pure sunshine of the new-born day. Somewhere in the yard a cock crows. Cissie looks down into her child's face and speaks quietly.*)

CISSIE. Hit's mawnin'!

(*And from her throat there comes a cry of anguish as she falls to her knees.*

(*Above her, on the door, a single spray of mistletoe sways in the morning breeze and then falls gently on the upturned face of the child.*)

CURTAIN

I GOTTA HOME

A Comedy in Three Acts

CHARACTERS

REV. ELIJAH J. COBB,   last of a line of simple souls who, having heard "the call" to preach, does nothing else

MRS. COBB,   formerly Liza Dell of Louisville, Kentucky

E.J.,   his oldest son and namesake

MIRAH,   the oldest daughter

TOUSSANT,   a second son

LILACS,   another daughter

BEN-HUR,   totally unexpected and unprepared for, another son

SISTER SABOY (pronounced "Sayboy") } stewardesses
SISTER WHITE

BROTHER PERKINS,   a Deacon

"DR." CALAB GREEN, the Presiding Elder. One of those hierarchical left-overs from the days of overseers.

MRS. SWAN,   the doctor's wife. Not "Dr." Green.

MISS HALL,   a school teacher

BUTCH JOHNSON,   merely a "friend" of Mirah's

MATTIE COBB,   the enigma

JASPER JONES AND PEEWEE, gentlemen of Harlem. They make themselves at home anywhere

LEO,   a number "runner"

BROTHER PUGH,   Pastor of a little church in Flat Hollow

A POLICEMAN

TWO REPORTERS

Reprinted by permission of David G. DuBois.

Time: 1938.

Scene: The combination parlor/sitting-living room of a Negro church parsonage. Laid in a large, Midwestern town.

ACT ONE
 Scene 1: A bright Saturday morning. About ten o'clock.
 Scene 2: One week later. Saturday afternoon.
ACT TWO
 Scene 1: Same as Act 1, Scene 2. Later in the evening.
 Scene 2: The following Sunday morning.
ACT THREE
Three days later. In the afternoon.

A C T   O N E

SCENE ONE: *The large combination parlor/sitting-living room of the Church Parsonage. In some far-off day perhaps it has been a home. Now, definitely it is a parsonage. Evidences of former preachers and preachers' families linger. The house has been furnished at different times by various committees of various and conflicting tastes. Much of the furniture in the room has been donated. In striking contrast is a high tier of bookcases running along the right wall. They are new, simple, and in good taste. They are filled with old and battered books. A staircase comes down along the back wall ending at the doors back left which open into the hallway. A narrow window, central frame surrounded by small frames of colored glass, is in the back hall above the stairs. Back right, double doors open into the dining room. Through the doors may be seen the dining table. Under the stairs on a small stand is the telephone. A bay window is in the left wall. Close to the window is an upright piano and stool. The top of the stool is never quite balanced. Door down right leads into what Rev. Cobb calls his "study."*

AT RISE: *It is a bright, cheerful morning. The room has the appearance of having been straightened.*

MRS. COBB *is ascending the stairs. She is just past forty. A woman of light complexion and good features in which linger traces of what might have been real beauty. When in repose, her face is still very attractive, but she usually wears an expression of harried anxiety that spoils her appearance. She wears a house dress with dust cloth tied about her head and is carrying broom, dustpan, and brushes. Over her arm hang a number of fresh bathtowels.*

MIRAH *may be seen in the dining room. The table is set apparently for one person. Mirah is doing something at this table. She is about sixteen and does not inherit her mother's good looks. Her face is broader and more solid, but there is a placid sweetness about her which is appealing.*

E.J. *(so called by his family) is seated before a desk right. He is about eighteen. He has not yet filled out into the lines of manhood, but he resembles his mother. His fine olive skin over sharp features and thick, waving hair are from her. Resembling her also are his petulant, nervous movements and the frequent curl of his thin lips. He seems to be copying into a notebook something he is reading from small slips of paper. He takes the slips of paper from his pocket one by one and seems anxious to keep them out of sight. He is working rapidly.*

LILACS *is at the piano practicing five finger exercises, swaying on the wobbly stool. Lilacs is eight and except in this type of American family could not be related to either Mrs. Cobb or E.J. She is very dark and very thin—tight skin stretched over prominent bones, long-fingered hands like claws, and bright eyes which dart from place to place. Her hair, though carefully braided, is stiff and rebellious. She is never quiet unless forcibly restrained and even then her eyes fasten upon persons and things with avid curiosity.*

MRS. COBB. (*almost at top of stairs*) Not so loud, Lilacs! You'll wake the Presiding Elder!

LILACS. (*hopefully*) Wan' me to stop?

MRS. COBB. (*positively*) No! Hold down the soft pedal—but keep right on practicing!

LILACS. (*after her mother has disappeared*) Hope Ah do wake 'im! Fat ole pig!

E.J. Oh, no! Keep down the soft pedal so His Majesty can go on snoring. . . . I'll have to turn my mattress when that pot-bottom leaves!

MIRAH. You shouldn't talk that way in front of Lilacs. She'll be saying it to some of the members.

E.J. (*grimly*) I'd like to!

MIRAH. Yes—and make things worse than they are!

E.J. Lot o' difference that would make. (*He gets up sweeping several tickets into his pocket, dropping one which he does not notice. As he moves he winces and quickly puts his hand to his neck.*)

MIRAH. What's the matter?

E.J. (*bitterly*) Matter? Oh, nothing—nothing at all. I just got a crook in my neck from sleeping on this old sofa last night. (*He gives the sofa a vicious kick*) But, what's that? It's Quarterly Conference—my bed isn't my own—we can sleep on the floor—Presiding Elders, Bishops, Doctor This and Doctor That—and when they do leave my room stinks!

LILACS. (*having swooped down on the ticket E.J. dropped*) What's this? Is it a ticket to som'nm?

E.J. (*turning quickly and grabbing it out of her hand*) Gimme that!

LILACS. Looks kinda like a movie ticket!

E.J. Well, it isn't! (*His sudden turn has again winced his neck and he puts up his hand*)

LILACS. (*watching him sympathetically*) What's a crook in the neck?

E.J. It's a stiff neck—it's a pain in the neck—it's what I get every time they have a conference here!

LILACS. (*connecting thoughts*) I didn't git nothin' but a chicken neck las' night at supper. He (*gesturing up stairs*) took all the white meat—Rev. Kelly took tha second joint—Deacon Black took tha—

(*The telephone rings. Mirah starts towards it with a little nervous gesture, but E.J. is there before her. Lilacs has checked her speech—listening*)

E.J. Yes . . . yes . . . it's me. What? . . . No—it ain't out yet . . . And don't call up here askin' questions. Do you get me? (*He slams up the receiver*)

MIRAH. Who was it?

E.J. (*indifferently*) Just a fellow.

MIRAH. (*with a little sigh*) Go on with your practicing, Lilacs.

E.J. (*his eyes on Mirah*) Say—what's on your mind? You look sorta down.

MIRAH. You never know what's going on at the church.

E.J. I get it soon enough—living practically in the lobby. When you live in a parsonage all you have to do is stick your head out the window—that is when they don't bring the meetings right into this room! I should drag myself inside a pew to listen to a lot of—

MIRAH. Oh, E.J. You never think about anybody but yourself.

E.J. Oh, I don't—don't I!

MIRAH. No! (*She turns away*)

E.J. Well, spill it, sis. I'm listening.

MIRAH. (*softly*) Pop's behind with his dollar money again. You should have heard the Presiding Elder last night.

E.J. (*bitterly*) The old slave-driving act!

MIRAH. And pop just sat there—saying nothing.

E.J. As ususal! (*E.J. makes a gesture of acceptance*)

MIRAH. (*earnestly*) And, E.J. you know what that means. Moving again! Moving—Moving! I don't want to move now. After painting all that old furniture in my room—painting the woodwork—trying so hard to make it look like a room in a real home!

E.J. Yeah—I know.

LILACS. (*who has been listening*) Ah likes to move!

E.J. (*thinking*) It'll be tough on Toussant, too. Have to leave his team— just been made captain . . . Aw, hell!

LILACS. You said a bad word! (*The telephone rings. Again Mirah starts towards it, but E.J. picks it up*)

E.J. Hello. . . . (*cordially*) Oh, hello, Butch! (*Mirah comes nearer*) How's everything? Gonna clean up Arnold this afternoon? Sure, I know it'll be a swell game . . . Yes . . . Yes . . . yes, she's here. Just a minute. (*Mirah tries to grab it out of his hand, but he makes an elaborate bow, evading her*) Miss Cobb.

MIRAH. (*eagerly*) Yes . . . hello, Butch. . . . I asked her. She said it's all right. Yes—I'm glad, too. I'll be ready. Yes . . . it's a beautiful day. Sure . . . yes . . . Good-by. (*She hangs up the receiver and looks at her brother*)

E.J. (*mocking*) It's a beau—ti—ful—day ! Well, pick me up! How long has this been going on?

MIRAH. I told you you ought to go to church sometimes. Butch does—now.

E.J. (*disgusted*) A paw snatcher! Just a ninny paw snatcher! And him the only colored player on the team. It's sickening! Go on with your practicing, Lilacs. Nobody's talking to you.

LILACS. (*resuming the scales*) How can I practice when you all keep yellin' all the time? I can't hear myself counting.

(*For a moment nothing is heard but the thump of the piano and Lilac's "one—two—three—four—. Mirah is thinking happily and E.J.'s head is buried in his notebook. Then—comes a loud crash in the dining room—the shatter of falling glass and a hard thump. This is followed by loud voices outside which in turn are suddenly hushed. Mirah rushes into the dining room, followed by E.J. and Lilacs. Lilacs, after a startled exclamation, runs back to the bay window, flings it up and hangs perilously out.*)

MRS. COBB. (*upstairs*) Mirah! Mirah—what was·that? (*Again loud voices outside are heard. "I didn't do it! "You did!' Didn't' "I seen you". They blur. Mirah comes slowly back into the living room. Mrs. Cobb is hurrying downstairs*) Mirah, it wasn't a window? Say something! (*sees Lilacs and almost screams*) Lilacs! Get back, you're going to fall! Lilacs, do you hear me? Shut that window. Where is it? Where is it—this time?

MIRAH. In the dining room.

MRS. COBB. The dining room! Those boys again—here, on Saturday—Conference going on! It's just too much!

LILACS. (*matter of fact*) Ben-Hur done it. Toussant's makin' him come in.

MRS. COBB. Your father's got to do something about it—this time, he's got to. (*She is upstage, gazing at the wreckage*) Shattered—glass over everything. I won't stand it! I—

(*An outer door has slammed and scuffling feet are heard in the hall. TOUSSANT flings open the hall door and pulls BEN-HUR through it. Toussant is fourteen, stocky build, brown skin, determined. He is fully conscious that he was named after Toussaint L'Ouverture and knows he is destined to be a "leader of his people." Ben-Hur, ten—a fat little brown boy, he charms without the least effort. Now, his cap half over his ear, he still carries his bat.*)

TOUSSANT. Might as well face it! Everybody saw you. Come on!

MRS. COBB. (*Trying to keep down her voice, but failing*) How many times have I told you boys not to play in front of the church? Now, look what you've done. Look at it!

BEN-HUR. Wasn't my fault. Why didn't he catch the ball? I hit it right at him—wasn't no sense in missin' it—(*He is crying*) Why didn't the ole fool catch it?

(*A sonorous voice calls from upstairs*)

VOICE. Sister Cobb! What is all that racket? Has something happened?

MRS. COBB. (*changing her voice completely*) Oh! Dr. Green. I'm so sorry—those boys—it is awful! Toussant, go out and get those boys away from the church immediately. Right away—do you hear? (*Toussant goes out*) Did they wake you, Dr. Green?

VOICE. (*pompously*) They aroused me from mah meditations—mah morning meditations wid da Lawd—mah meditations what give me strength an' comfort for the day. Is breakfast ready?

MRS. COBB. Oh, yes. As soon as you'd like it.

MIRAH. (*quickly*) Don't let him come down now!

E.J. No—keep him up there until we can clean this up.

MRS. COBB. Oh—Dr. Green. You'll find your towels and everything in the bathroom. If you'd like to take your bath before breakfast.

VOICE. (*shocked*) Ah takes mah bath on Saturday night!

MRS. COBB. Yes—I know—but this is Saturday morning—And I thought—well—with a large family, Saturday night is always kinda crowded. . . . So, if you'd like—nobody's using the bathroom now, you see. I'm sure the water's hot.

VOICE. (*reluctantly*) Well—Ah might see . . . but, Ah donno how Ah'd feel—takin' a bath Saturday mawnin'! (*There is the sound of a closing door*)

E.J. Wish it would kill him!

(*Toussant has returned. He now goes resolutely to dining room*)

TOUSSANT. It's gotta be fixed right away.

MRS. COBB. Fixed! Yes, of course, fixed. Your father's not here. I can't call Deacon Perkins. He'd be sure to say something to the Presiding Elder.

TOUSSANT. Aw, ma, it won't cost much.

MRS. COBB. The church is supposed to keep up repairs. We don't have any money to keep this old shell from falling down about our ears.

BEN-HUR. We ain't wreckin' the parsonage—don't care what they say—we ain't!

MIRAH. (*who is busy sweeping up the glass*) Maybe I could hang a curtain so it wouldn't show.

MRS. COBB. If it'd only been in the basement—or even the kitchen. But, you can't cover it up right here! No, it won't cost much. But everything in the world costs something—and something means money!

E.J. (*bursting out*) It's all you talk about! If money's so important why don't you let me go out and get a real job instead of all that dam study. I can make money!

MRS. COBB. (*drawing herself up*) E.J., I'll appreciate it if you don't use such language before your sisters. And, I'll tell you why you're going on with that—that—studying. It's because you're a Dell—that's why, and Dells always amount to something. Even if I did marry a poor preacher my children are going some place in life. I thought he was going to be something—a Bishop, maybe, or something—but he just goes on preaching . . . dragging his family from pillar to post—but, I don't care—you're going to be somebody. (*The children have heard all this before. E.J. turns away suddenly.*)

MIRAH. (*trying to be practical*) Ben-Hur, have you got any money?

(*Ben-Hur drags himself across the floor to the desk and from somewhere within its depths draws forth a brown jug. He shakes it. Everybody brightens at the unmistakable jingle of coins.*)

BEN-HUR. (*stoically*) I was savin' fur the circus. (*Shoulders sag again*)

TOUSSANT. (*digging in his pocket*) I gotta quarter. (*He lays it on the desk. Ben-Hur clutches it and looks around hopefully.*)

BEN-HUR. Aw, thanks, Toussant.

TOUSSANT. We'll have the money. You run get Jake Smith. Tell him to come right over and fix that window. Can you make him see he's gotta come right away?

BEN-HUR. (*starting out*) Sure thing! I'll bring him. (*He hurries out*)

MRS. COBB. If the Presiding Elder just stays upstairs now. (*She goes out towards the kitchen*)

E.J. It'll take some time for that rusty walrus to scrub his hide.

MIRAH. Some day I'm gonna have a home of my own and I'll do just what I want to in it.

E.J. (*teasing*) I suppose you're dreaming about the bungalow Butch is going to build for you!

MIRAH. (*intensely*) You're hateful—that's what you are. You never think any happiness can come in this home . . . You never even imagine any good coming to us.

E.J. Pop does enough imagining for all of us.

MIRAH. You let pop alone.

TOUSSANT. (*stoutly*) That's what I say. Lot o' great men was poor—and—and—Well, anyhow I like to listen to pop preach. He sounds like a—(*He stops lamely*)

E.J. Well, go on. Why don't you finish?

MIRAH. You ought to be ashamed of yourself. Your name's Elijah, too.

E.J. You telling me! But, I don't go around talking about how the ravens fed my patriarchal namesake in the wilderness. I been hearing that ever since I was born. Say, have you ever seen any ravens lighting around this house? I saw one once and of all the evil, vicious, wicked-looking creatures—

MIRAH. Stop! I won't listen to you.

E.J. (*starting upstairs*) Pop's just got his birds mixed: T'ain't Elijah's raven that sits over our doorway—it's Edgar Allan Poe's—and all he does is croaks! (*Exit upstairs*)

TOUSSANT. Smart guy!

LILACS. (*who has been looking out the window*) Here comes the committee—now—Ma—Ma! Here comes the committee.

MRS. COBB. (*hurrying in from the kitchen*) Oh, my goodness! So early. No use trying to fix anything now. They'll see it!

MIRAH. No—they needn't. We'll just close these doors.

TOUSSANT. (*helping Mirah close the double doors*) Sure—Keep 'em in here. Won't take but a minute. This is our affair. (*The doorbell is ringing*)

MRS. COBB. (*entering the spirit*) Let's see—what can I be doing? Mirah, where's that choir drape I was going to hem?

MIRAH. In pa's study—all pressed. All together, now. Hold the fort! (*She closes the doors*)

MRS. COBB. Get back to your practicing, Lilacs. Toussant, answer the door. (*She disappears within the study as the piano takes up its uneven course. Voices are heard in the hall.*)

(*Enter* SISTER SABOY, *The rawboned, dictatorial captain of all church committees,* SISTER WHITE, *a large, comfortable, round-faced black woman, and* DEACON PERKINS, *a sour-faced little black man.*)

SISTER SABOY. Thought we'd better get here early. Ah believes in tendin' to tha Lawd's work fust! How do yo' do, Lilacs?

LILACS. (*noncommittal*) Mornin'!

(*Mrs. Cobb enters from study. She is carrying some stiffly starched white material and a sewing basket.*)

MRS. COBB. Good morning, sisters and Brother Perkins. Hope you're well.

PERKINS. Fair to meddlin', Sister Cobb. You' lookin' perk as ever.

(*He grins. The sight of a good-looking woman visibly cheers him. Sister White merely smiles, but her whole face lights up warmly*)

SISTER SABOY. Ah brought some clean sheets. Thought you might need 'em. (*She extends a bundle*)

MRS. COBB. (*pleasantly*) Now, that's real nice of you. Lay them on the sofa there and let's sit down. Dr. Green isn't down yet, but his breakfast's all ready. I was just starting to hem this choir drape. (*She prepares to sit down*)

PERKINS. I'll go out in the kitchen an' take a look at that faucet. (*He starts towards the dining room*)

MRS. COBB. (*heading him off*) The faucet? Why—

PERKINS. Yo' said las' night tha hot water was leaking. I brung along a new washer.

MRS. COBB. (*hard pressed*) Oh—now—that's too bad—as a matter of fact—that is—E.J.—

PERKINS. What's that?

MRS. COBB. Why, E.J. said he'd fix it.

PERKINS. Oh, well, I got tha washer right here. Might as well—(*he moves on*)

MRS. COBB. That's just it. E.J. said last night he'd fix it and—this morning—he did.

PERKINS. You mean tha faucet's fixed?

MRS. COBB. (*committed now*) Why—yes.

(*Lilacs slips on the stool bringing her elbow down hard on the keyboard. Mrs. Cobb gives her a sharp look, but says nothing.*)

PERKINS. (*disappointed*) Well, I guess I'll drop down a bit. Needn't have come.

MRS. COBB. (*eagerly*) Yes, do sit down.

SISTER WHITE. Ain't there nothin' Ah kin do, Sister Cobb?

MRS. COBB. Just take one end of this. We'll git the hem fixed in a jiffy. (*Sister White threads her needle and begins to sew*)

SISTER SABOY. (*who has wandered over to the window and is now observing a scrawny plant hanging in pot*) This plant needs water. Ain't had a mite for days. I'll git some. (*She makes a move towards dining room*)

MRS. COBB. Oh, no, I'm sure. That's one of those plants you water once a week. This isn't the day. Wasn't this your idea, Sister Saboy—to put something in front of the choir?

SISTER SABOY. (*coming over*) Deed, yes. Ah jus' couldn't stand it no longer. Legs crossin' an' a-crossin' all durin' tha meetin. That long, skinny Sally Brown hitchin' huh skirts higher an' higher. It was gettin' disgraceful!

PERKINS. Yo' means tha choirs gonna sing behind curtains?

SISTER SABOY. (*still eye on him*) Jus' hide tha legs!

PERKINS. Oh! (*he coughs*) Er—a—guess I'll—Oh—no—you said the faucet's fixed. Yo' sho he put in a new washer?

MRS. COBB. You needn't worry about anything E.J. fixes.

SISTER SABOY. How is E.J.? I haven't laid eyes on him lately.

MRS. COBB. He's fine, thank you, but he's awful busy.

SISTER SABOY. (*having finally seated herself*) Is he workin'?

MRS. COBB. Well, he doesn't have a job—but, he is working. He's reading law.

PERKINS. Readin' law?

MRS. COBB. Of course, we couldn't afford to send him to the university, but Clark and Simon's said they'd take him in their office this fall. He's studying hard to make a good showing.

MRS. SABOY. Sounds powerful highferlutin' to me!

MRS. COBB. My brother was a lawyer. (*Silence*) He went out to Liberia and—

PERKINS. Ain't that there where that missionary was from spoke las' week?

MRS. SABOY. Yes—she said it was a awful country. Folks don' wear no clothes attal!

PERKINS. Yo' say yo' brother lived out there, Sister Cobb?

MRS. COBB. He was just sent to—Lilacs, it's time you went to your lesson. It's after ten.

LILACS. (*sliding off stool*) Yassum.

MRS. COBB. Run change your dress. Hurry now, you'll be late.

SISTER SABOY. (*sweetly*) How d'yo' like takin' music lessons. Lilacs?

234 / SHIRLEY GRAHAM

LILACS. Yassum.

MRS. COBB. Lilacs, Sister Saboy asked you a question—Pay attention.

LILACS. Yess. I—like 'em. Only— (*She is going up the stairs*) Only—I ain't gonna play no piano when I grows up!

MRS. COBB. Lilacs!

LILACS. I'm gonna be a dancer! (*She vanishes in the upper region*)

MRS. COBB. (*trying to treat it lightly*) That child's a caution!

PERKINS. (*lugubriously*) Them kind o' thoughts is dangerous, sister—they's dangerous.

SISTER SABOY. I hopes you're not throwing away money! (*There comes the unmistakable sound of hammering from the dining room*) What's that? (*Sister Saboy strains her ears*)

MRS. COBB. (*quickly*) What? I didn't hear anything—My goodness—the time does fly—You know, I was sayin' to Sister Quince last night that it doesn't seem possible we been here—

SISTER SABOY. There it is again . . . Sounds like one of the boys is beatin' on the woodwork! Ah bettah go—(*She is getting up*)

MRS. COBB. I think that's in the basement. But, you sit still—I'll—

SISTER SABOY. We can'—(*a pompous tread is descending the stairway. She looks up*) Oh—Good mawnin', Elder.

(*Her attention is wholly captured by* CALAB GREEN, *the Presiding Elder. He is large, black and shining. Ministerial garb encases layers of fat. He is bald-headed and he wheezes both from much talking and eating. He beams upon the loyal parishioners who return his gaze with adoration. Mrs. Cobb tries to hide her agitation*)

ELDER. (*rubbing his hands*) Faithful souls, toilin' in the mastah's vineyard. God bless yo', mah children! (*He shakes hands with each*)

MRS. COBB. Elder—you did get dressed in a hurry. We weren't expecting you down so soon.

ELDER. Sistah, wen' de inner sun calls (*he pats his stomach*) mortal flesh must leave obey!

MRS. COBB. Yes—yes—You know these members. Sit right down while I get your breakfast on the table. Oh, yes—I believe—er—Brother Perkins wanted to see you about a little matter. (*brightly*) You did want to talk to the Elder, didn't you, Brother Perkins.

PERKINS. Why—why—

ELDER. Hit can wait. Ah nevah feels up to serious discussion befo' Ah eats. This mawnin', 'specially, Sister Cobb. I—I—(*he sneezes*)

SISTER SABOY. (*solicitously*) Yo' catchin' cold, Eldah.

ELDER. Ah don' feel so good—that hot bath—(*he sneezes again*)

MRS. COBB. Oh—dear. I'll get you something right away. I—(*The doorbell rings*) Now, what. (*she calls*) Mirah—Mirah—

MIRAH. (*appearing in dining room door*) Yes, ma. Good morning, everybody.

MRS. COBB. Is it—is—(*Mirah is pushing the door back. She is smiling sweetly*)

MIRAH. Your breakfast's all ready. Dr. Green, Come right out.

GREEN. (*beaming on her*) Them is sweet words—daughter. (*Bell rings again*)

MRS. COBB. (*relaxed*) See who's at the door, Mirah. I'll look after the Elder. Now, we've finshed this half. (*She indicates sewing*) If you ladies want to start on the other piece it's in Reverend's study.

(*Sister White folds piece which she takes into study*)

ELDER. (*squeezing himself into a chair, his back to the door*) Blessed are the pure in heart—for they shall see God. Come right out, Brother Perkins. Ah can talk when food's in front o' me.

PERKINS. Ah reckon Brother Cobb's out collectin' his quarterly envelopes.

SISTER SABOY. No—I met him on the way over to Mother Reed's. Said she was took bad this morning.

PERKINS. Seems lak Reverend be awful busy gettin' up them back dues. Hit's tha las' quarter.

(*He joins the Elder and Sister Saboy goes into study. Down the steps moving softly comes E.J. He meets Mirah coming in from the hall. She is carrying a letter and a newspaper.*)

E.J. (*speaking softly*) The buzzards are gathering! Say, do you think if I—could—knock around an' gather up a few dollars—you could slip 'em in the church envelope without pop knowing?

MIRAH. Why, E.J. If you put money in the church why shouldn't he know? It's a grand idea, but where can you raise money?

E.J. Might get some—donations. But, no, it's got to be kept quiet. The people I'll get it from won't want their names signed.

MIRAH. Course I can git in. It'll be wonderful if you do try. Oh, E.J., we don't want to move—now.

E.J. I see you don't. Tell your boy friend even if I ain't a pew warmer I wouldn't mind havin' a home to drop in on—even if it's—my sister's. (*He laughs silently and exits to hall*)

SISTER SABOY. (*in study doorway*) Weren't that E.J. jus' went out?

MIRAH. Yes, mam.

SISTER SABOY. (*acidly*) Looks lak he might o' come in and speak. Readin' law, Humph!

MRS. COBB. (*calling from dining room*) What is it, Mirah?

MIRAH. A "special delivery" for pa.

MRS. COBB. Well, I'm glad it's not a telegram. I'm always fraid to open them. Put it over there on the desk. Reverend will see it the minute he comes in.

SISTER SABOY. Hope it's not bad news!

MRS. COBB. (*indifferently*) Oh, I never worry about Reverend's mail. Don't see why so many people write him.

MIRAH. Here's the paper. (*She tosses it on the table*)

PERKINS. Is that there the "Chicago Watchtower"?

MRS. COBB. Yes. Would you like to see it? (*She hands him the paper*)

PERKINS. (*coming down bringing the paper*) Ma wife's allus after me to subscribe for it, but I tells her we jus' can' afford them weekly papers.

SISTER SABOY. The headlines is simply scandalous. Old Reverant Watts always said he wouldn't allow that paper in his house—Till tha day he died, he said it. . . . (*She gazes soulfully up at the stained glass window*) I nevah look at that window without thinking about his dear, departed wife. Them pieces was from her memorial window—bit left over. He thought it would be nice to put them in here. (*shaking her head*) She breathed her last right upstairs in the front room.

MRS. COBB. (*a bit nervously*) Yes—I know. Er—a—did you finish the choir piece? I think we'd better get it up.

BROTHER PERKINS. (*reading*) "Howard Professor's Wife Sues Scholar—Love Nest Exposed" Humph! Such carryin's on!

SISTER SABOY. (*sadly*) He never let that paper come in tha parsonage.

MRS. COBB. It does carry lots of national news. Reverend wants the children to read about what Negroes all over the country are doing.

PERKINS. Here's something would interest Mirah. (*reads*) "Colored Maid Left Fortune by Movie Star"!

MRS. COBB. I don't see—(*she bites her lips*) I must run upstairs and straighten the Elder's room. He's finishing his breakfast. Just make yourselves at home. Lilacs! Lilacs, you're not ready yet? (*She goes up*)

MIRAH. (*from dining room*) Did you say something to me?

PERKINS. Jus' said you'd read this. Here, take the paper. I've had enough of that trash. Look at that! (*He points with his finger to the article. Mirah glances down with little interest*)

TOUSSANT. (*just entered from hall*) What is it?

MIRAH. (*reading*) Nothin' much.

SISTER SABOY. You might read it aloud, Mirah.

MIRAH. Oh, excuse me, Mis' Saboy, I didn't know you wanted to hear it. (*reading*) The publication of Sadie Kessler's will yesterday revealed the fact that Miss Kessler, recent beloved star of stage and screen, had provided most generously for all the members of her household. Particularly favored was her personal maid, Mat—(*The telephone rings brightly. Mirah turns to answer it, but Sister Saboy is there before her.*)

SISTER SABOY. Yes—yes, this is tha parsonage. . . . I said this is tha parsonage . . . Yes, Rev. Cobb lives here . . . He ain't home . . . What? What? Who do you want . . . the son? Which son . . . young Mr. Cobb . . . I suppose you mean Elijah. (*Mirah and Toussant are exchanging agonized glances*) Well, he ain't home, neither. (*She slams up the receiver*) It was a girl!

(*Mirah and Toussant draw together saying nothing*)

PERKINS. They will run after a good lookin' preacher's son!

MIRAH. (*brightly*) It says here this maid traveled all over Europe with Sadie Kessler. That musta been grand! She was with her fifteen years—and before that she was with Williams and Walker.

PERKINS. (*perking up his ears*) Williams an—? Was she a show girl?

TOUSSANT. (*amused*) Yes. She was a dancer!

MRS. COBB. (*upstairs*) All right, Lilacs. No more talk. Now go!

LILACS. (*creeping down the steps and out*) Yessum. Ah'm goin'.

MRS. SABOY. If some of yo' lil' friends was callin' yo' out to play, yo' would move faster 'n that, Lilacs. (*Lilacs gives her a dirty look and exits*)

MRS. COBB. (*calling down*) Mirah—have you dusted the hall?

MIRAH. Yes, mam. I will. (*to Perkins*) See, here it is. Mattie Cobb had been a member of the old Williams and Walker company. She—

TOUSSANT. I guess there's lots of "Cobbs."

MRS. COBB. Toussant, bring up those blankets hanging out on the back line. And hurry.

TOUSSANT. Yessum.

(*He exits through dining room. Mirah goes into hall. The Elder, stuffed, is pushing back his chair and turning slightly around, picking his teeth. Perkins grabs the paper.*)

PERKINS. I speck I've seen this hyear Mattie Cobb!

SISTER SABOY (*taken back*) What?

PERKINS. Yes, mam—hit say right here she danced with Williams and Walker—don't hit?

SISTER SABOY. Yes, but—

PERKINS. Well, (*leaning closer*) once I went to Indianapolis to see that there Williams and Walker show!

SISTER SABOY. You did! Why, Brother Perkins!

PERKINS. Hush! That was 'fore I got religion, of course. I was a pretty gay young buck in them days and that show—Lawdy, Lawdy! I allus was glad I seen it—course, 'fore I was a Christian. If Mattie Cobb was in dat bunch—she sho' was a pippin!

ELDER. (*from dining room*) What's dat yo' sayin', Brother Perkins! Why, yo' ole rooster! Ha! Ha! Ha! Gimme dat paper!

(*Sheepishly Brother Perkins goes up to the door and hands him the paper. Mirah is heard speaking in hall*)

MIRAH. Hello, Pa.

(*In the hall appears* REVEREND COBB. *He is fifty years old. The years have slightly rounded his shoulders, but have given him no superfluous flesh and no wrinkles. Slightly nearsighted eyes, strained by much reading, peer out with a bland, smiling confidence. He is brown-skinned, with soft, graying hair and a trimmed beard. He wears a plain, dark suit, slightly wrinkled. He smiles warmly at his visitors.*)

REVEREND. Sister Saboy, I greet you again this lovely morning. And how's my good brother?

PERKINS. (*coming down*) Toler'ble, Reverend, Jus' tolerable. How's Mother Reed?

REVEREND. We had a glorious hour together. She's going down without a murmur—dying like she lived—beautifully!

MRS. SABOY. (*anxiously*) You mean—?

REVEREND. Not yet, but soon—soon.

PERKINS. (*willing to change the subject*) There's a special for you, Reverend.

REVEREND. Oh, thanks, Brother. I'll take it in the study. (*Crossing to pick up his letter he sees the Elder*) Good morning, Elder. Hope you rested well.

ELDER. (*generously*) Ah did, indeed, suh, Ah did, indeed. (*He continues reading. Reverend picks up his letter and goes into study*)

MRS. COBB. (*calling down*) Was that Reverend just came in?

SISTER SABOY. Yes, it was, Sister Cobb.

MRS. COBB. I'm coming right down. Everything's in shape now.

PERKINS. Well, I guess we'll be going along.

SISTER SABOY. Sister White's in the kitchen. She said not to wait for her.

PERKINS. Sure you don't want me to look at that faucet?

MRS. COBB. The faucet? Oh, no, no! I'm certain it's all right. E.J . . .

SISTER SABOY. Some gal just called up here for E.J.

MRS. COBB. Oh—did she leave a number?

SISTER SABOY. They never do.

MIRAH. (*coming in from hall*) E.J.'ll be back in a little while.

(*Reverend enters from study. He holds the open letter in his hand and is beaming with pleasure.*)

REVEREND. Oh, my dear—listen to this—you're not going, folks—I was coming out—stopped to read my letter—mamma, it's from my sister—she's coming here to see us!

MRS. COBB. (*faintly*) Your sister—coming here—your sister—(*There is unspoken meaning behind her words*)

MRS. SABOY. Coming here? When? (*The Elder looks up, interested*)

REVEREND. Real soon. The letter's from California—it seems she's been out there quite a spell—she's been trying to locate me—Imagine—She says she wants to get away and talks about coming home.

MIRAH. Pa, I didn't know you had a sister in California. (*Toussant has started in, his arms full of blankets. The Elder is standing in the dining room doorway.*)

REVEREND. Neither did I—that's what's so wonderful. . . . I haven't heard from her for so long—It's been years—I didn't dare think.

MRS. SABOY. She probably got a big family.

REVEREND. Well, really I don't know—she doesn't say—that is funny—she doesn't say a word about anybody.

ELDER. Is she a widow?

REVEREND. She just says (*he consults the letter "My dear Brother, I"*)—

MIRAH. Papa—what is—your sister's name? (*She and Toussant are gazing hard at one another. Toussant clutching the blankets.*)

REVEREND. Eh, what? Why, it's—Mattie—It's your Aunt Mattie. She's never even seen you. Think of it! It's just Mattie Cobb, of course—that is—if she's never married—maybe—

(The blankets slip from Toussant's stunned arms. The Elder is staring open-mouthed at the paper which he is holding as the curtain falls.)

CURTAIN

SCENE TWO: *The same. One week later, mid-afternoon.*

Effort has been made to improve the appearance of the room. Curtains now hang at the door between sitting and dining room. Elegant doilies have been placed on the backs of chairs, new cretonne drapes are at the windows.

AT RISE: *Mrs. Cobb and Mirah are arranging a new rug on the floor, being very critical about the job. Two moving men (white) are bringing in from the hall a sofa which is still partly wrapped. At the moment they are having difficulty getting it through the door. Half up the stairway stands Toussant, several sheets of paper in his hand. He is declaiming with sweeping gestures.*

Ben-Hur just appearing in the dining room is industriously applying himself to a large slice of bread.

TOUSSANT. And now ladies and gentlemen I come to the stirring lines of our immortal poet, Paul Lawrence Dunbar—the poet who might well be called the pride of his race, the people's choice of Ohio, the black barber of—of—What do I want to say, Mirah? *(no answer from Mirah)* Mirah! "the black barber of—what?' Mirah!

MRS. COBB. Leave Mirah alone. We're trying to get this rug straight. There—I think that's right—no—a little further over this way.

TOUSSANT. I gotta finish my speech! Boy, I hope she gets here in time to hear this. Believe me, it's a pippin! Say, do you suppose she likes speeches?

MRS. COBB. I don't know.

TOUSSANT. *(not discouraged)* Course she would—her being around actors and things. Say, I might decide to be a actor.

BEN-HUR. How you gonna be a leader if you a actor? Actors ain't nobody.

TOUSSANT. That's all you know. Paul Robeson's a actor!

BEN-HUR. Well, his name ain't "Toussant"!

MRS. COBB. Keep quiet, boys!

TOUSSANT. *(injured)* Well, can't nobody listen to me?

LILACS. *(swinging over the banister above Toussant and balancing herself perilously on the steps)* Go head, Toussant—I'm hyear!

MRS. COBB. Lilacs! You'll tear your dress! Get down, instantly! *(to Ben-Hur)* Don't come in here with those crumbs. *(to the men)* Oh, Mercy! you'll scratch it! *(She assists the furniture men)*

TOUSSANT. Now, Mirah, black barber of what? You heard what I said—bout Dunbar—

MIRAH. *(absentmindedly)* Dayton—I guess.

TOUSSANT. *(again declaiming)* —the choice of Ohio, the black barber of Dayton—*(pause)* That don't sound so good!

BEN-HUR. It sure don't. Paul Lawrence Dunbar wasn't no barber!

TOUSSANT. I didn't say he was!

BEN-HUR. (*amazed*) You did so! You jus' said it—"black barber of"—

TOUSSANT. Crazy, I'm not talkin' 'bout that sort of a barber. Miss Nelson said—

LILACS. (*still balancing herself prettily*) Black Barber! Black Barber!

TOUSSANT. (*annoyed*) Shut up! You! (*He slaps out at Lilacs who expertly evades him by sliding down the banister and landing in a heap on the floor*)

MRS. COBB. Children!

TOUSSANT. Miss Nelson was tellin' me about poets and she called Shakespeare the barber of—

MIRAH. Oh, Toussant, you're mistaken!

TOUSSANT. I am not! It sounded grand when Miss Nelson said it. She—

LILACS. (*dusting herself off, speaks decisively*) White folks is crazy!

(*The men have finally set the sofa in the middle of the floor and are tearing off the wrapping*)

MRS. COBB. Lilacs! (*admiring sofa*) It's beautiful! But, where shall we put it?

MAN. Guess that's all, lady.

MRS. COBB. Yes, yes. I'm so glad they sent it right up. (*Exit men*) That was quick work for the committee.

MIRAH. I'll say it was.

MRS. COBB. I told them your father's sister was coming and we had to fix up this place a little. And, I didn't bite my teeth about it, either.

LILACS. (*chanting*) I gotta rich ant—I gotta rich ant—

MRS. COBB. (*tolerantly*) Be still, Lilacs. (*Ben-Hur has been examining the old sofa. Now, he speaks suddenly.*)

BEN-HUR. Ma, can I have this?

MRS. COBB. You don't need that sofa.

BEN-HUR. I'll put it in the basement. Please, ma—I'll just—(*He starts to pull it towards the door*)

LILACS. (*shrill*) He wants to sell it!

BEN-HUR. You shut your mouth, Miss Smarty!

LILACS. He sells everything—You just look in the basement, ma—just look in the basement—regular old junkshop. I seen—

BEN-HUR. (*fiercely*) Pokin' 'round in my things, eh? I'll fix you for this—you little—(*Starts towards her*)

MRS. COBB. Ben-Hur, let her alone. And I don't think you'd better sell that sofa. The members might talk.

BEN-HUR. Did I say I was going to sell it? Did I? I guess it don't make no difference what our aunt thinks about me—I don't count—Toussant can make his speeches—an' E.J.'s goin' in a law office and Mirah's in a new dress, but me—I don't—

MRS. COBB. Oh, for heaven sakes—be still. This sofa's going in your father's study.

MIRAH. There isn't room in there.

MRS. COBB. It'll be another place to pile books. (*Again threatened by Ben-Hur, Lilacs runs to the hall door, bumping into E.J., who is just entering*)

E.J. (*catching her*) Hey, where you going so fast?

LILACS. (*pulling away*) Lemme go—lemme go—Ben-Hur—

E.J. (*grabbing Ben-Hur, as she slips out*) Wait a minute, fellow. A man doesn't strike a lady, you know.

BEN-HUR. (*raging*) Lady! She ain't no lady—she never was a lady—she never will be a lady—I'll smack her head off—I'll—

E.J. Hold it! hold it! We have company!

BEN-HUR. Oh, gosh!

(*He flings himself into a chair as* BUTCH JOHNSON *comes in behind E.J. Butch is a stocky young fellow, good football material, brownskinned, awkward. He immediately fastens his eyes on Mirah.*)

MRS. COBB. How do you do, Richard. I guess you've come to see Mirah, but I'm afraid you find us all busy this evening. You know, we expecting company.

BUTCH. (*dropping down on the old sofa*) Yes, mam, I know.

MRS. COBB. No, don't sit there. We were just getting ready to move it. Here, E.J. help Toussant put this in your father's study. You see, we have a new one.

MIRAH. You won't mind sleeping on this. See, it's soft as—(*sitting on it she bounces up and down*)

MRS. COBB. Sleeping on it! We didn't get this for E.J. to sleep on.

MIRAH. I mean when the Presiding Elder or the Bishop comes.

MRS. COBB. Things are going to be very different from now on. E.J.' s not going to be giving up his room for every Tom, Dick and Harry—

E.J. Harry! Is that his name—Harry?

MRS. COBB. Who?

E.J. The Presiding Elder, bless him!

MRS. COBB. You know his name's Calab Green.

E.J. Calab! (*He shakes his head*) No, I'm afraid he'll have to change it. I'm sure she won't like that.

MRS. COBB. What are you talking about?

E.J. Haven't you heard?—The Presiding Elder's setting his cap for our rich aunt!

(*Mirah titters and even Butch grins.*)

MRS. COBB. Don't talk nonsense!

E.J. You heard his talking about how he missed his wife and how lonely he is now—when he left here he was purring like a cat. He even shook hands with me!

BUTCH. Have you heard when she's coming, Mis' Cobb?

MRS. COBB. No, but I feel it in my bones she'll be here tonight or in the morning. Here, boys, get this moved. Toussant!

(*Toussant has paid very little attention. He has been busy writing and erasing on his paper. Now, he speaks, his mind still busy*)

TOUSSANT. I've cut out this last part. Listen "We wear the mask that grins and lies—It hides our cheek and shades our eyes—this debt we pay to human"—

MRS. COBB. Toussant, did you hear me.

TOUSSANT. (*resigned*) Oh, well, I might as well give up. How you, Butch. I guess your family is proud of you playing football, but my family doesn't care about what I'm doing. I can't even get 'em to listen to me—not even when I spend my whole Saturday afternoon working on something—not even—

MRS. COBB. Toussant, stop that nonsense. (*She looks up, sniffing the air*) Mercy! Something's burning! (*Rushes out through dining room*)

TOUSSANT. (*picking up one end of the sofa*) Fat chance I'll have to be anybody! Might as well be named Sam. (*E.J. laughs as they carry sofa into study.*)

MIRAH. (*to Butch*) I guess we're all kinda excited—sorta crazy like.

BUTCH. Aw, well. I guess anybody'd be—kinda—excited—having a aunt comin' from Hollywood an' everything!

MIRAH. I got some new things.

BUTCH. Yes—you don't suppose—maybe—you could—we could go some place—tonight?

MIRAH. Where could we go?

BUTCH. I think there's a good movie on—at the Palace. Wouldn't make no difference to me—where we went.

MIRAH. Wouldn't it.

BUTCH. What'd you say? Havin' a famous aunt wouldn't make no difference in the movies—would it?

MIRAH. I don't know—I might ask—

BUTCH. Do you always have to ask—somebody?

MIRAH. Well—I—

BUTCH. Looks to me like you kinda—old fashioned—None of the girls I know—

MIRAH. (*flaring up*) I am not old fashioned!

BUTCH. Oh—I didn't mean—er—old fashioned. I just—You know—askin'—and—everything—

MIRAH. My father says—

BUTCH. Sure, I know—your father's a preacher and everything. But, most of the time they say preacher's children are—

MIRAH. It's not true!

BUTCH. I don't think you're fast. I—I—think—

(*Lilacs suddenly puts her head into the hall door and announces*)

LILACS. Mis' Swan's gettin' outta her car. Somebody's with her. I'll let 'em in. (*Head disappears*)

MIRAH. Lilacs, come back here! Oh, dear!

BUTCH. Guess I'll be going. Will you find out about—er—what we said?

MIRAH. Yes, I'll—

TOUSSANT. (*in study door*) Who'd Lilacs say was coming?

MIRAH. Mis' Swan.

E.J. (*behind Toussant*) Is Dr. Swan with her?

MIRAH. I don't think so. (*Ben-Hur heaves himself out of the deep chair in which he has been sitting unnoticed.*)

BEN-HUR. (*grinning at Butch*) She better ask!

BUTCH. Oh—hello, fellow. I guess you couldn't use a ticket to the game next Saturday.

BEN-HUR. For a ticket to the game, I ain't heard nothing. I was sound asleep!

BUTCH. Okay. I'm running along before the company comes. Bye. (*Mirah follows him into the hall where voices are now heard.*)

E.J. Lemme get upstairs. That voice of hers gives me a pain. (*Going up*)

TOUSSANT. Me, too. (*to Ben-Hur, who is crossing the room*) Where you going?

BEN-HUR. To the basement.

MRS. COBB. (*calling from the kitchen*) Toussant! Toussant!

TOUSSANT. (*turning back*) Oh, darn!

(*He goes through dining room as* MRS. SWAN *enters from hall. Being "the doctor's wife" is a responsibility which she never forgets. She attempts to act and dress up to this fact. The results are highly individual. Behind her comes* MISS HALL, *a young and attractive school teacher.*)

MRS. SWAN. Wasn't that that there Butch Johnson out there with Mirah?

MISS HALL. Yes, I think it was. He's a very nice boy.

MRS. SWAN. Humph! (*walking to the center of the room*) Well, how they have fixed up this room is elegant—positively elegant!

MISS HALL. It isn't every day a Hollywood heiress visits our parsonage.

MRS. SWAN. Maybe. But, it behooves us people what represents the real Society of this town to remember that she was only a maid. (*Miss Hall tries to say something*) Naturally the money makes a difference, but there is such a thing as po-sition!

MISS HALL. I don't see exactly how we can—

MRS. SWAN. You wouldn't. You're not the wife of one of the profession. A school teacher has to come in contact with all the—er—classes. There are people what recognizes distinctions. The club was asking me did I think we oughtta entertain her. And I says we gotta give the matter careful de-liber-ation.

MISS HALL. But—

MRS. SWAN. Miss Hall, the Daughters of the New Revolution stands for something—it's gotta long line of standin' fur something—an' we ain't picking up some presuming nu-vo-rich and presenting 'em on our plane. We gotta keep our culture pure.

(*Mirah has just entered from the hall.*)

MIRAH. Oh, hasn't ma come?

MRS. SWAN. We ain't seen her.

MISS HALL. (*laughing*) She probably doesn't know we're here.

MIRAH. I'll tell her. (*She goes out through the dining room*)

MRS. SWAN. (*calling*) And, Mirah—tell one of your brothers to bring that lamp outta my car. (*to Miss Hall*) That lamp will give just the finishing touch. We'll sit here by the window. . . . Do you suppose Sadie Kessler really left her a fortune?

MISS HALL. That's what the papers say. (*eagerly*) And she traveled with her—everywhere. Oh, How I'd love to talk to somebody who's really seen London and Vienna and—Paris! I've tried so hard to save enough money to go places.

MRS. SWAN. Humph! Thank God I ain't got no cravins to be trapasin' 'round with a lot of fureigners! I ain't got no time for jibbering Frenchmen and smelly Dagoes. This country's good enough for me. Us Daughters of the New Revolution is taught to 'preciate ourselves! (*Miss Hall has been surveying the room*)

MISS HALL. Even the rug doesn't help this room much.

MRS. SWAN. (*snapping*) She lets the children climb all over everything. What can you expect. It's laziness—just pure laziness—this thing of preachers having so many children.

MISS HALL. Laziness?

MRS. SWAN. And all those old books! Makes the whole room shabby. Rev. Cobb spent all that money for cases—he bought 'em himself, you know—and then stuffs them with a lot of torn, rusty old books.

MISS HALL. (*regarding the bookcase*) They have been used.

MRS. SWAN. Used! It's disgraceful, right here in the front room. I was telling the doctor just the other day—(*Breaks off as Mrs. Cobb enters, wiping her hands on her apron*) Oh, how do you do, Sister Cobb?

MISS HALL. Good afternoon, Mrs. Cobb.

MRS. COBB. Sorry I couldn't come in sooner. My meat was burning. I had to put it in another pan. Do sit down.

MRS. SWAN. We just ran by to bring the lamp I promised the committee.

MRS. COBB. That's very kind of you. Toussant's gone out after it.

MRS. SWAN. You must be very happy over the improvements we've made. (*She indicates the elegance of the room*)

MRS. COBB. (*calmly*) Yes, it will do very well for the present, I guess.

MRS. SWAN. (*taken back*) For the present—?

MRS. COBB. Of course when my sister-in-law arrives we'll probably make some changes. We may move!

MRS. SWAN. (*incredulous*) Move? From the parsonage?

MRS. COBB. We'll need a larger house.

MISS HALL. (*to fill in the gap*) You're expecting Miss Cobb soon?

MRS. COBB. Any day, now. Reverend heard from her the first of the week saying she was leaving California. She didn't say how she would travel. Of course, she may be flying. (*impressive pause*) We're all anxiously waiting for her.

MRS. SWAN. (*a bit acidly*) I'm sure you must be. (*Toussant enters from hall carrying a floor lamp*)

MRS. SWAN. Here's the lamp. It's been in the attic for some time, but if you clean the shade, it will do very well. Put it right over there, Toussant, by the window.

MRS. COBB. (*getting up*) No, Toussant, put it here. The shade is a little worn, but I'll get a new one next week.

MRS. SWAN. (*gasping*) Well, really—

MRS. COBB. (*continuing*) By the way, how is Dr. Swan? We haven't seen him for some time.

MRS. SWAN. (*recovering herself*) Natchally, he ain't got time to go to church.

MRS. COBB. I suppose he is pretty busy.

MRS. SWAN. Reverend Cobb was by the office the other day and doctor paid his dues. He always keeps up his obligations.

MISS HALL. Has Mirah finished that book I loaned her?

MRS. COBB. Yes, indeed. She was talking about it last night.

MISS HALL. I think I'll go out and talk to her. I'd like to know how she liked it.

MRS. COBB. Certainly. (*She calls*) Mirah!

MISS HALL. Don't call her—I'll just go out there. (*She goes out through dining room*)

MRS. SWAN. (*looking after her*) So much reading ain't good for a girl Mirah's age.

MRS. COBB. Oh, she's like her father. (*Voices in the hall*) There's Reverend now. Gracious! He has somebody with him. I know what that means.

REVEREND. (*still in hall*) Come right in, now, Brother Pugh. Not another word. Dinner's ready to sit on the table. You must have a bite. (*In doorway*) Mamma, here's Brother Pugh, from over at Flat Hollow. Put another plate on, Mirah. Howdy, Sister Swan. Good to see you!

(*He is ushering in* BROTHER PUGH, *an older, bent and shabby counterpart of himself. Brother Pugh's hair is white and his voice thin as a worn reed.*)

MRS. COBB. (*going forward*) How are you, Brother Pugh. Come right in. Here, lemme dust your hat. (*She takes it*)

BROTHER PUGH. (*humble*) Thank yo', kin'ly, Sistah Cobb.

REVEREND. Dinner ready, mamma? Where's the children? Sit down, Brother Pugh, sit down. It's always good to get home!

MRS. COBB. I'll take it right up. You don't have to hurry, do you, Mrs. Swan?

MRS. SWAN. (*uncertain*) Well, doctor said he'd come by here for me.

MRS. COBB. Then come on out with me. We can talk while I'm doing this. (*They go out and Mrs. Cobb pulls together the dining curtains. The two men are left alone.*)

REVEREND. Well, how are things over at Flat Hollow?

BROTHER PUGH. Purty slow, Brother Cobb, purty slow.

REVEREND. That's a right nice little charge over there, though. Small, but faithful souls.

BROTHER PUGH. Yes—hit is. Mah wife an' me been real happy wid them members. But, ah speck we won't be there much longah, Brother. (*There is tragedy in his voice*) Mah dolla money's gonna come up short.

REVEREND. Oh, Pshaw! The Bishop knows these are close times. People don't have the money.

BROTHER PUGH. Ah can' tell 'im dat. Da Presiding Elder say a youngah man can git hit.

REVEREND. (*protesting*) Come now, Brother Pugh—

BROTHER PUGH. (*Laying his wrinkled hand on Reverend's arm*) T'ain't no use. Ah ain't up wid dese new times. Ah ain't got no edication lak yo'. Ah learned to read right outta mah ole Bible. Hit ustta be all right cause Ah knows 'bout sorrow an' sufferin'—knows 'bout da love o' Jesus, but—(*He turns away, discouraged*)

REVEREND. (*fervently*) You know the things that count.

BROTHER PUGH. (*shaking his head*) Nobody wans to hyear dos things no more. Ah can' raise money. Ah'm gettin' ole—what'll become of us—me an' mah ole lady?

REVEREND. Brother Pugh I'm ashamed of you . . . A God-fearing man, if ever there was one. You led our people when they didn't have books and fine churches; you been a true soldier and here you are doubting God's love. Why, you're like the prophet Elijah. Remember that time he ran away—discouraged—afraid, even. He thought the Devil himself was running everything. But, our Lord didn't get angry at his prophet—not Him. He knowed Elijah was just a little beat and tired. He just showed him a quiet place to rest and He sent His ravens to feed him. Remember? God sent his ravens to feed Elijah!

BROTHER PUGH. You're a good man, Brother. Ah knows Ah hadn't oughtta worry. Only—sometimes—when Ah sees 'em lookin' at me—Ah feels so worn an' shabby (*his voice quivers*) lak dis ole coat—(*he holds up his arm*)—frayed at da sleeves—thin and patched.

REVEREND. Old coat? (*slapping his knee*) Why, bless me—How glad I am you mentioned it. I've got a coat that's been hanging here for ages (*He goes into the study continuing talking. Mirah appears in dining room door to call them. She hesitates*) Mamma would've cut it up long ago for one of the boys—only you can't do a thing with these old preacher coats—not a thing—(*comes out taking a frock coat from its hanger*) It's too small for me, but I shouldn't be at all surprised if it would about fit you. Here, let's try it. (*Mirah makes a motion of protest, but is not seen. E.J. has started down the steps and stops*) Take yours off. . . . (*suiting action to words*) Now, slip this on.

BROTHER PUGH. (*running his hand over coat*) Hit's a real broadcloth!

REVEREND. Sure. I been worried about it hanging up there in the dust. There—a little full across the shoulders, but a pretty good fit. Wish there was a glass in here so you could see. How does it feel?

BROTHER PUGH. (*lifting his shoulders*) Wonderful! Hit's—hit's—lak a new man!

REVEREND. There you are!

BROTHER PUGH. I donno how to thank—

REVEREND. Don't thank me. Just go on doing the Lord's work. I'm just passing on a little of his blessings. Something wonderful happened to me just this week. You know, I thought I was behind in my dollar money too. My wife was awful upset, but I wasn't. And Sunday night when we counted the envelopes for the last time—what do you suppose happened?

BROTHER PUGH. What, Brother Cobb?

REVEREND. I found an envelope I'd never seen before, just signed "A friend" and in that envelope was fifty dollars—Fifty dollars, Brother Pugh—That brought my report up so far that every class was encouraged—fifty dollars! I don't know who that friend is—and I don't ask. I know the Lord touched his heart.

MIRAH. (*softly*) Dinner's ready, pa.

REVEREND. That's good news! Come on, Brother Pugh. Um-um—it smells good! (*Brother Pugh passes on into the dining room. Mirah grabs her father's arm, pulling him downstage*)

MIRAH. Papa! That was your good coat! What will you wear tomorrow?

REVEREND. Sh-sh-sh! I've got plenty of coats.

MIRAH. You haven't—you know you haven't . . .

REVEREND. (*smiling*) Honey, that wasn't my coat—That was a mantle! (*He exits to dining room. E.J. comes down to steps. Through the portieres may be heard voices and dishes.*)

MIRAH. You saw?

E.J. Yes—and I heard. It's the ravens again. (*clapping his head and grinning*) Hey, sis, do we look like ravens?

MIRAH. (*giving him a little hug*) We should worry!

MRS. COBB. (*from dining room*) Come on, children—Pa's waiting to say the blessing. Where's Lilacs?

E.J. (*calling upstairs*) Lilacs! Come on. We're waiting.

LILACS. I'm commen!

MRS. COBB. Go on, pa. She'll be here in a minute.

(*At this moment comes a loud, hard ring of the doorbell. E.J. dashes back the curtain. Everyone is tense*)

TOUSSANT. Maybe it's her!

MRS. SWAN. Want me to go, Sister Cobb?

MRS. COBB. No, no! I'll go.

E.J. Keep calm, everybody.

LILACS. (*running full speed downstairs*) I'll go! (*Before anyone can stop her, she is out through the hall door. There is expectant waiting. In a moment Lilacs rushes back—her eyes wide, short of breath*) Pa—pa—it's—a—it's—a—(*Speechless, she points as from the hall strides a policeman.*)

E.J. (*giving a start*) What—what—!

(*The policeman fixes the staring group with a hard eye and asks*)

POLICEMAN. Is this where (*he consults a paper*)—Rev. Cobb lives?

REVEREND. Why—why—yes.

POLICEMAN. Are you Rev. Cobb?

REVEREND. Yes.

POLICEMAN. Do you know a (*again consulting paper*) a Mattie Cobb?

REVEREND. Yes—of course—Mattie—you've come about Mattie? That's my sister.

MRS. COBB. His sister? Oh, what has happened—what has happened—now?

POLICEMAN. (*gazing at the little man in surprise*) It is? Well, I'll be—(*he stops*) I guess it'll be all right—only you'll have to come get her.

MRS. COBB. Come get her?

MRS. SWAN. Get Her? Where is she?

REVEREND. She's not hurt? Officer, she's not hurt?

POLICEMAN. Naw—she ain't hurt—much. Considerin' what she did to the other fellow!

REVEREND. (*excited*) Oh, where's my hat? Mamma, what do you suppose is the matter?

MRS. COBB. I can't bear it! I can't bear it! E.J. you'd better go, too.

POLICEMAN. The car's outside. Won't take long.

MRS. SWAN. Not a patrol wagon? Oh, Miss Hall, a patrol wagon in front of the parsonage! (*She rushes to the window*)

POLICEMAN. (*unimpressed*) Naw. (*to Reverend, who has found his hat*) Ready?

REVEREND. Yes, yes—I'm ready. Are you coming, E.J.?

MRS. COBB. But where? Where is she?

POLICEMAN. Her? Oh—Mattie Cobb's in jail. (*He leads the way out*)

CURTAIN

ACT TWO

SCENE ONE: *Two hours later. It is dark outside, but the room is brightly lighted. The guests have gone.*

At Rise: *Ben-Hur and Lilacs are at the window down left straining their eyes and pushing each other in their eagerness to see. Lilacs is fairly jump-*

ing up and down with excitement. Toussant at the table is trying to give some attention to his papers. He is hardly succeeding.

LILACS. Look! Look! There's a car. It's stopping!

BEN-HUR. No! It's going by . . . Wait . . . wait a minute. I think it is slowing down. (*Toussant hurries to window*)

MIRAH. (*running down the stairs*) Was that the doorbell? Quick—was that the bell?

TOUSSANT. No—the bell didn't ring. We thought . . .

BEN-HUR. Nobody's gettin' out. It stopped. It can't be them. Nobody's getting out!

TOUSSANT. Well—what's it stopped for?

LILACS. (*turning towards door*) I'm gonna see!

(*The telephone rings. Everybody rushes to it. Mirah grabs receiver.*)

MIRAH. Yes . . . Yes. Oh, E.J.! Where are you? It's been an hour since you called and you said then. . . . Yes. . . . Yes . . . Reporters? Oh, E.J.! Yes. . . . Yes . . . Hurry, hurry. Yes, I'll tell her. Good-by. (*hanging up*) I'll die! Simply die!

TOUSSANT. What did he say?

BEN-HUR. Tell us!

LILACS. (*screaming*) Ma-ma! Ma-ma!

MIRAH. Shut up!

MRS. COBB. (*calling down*) Who was it, Mirah? Are they coming?

MIRAH. Wait a minute. Let me tell you.

TOUSSANT. Well, go on! (*Mrs. Cobb comes halfway downstairs, leaning over banister.*)

MIRAH. E.J. said we gotta watch out for reporters. He said they're trying to dodge them. That's why they're so long. He said—

TOUSSANT. Reporters! Bigshots! This is something!

BEN-HUR. Dodging reporters! Gosh!

MIRAH. It's like a movie. I never was so excited in my life!

MRS.COBB. But when he called before he said—

MIRAH. I know, but somebody at the police station recognized her and he said it was awful—just awful!

TOUSSANT. She musta been driving some car to run that cracker right in the ditch and smash him all to pieces.

MIRAH. (*eagerly*) A special make—E.J. said that—it was a special make car.

LILACS. (*hopefully*) Maybe he'll die!

MRS. COBB. Oh, hush Lilacs. The man's all right. Naturally they couldn't figure out a colored woman driving such a car—especially with a California license. (*Heartily*) Well, they'll see.

MIRAH. They have seen! She figured by sending for pop nobody'd question her. Guess it didn't work.

TOUSSANT. How they find out?

MIRAH. He didn't say.

BEN-HUR. Reporters!

LILACS. (*throwing up window*) Look here comes another car!

MRS.COBB. Lilacs get out of that window. We'll see them when they get here. (*turning back upstairs*) I'm getting the room all ready. She'll probably need to lie right down. No telling how badly shaken up she is by the accident and everything. Mirah, see that the kettle's on so she can have something hot.

(*The doorbell rings. Everybody starts*)

MIRAH. That can't be them.

TOUSSANT. They wouldn't ring.

BEN-HUR. Maybe it's your movie date!

MIRAH. I'm not—Do you think we ought to answer?

LILACS. I'll—(*Toussant lays a firm hand on her, plunking her into a chair*)

TOUSSANT. You sit still!

(*Mrs. Cobb gathers up her courage and goes to the door. Outside an auto horn sounds and the window curtains blow back in a lazy evening breeze. Voices in hall*)

MRS. COBB. This is a surprise, Elder! (*Sonorous voice*)

TOUSSANT. (*horrified*) The Presiding Elder!

BEN-HUR. Aw, rats!

ELDER. (*at door*) Wouldn't go through without dropping in to see yo' all. How's everybody? (*Expansively*) How you all, children?

TOUSSANT, BEN-HUR, LILACS. (*chorus*) How-do. (*The Elder's eyes are darting about the room*)

ELDER. (*to Mirah*) And how is the little lady this evening?

MIRAH. (*primly*) Quite well, thank you.

ELDER. Fine! Fine! Ah—see you've made quite a few changes—Ah—yes— tha touch of a woman's hands—Precious—precious! Yes, yes, (*he sighs deeply*) and is tha good Reverend in? (*Making himself comfortable in the armchair*)

MRS. COBB. No—ah—that is—we're expecting him any minute. Arn't you holding Quarterly Meeting at Pineville tomorrow?

ELDER. Yes—yes—jus' stopped on my way over—wouldn't pass through without droppin' in to see Brother Cobb—I tell you—he's a fine man—a fine man—always out—tendin' his flock . . . His sister—has she—er— (*There is a noise in the dining room. Everyone jumps*)

MIRAH. (*starting out*) I'll see—

MRS. COBB. No—I'll—(*Sister Saboy appears in the doorway*) Oh!

SISTER SABOY. 'Scuse me! Thought Ah'd jus' slip in tha back way so as not to disturb you. I thought—maybe—(*She stops, staring at the Presiding Elder.*)

ELDER. Good evening, sistah. Always glad to see the good ladies of the church.

SISTER SABOY. (*bluntly*) We ain't expecting you. Mis' Swan said—that is— she said—(*whispering mysteriously*) Has she come?

MRS. COBB. (*crossly*) No, she hasn't.

ELDER. (*alert*) Yo' means—

MRS. COBB. Reverend has gone after his sister. She had an automobile accident.

ELDER. A accident? Why, why didn't yo' tell me—here Ah am—Oh my—

LILACS. (*offering information*) Smashed a man's car to smithers!

ELDER. Oh, Lawd! She's hurt? How terrible! Is she badly injured?

MRS. COBB. E.J. phoned she wasn't. They're on their way now.

SISTER SABOY. Never can' tell 'bout them things!

ELDER. How true! A man can't—oh! This is awful—maybe broken an— Poor, lonely little thing. . . . she will need somebody to—God works in mysterious ways—Well, Ah'll jus' . . .

(*There is a sharp report in the hall outside. Followed immediately by a thump and crash. Then a rich, husky voice is heard exclaiming*)

VOICE. You will—will you? Yo' little weasely pop-eyed worm of a printer's devil! Sneaking out of corners—snooping down on people 'n' grabbing pictures! Oh! no, yo' don't. I'll break every bone in your—

(*Sound of scuffling and strain. Then through the door comes hurling the body of a little man. He is clutching a camera and falls in a heap on the floor. After him comes a formidable female whose red hair is only partly concealed by a rakish hat, now almost falling off. The female swoops down on the camera and standing erect tears it with her two hands. In that moment there is a blinding flash. A gleeful voice from the window causes them to turn. There, framed in the opening, is a camera backed by the head and shoulders of another man. He shouts*)

REPORTER. Atta Firebrand! Couldn't a been better if you'd come down and posed! Tough luck, Charlie! (*disappearing*) Be seeing you on the front page, sweetheart! (*The female strides across the room, seizes the flower pot hanging beside the window. There is a crash followed by a whoop of laughter from outside*) Missed me, baby!

FEMALE. Damnation! (*She turns and eyes the cowering creature who is making a move to get up. Through set teeth she speaks*) You—get outta here—before—I—break—your goddam neck! (*Terrified, he scrambles by E.J. who, loaded with baggage, stands grinning in the doorway. Then, the lady turns and speaks casually to the group.*) Well, hello, everybody!

E.J. (*endeavoring to shake their stupor*) Here we are, ma! Pops bringing in the rest of the things.

MRS. COBB. (*feebly*) Mattie—

(*MATTIE COBB has sunk down on the sofa, dragging off her hat. She is a large woman, clad in a sensible suit for driving. Her feet stick straight out in front of her. She is completely dejected. Her appearance is not improved by several strips of court plaster which have been pasted on her forehead.*)

MATTIE. Ain't this the dammedest mess! I'm beat. Gimme a drink, somebody!

E.J. (*while the others gasp—Lilacs slips out*) Howdy, Elder. Everything's all right, ma. They had to dig Aunt Mattie out of a wreck—but, oh, boy, what a wreck!

MRS. COBB. (*trying hard to recover*) We'er—we'er—so glad you're not hurt.

E.J. Here, Toussant, help me. Watch out, that's a radio.

TOUSSANT. Gee! A portable!

MRS. COBB. Boys, you can take the bags right upstairs. (*She bustles about.*)

ELDER. (*clearing his throat*) Well, Ah reckon Ah'll . . .

(*Lilacs has entered from the dining room with a brimming glass of water. She offers it to her aunt*)

LILACS. Hyear's your drink!

(*Mattie has been lying back her head on the sofa. She lifts up quickly and stretches out her hand. It pauses in mid-air as she stares at the glass.*)

MATTIE. (*in amazement*) What?

LILACS. (*extending it closer*) You asked for a drink. Hyear it is . . . it's nice and cold. I let the faucet run a long time.

MATTIE. (*throwing back her head—uproariously*) Ha! Ha! Ha! Will you look at this? Water! Honest-to-God water! What d'yo' know about this? (*Lilacs backs away disappointed.*) Hey, no! You're a cute little tike. Lemme try it. (*Standing, she takes the glass, closes her eyes, and puts it to her lips. A shudder shakes her frame*)

MRS. COBB. Lilacs, you—

MATTIE. (*sputtering*) No—no—good—kid. Can't take it. (*She observes the Presiding Elder gaping at her*) Here, big boy, got anything on you? I'm dying for a drink!

MRS. COBB. Oh!

PRESIDING ELDER. (*choking*) Why—why—How dare—I—I—No—

MATTIE. Okay, pal. You look like the kind of guy that'd always be hipped. (*With a wink*) Maybe not when you're visitng the preacher—eh? Ha! Ha! Ha!

(*The gasp is cut short by Reverend's appearance*)

REVEREND. (*beaming*) Here we are, folks! Here we are! Well! Well! (*He begins dropping bags*) Why, Elder! When did you get in?

MATTIE. Elder?

SISTER SABOY. Dat's our Presiding Elder!

MATTIE. Tie me for a hog!

REVEREND. Yes, indeed. Dr. Green, we're having a wonderful reunion. Haven't seen my sister for twenty years. Now, here she is! You've met her!

PRESIDING ELDER. (*rising with dignity*) Well, Brother Cobb, I—

MATTIE. Sure—sorta informal like. I ain't seen much of preachers in my crowd. You see, I—don't always recognize 'em!

MRS. COBB. Miss Cobb has been living in Hollywood and abroad most of this time.

MATTIE. I been around!

MRS. COBB. Now, if you'll just excuse me—I'll run out and get you something to eat. Come on, Sister Saboy. (*She hurries out, followed by a reluctant Sister Saboy*)

PRESIDING ELDER. (*pompously*) T'was the little lamb that strayed far from the fold that was most welcome. We shall keep you safe!

MATTIE. Eh, what? Ha! Ha! Ha! Think o' that! Where's that water, baby. I gotta drink something!

REVEREND. Won't you stay and have a bite with us, Elder.

ELDER. I'd better be gettin' along. Brother Simon's lookin' fur me.

MATTIE. (*staring at him*) Funny, how much yo' reminds me o' Pete Gill. Pete sho' had a way with women!

ELDER. (*flattered*) Well—I—

MATTIE. That is—till one o' 'em caught him wid a razur. Reckon he's cuttin' up with tha angels now!

ELDER. I must be going . . . even with money . . . No . . . Good evenin'.

REVEREND. (*following him into hall*) What's that? Sorry you won't stay. But, we'll be seeing you again. My sister . . .

(*Mattie grins after them as the voices become indistinct. Mirah has followed her mother to the kitchen. The boys have taken luggage upstairs, leaving the radio below. Now, only Lilacs watches as Mattie again sips the glass of water. Mattie groans, closing her eyes*)

LILACS. (*solicitiously*) Does something hurt you, Ant Mattie?

(*Mattie freezes. Her eyes fly open*)

MATTIE. (*hoarse*) What? (*She strangles*)

LILACS. Ain't you feelin' well?

MATTIE. Did you say—Ant Mattie? Is that what I'm gonna be called round here?

LILACS. (*smiling broadly*) Yessum—Ant Mattie.

(*Again Mattie closes her eyes. She gently sets down the glass*)

MATTIE. (*feebly*) Go away. I think I'm gonna be sick.

LILACS. (*alarmed*) Oh! I'll call—

MATTIE. No—no! Jus' lemme be quiet. That's a good girl. I gotta think. I'm dizzy.

(*Lilacs tiptoes off as Reverend returns from the hall. She motions to her father to be quiet and goes out. He starts softly across the room towards his study, but Mattie calls out to him.*)

MATTIE. Come over here, Eli. Lemme look at you. Haven't had a chance, yet.

REVEREND. You must rest. All this excitement. Poor Mattie, you're worn out!

MATTIE. Nobody calls me that now. It—it carries me back.

REVEREND. What? Mattie? (*She nods*) That's your name!

MATTIE. Who know that!

REVEREND But, what do they call you?

MATTIE. (*vaguely*) Oh—lot's o' things. Rusty—mostly.

REVEREND. Rusty! I—see—your hair. I wouldn't have known you. But, it's so good to see you again.

MATTIE. I got to wondering about your wife and you havin' kids and every-thing—It's been so long ago, but I remember Liza Dell from way back. Those Dells was always mighty tony!

REVEREND. I'm fraid I've kinda disappointed her. I don't seem to get ahead very fast.

MATTIE. And I reckon she ain't never forgot that your sister went off with a show man and him married.

REVEREND. Don't, Mattie. We're all glad you've come home. Why didn't you ever write? I was afraid—I thought—

MATTIE. For a long time it didn't make no difference. Then, in London I met Sadie . . . and . . .

REVEREND. Oh, Pshaw—we're happy you're here now. You tell us all about your travels when you're rested.

MATTIE. (*fondly*) Haven't changed a bit, have you?—I'll bet you're still slippin' out nights and climbin' trees—to be alone.

REVEREND. (*embarrassed*) What nonsense!

MATTIE. (*getting up and walking about*) I'd forgotten there were places like this in the world—honest to God, I had. (*E. J. and Toussant are coming down the stairs*) A swell pair of kids!

REVEREND. (*proudly*) You've met E.J. (*E.J. gives his aunt a broad under-standing grin*) Now, this is Toussant—Named after Toussaint L'Ou-verture.

MATTIE. What'd yo' know 'bout that!

TOUSSANT. Aunt Mattie—may we—can we—attach the radio downstairs?

MATTIE. Sure—go 'head. Set it any place.

TOUSSANT. (*overjoyed*) Oh, Boy! (*With E.J. he begins searching for the best place to make the attachments.*)

MATTIE. (*watching them*) You gonna be a soldier, too, Toussant?

TOUSSANT. No, mam. I'm goin' be a leader.

MATTIE. A leader—of what?

TOUSSANT. Oh—folks. I can make speeches now. (*dropping cord and look-ing up eagerly.*) Would you like to hear one—I jus' finished—(*He starts up*)

E.J. (*firmly*) Not now, Toussant.

REVEREND. Where's Ben-Hur?

MATTIE. Ben-Hur?

REVEREND. He's next to the baby.

E.J. Our sister named him. She was reading the book when he was born.

MATTIE. (*faintly*) Ben-Hur! (*Enter Mrs. Cobb from dining room.*)

MRS. COBB. Now! I see you're feeling better.

MATTIE. (*appreciating her effort*) Sure! I managed to pick myself up. If there's anything can get my goat it's them stinkin' little reporters buttin' into every breath you draw! You know how 'tis, Eli.

MRS. COBB. (*touch of bitterness*) Him? No, he wouldn't know. Never mind. Come on out and eat. You must be starved.

MATTIE. Well, I could put some good home cookin' underneath my belt. (*A burst of music behind them from the radio. It is a good jazz orchestra. Lilacs comes bursting from the dining room—bumping into Mattie in her eagerness.*)

LILACS. Music! Music! A radio! Oh! Glory be! (*She begins to dance. Mattie watches with growing amazement and appreciation—Reverend with growing consternation. The rest of the group with varying and conflicting emotions.*)

MATTIE. What d'you know about that? She's got something!

REVEREND. Lilacs!

LILACS. (*continuing to dance and making a song of it.*) Lemme 'lone— lemme dance—My feet jus' won't stay still!

REVEREND. Toussant—stop that music. (*Toussant shuts off radio. To Lilacs*) Is this any way to carry on before your auntie?

LILACS. (*almost in tears*) She was a dancer! She was a dancer! I know it! E.J. said so! Tell 'em, Ant Mattie, tell 'em. (*She runs to her*)

MATTIE. (*touched*) It's—been a long—time—Lilacs.

LILACS. But you knows—you knows . . . You knows how it is when the music come—when you can't stay still. Oh! I wanna dance! I wanna dance! (*She is crying*)

MATTIE. (*Putting her arms around her.*) Yes, yes, baby . . . I know.

REVEREND. Well, well . . . what is all this. I guess old King David had some of the same feelings—but right now your auntie's got to eat.

E.J. If King David had a ever got with Benny Goodman—Well, that gay old—

REVEREND. Never mind. He was dancing before the Lord!

E.J. Um-um!

REVEREND. Such a face, Lilacs. I'm sure your auntie would love to hear you play her a piece after while.

LILACS. Don' wanna play no piece. I wanna dance!

MRS. COBB. (*a bit weary*) Oh, come on and eat.

E.J. Just one of our little daily dozens, Aunt Mattie. You'll get used to 'em.

MATTIE. (*laying her arm affectionately over his shoulder*) It's a home, kid—it's a home!

(*They all accompany their guest to the dining room*)

REVEREND. Let's have some more music—a little less—er—a—jumpy!

(*They laugh and E.J. comes back into the living room to turn on radio. While he is doing so, Ben-Hur puts his head in at the hall door and calls in a whisper*)

BEN-HUR. E.J . . . (*urgently*) E.J.! (*E.J. turns quickly. Ben-Hur signals him to be quiet*)

E.J. What do you want?

BEN-HUR. (*still whispering*) There's a fellow here to see you. He said— (*E.J. is alert. He goes to the door as LEO slips in pushing Ben-Hur out of the way.*)

E.J. What are you doing here? Get—

LEO. Don' wan' yo folks to know, do you, Mister Good Guy? (*Ben-Hur makes a lunge to strike him. E.J. prevents it.*)

E.J. No! Ben-Hur, go on in the dining room. They been asking for you. Keep them talking. It's all right. I'll take care of this. Keep the folks out there. (*Ben-Hur understands and exits to dining room. He is heartily greeted.*)

REVEREND'S VOICE. Ah! Here's Ben-Hur, Mattie. Where you been, son?

MATTIE. Helly there, Ben-Hur. (*Other voices as they become indistinct*)

E.J. (*speaking low*) Now, then. What do you want?

LEO. Askin' me after yo' ain't been 'round for a week! What kind of a number runner do you think yo' are?

E.J. I'm not a regular number runner. I tried it, but for me it don't work. You know I did nothing to lose.

LEO. (*agreeing*) You did have the damdest luck for a beginner. But, that ain't—

E.J. I know—That's not your concern. But, I don't have to keep on doing it . . . Now, I don't need to!

LEO. Oh! Droppin' us, eh? Jus' like that! Well, Mr. Big Time, have you forgotten a little matter of fifty bucks that—

E.J. What do you think I am? Jake'll get it back—every penny of it.

LEO. Maybe! But that ain't the way we handles things. Wid number runners everything's gotta be open and above board. What kind of a reputation d'you think we'd get if we walk out without makin' reckonings. Jake's particular 'bout things like that.

E.J. Yes, I know—but—

LEO. Look, kid. I didn't come here to stick you up. Jake's a all right guy— white. He happened to be passin' by this afternoon and seen a cop come in here. Believe it or not, he comes right down to my place—worried. He says, "Leo, looks kinda like that boy's in trouble." Seems he heard your ole man preach once and he thinks he's tops—so he don' want yo jammed. Says for me to come up here and hang 'round till I found out what's up. Now then, spit it! You in bad?

E.J. Man! That's swell of Jake. Now, I can tell you. That policeman—it wasn't trouble! He just came to notify us that our aunt had an automobile accident—nothing serious, but she sent for my dad. Leo, she was driving from California—from Hollywood. She's rich! It'll be in the papers tomorrow. Tell Jake to read it. He needn't worry about his money. I'm sitting on top of the world—and—say, I won't forget him!

LEO. Jesus! From Hollywood! Is she in there? (*He strains to catch a glimpse. Mrs. Cobb returning from the kitchen with another dish sees him*)

MRS. COBB. (*pausing*) Oh! E.J., is that someone to see Reverend?

E.J. No, ma, just one of the fellows. I'll be right there.

LEO. Yes, mam. I'm going. (*lowering his voice again*) Okay, bo. I'll tell Jake. Drop 'round and see us.

E.J. (*going out hall with him*) Sure. You needn't worry. (*They sit. Voices come up in dining room*)

MATTIE. No! No! Don't show me any more food. Let's take these dishes out and then I'll eat my dessert. It's too good to bolt right down and I need the exercise.

MRS. COBB. Gracious! It is getting late. Lilacs, you should be in bed. (*The young folks come down while the table is being cleared*)

TOUSSANT. Darn it! I haven't finished that speech. (*He dives for his papers*)

BEN-HUR. My goodness! I'll bet it's too long anyway.

TOUSSANT. (*indignantly starting upstairs*) It is not. I've got all but the last part. Now, let's see—(*He disappears, his eyes fast on the sheets. In a second he sticks his head over the banister*) Turn off that radio. I gotta concentrate. (*Exits. Ben-Hur is busy at the desk. He takes out the brown jug. There is a sound of coins dropping.*)

LILACS. (*curious*) Whatchu doin'?

BEN-HUR. (*crisply*) Tendin' to my own business, Miss Nosey.

E.J. (*also observing with interest*) Gosh! You sound like you're in the money!

BEN-HUR. (*important*) I'm a business man!

REVEREND. (*as they come down from the dining room*) You'll excuse me, won't you. I must get ready for tomorrow.

MATTIE. (*smiling*) I know, Eli. Go—climb—your tree. (*Reverend smiles and goes into study, closing door.*)

MATTIE. (*to Mrs. Cobb*) A good meal does set me up! And lady, that was the best all-round meal I've had in a long time.

MRS. COBB. (*deprecating*) Oh, Mattie! A woman in your position hadn't ought say such things.

MATTIE. (*raising her eyebrows*) My position! Humph! Well, anyhow, it's a long drive from Hollywood.

MRS. COBB. That's true. And I suppose you couldn't always find good hotels.

MATTIE. You got something! I found the hotels all right—but, a lady of my complexion does run into complications. Now, you high yellows—(*She waves her hand*)

MRS. COBB. I never talk about—well, you know.

MATTIE. (*her eyes on Lilacs*) Yeah. It might be embarrassing. Some of us sho do take back! Well, as I was saying—I sure missed Sadie on this trip. Her being along would have simplified matters.

MIRAH. Oh, tell us about her!

MRS. COBB. (*firmly*) Not tonight, Mirah. We've all got to be thinking about getting to bed. Tomorrow's Sunday. Lilacs! Ben-Hur! Come right now and say good-night to your auntie. You must go up. (*She picks up her sewing basket*) There's always something to do.

BEN-HUR. Aw, not yet, ma.

MRS. COBB. Yes—right away.

LILACS. Good-night, Ant Mattie. I'll play for you tomorrow.

BEN-HUR. (to Lilacs) That'll be a treat! (Lilacs kicks him. To his aunt) Goo'night!

MATTIE. Goodnight, children. Sleep tight—

LILACS. An' don' let tha bedbugs bite! (Mattie laughs as they disappear)

MATTIE. Sure is a shame I had to smash that car after coming all this way. You kids couldn' of had some fun with it. Wouldn't of happened if I hadn't gone by Louisville. That extra hundred miles was too much for the old wreck.

MIRAH. Wreck!

MRS. COBB. You stopped at Louisville?

MATTIE. Yes! Worse luck!

MIRAH. Did you have an accident there, too?

MATTIE. Yeah—I had an accident—a real accident. I picked the wrong horse!

MRS. COBB. (puzzled) Picked the wrong horse?

E.J. (catching his aunt's eye) That an expression, ma. It means—made a bad investment. That's what you mean, isn't it, Aunt Mattie?

MATTIE. You tell it!

MRS. COBB. That's too bad. A woman with money always has to be on her guard. People are out to take advantage.

MATTIE. Yeah! (suddenly taking it in) With money! My God! You don't— (She stops)

MRS. COBB. Mattie, what's the—

MATTIE. Don't tell me you all been taken in by that newspaper blah! I'll bet Sadie has laughed herself sick over that fortune she's left her "people." I know we have!

MRS. COBB. You mean—?

MATTIE. No—no . . . Sadie was a grand gal, the best in the world, but she never did know nothing about money. The wonderful times we've had matchin' pennies to see who'd get the last one—sleepin' in the theatre dressin' room cause the hotel was so cold—or maybe there weren't no hotel! When she got in the movies and begin to make money so much was hanging over from the lean years—we couldn't catch up. And she didn't have no sense—bought everything anybody offered her! Sometimes she'd give me a great roll to keep. "Bury it," she'd say, "next week we might be pressin' bricks." Never could get through her head she was a star. Then, one day she'd rush in and demand the money. When I'd try to hold out she'd scream and yell and say I was robbin' her. Finally, I'd have to give in and off she'd go, happy as a kid and spend every dam cent of it. Her long illness stripped all of us. That worried her. Till one day she made a joke of it. Looked up from her pillow and said with her wide grin. "Tell 'em," she said, "I'll leave 'em my fortune! I'll make a will!" God! She was a fool! (Roughly she wipes the back of her large hand across her eyes)

MRS. COBB. (wetting her lips) What are you going to do?

MATTIE. Me? Oh! I ain't worried. We always kept in touch with Lew Simons. I wired him after I got everything straightened out and he wired right back that if I could get to New York by the 15th I'd have a job. Then, I thought 'bout stopping to see you all so I packed my things in Old Faithful and set out. Everything was swell too, till I started running into these "accidents." Hell! (*There is a loud pounding out back*)

MRS. COBB. (*it is the last straw*) Now what? At this hour of the night! It's the back door—Go see who it is, E.J.?

(*E.J. goes out back. In a moment there is a loud voice answered by E.J.'s*)

E.J. He's busy, I tell you. We can't bother him now.

BROTHER PERKINS. (*drawing nearer*) Young man, git outta mah way. Ah'm a-tendin' to the Lawd's business an' Ah'm tellin' yo' I gotta see the Reverend right now.

E.J. Can't I do something.

PERKINS. Mabbe yo' can and mabbe yo' can't, but I gotta see Reverend.

REVEREND. (*opening the study door*) What is it, E.J.?

PERKINS. (*pushing through into living room*) Howdy, everybody. Ah'm fit to be tied an' yo'all have to 'scuse me, but somebody has done desecrated the house of the Lawd!

REVEREND. Brother Perkins!

MRS. COBB. What?

PERKINS. Yes, mam! Tha collection plates is stole!

REVEREND. No?

MATTIE. Collection plates!

MRS. COBB. Stolen?

BROTHER PERKINS. Yessuh! Yesmam! Ah put 'em out in the back lobby this morning tendin' to clean 'em. When Ah went back this afternoon they wasn't there, but Ah figured tha janitor had moved 'em—maybe took 'em home. So, I waited till Ah could see him. But, he tells me he don' know nothin' bout 'em. An' now—Reverend—Ah comes to tha queer part. Sister Saboy's little gal, Carrie, say she seen somebody with 'em this very afternoon.

REVEREND. Did she know who it was?

BROTHER PERKINS. Yes, she knowed.

REVEREND. Well, it's all right then. Somebody had put them away.

BROTHER PERKINS. No—they ain't put 'em away. They took 'em.

REVEREND. Why—who could have done such a thing—Who was it.

PERKINS. Yo' boy—Ben-Hur!

REVEREND. Ben-Hur!

MRS. COBB. No!

REVEREND. You mean she saw him take them away?

PERKINS. Yessuh! She says he was carryin' 'em away.

REVEREND. (*looking around*) Where's Ben-Hur?

MRS. COBB. Pa—he's gone to bed. You know he wouldn't take the collection plates!

(*Reverend walks to the foot of the steps and calls*)

REVEREND. Ben-Hur! (*there is no answer*) Ben-Hur!

BEN-HUR. (*in distance*) Yessuh.

REVEREND. Come down here!

(*There is a pause. Then, in a surprised voice*)

BEN-HUR. (*nearer*) But—I'm undressed.

REVEREND. Slip on your trousers and come down here!

BROTHER PERKINS. (*shaking his head*) Powerful sorry 'bout this, Sistah Cobb. But—

MIRAH. (*breaking in*) Ben-Hur didn't steal those plates!

MATTIE. (*patting her arm*) Good girl!

(*Now down the steps comes Ben-Hur. He has pulled on his trousers over his nightshirt and is barefoot. His eyes are wide. His father's voice warns him of pending trouble. After him at the top of the stairs partly hidden by the banister may be seen the white-robed figure of Lilacs.*)

REVEREND. Ben-Hur, the collection plates are missing from the church. Have you seen them?

BEN-HUR. (*slowly looking around the room*) Ain't you got new ones?

REVEREND. (*sharply*) New ones? What do you mean?

BEN-HUR. I thought—Didn't somebody throw the old ones away?

REVEREND. (*anxiously*) Ben-Hur, what are you talking about—old ones— new ones? There's only one set of collection plates. Have you seen them?

BEN-HUR. (*after a pause*) Yes—sir.

PERKINS. Ah knowed it! Ah knowed it! You stole 'em!

LILACS. (*shrieking out on the steps*) He didn't! He didn't! You ole—ole crow! He didn't steal 'em!

MRS. COBB. Lilacs! Lilacs! Go back to bed!

LILACS. (*running down*) No! No! Papa, he didn't steal 'em. I know. He sells things. I tole you, ma! He collects things—everywhere. Things people don't want—things they threw 'way—Go look in the basement. I tole you! I tole you!

PERKINS. (*furious*) Yo' lil imp o' Satan! You oughtta be—

REVEREND. (*softly*) Ben-Hur?

BEN-HUR. It's like she says. I sold 'em! They was out in the back lobby and I figured you all was throwin' em away so I better take 'em before somebody else did. They was pretty rusty, you know. I couldn't get much for 'em. The man said they was too old.

PERKINS. Sold tha collection plates! Young scallawag! You need a good—

REVEREND. Just a minute, Brother Perkins! Thanks for coming in and telling me. I'll see that we get new plates. Ma, I guess you can find something here to use tomorrow. E.J., go to the door with Brother Perkins. Good night, Brother.

MRS. COBB. Yes—yes—I'll find something. (*She hurries out to dining room*)

BROTHER PERKINS. Don' think tha Presiding Elder won't hear o' this! Can' manage yo' own young ones! Time we was gettin' rid o' the whole part an' parcel o' youse!

REVEREND. (*repeating*) Goodnight, Brother.

MATTIE. (*stepping forth*) He said "goodnight, Brother." Just why, I don't know. I'll show you the door. Get out—before I forget to be a lady! I'm tryin' to remember that this is a parsonage—get out! (*Exit Perkins. Reverend looks hard at Ben-hur. E.J. follows Perkins out*)

REVEREND. Tell me, son. Why did you do this? Why do you sell things?

BEN-HUR. (*returning his gaze earnestly*) It's a business! Everybody else is doin' something—I wanted you all to know I'm a good business man. Can't you understand?

(*Reverend stares at him a moment and then without speaking turns and enters his study closing the door behind him. Ben-Hur's drooping figure crosses the floor to the stairs. Lilacs goes along comforting him.*)

LILACS. Never mind, Ben-Hur. Don't you care what old pickle face said. You don' need to worry. We gotta rich ant now. She'll fix things. You'll have a big business. We gotta rich ant! (*They are half up the stairs— Lilacs looks down at Mattie giving her a wide grin.*) An' maybe I can dance!

(*The telephone rings as they disappear. Listlessly Mirah answers it. E.J. returns from hall.*)

MIRAH. Yes—yes—I'm sorry, Butch, I couldn't go . . . No . . . Yes . . . she . . . did come . . . Yes . . . No, nothing's the matter. I don't know. . . . No . . . I really don't know. Things are—different. No . . . No . . . We— may—not be here. . . . No, Butch. I—I—can't talk. No, no, don't come over. I—I—good-by.

(*E.J.'s eyes meet hers in sympathy. With a little catch of breath, she turns and runs upstairs. Enter Mrs. Cobb from the kitchen.*)

MRS. COBB. Well, let's go to bed. It has been a day. (*She turns out the lights, leaving only the small reading lamp on the table.*) I'll see that everything's placed in your room, Mattie. You needn't hurry. Reverend will probably be in there for some time. Are you coming, E.J.?

E.J. Yes, ma.

MATTIE. I'll be along.

(*They disappear upstairs leaving Mattie sitting on the sofa. The room is in shadows. Through the colored glass of the window above the stairs comes the reflection of a street lamp. Slowly Mattie gets up and starts up the stairs. She pauses looking towards this window.*)

MATTIE. You oughtta been here tonight, Sadie. This was your joke! Rich aunt! It's good! But, now you gotta help me out. Look, Sadie, we've been through so much together and you always found a way. There must be one now. Did you hear him?. . . . He sold the collection plates! Ain't it funny? Did you ever hear anything funnier? Well, why don't you laugh? (*Her voice breaks*) Oh, Sadie!

CURTAIN

SCENE TWO: *The same. The following morning.*

It is Sunday and the room shows the disorder of the regular Sunday morning rush. Through the door may be seen the breakfast table, chairs pushed back, dishes scattered. The window above the stairs is raised and as the curtain lifts the sound of church bells may be heard.

At Rise: Ben-Hur, dressed for Sunday School, his cap on his head, is sprawled in a chair eagerly reading the funny paper. Toussant, standing near the dining room door, is reading the news sheet. Mirah, wearing a hat, is looking over his shoulder as she draws on a light wrap. E.J. is still sitting at the breakfast table, eating.

MIRAH. (*calling*) Hurry, Lilacs. We'll be late!

TOUSSANT. It's all here! And *look* at this picture!

E.J. Who can help looking at it? (*The phone rings. Mirah answers it.*)

MIRAH. (*at phone*) Hello . . . yes . . . he's here . . . It's for you, E.J. (*E.J. takes receiver with utter lack of enthusiasm.*)

E.J. Yes . . . yes . . . (*Trying to speak lightly*) Yes, I told you it would be there . . . Sure is . . . (*mirthlessly*) Ha! Ha! . . . Well, now, you know . . . Er—a—say, I was just thinking about coming down your way . . . Oh, no, I haven't got that yet . . . You know how 'tis, fellow can't hop on that the first thing . . . Sure . . . But, I was wondering if maybe Jake couldn't use me again this week . . . Oh, no, but I'm sorta onto the ropes now . . . Might have better luck and everything. Sure . . . well, it's kinda fun. Never can tell what might happen . . . Sure can't . . . You ask him, will you? . . . He is a swell guy. So long . . . I'll be seeing you. (*He hangs up*) And how!

TOUSSANT. (*casually*) Bad news?

E.J. (*bitterly*) Read your paper and find some good news! Maybe the Republicans are going in—maybe Hitler's dead—maybe—Aw, hell!

MRS. COBB. (*Interrupting as she comes in from kitchen. She is carrying two silver trays.*) I guess I'll have to let you take these. I can't find anything else that matches. There's going to be enough talk about those collection plates as it is.

TOUSSANT. Couldn't you just scour out a couple of pie plates? These are—

MRS. COBB. Yes, I know. They've been in the family so long. If one of them should get lost or anything. But—

E.J. Some of those old deacons might recognize them for what they are—mint julip service . . . the old colonel will turn over in his grave.

MRS. COBB. (*haughtily*) Well, if any of that scum does know they'll know they come from a family that's use to serving mint julips.

E.J. (*Peering through an imaginary glass and imitating the traditional colonel.*) Look at it, suh—frosted round the brim—cool an' sweet—nothin' like it in yo' Yankee lan'—nothin' like it in the world—Have one, suh! (*He sips from the glass*)

MRS. COBB. (*proudly*) Stop that nonsense, E.J. You've got blood in your veins and don't you forget it. Here, Toussant, take these and keep an eye on them. (*Toussant takes trays and exits through hall. Mrs. Cobb returns to kitchen.*)

E.J. (*looking after her*) Some of that blood's gonna get spilt if I don't do some fast thinking. Mirah, I don't suppose you could slip something *off* those plates . . . no, there wouldn't be enough.

MIRAH. What are you talking about?

E.J. Well, you didn't have any trouble slipping an envelope in last Sunday . . . Now, I'm wondering if you could slip an envelope *out* this Sunday.

MIRAH. (*in amazement*) Steal from the church funds?

E.J. No, nitwit—just get back my fifty dollars—oh, forget it!

MIRAH. But—

MRS. COBB. (*calling*) You're going to be late. Put that paper down Ben-Hur, and go along.

BEN-HUR. (*slamming down paper*) Aw, shucks! (*He follows Mirah out as Lilacs runs downstairs. She is a very much bestarched and tucked little lady. Carries her hat in her hand and a hair ribbon*).

LILACS. I can't tie my ribbon! (*She looks around for Mirah*)

E.J. Didn't you hear the bell ringing? She can't wait all day.

LILACS. I wouldn't be no ole Sunday-School teacher, no how! (*Starting for kitchen*) Ma-ma!

E.J. Come here! I'll tie it.

LILACS. You can't! Ma—(*E.J. snatches the ribbon and jerks her in front of him*)

E.J. Stand still! (*With much effort he manages to get the bow tied at a rather grotesque angle.*)

LILACS. If my bow don't look right, I'll bust you!

E.J. Ma oughtta keep you in the house. You talk like an alley rat.

LILACS. I don't neither, I—Ma, aunt Mattie's getting up. She looks funny . . . she's got—

MRS. COBB. (*Entering*) Haven't you gone yet? Stop talking about your aunt!

LILACS. (*trying to put on her hat over the bow*) It *feels* funny!

MRS. COBB. Come here. (*Expertly Mrs. Cobb straightens the bow, puts on the hat and gives a few pulls to the little dress.*) Now, hurry!

(*Lilacs hurries out. Mrs. Cobbs sighs as she observes the disorder of the room. She picks up the funny paper, arranges a window shade, etc. She pauses beside the table looking at the paper Toussant has tossed down. She has evidently seen it before, but she reads again while the weight of the disaster beats upon her. E.J. eats silently without turning his head. The study door opens and Reverend enters. He also is ready for church—clean and neat—but wearing a frock coat which shows signs of much wear.*)

REVEREND. Ma, I can't find a clean handkerchief. Don't seem to be none in the drawer.

MRS. COBB. (*Without looking up*) Maybe they got pushed back. (*Reverend returns inside study and in a moment calls back brightly*)

REVEREND. Yes—here they are. Now, I'm all ready. (*Entering, looking at watch*) Better be getting along. (*He notices her sharply*) You're not dressed yet, ma. You'll be late!

MRS. COBB. (*bluntly*) I'm not going to church. (*Reverend stares at her in amazement. Mrs. Cobb speaks with gathering intensity.*) No, I'm not going . . . You've seen this picture. Maybe it means nothing to you! (*reads*) Sadie Kessler's Maid Socks Reporter! Preacher's Sister Left Fortune! Read it! Everybody else has!

REVEREND. Now, ma, I know that's too bad. Poor Mattie always did have a temper. We must—

MRS. COBB. (*savagely*) What do I care about her temper!

REVEREND. But—

MRS. COBB. They'll laugh at it because they think she's got a fortune! She can afford to have a temper . . . But, it's this lie about her money . . . That's what will ruin us . . . All these things will come out . . . everything . . . everything . . .

(*She turns away with a gesture of despair. Through the open window come sounds of the Sunday School. Children are singing: "Bringing in the sheaves, bringing in the sheaves. We shall come rejoicing, bringing in the sheaves."*)

REVEREND. (*gently*) Now, ma. I told you the money couldn't make any difference. It would of been *her* money, anyhow, and—(*Mattie has started down the steps. She draws back.*)

MRS. COBB. (*bursting out*) For twenty years I've listened to you tellin' me why other people should have so much and we have so little—for twenty years I been seein' other men pass you one by one—while you talk, talk, talk. These other men think about their families . . . their wives can have something—their children can be somebody. You know what all this means to us. When the Bishop hears about these disgraceful—

REVEREND. My dear, my dear. Don't worry. The Lord will—

MRS. COBB. Stop it! I can't stand it! I've heard it too many times—I can't stand it again. He's provided! He's provided all right. He's provided you with a series of parsonages to live in and five children you can't even educate!

REVEREND. Liza!

(*She rushes out through dining room. Reverend stands a moment, bewildered. Then, going to the desk, he picks up his Bible, takes his hat and slowly goes out to hall. Through the window still comes the young voices singing "They will come rejoicing, bringing in the sheaves." Coming down, Mattie softly closes the window—shutting out the singing. E.J. getting up from the table sees her and realizes she has heard.*)

MATTIE. (*softly*) Poor Liza!

(*E.J., his hands in pocket, shoulders sagging, walks to window down right and stands looking out.*)

E.J. Sorry you heard.

MATTIE. That's all right by me, boy. She's jus' a female, puttin' up a fight for her young ones. I don't blame her. It *is* hell.

E.J. I guess pop can't be no different.

MATTIE. No—Eli would o' been tops in a monastery, but in a parsonage— he's jus' a cockroach! (*The door bell rings*)

E.J. I'll see who that is.

(*He goes out hall. Mattie walks to dining room, picks up an orange and starts peeling it. E.J. returns followed by* JASPER JONES—*resplendent in the finery of the Seventh Avenue and Harlem.*)

E.J. It's for you, Aunt Mattie.

MATTIE. (*looking up in surprise*) For me? (*coming down*) Jasper!

JASPER. (*making an elaborate bow*) It ain't nobody else but!

MATTIE. (*seizing his hands*) Why, yo' little ole sweet tooth! What d'you mean by popping up like this?

JASPER. Same ole Rusty! When I seen that picture I says "Peewee—it can't be—but there she is—big as life. Rusty!" you remembers Peewee?

MATTIE. Peewee! You don' mean Peewee! He here, too? Say, have they blasted Seventh Avenue? Harlem must be quiet as Grant's tomb! I sho am glad to see you! Sit down.

JASPER. (*looking around room as he seats himself*) Cripes! I was scared to ring the bell. You here—living in a church building. (*observing stained glass window*) Look at dat window! Jerusalem!

MATTIE. (*laughing*) I know. It gimme an awful shock, too. Jus' forget it. (*E.J. has gone to dining room and may be seen carrying out the dishes to kitchen*)

JASPER. (*regarding Mattie fondly*) Thank Gawd! Yo' ain't gone high hat— even wid all dat money! Hit sho is wonderful!

MATTIE. (*remembering*) Oh!

JASPER. Take hit easy, baby, take hit easy. I didn't come round to make a touch. Peewee an' me doin' right well here—right well.

MATTIE. Sure nuff? Big boy, maybe you're my savin' grace! Maybe you all can help me.

JASPER. (*heartily*) Help yo! Of course! Anything yo' say, sweetheart. Spill it to papa. Thought you looked sorta low when I come in.

MATTIE. (*earnestly*) Low! Listen—I could put on a silk hat an' walk right under a snake's belly!

JASPER. (*impressed*) Do tell!

MATTIE. (*slowly*) Jasper—I got to have some money.

JASPER. (*astonished*) Money!

MATTIE. Yes, money! A whole lot of money.

JASPER. But—

MATTIE. (*waving it aside*) It's all huey!

JASPER. Yo' means—?

MATTIE. I mean Sadie Kessler ain't never had no fortune in the first place an' she didn't leave it to me, in tha second!

JASPER. Well, Ah'm a pick-eyed watah lily!

MATTIE. You are—if Sadie left me any money! She gimme a house—one of those crazy pie boxes out in Hollywood. I can't live in it—an' I can't sell it. Nobody but a dam fool like Sadie would buy it! She left me a car—It was a good car—in its day, but now it's smashed up in a garage and will cost more 'an it's worth to get it out. What I needs is money—an' plenty of it!

JASPER. (slowly) Well—now—about tha car. I reckon we could arrange to—

MATTIE. Dam the car! I can get where I'm going! T'ain't that. When did you ever hear me gripin' about being broke? Hell! Sadie an' me was broke mos' of tha time. This is somethin' different.

JASPER. (painfully) Yo' means cold cash?

MATTIE. Look, Jasper, whatcha doin' out here? What kind of scheme you an' Peewee workin' on. I feels my luck comin' up like a heat. Lemme in on something. What's on tha ball?

JASPER. Not so fast, girlie. I gotta think. Yo' sorta knocked me for a ringer. I can't get it.

MATTIE. (tersely) Don't strain your head, honey. That'd be fatal.

JASPER. Is yo' in trouble, Rusty, dat yo' gotta have a pile o' dough all in a lump?

MATTIE. Jasper, you wouldn't understand. It's sorta outta your line. But, there's something I gotta do, that's all.

JASPER. Well, maybe I could nose 'round and pick up a good horse—

MATTIE. (disgusted) Horses is out. That's how I lost my las' two hundred down in Louisville the other day. (Goes to door and calls) E.J. Come here a minute. (E.J. appears) This is my brother's boy—E.J. E.J., this is Jasper Jones—a—er—a ole friend.

E.J. How do.

JASPER. How ar' yo', kid.

MATTIE. Sit down, E.J. Jasper here knows a lot o' things you don't know. But right now we need some heavy thinkin' done and we're sorta short on brains.

E.J. (laughing) Okay, Aunt Mattie. I'll do what I can. (Jasper stares at him.)

MATTIE. Sure—that's my name. Any comments?

JASPER. Ah ain't opened mah mouth.

MATTIE. Don't.

JASPER. (grinning at E.J.) She wants big money—quick.

E.J. Don't we all!

MATTIE. Boy, I'm the world's best gambler. I know sometimes we have to go run down our luck. We gotta shake a leg and go find it.

E.J. (shaking his hand) Fraid I can't be a bit of help. I never made any

quick money—I never made any kind of money. In fact, I never even saw
any made!

MATTIE. But, you must have some ideas!

E.J. If I had any ideas I could use—No, I just read about 'em Irish Sweepstakes and—

JASPER. (*slapping his knee*) That's it!

MATTIE. (*sarcastically*) What's it? Your mind sho runs in grooves. I said
horses was out—anyhow where we gonna get hold of a Sweepstake ticket
all of a sudden?

JASPER. (*leaning forward*) Rusty, for nobody else in tha world would Ah do
this.

MATTIE. (*regarding him suspiciously*) What?

JASPER. Ah'll let yo' all have one of mah tickets!

MATTIE. (*interested, but wary*) You gotta Sweepstakes ticket?

JASPER. Three of 'em.

MATTIE. Um-um. How you know they ain't fakes.

JASPER. (*injured*) Do Ah look lak a chipmonk? Ah deals with tha big shots!
Fact is—Ah was sellin' tickets myself.

MATTIE. You was?

JASPER. Sure—Ah had a whole book. Yo' get two free tickets with every
book yo' sell. Then, I paid for one mo'—Iffen yo'd like, yo' can have that
there third ticket.

MATTIE. (*promptly*) Two-fifty.

JASPER. Now—look, Rusty, yo' knows yo' can' get no Sweepstakes ticket
out here for two-fifty.

MATTIE. That's what you paid for it. Run upstairs, E.J. and get my pocket
book. I oughtta have that much rattlin' round' loose. (*E.J. goes upstairs*)
Lemme see that ticket. (*Jasper draws folder from his pocket and carefully extracts a ticket which he hands her. She studies it—more and more
intently.*) Why! This here race is the 23rd. That's—that's Wednesday!

JASPER. Sure.

MATTIE. Whatchu tryin' to do? It's past time for the drawing.

JASPER. You're wrong. Tha drawin's today. Read it!

MATTIE. (*again studying it*) Um-m—um.

JASPER. Course—if yo' don' want hit.

MATTIE. Oh! I'll take it. It's a chance—though I ain't so strong for horses.
They notifies you right away, don't they?

JASPER. By cable.

(*E.J. has returned and hands Mattie pocketbook*)

MATTIE. (*searching for money*) So, if we don't hear nothing by night—we
won't have nothin' to think about.

JASPER. Not a thing!

MATTIE. Well, that's good—we won't lose much time. Here, E.J. (*Hands
him ticket*)

JASPER. (*generously*) Iffen it'll strain yo', Rusty, yo' can give me that two-fifty some other time.

MATTIE. (*finally counting out the change*) No—here—take it! (*She hands it to him*) Fact is, Jasper, I gotta hunch! (*He starts forward*) I don' wanna cheat you, Jasper—an' that ticket might win.

JASPER. (*anxiously*) Whatchu mean?

MATTIE. (*continuing*) So I'm gonna give you more than two-fifty. My car what's busted up still has a swell engine. It was made special. Here's the garage ticket for it. Take tha car, too.

JASPER. (*worried*) Why yo' doin' this, Rusty.

MATTIE. (*calmly*) You see, I dreamed about numbers last night—numbers floatin' on the water—black numbers floatin' right on silver water. It was plain as day.

JASPER. But this—

MATTIE. Yes, I knows. That's why I wasn't thinkin' bout no horse—I was trying to find a number. Well—I found it.

JASPER. What?

MATTIE Yes! Tha first an' las' numbers on that ticket! A four and a seven! Them was what I seen floatin' on tha water—black numbers on the water. (*E.J. stares at ticket*)

JASPER. (*hoarsely*) Gimme that ticket!

MATTIE. Put it in your pocket, E.J. It's paid for.

E.J. (*excitedly*) That colored woman in Baltimore—she won first prize!

MATTIE. Well, tha government took its slice!

E.J. But—out of a hundred and fifty thousand—oh, boy! (*Doorbell rings*)

MATTIE. (*as if welcoming fate*) Go to the door, E.J.

(*E.J. laughs and goes out. In a moment returning with* PEEWEE—*a smaller, but even more elaborately turned out edition of Harlem.*)

PEEWEE. (*jubilantly*) High, Rusty!

MATTIE. (*still quiet*) Hello, Peewee. (*Peewee somewhat dampened turns to Jasper*)

PEEWEE. Jasper! Ah couldn't wait. Ah rushed right over! Hit's come!

JASPER. (*swallowing*) What?

MATTIE. (*calmly*) The cable.

PEEWEE. (*staring at her in amazement*) Golly! Yo' knows 'bout it!

JASPER. (*Terror gripping him*) Niggah—whatchu talkin' bout?

PEEWEE. (*looking from one to the other*) She tole yo'—the cable!

JASPER. Where's hit from?

PEEWEE. Has yo' been kicked in da head by a mule? Hit sho ain't Hitler sendin' for his black baby tuh come home!

JASPER. Mah Gawd!

MATTIE. Give him the cable, Peewee. Maybe, he'll open it. (*Peewee hands cable to Jasper, who takes it with shaking hand.*)

PEEWEE. Sufferin' catfish! Ah'm excited too, but dis ain't no time to fall to pieces. Wait till tha' race! Lawd! Lawd! Gotta horse in da Irish Sweep-stakes! (*With trembling fingers Jasper is trying to open cablegram.*)

E.J. (*unable to stand the suspense*) Let me help you!

JASPER. (*savagely*) Go away from hyear! (*He unfolds it while they lean forward*)

PEEWEE. (*almost jumping up and down*) Get out your ticket! Where's your tickets! (*Jasper is reading painfully—mouthing the words.*)

MATTIE. (*tense*) Out loud—you idiot—out loud!

JASPER. (*still mumbling*) Ar—a—(*inaudible—reading*) ticket number—(*He stops*)

E.J. Go on! Go on!

JASPER. (*reading*) Number 4—0—8—7—7!

PEEWEE. (*rejoicing*) Hot dawg!

(*Jasper collapses in his chair. Mattie sinks back with a sigh of pure content. E.J. stares at ticket he is holding in his hand—a slow grin spreading over his face. Peewee is so happy that it is a moment before he realizes something unusual. Then he stares at E.J. and at the ticket he is holding.*)

PEEWEE. What—what—?

JASPER. (*miserable*) Ah sole—hit!

PEEWEE. Tha ticket?

JASPER. Fur two-fifty an' a busted car!

PEEWEE. (*pointing at E.J.*) To that kid?

JASPER. To Rusty!

MATTIE. Keep your shirt on, Peewee. This is for a good cause.

E.J. Aunt Mattie! Aunt Mattie, even if our horse don't win, we get somethin' don't we.

MATTIE. You bet . . . Several hundred dollars just on the drawing. We're ridin' a wave, sonny. I know now, my dreams don't fail me!

PEEWEE. (*rather grimly*) Big Boy, Ah'll give you five hundred dollars for that ticket.

E.J. Five hundred—

JASPER. (*dolefully*) Where yo' gonna get any—

PEEWEE. Shut yo' trap, wise guy! (*to E.J.*) Well—what'ar ya sayin'?

MATTIE. Nothin'. He ain't sayin' a word. That's my ticket and I'm taking a shot at that hundred an' fifty thousand. Gimme that ticket. Reckon I better keep it myself.

PEEWEE. (*admiringly*) Ole Rusty! Gets all tha luck!

JASPER. (*disgusted*) She ain't got no fortune!

MATTIE. Tell him bout it, Jasper. We got another little knot to untie, E.J. and me.

E.J. (*eagerly*) What now, Aunt Mattie?

MATTIE. How the hell we gonna make Eli take this? He's the one it's for.

E.J. That's right. He wouldn't touch—

MATTIE. Save your breath, boy. I been knowin' him longer than you have. Just keep still and think!

(*Peewee has been walking around. Now he looks up*)

PEEWEE. An' yo' brother's a preacher!

MATTIE. Yeah! Our old man was a sort of preacher, too—went around to different towns. We didn't even have a parsonage to live in.

JASPER. Mah Gawd! If Ah'd a known yo' was a preacher's kid, Ah'd a—

MATTIE. (*finishing with a grin*) Steered clear o' me! No hard feelin's, Jasper. But, that's why me an' E.J. here understands one another so well.

E.J. (*jumping up*) I've got it! (*He hurries over to the old desk, flings it open and begins rummaging through the papers as he talks*) Some stock pop bought—years ago—for land, out in California. Ma found out about it—took it to a lawyer—it wasn't worth the paper. It's in here some place—I saw it the other day—Lord, how she raved! Poor pop—that was the one and only time he ever tried to make some money—Yap, yap. Here it is! (*He has flung things right and left, at last pulling out a long envelope.*)

MATTIE. Sounds just like Eli. But, I don't see—

E.J. Listen. You talk to him about land in California. Just bring up the subject.

MATTIE. That'll be easy. They play regular Chinese checkers with lots out that way . . . Jump in any direction!

E.J. Well, then I'll tell you about this stock. You ask to see it. When I give it to you, say you'd like to have a friend of yours look it over. It might be good, after all. Jasper here, he can be the friend.

JASPER. No—no! Ah ain't havin' nothin' to do with this. I'm out and I'll stay out.

MATTIE. (*patting his arm*) Aw, Jasper!

E.J. Then—whatever we get—we can tell him the stock was good and that it brought in so much. You see!

MATTIE. (*admiringly*) That's what having brains means! Just like that!

PEEWEE. Humph! Even a preacher ain't that dumb!

MATTIE. Eli's is a special kind of dumbness—God-given! It'll work.

JASPER. (*heavily*) Well, here. (*he hands cable to E.J.*) Yo' might as well have this. Yo' got everything else—even, brains.

(*E.J. takes cable and eagerly begins to read it. Suddenly, he gives a gasp*)

MATTIE. What's the matter, E.J.?

E.J. (*his face drawn—shaking the cable*) This—this—(*He cannot speak*)

PEEWEE. Is everybody round here batty?

MATTIE. E.J.!

E.J. (*gasping*) Aunt Mattie—let 'im have tha ticket—let 'im have it—five hundred dollars—oh, let 'im have it?

MATTIE. Are you crazy? What's wrong with that ticket?

E.J. (*trying to control himself*) It's this—this cable—the horse—the name—Oh, we'll never—

MATTIE. (*to Jasper*) What's the matter with it—what does it say? Gimme that cable! (*She snatches it from E.J.*)

JASPER. The horse? Sho, hit tells the horse your ticket drew.

E.J. The name—the name—

JASPER. What's wrong with this horse? What do you know about horses anyhow?

E.J. It's called—Raven!

MATTIE. (*eagerly*) Yes—that's the name. I never heard of him—but glory be! (*Her face is beaming*) It's another sign—black letters they was on the water—*black*—and now—Raven.

E.J. (*almost hysterically*) No—no—you don't understand. Pop—he's always talkin' 'bout them. His name—Elijah—Elijah and the ravens!

PEEWEE. Lemme out of here! Hit's a bughouse!

MATTIE. What? What—Wait, wait. I do remember. Yes, yes. Something about—

E.J. The ravens fed Elijah!

MATTIE. Why—why—it's perfect—it's absolutely—perfect!

E.J. No—no!

(*The dining curtains are suddenly parted and Mrs. Cobb hurries in. She stops embarrassed, wiping her hands on her apron.*)

MRS. COBB. Oh! Excuse me, Mattie, I didn't know you had callers. No—no—I won't stop a minute. (*She is hurriedly crossing room to stairs*) I'm going to be late for church. I must hurry. Do make yourself right at home. You understand—I'm—I'm late now.

MATTIE. Liza, I'd like you to meet these friends.

MRS. COBB. (*not stopping*) How do you do. You will excuse me, won't you? (*She is already half up the stairs*) You see, I haven't missed pa's sermon on Sunday morning in twenty years. This morning—I—I was delayed—but—if I hurry—

MATTIE. (*standing close to her*) You're a good scout, Liza.

MRS. COBB. (*to her*) No—no, Mattie—I'm a wicked woman—I don't deserve—but, if I can only get there before he starts to preach . . . (*She hurries upstairs*)

MATTIE. (*looking up after her*) That's a good idea! (*gaily*) Run upstairs, E.J., and grab my hat and coat. Pick up your flat feet boys—we're going to church!

JASPER AND PEEWEE. (*in consternation*) To—church?

MATTIE. Sure—don't get scared and I'll vouch for your good behavior! Hurry, Liza, we'll wait for you!

MRS. COBB. What did you say, Mattie?

MATTIE. I said, hurry! We're all going to church. We're all going to church and hear Eli preach about the ravens!

(*The hall door opens and Ben-Hur slouches into the room*)

E.J. (*starting upstairs*) Why, Ben-Hur, church isn't over?

BEN-HUR. Naw.

MATTIE. Has your pa started to preach yet?

BEN-HUR. Pa ain't gonna preach.

E.J. What?

BEN-HUR. Tha Sliding Elder just rolled in. He's gonna preach. I don't wanna hear 'im.

MATTIE. *Sliding* Elder?

E.J. He means the Presiding Elder, but what's he doing here?

BEN-HUR. I donno. (*calling*) Ma! Ma!

(*Mrs. Cobb, ready for church, starts down the steps.*)

MRS. COBB. What is it, Ben-Hur? Why aren't you at church?

BEN-HUR. Pa said to tell you the Presiding Elder's here. He'll be here for dinner.

MATTIE. Now, I know we gotta go to church. Come on! "Onward Christian Soldiers"—I gotta gird my loins—for the fight!

(*Exit. Others follow her as curtain falls*)

CURTAIN

ACT THREE

Scene: Wednesday afternoon.

At Rise: Mattie enthroned on the sofa has evidently been entertaining Brother Perkins. He is slapping his knee and laughing uproariously.

BROTHER PERKINS. Ha! Ha! Ha!

MATTIE. (*in conclusion*) An' that's that!

BROTHER PERKINS. Ah never did in all mah life—Ha! Ha! Ha!

(*Sister Saboy appears behind them in the dining room door. She takes in the scene with utter disapproval and speaks severely.*)

SISTER SABOY. Brother Perkins!

BROTHER PERKINS. (*trying to control himself*) Oh—er—yes—Sister—What?

SISTER SABOY. Has yo' forgot the prayer service dis afternoon?

BROTHER PERKINS. Oh—why—er—no. t'ain't time yet.

SISTER SABOY. It's past time—and the church is still locked—an' you has that key.

BROTHER PERKINS. Oh—my goodness. I'll be right over—Mercy—Is Reverend there?

SISTER SABOY. He ain't—an' members is standing out in the street—waitin' to git in. . . . Certainly don't speak well for our *deacons*.

MATTIE. Don't be too hard on him, Mis' Saboy. He just stopped in to chat a while and we got to talkin' bout—ole times.

SISTER SABOY. Humph! He tole me about some of his scandalous carryin' ons.

MATTIE. (*raising her eyebrows*) He did?

BROTHER PERKINS. (*hastily*) No—no—I jus'—(*he shakes his head at Mattie*)

MATTIE. I didn't think you did.

BROTHER PERKINS. Ah gotta run along, Miss Cobb. I'll—I'll stop in again—some time.

SISTER SABOY. You wouldn't be comin' over to prayer meetin'—would yo'—*Miss* Cobb?

MATTIE. No—er—no—(*sweetly*) I enjoyed service Sunday morning—*so much*—but, this afternoon—I'm just awfully busy.

SISTER SABOY. Ah thought yo' would be. Come, Brother Perkins. (*They exit almost bumping into E.J. who is entering hastily. Sister Saboy stops.*) *You* wouldn't be comin' to prayer meeting—would yo', E.J.?

E.J. (*wiping his forehead*) *Me?* What for? Oh, excuse me—no. (*Sister Saboy takers her leave*) Good heavens! Look, I've just finished fastening the aerial. Let's see if it comes over any clearer. (*He turns on radio*) It's getting on toward four o'clock.

RADIO. (*strident voice*) . . . and in the cause of democracy it behooves every citizen of the United States to leave every consideration and—

E.J. (*switching it off*) That's better. Now, I believe that short wave will work. (*Mirah is hurrying downstairs*)

MIRAH. Is it time?

E.J. Not yet—I'm just trying out the aerial. (*Toussant has entered hastily from hall*)

MIRAH. How'd you get here so soon, Toussant?

TOUSSANT. Sneaked out of my last class! Oh, Mirah, here's somebody to see you.

(*Butch has come quietly in behind him stopping at the door.*)

BUTCH. Hello, Mirah.

MIRAH.. Oh, hello.

E.J. There's plenty time yet. Come on, Toussant, and look at this aerial. (*They go out. Mattie, after a glance at Mirah and Butch, also slips out.*)

BUTCH. What's the matter, Mirah?

MIRAH. I—nothing.

BUTCH. But look, Mirah. . . . I been trying to see you . . . You sound so funny over the phone . . . Like you don't want to talk to me.

MIRAH. I been awful busy.

BUTCH. (*bitterly*) I guess that's it. The fellows at school told me. I guess you'll be going away from this town with your rich aunt. We're too small for you now. Well, if that's the way you feel about it—don't let me stop you.

MIRAH. Maybe—maybe everything will be all right—now.

BUTCH. What d'you mean all right. Nothing's been all right since she came here—Her with her special made car, reporters running after her and all that money!

MIRAH. That's just it—she hasn't any money.

BUTCH. What?

MIRAH. No—everybody thinks wrong—We haven't any rich aunt—it's all—all a mistake!

BUTCH. (*his face breaking with smiles*) Mirah—is that true? She's not a rich aunt—not at all?

MIRAH. No.

BUTCH. (*seizing her*) Oh, Mirah—I'm so glad—so glad!

MIRAH. Glad!

BUTCH. Yes—look—look, Mirah. I've made the fraternity—I've been trying to tell you all week—Look—look, I've got a pin. Will you wear it? Mirah, I wanted so to show it to you—Look—look.

MIRAH. Oh, Butch!

(*Through the door bursts Ben-Hur, flinging his books across the room*)

BEN-HUR. (*out of breath*) Am I late? Has it started? (*seeing the two*) Say, what goes on here? It's most time for the race—Where's everybody?

BUTCH. (*grabbing him around the neck and dancing*) Everything's fine! Everything's wonderful! Want a ticket to the game? Want ten tickets to the game? Want to play in the game? What do you want?

BEN-HUR. (*struggling*) Hey, are you crazy! Let me go! An' you stay away from my sister. I'm gettin' sick of you!

MIRAH. Ben-Hur!

BUTCH. Pay him no mind, beautiful! (*approaching Ben-Hur, threateningly*) Brother—you're gonna love me. You're gonna—(*Enter E.J. and Toussant. Ben-Hur slides over to them saying*)

BEN-HUR. You big chump!

E.J. Such language, little brother!

BEN-HUR. Aw, he—

TOUSSANT. Never mind that now. Turn on the radio!

MATTIE. (*calling over her shoulder as she enters*) C'mon, Liza. Leave that— it's almost time!

(*The window above the stairs is open and now comes singing from the church next door.*)

PRAYER GROUP. (*singing*) Oh! walk together chillun, don' yo' get weary, Walk together, chillun, don' yo' get weary, There's a great camp meeting in the promise land.

MIRAH. Aunt Mattie, I'd like you to meet a—friend of mine.

MATTIE. Sure, I'd be glad to.

MIRAH. This is Butch Johnson—my aunt, Miss Cobb.

BUTCH. I'm glad to meet you, Miss Cobb—I—er—really am.

MATTIE. (*grinning*) You sound like you mean that, Butch. I think we'll get along.

MRS. COBB. (*coming in wiping her hands*) I should have gone to prayer meeting this afternoon.

E.J. That's all right, ma. This one time won't hurt.

(*Toussant has turned on the radio and it is making strange and discordant sounds*)

E.J. Put it on seventy and wait.

BUTCH. What you trying to get?

E.J. The Irish Sweepstakes race.

BUTCH. What?

MIRAH. What if we can't get it!

E.J. Aw, the paper said BDF. Find seventy!

RADIO. (*female voice*) . . . the little Handel would not be discouraged. And one night way in the middle of the night when all the household was fast asleep, he—

MRS. COBB. Oh, my goodness! Shut that off. I'll scream.

E.J. (*snapping it off*) That's the station. Remember everybody and don't touch it.

BUTCH. (*to Mirah*) But why is everybody so excited? I shouldn't think a race would—

MIRAH. Butch, we've got a horse in.

BUTCH. What?

MIRAH. Yes—That's why I said everything might be all right, after all. Aunt Mattie entered it for us. She bought a ticket.

BUTCH. Oh . . . I see.

MIRAH. I couldn't sleep a wink last night!

MATTIE. Now, keep cool, honey.

MIRAH. But—a hundred and fifty thousand dollars! (*Her voice is awed*)

MATTIE. That's number one.

TOUSSANT Well, the second prize is seventy-five thousand and—

E.J. —the third fifty thousand.

TOUSSANT. And there's just lots of ten and twenty thousands running around loose. Any one of them would set us up.

BUTCH. Money—Just plenty of money—I guess I—

MIRAH. (*taking his hand*) It's just a race, Butch. (*Laughing*) we're all counting chickens before they hatch.

MRS. COBB. It would mean a *home*! Children, I do hope we're not doing wrong.

E.J. Mom, the money goes to hospitals, anyhow.

MATTIE. And somebody gets them prizes!

MRS. COBB. I should've gone to meeting this afternoon. (*Doorbell rings*)

TOUSSANT. Darn it! Now, who's that?

MIRAH. Maybe somebody thinks the meeting is in here. I'll see. (*She goes out*)

MATTIE. Speck it's Jasper and Peewee. They said they'd be over.

(*From the hall comes the sonorous voice of the Presiding Elder*)

PRESIDING ELDER'S VOICE. Ha! Ha! An' how is the little lady? (*a murmured response*)

E.J. Holy Smoke! Can't that clink do his courting some other afternoon?

TOUSSANT. He sure is on the job!

MATTIE. I've stood all that I can stand. Enough's enough. I'll get rid of him.

TOUSSANT. But how?

MATTIE. By telling him the truth. That'll fix him.

MRS. COBB. (*fearful*) But Mattie, he might—

MATTIE. Don't worry about what he can do to Eli. I'll take care of that too.
(*Enter the beaming Presiding Elder, followed by a distressed Mirah.*)

PRESIDING ELDER. Good afternoon, everybody.

MRS. COBB. How do you do, Elder. Reverend wasn't expecting yo.

ELDER. A embassy of the Lawd must ever be expected. The ladies are
present. That's enough!

MRS. COBB. Reverend is over at the Church. He's holding prayer services.

ELDER. In the afternoon? A noble soul—but really, I don't see how he finds
the time from his other duties. Well, well! And, how are you, Miss Cobb?

MATTIE. (*smiling wanly*) I'm awful glad to see you.

(*The Elder seats himself comfortably on the sofa. E.J. manages to get
everybody else out of the room. Then he and Toussant stroll very conspicu-
ously out into the hall.*)

ELDER. Daughter, yo' looks burdened this afternoon. Is anything wrong?

MATTIE. Elder, you don't know what it is to carry such a load as I carries—
so much responsibility—so many things I has to think about.

ELDER. Yes, indeed. It must be pretty hard for a lone woman.

MATTIE. It is—sometime I just don't know which way to turn. (*She sinks
down on the sofa beside him, sighing deeply*)

ELDER. (*impressively*) Daughter—tha hand o' the Lawd is in this. He sent
yo' here.

MATTIE. (*soulfully*) Did he?

ELDER. He did indeed. He looked down an' he saw me toiling in his vineyard—toiling all by myself—He had taken my dear, sweet wife to himself—but he knowed Ah needed a helpmate.

MATTIE. Oh, Elder!

ELDER. Madame—er—Miss—I'll be happy to share yo'—er—burdens. Will
you be mah—

MATTIE. (*eagerly*) Yo' means yo'll look after everything for me?

ELDER. (*fervently*) I will.

MATTIE. An' I won't have to worry my head with no figures or nothing.

ELDER. Not a figure.

MATTIE. Oh, that's wonderful! Now, I can get my car out of the garage and
everything.

ELDER. Your car?

MATTIE. (*talks rapidly*) Yes—Oh, I been so worried. I didn't have no
money to get my car out. And it's wrecked. Honestly, I need a new one,
but this is a good engine—though the body is falling to pieces. That's why
it costs so much. I've been crazy trying to figure out where I'd get the
money. Oh! (*throwing her arms around his neck*) you wonderful man!

ELDER. (*struggling out of the embrace*) No money? yo' mean your money's
still tied up—Yes, of course—lawyers an' things—sure—sometime it
takes a while to—

MATTIE. I'll say lawyers! After those skinflints got through there wasn't a cent—not a cent—Oh, I've been wild. Now, I can—(*She makes another lunge towards him, but he evades her.*)

ELDER. Wait a minute—sistah—Ah'm fraid—Ah don't understand—

MATTIE. (*cooing*) Don't be modest! I understands. Just let me look at you! (*She gazes at him soulfully while he twists and squirms*). Yes—you're just like my—my—my—my—(*She covers her face and her shoulders shake*)

ELDER. (*backing away and trying to rise*) Mis Cobb—really—Ah must— Ah must—

MATTIE. Oh! I'm so happy! (*The Elder is looking about wildly. The doorbell rings*)

ELDER. Please—please—here comes somebody—Ah'm afraid you misunderstood me—Ah—thought yo' needed a—er—a manager—Ah thought—

MATTIE. (*looking up wildly*) What? You wasn't—Why, you said—

(*Sound of E.J. talking to somebody. The Elder is now on his feet— backing towards hall door. He nearly bumps into Jasper*)

ELDER. Oh!

JASPER. What the—

(*Peewee is behind him. The Elder is trapped*)

MATTIE. (*tearfully*) Boys—I'm glad you came. You're my only friends. This man—

ELDER. Please—please—Ah think Miss Cobb ain't feeling so well.

MATTIE. Just a broken heart—that's all—Just a broken heart.

JASPER. (*gallantly springs forward*) Mattie—tell me—Has this man dare to—

ELDER. (*terrified*) No—No! They're waiting for me at the church—I must go. Miss Cobb, I'll be back. Please, I'll be happy to do anything I can about that little matter. Maybe—Ah—can—get the car fixed. Now— don't worry—don't worry. (*He backs out, Peewee having stepped aside. He glares at him*) Goodby, Miss Cobb—er, goodby gentlemen.

(*He vanishes—there is a moment's pause. Then a mad dash for the radio*)

MATTIE. Come on! Come on! Everybody.

TOUSSANT. He's gone!

E.J. Ma-ma! Mirah!

JASPER. (*at the radio*) It's started!

E.J. We've missed the first part! (*The radio buzzes and clicks several times. Indistinct noises—Low singing now again may be heard in the church. It continues throughout the race.*)

RADIO. (*announcer*) . . . the crowds going wild . . . Can you hear them? (*sound of cheering*) look at those horses . . . running neck to neck . . . coming to the last run . . .

JASPER. My Gawd . . . which horses?

MATTIE. What horse?

E.J. Wait! Wait!

RADIO. What's that . . . There's a horse . . . breaking away from the group in the back . . . he's coming up . . . he's coming . . . it's a black horse . . . let's see . . . what's the number?

TOUSSANT. (*screaming*) A black horse!

RADIO. No. 4! Must be a dark horse in the race. Don't know about it. Come on! Come on! No 4! Raven! That's the name. Now, Lone Star is breaking away . . . he's out front . . . What motion! What rhythm! Ladies and gentlemen . . . you should see it. There—Empire is gaining—her jockey is using the whip—we're coming to the last turn.

PEEWEE. What 'bout Raven? What 'bout Raven?

RADIO. This is a race! What! What! No! Yes! Yes, Raven, the black horse has the inside! . . . the jockey is riding high . . . the crowd's going wild. Raven's a new horse! It's the home stretch and Raven is gaining . . . he's gaining . . . Lone Star is still in the lead, but that thundering black menace is coming up. . . . Only a little further to go! Empire leaps forward. It's the goal—the goal—and the race is finished! Lone Star first—Empire second and Raven third! Listen to the crowd! They're cheering Raven—the unknown—Lord, how that black horse did—

MATTIE. Shut it off! That's enough!

(*In the sudden stillness there is a gasp and Toussant sinks to the floor*)

E.J. He's fainted!

MATTIE. (*softly*) We did it—Sadie—we did it!

MIRAH. It is all right, now, Butch. Can I keep my pin?

BUTCH. Yes, Mirah. (*In the doorway at hall appears Reverend*)

REVEREND. Sister White said the Presiding Elder was here. I came to take him over to the meeting. Has he gone? (*They are staring at him*)

MATTIE. (*gently*) Eli—I just got some news for you!

REVEREND. News! Well—that's nice. Did Dr. Green say—

MATTIE. It's about that investment you made—you remember—the one I was looking into.

REVEREND. (*a little disappointed*) Oh—that—well, I wouldn't worry about that—as ma says I'm no business man—but, I do appreciate your trying to see about it.

MATTIE. But, it's all right, Eli. You've just made fifty thousand dollars! There will be some—er—fees to pay, but it will be quite a lump.

REVEREND. (*bewildered*) Fifty—fifty—what?

MATTIE. Mr. Jones—here—just brought the—news.

JASPER. (*getting up and bowing*) Congratulations—ole—er—Reverend!

PEEWEE. (*following his example*) Same here!

REVEREND. (*his face breaking into happy smiles*) Ma! Ma! (*He starts upstairs.*)

(*Above him, through the open window comes a new song. It is:*

I gotta home in that rock
Ain't that good news

I gotta home in that rock
Ain't that good news
Let the billows o'er me roll,
I can safely hide my soul,
I gotta home in that rock
Ain't that good news.

MRS. COBB. (*near radio*) Here I am, pa.

REVEREND. (*Leaning over the banister—eagerly—like a happy child*) You see—you see, ma—I was right—I was right all the time.

MRS. COBB. Yes, pa—you was right!

E.J. It *was* the ravens, Pa.

MATTIE. (*raising her hand with an imaginary toast*) Good ole Raven!

(*Slow curtain as the voices still sing "I gotta home in that rock"*)

THE CURTAIN FALLS

PLAYS AND PAGEANTS BY BLACK WOMEN BEFORE 1950

ABBREVIATIONS

FK   Fisk University Library, Special Collections, Nashville, Tennessee
FTP   Federal Theatre Project Research Division, Fenwick Library, George
          Mason University, Fairfax, Virginia
HBC   Hatch-Billops Collections, Archives of Black American Cultural His-
          tory, New York
HU   Howard University, Moorland-Spingarn Research Center, Washington,
          D.C.
KT   Karamu Theatre, Cleveland, Ohio
LC   Library of Congress, Washington, D.C.
NYPL   New York Public Library, New York
PALLC   Performing Arts Library at Lincoln Center, New York
SCHOM   Schomburg Center for Research in Black Culture, New York
UFLA   University of Florida, Rare Books and Manuscripts, Gainesville,
          Florida
YL   Yale University, Beinecke Rare Book and Manuscript Library, New
          Haven, Connecticut

Andrews, Regina
  Climbing Jacob's Ladder (1931). SCHOM
  The Man Who Passed. SCHOM
  Matilda. SCHOM
  Underground (1933)
Banks, Lucille
  The Desert Son (192?). HU
Bonner, Marita
  The Pot Maker (1927). *Opportunity*, Feb., 1927
  The Purple Flower (1928). *Crisis*, Jan., 1928
  Exit: An Illusion (1929). *Crisis*, Oct., 1929
  Muddled Dream
Burke, Inez
  Two Races (1930). *Plays and Pageants from the Life of the Negro*, Willis Richard-
    son, ed. Washington, D.C.: Associated Publishers, 1930
Burrill, Mary P.
  Aftermath (1919). *Liberator*, April, 1919
  They That Sit in Darkness (1919). *Birth Control Review*, Vol. III, No. 9, Sept.,
    1919
  Unto the Third and Fourth Generation (1930). *The Emersonian Yearbook of 1930*.
    Emerson College, Boston
Burroughs, Nannie Helen
  Slabtown District Convention (1942)
Busey, De Reath Irene Byrd
  The Yellow Tree (1922). HU

Bush, Olivia Ward
Memories of Calvary: An Easter Sketch. Philadelphia, Pa.: A.M.E. Book Concern (c. 1915)

Childress, Alice
Florence (1949). *Masses and Mainstream*, Vol. III, Oct., 1950

Cooper, Anna J.
Christmas Bells. HU
From Servitude to Service (1940). HU

Cuney, Maude (Hare)
Antar of Araby (1929). *Plays and Pageants . . . ,* Richardson, ed.

Delany, Clarissa Scott
Dixie to Broadway (1924)

Duncan, Thelma
The Death Dance (1923). *Plays of Negro Life*, Alain Locke and Montgomery Gregory, eds. New York: Harper, 1927
Sacrifice (1930). *Plays and Pageants . . . ,* Richardson, ed.
Black Magic (1931). *The Yearbook of Short Plays*, First Series, Wise and Snook, eds. Evanston, Ill.: Peterson, 1931
Drifting. HU
Full Moonlight
God's Own
Jinda. HU
Payment. HU
Scarlet Shawl

Fuller, Meta Vaux Warrick
By Special Appointment (192?). Fuller Estate
A Call after Midnight (192?). Fuller Estate
The Emerald Pendant (192?). Fuller Estate
The Touch of Gold (192?). Fuller Estate
Redemption: A Pageant of Negro Achievement in Five Episodes (n.d.). Fuller Estate
The Hidden Sack (n.d.). Fuller Estate

Gaines-Shelton, Ruth
The Church Fight (1926). *Crisis*, May, 1926

Graham, Ottie
Holiday (1923). *Crisis*, May, 1923
King's Carpenter. Stylus, Vol. I, No. 1, May, 1926

Graham, Shirley (DuBois)
Tom-Tom (music-drama) (1929)
Tom-Tom (three-act opera) (1932). HBC, also at SCHOM
Coal Dust (1930). FK
Elijah's Ravens (1930). KT
I Gotta Home (1939). FK
Dust to Earth (1940). KT
Track Thirteen (1940). *Yale Radio Plays: The Listener's Theatre.* Boston: Expression Company, 1940
It's Morning (1940). FK

Grimké, Angelina Weld
Rachel (1916). Boston: The Cornhill Co., 1920
Mara (192?). HU

Guinn, Dorothy
Out of the Dark (1924). *Plays and Pageants . . . ,* Richardson, ed.

Gunner, Frances
The Light of the Women (1929). *Plays and Pageants . . .* Richardson, ed.

Harris, Helen Webb
   Genifrede (1922). *Negro History in Thirteen Plays*, Willis Richardson and May
     Miller, eds. Washington, D.C.: Associated Publishers, 1935
   Frederick Douglass
Hazzard, Alvira
   Mother Like It (1928). *Saturday Evening Quill*, No. 1, 1928. LC
   Little Heads (1929). *Saturday Evening Quill*, No. 2, 1929. LC
Helmsley, Jeroline
   Wade in the Water (1931)
Hirsh, Carlotte Teller
   Hagar and Ishmael (1913). *Crisis*, 1913
Hopkins, Pauline Elizabeth
   Slave's Escape (1879). FK
   One Scene from the Drama of Early Days
Hurston, Zora Neale
   Color Struck (1925). *Fire*, Nov., 1926
   Spears (1925)
   Meet the Momma (1925)
   The First One (1927). *Ebony and Topaz*, Charles S. Johnson, ed., 1927
   De Turkey and De Law (1930)
   Cold Keener (1930)
   Mule Bone (1930). With Langston Hughes. HU
   Poker (1931)
   Great Day (1931)
   Woofing (1931)
   Jungle Scandals (1931)
   Singing Steel (1931)
   Lawing and Jawing (1931)
   Fast and Furious (1931). Coauthored with a host of playwrights. *Best Plays of
     1931–1932*, Burns Mantle, ed. New York: Dodd, 1932
   Forty Yards (1931)
   From Sun to Sun (1932)
   Fiery Chariot (193?). UFLA
   Lysistrata (193?)
   Polk County (1944). With Dorothy Waring. PALLC
Jeannette, Gertrude
   A Bolt from the Blue (1946). Author
   This Way Forward (1949). Author
Johnson, Georgia Douglas
   Blue Blood (1926). *Fifty More Contemporary One-Act Plays*, Frank Shay, ed.,
     New York: Appleton, 1928
   Plumes (1927). *Plays of Negro Life*, Locke and Gregory, eds.
   A Sunday Morning in the South, 1st version (1925). FTP
   A Sunday Morning in the South, 2nd version (1926?). *Black Theatre USA*, James
     Hatch and Ted Shine, eds. New York: Free Press, 1974
   Frederick Douglass (1935). *Negro History in Thirteen Plays*, Richardson and
     Miller, eds.
   William and Ellen Craft (1935). *Negro History in Thirteen Plays*, Richardson and
     Miller, eds.
   A Bill to Be Passed
   Popolikaku (1926?)
   Safe (193?). FTP
   Blue-Eyed Black Boy (193?). FTP
   Red Shoes (1947)

Brother's All (1948)
The Starting Point. YL
Well-Diggers
And Still They Passed
Holiday
Midnight and Dawn
Little Blue Pigeon
One Cross Enough
Sue Bailey
Attucks
Livingston, Myrtle Smith
  For Unborn Children (1926). *Crisis,* July, 1926
Marshall, Harriet Gibbs
  The Last Concerto (1936). HU
McBrown, Gertrude P.
  Bought with Cookies (1949)
McClendon, Rose
  Taxi Fare (1931). With Richard Bruce
Miller, May (Sullivan)
  Pandora's Box (1914). *School's Progress,* 1914. Author
  Within the Shadows (1920). Author
  The Bog Guide (1925). *Plays and Pageants* . . . , Richardson, ed.
  Riding the Goat (1925) *Plays and Pageants* . . . , Richardson, ed.
  The Cussed Thing (1926). Author
  Scratches (1929). *Carolina,* No. 49, April, 1929
  Graven Images (1929). *Plays and Pageants* . . . , Richardson, ed.
  Stragglers in the Dust (1930). Author
  Nails and Thorns (1933). Author
  Sojourner Truth (1935). *Negro History in Thirteen Plays,* Richardson and Miller, eds.
  Samory (1935). *Negro History in Thirteen Plays,* Richardson and Miller, eds.
  Harriet Tubman (1935). *Negro History in Thirteen Plays,* Richardson and Miller, eds.
  Christophe's Daughters (1935). *Negro History in Thirteen Plays,* Richardson and Miller, eds.
  Freedom's Children on the March (1943). Author
  Moving Caravans. Author
Milton, Muriel
  Via Underground (1923). HU
Nelson, Alice Dunbar
  The Author's Evening at Home (1900). *Smart Set,* Sept., 1900
  Mine Eyes Have Seen (1918). *Crisis,* April, 1918
  Gone White (192?). *The Works of Alice Dunbar Nelson,* 3 vols., Gloria T. Hull, ed., New York: Oxford University Press, 1988
Norman, Dora Cole
  The Niche
Price, Doris
  Two Gods (1932). *Opportunity,* Dec., 1932
  The Bright Medallion (1932). *University of Michigan Plays,* K. Rowe, ed. Ann Arbor, Mich.: George Wahr, 1932. NYPL
Spence, Eulalie
  Brothers and Sisters of the Church Council (1920)
  The Starter (1926) *Plays of Negro Life,* Locke, ed.
  Foreign Mail (1926). New York: Samuel French, 1927

The Hunch (1926). *Carolina*, Vol. 4, No. 7, May, 1927
Fool's Errand (1927). New York: Samuel French, 1927
Her (1927). FK
Hot Stuff (1927?). HU
Episode (1928). *The Archive*, Vol. XL, No. 7, April, 1928
Wife Errant (1928)
La Divina Pastora (1929). Spence Estate
Undertow (1929). *Carolina*, No. 49, April, 1929
The Whipping (1932). Optioned by Paramount Studios. Spence Estate
Being Forty
Terrell, Mary Church
  Phillis Wheatley: A Bicentennial Pageant (1932). HU
Thomas, Marguerite, C. E.
  The Barrier Broken (192?). HU
Thompson, Eloise
  Africannus (1922?)
  Cooped Up (1924)
  Caught (1925)
Tillman, Katherine David
  Fifty Years of Freedom; or, From Cabin to Congress (1910). Philadelphia, Pa.:
    A.M.E. Book Concern, 1910; SCHOM
  Aunt Betsy's Thanksgiving (n.d.). Philadelphia, Pa.: A.M.E. Book Concern;
    SCHOM
  Thirty Years after Freedom
Townsend, Willa A.
  Because He Lives (1924). Nashville, Tenn.: Sunday School Publishers, Board of
    Baptists Convention, 1924
Trent, Hattie
  Founding and Progress of the A.M.E. Zion Church (1945). HBC
Weber, Amy L.
  Off Col'uh (1926)
  Wine of Life (1927)
White, Lucy
  Bird Child (1922). *Plays of Negro Life*, Locke, ed.
Winter, Ella
  Blood on the Fields (1935). With Langston Hughes. YL

SELECTED BIBLIOGRAPHY

Abramson, Doris E. *Negro Playwrights in the American Theatre 1925–1959*. New York: Columbia University Press, 1969.

Arata, Esther Spring. *More Black American Playwrights*. Metuchen, N.J.: Scarecrow Press, 1978.

Arata, Esther Spring, and Nicholas John Rotoli. *Black American Playwrights, 1800 to the Present*. Metuchen, N.J.: Scarecrow Press, 1976.

Belcher, Fannin S., Jr. "The Place of the Negro in the Evolution of the American Theatre, 1767 to 1947." Ph.D. dissertation, Yale University, 1945.

Bond, Frederick W. *The Negro and the Drama*. Washington, D.C.: Associated Publishers, 1940.

Brown, Sterling. *Negro Poetry and Drama and the Negro in American Fiction*. New York: Atheneum, 1978.

Brown, Sterling, Arthur Davis, and Ulysses Lee. *Negro Caravan*. New York: Dryden Press, 1941.

Brown-Guillory, Elizabeth. *Their Place on the Stage*. New York: Greenwood Press, 1988.

Cooper, Anna J. *A Voice from the South*. Xenia, Ohio: Aldine Printing House, 1892.

Craig, E. Quita. *Black Drama of the Federal Theatre Era*. Amherst: University of Massachusetts Press, 1980.

Flanagan, Hallie. *Arena: The Story of the Federal Theatre*. New York: Duell, Sloan and Pearce, 1940.

Flynn, Joyce, and Joyce Occomy Stricklin. *Frye Street and Environs: The Collected Works of Marita Bonner*. Boston: Beacon Press, 1987.

Harris, Trudier, ed. *Afro-American Writers before the Harlem Renaissance*. Dictionary of Literary Biography, Vol. 50. Detroit: Gale Research Company, 1986.

———. *Afro-American Writers from the Harlem Renaissance to 1940*. Dictionary of Literary Biography, Vol. 51. Detroit: Gale Research Company, 1987.

———. *Afro-American Writers, 1940–1955*. Dictionary of Literary Biography, Vol. 76. Detroit: Gale Research Company, 1988.

Hatch, James V. *Black Image on the American Stage, 1770–1970*. New York: Drama Book Specialists, 1970.

Hatch, James V., and Abdullah Omanii. *Black Playwrights, 1823–1977: An Annotated Bibliography of Plays*. New York: R. R. Bowker, 1977.

Hatch, James V., and Ted Shine, eds., *Black Theatre USA: Forty-Five Plays by Black Americans, 1847–1974*. New York: The Free Press, 1974.

Hemenway, Robert E. *Zora Neale Hurston, A Literary Biography*. Urbana: University of Illinois Press, 1978.

Hill, Errol. *The Theatre of Black Americans*, Vols. I and II. Englewood Cliffs, N.J.: Prentice-Hall, 1980.

Hull, Gloria T. *Color, Sex, and Poetry: Three Women Writers of the Harlem Renaissance*. Bloomington: Indiana University Press, 1987.

Hull, Gloria T., ed. *The Works of Alice Dunbar Nelson*, 3 vols. New York: Oxford University Press, 1988.

Hundley, Mary Gibson. *The Dunbar Story 1870–1955*. New York: Vantage Press, 1965.

Hutchinson, Louise Daniel. *Anna J. Cooper: A Voice from the South*. Washington, D.C.: Smithsonian Institution Press, 1981.

Isaac, Edith J. R. *The Negro in the American Theatre.* New York: Theatre Arts, 1947.

Johnson, Abby Arthur, and Ronald Maberry Johnson. *Propaganda and Aesthetics: The Literary Politics of Afro-American Magazines in the Twentieth Century.* Amherst: University of Massachusetts Press, 1979.

Lawson, Hilda J. "The Negro in American Drama: Bibliography of Contemporary Negro Drama." Ph.D. dissertation, University of Illinois-Urbana, 1939.

Locke, Alain, ed. *The New Negro.* New York: Atheneum, 1925.

Locke, Alain, and Montgomery Gregory, eds. *Plays of Negro Life.* New York: Harper and Row, 1927.

McKay, Nellie. "Black Theatre and Drama in the 1920s: Years of Growing Pains," *Massachusetts Review* (Winter 1987): 615–626.

———. "What Were They Saying? Black Women Playwrights of the Harlem Renaissance." *The Harlem Renaissance Re-examined.* ed. Victor A. Kramer. New York: A.M.S. Press, 1968: 129–147.

Miller, Jeanne-Marie. "Black Women Playwrights from Grimké to Shange: Selected Synopses of Their Works," in *But Some of Us Are Brave*, ed. Gloria Hull, Patricia Bell Scott, and Barbara Smith. Old Westbury, New York: Feminist Press, 1982: 280–296.

Miller, May, and Willis Richardson. *Negro History in Thirteen Plays.* Washington, D.C.: Associated Publishers, 1935.

Mitchell, Loften. *Black Drama: The Story of the American Negro in the Theatre.* New York: Hawthorn Books, 1967.

———. *Voices of the Black Theatre.* Clifton, N.J.: James T. White & Co., 1975.

Monroe, John Gilbert. "A Record of the Black Theatre in New York City, 1920–1929." Ph.D. dissertation, University of Texas at Austin, 1980. Ann Arbor: University Microfilms International, 1982.

Poag, Thomas Edward. "The Negro in Drama and the Theatre." Ph.D. dissertation, Cornell University, 1943.

Richardson, Willis. *Plays and Pageants from the Life of the Negro.* Washington, D.C.: Associated Publishers, 1930.

Sampson, Henry T. *Blacks in Blackface: A Source Book on Early Black Musical Shows.* Metuchen, N.J.: Scarecrow Press, 1980.

Sandle, Floyd Leslie. "A History of the Development of the Educational Theatre in Negro Colleges and Universities from 1911 to 1959." Ph.D. dissertation, Louisiana State University, 1959.

Thompson, Sister Francesca. "The Lafayette Players: 1915–1932." Ph.D. dissertation, University of Michigan, 1972.

Wilkerson, Margaret B., ed. *Nine Plays by Black Women.* New York: Mentor, 1986.

Woll, Allen. *Dictionary of the Black Theatre.* Westport, Conn.: Greenwood Press, 1983.

SELECTED PERIODICALS

Crisis
Opportunity
Colored American
Saturday Evening Quill (Boston)
Pittsburgh Courier
New York Age
Afro-American (Baltimore)